EASTERN BENGAL BALLADS

Eastern Bengal Ballads

(Ramtanu Lahiri Research Fellowship Lectures for 1926-28, in Two Parts)

Vol. III : Part I

Compiled and Edited by
Dineshchandra Sen, Rai Bahadur, B.A. D.Litt. (Hons.)

GYAN PUBLISHING HOUSE
NEW DELHI-110002

Eastern Bengal Ballads

ISBN: 81-212-0906-4 (Set)
ISBN: 81-212-0909-9 (Vol. III)

Published in 2006 in India by
Gyan Publishing House,
5, Ansari Road, Daryaganj, New Delhi-110002
E-mail: books@gyanbooks.com

Laser Typesetting at: Vinayak Printers, Delhi
Printed at: Salasar Imaging System, Delhi

CONTENTS

GENERAL INTRODUCTION

1. *Our Ballads and Ballad-Collectors.*

I am glad to say that the Ballads published by the Calcutta University have elicited appreciation from many distinguished orientalists and scholars of Europe. Some of the opinions will be found quoted in the Appendix. Altogether 34 Ballads have been published of which the first volume contains 10, the second 12, and the third (the present one) 12. The Ballads comprised in these three volumes are: (1) Mahua (the gipsy girl), (2) Malua (the true wife), (3) Chandravati (the saintly daughter of Banshi Das), (4) Kamala (the patient sufferer), (5) Dewan Bhabna (the cruel tyrant), (6) Kena Ram (the robber who was reformed), (7) Rupavati (the betrothed maiden), (8) Kanka-o-Lila (the loving couple), (9) Kajalrekha (the banished girl), (10) Dewana Madina (the lady killed by love), (11) Dhopār Pāth (the washer-maiden), (12) Mahisal Bandhu (the herdsman-lover), (13) Kanchanmala (the bride of a blind baby), (14) Santi (the tempted one), (15) Bhelua (the beautiful one), (16) Rani Kamala Devi (the queen who courted a tragic death), (17) Manik Tara (the adventurous career of a young dacoit), (18) Santal Insurrection, (19) Nizam (the robber), (20) Isha Khan (the Dewan of Jangal Bari), (21) Surat Jamal and Adhua (a love-tale and tragedy), (22) Firoj Khan (the descendant of Isha Khan), (23) Manjurma (the wife of an old quack), (24) Kafen Chora (the coffin-stealer), (25) Bhelua (the true wife of Amir the merchant), (26) Hati Kheda (the capture of elephants), (27) Ayana Bibi (the forsaken lady),

(28) Kamal (the unhappy merchant), (29) Shyam Ray (the lover of a Dom girl), (30) Chaudhuri's Larai (the fight between the Chaudhuris), (31) Gopini Kirtan (the tale of Krishna's early life), (32) Sujā-tanayār Bilāp (the lament of the daughter of Shaha Suja), (33) Bara Tirther Kabita (the lay of the twelve shrines), (34) Manipurer Larai (the fight at Manipur). By far the best ones of these were collected by Babu Chandrakumar Dey of the village Aithar in the District of Mymensingh (P. O. Kendua). It is from him that we have got 'Mahua,' 'Malua,' 'Kamala,' 'Dhopār Pāth,' 'Dewana Madina,' 'the Herdsman Lover,' 'Kanka-o-Lila,' 'Chandravati,' 'Shyam Ray,' in fact, the best of the Ballads yet collected. He has besides given us numerous Ballads of humbler poetic merit such as 'Dewan Isha Khan,' 'Firoz Saha,' 'Alal Dulal' and others, which are, however, redeemed by a wealth of historical references which make up for their mediocrity as lyrical poetry.

Babu Chandrakumar's health has been shattered by his excessive work, but still he is carrying on with unmitigated zeal the task of recovering these rural songs of his district. It will be, I presume to say, a bare act of justice if we release him from further obligations as a servant of the University, turning the small pittance that he draws into a life-pension. He has already done a great work to deserve this favour. And I am sure whether my suggestion be complied with or not, he will pursue his work in the field of Ballads till the end of his life, as it is a labour which requires no other incentive on his part than his own inspired devotion and love for the work.

The other Ballad-collectors appointed by the University have also given a good account of their work, and the name of late Babu Beharilal Roy should be thankfully mentioned in this connection. He died, so to speak, in harness. Three days before he died, he had sent me the incomplete Ballad of 'Manik Tara' ('The adventures of a young dacoit') published in the second volume. It is a Ballad of unique interest and the picture of the domestic life of Bengal that it gives combines romance with realistic scenes full of vivid imageries. Unfortunately, in spite of my utmost efforts, I have not been able to get the entire Ballad, but I have no reason to despair and give up my pursuit. This Ballad deals with incidents alleged to have occurred in Dash-Kahaniya and its adjacent localities in the Subdivision of Jamalpur in Mymensingh, and I have appointed some earnest workers to try their best to recover the missing cantos from those places. Of the rest of the Ballad-collectors Babu Ashutosh Choudhuri's work deserves by far the most prominent notice. He is an enthusiast in the cause, and some of the Ballads collected by him, are of high value and are almost on a par with Chandrakumar's collections. Ashu Babu is a born researcher in the field he has chosen, and writes a commendably elegant and racy Bengali style. He has one qualification which Chandrakumar does not possess, *viz.*, a robust and sound health. He is not afraid of storm, rain or any other inclemencies of weather and is ready to face any difficulty in his way.

2. *Common Subjects treated in the Ballads.*

There are some familiar incidents in many of the Ballads which are a common poetical legacy to their authors. In some cases the accounts of these incidents are given in certain set and stereotyped expressions, common to many of the Ballads. Each poet when dealing with an episode of the nature uses these set phrases, so that we find them repeated in a number of Ballads.

Abduction of women.

The forcible abduction of women by ruffians may be traced in India from a pre-historic period,—from the time when the mother of **Shvetaketu** was dragged away by an outsider in the presence of his father. The lot of Sita has been shared by her sisters in this country from the Satya Yuga down to this Iron-Age of ours. In the first volume of Ballads we find **Mahua** and **Sonai**, in the second volume **Bhelua**, in the third the **Dom girl, Shvarupmala** and **Chandra-kala** abducted by profligate youngmen of aristocratic families. In the second volume **Sujata** the beautiful bride of **Dinghadhar** is carried away by **Meghua** the merchant. We have got many scraps of songs in which unfortunate Hindu girls lament their lot while in the grip of Burmese and Portuguese pirates. In the Bengali recensions of the Mahabharat, **Chinta** the faithful wife of Raja **Sribatsa,** falls into the clutches of a merchant. In the genealogical records of the Brahmins instances of such abductions are plentiful. It is thus a common situation described by many of the Ballad-makers, hence the accounts given of them generally agree in language. These abductions after a lull of half a century of peaceful British rule, have reappeared with a redoubled intensity owing to communal ill-feelings, and we hope that the Paramount Power which now rules the country,—which could send that lion of a man Napoleon to exile in St. Helena, humiliate the pride of the great Kaiser,—which justly takes pride in the title of "Lord of the Waves," and in whose Empire the sun never sets,—will be able to cope with the situation and save the poor Hindu girls from this age-long traditional oppression.

But to revert to our topic, there are set phrases in these ballads for other incidents also which have formed the themes of many a Ballad. As the bathing-ghat of a pond or a river practically gives an outsider the only opportunity of meeting a girl of a Hindu or Moslem family, it is quite natural that the place becomes often the meeting-ground of lovers. She is wooed and courted when found there all alone. In the first volume of Ballads, **Chandravati** and **Jaychandra** meet at

The bathing-ghat.

the bathing-ghat of Sutia at the village Patuair (Pt. II, p. 97). **Sonai** and her princely lover meet on the bank of a river close by her native village (Pt. II, p. 166). **Chandbinode** and **Malua** see each other for the first time at the bathing-ghat of a pond at the village of Arulia (Pt. II, p. 97). The washer-maiden **Kanchan** and her lover the prince, meet at the bathing-ghat of a pond in the Ballad of Dhopar Path (Vol. II, Pt. II, p. 3). **Isha Khan** and **Subhadra** (Sonamoni) exchange their love-glances on the bosom of the Padma at Sripur, when **Isha Khan** was on board his magnificent 'Kosha' and the princess was bathing in that noble river (Vol. II, Pt. II, p. 367). In the Ballad of **Santi,** her husband **Killan Sadagar** puts her fidelity to a test by his persistent temptations conducted through all the months of a year at the bathing-ghat of a public pond (Pt. II, p. 124). We have again such meetings in the Ballads of **Shyam Ray**, **Ayana Bibi** and **Manjurma** in the third volume. Shyam Ray, through the window of his palace, observes the Dom girl bathing and is over head and ears in love (Vol. III, Pt. I, p. 209). The merchant **Ujjal** is fascinated by the timid glances of **Ayana Bibi** when she is returning from the bathing-ghat to her home (Vol. III, Pt. I, p. 146). **Manjurma** and **Hassan** play their love amours at the bathing-ghat of a river, availing themselves of the absence of **Munir** the village-quack.

Temptation.

The temptations offered by an outsider for seduction of women have also a set phraseology, and in many situations of this kind the reader will be struck by a similarity of description. In most cases such temptations do not weigh with the heroines of the Ballads who are generally too high to yield to the allurements of filthy lucre. The tempting address of the treacherous merchant to **Mahua** (Vol. I, Pt. II, pp. 26-27), of the Kazi to **Malua** (p. 70), of Dewan **Jahangir** to the latter (p. 84), of the merchant **Bhola** to **Bhelua** (Vol. III,

Pt. I, p. 90) and of **Kazi Munaff** to her, all run on the same lines. Though the situations are the same, and the temptations held out are very similar, the way in which the women receive them is different in each case. **Mahua** does not answer a speech by a speech but springs on her tempter with the ferocity of a tigress. **Malua's** queen-like rage bursts forth in a glow of poetic language in which her love for her husband manifests itself in a rapid stream of flowery imagery and in an eloquent flow of felicitous expressions.

The lover's search for the beloved one, lost or abducted, forms another common theme. Poor **Manir**, the **Mahishal Bandhu** and **Nader Chand**, when separated from their consorts, address inanimate Nature, enquiring about the lost ones. In all this, not only are the situations the same but the very words are similar. This particular phase of a lover's trance and laments may be traced from the time of the Ramayana where Ram's search for Sita produces an intensely pathetic interest—the woods, the rivers, the hills and rivulets were addressed by the lover in a trance and the whole Nature seemed to respond to the appeal of the hero.

A lover's trance.

The textile work of Bengal and its excellence have been a source of her artistic fame all over the world from a remote antiquity. We find in the Maynamati songs, an account of the various dresses then in vogue, when **Aduna** the princess brings out from her chest *saḍis* of different kinds from which she had to make a selection. She first puts on one and then another, until the right one is found. The poet while delineating a lady's capricious whims and fastidious taste, so difficult to please, makes this the occasion for describing a rich variety of *saḍis* of wonderful artistic fineness, prepared by the Bengal weavers,—from the flame-coloured ones down to those bearing the transparent hue of the Ganges water. The dark

Saḍis of Bengal.

Nilambari interwoven with light blue threads, showing itself in the full glory of the colour of the Jumna, the **Udaitara** or 'the morning-star' and the **Megha-dumboor** or 'the fragments of clouds' and many such are described. What we find in the Maynamati songs in respect of these *saḍis* we see repeated in the Manasha-mangal Kabya by Jagajjiban Ghoshal (Typical Selections, Part I, p. 288), and also in several Ballads which have not yet been published. Perhaps the most graphic and artistic account of a lady's toilet in rich and aristocratic families occurs in the Govinda Mangal by Jadunandan Das (Typical Selections, Part II, pp. 1291-95).

Making of the hair.

Perhaps Bengal and Orissa owe their artistic manipulations of the hair forming into knots and chignons of various fashions, to the Tibeto-Burman races in the North. A very superb description of manifold arrangements of the long and curly hair of women in which it is made to imitate scenes from human society and animal-life is found in the Maynamati songs. Such descriptions are found repeated in some of the Ballads which are reserved for publication in the fourth volume of this work.

Sea voyage.

Description of ships is to be found in profusion in our old poetry. The 'Manasha-mangal' and the 'Chandi-mangal' poems give numerous picturesque accounts of these. Unfortunately the sea voyage was already forbidden when the best of these poems were written. The poets often depended on old traditions and fanciful stories related by the old men and women of the country-side. Their own imagination also found a full play in this matter and the result was that in most cases these descriptions were exaggerated beyond all measure, and facts and fiction struggled for expression "in a fantastic strife." Bangsidas, the poet of Manasha-mangal Kabya who flourished in the 16th century, is one of the few who have given us some reliable accounts of sea voyagës. The remedies adopted by the captain to save the ship from capsizing during furious storms in the sea and also from attacks by huge sea-monsters have been told by many a poet in a fanciful style which we are not inclined to credit. The cargo is often described in detail but there is also an element of fiction in this. Contrasted with the classical poems, the Ballads have this speciality that they give us first-hand observations and experiences from life. The names of the fourteen ships of Amir the merchant, in the Ballad of **Bhelua** and a full account of the cargo are interesting and do not look like fiction. It is interesting to note that the flag-ship of the Moslems generally carried the *Koran* and other scriptures. The propagation of a religious creed helped by a strong army and with the avowed object, apparently harmless, of defending the faith, was generally the plea by which the enterprisers on the deep commenced their aggressive operations, eventually resulting in the establishment of sovereignty over a foreign land. This is no new feature in the political history of the world.

What I have written above will, I hope, be sufficient to show that the Ballad literature in this country developed a set phraseology in respect of certain common incidents, which was gradually improved on by the succeeding generations of poets who described them. It is no wonder, therefore, that the reader is struck, every now and then, by common expressions and set phrases used in the Ballads when the aforesaid situations are described.

3. *A Bird's-eye View of the Characters described in the Ballads (Vols. I, II, III).*

Female Characters.

As Eastern Bengal Ballads have been prescribed by the Calcutta University as texts for the M. A. Examination in Indian Vernaculars, I should here like to append some notes analysing the characters contained in them for the benefit of my students. I have already dealt with the subject in my Introduction to Vol. I, Pt. I ; but there my notice has been rather short. The new volumes have brought to light a variety of characters, giving an opportunity for a critical study of them on a comparative basis.

The female characters in these Ballads are by far the most prominent deserving a full analytical criticism. I am not, however, going to take a considerable space and shall confine myself to a notice of only those characters that have some striking traits deserving a fuller treatment than given in the prefatory notes.

One of the most important of the female characters is **Mahua** (Vol. I, Pt. II, pp. 1-40). She is unique in this sense that while possessing the towering virtues of an ideal character, she is not modelled after Sita and Savitri who have usually inspired the poets of our country in the conception of lofty womanhood. She has a distinct place of her own and is without a peer in our literature. In her devotion to her chosen mate she is the ideal Brahmin girl that she is by birth. But in her resourcefulness, in the quickness of her action and cunning, verging on ferociousness, she plays the gipsy girl that she was trained to be. No Bengali maiden, however true to her lord, could do what she did in regard to the wicked merchant (Text, pp. 27-29). There she was wild like a tigress, and though her beauty was angelic, her glee was witch-like when she laughed in triumph over the murders she had committed (p. 28). No Bengali maiden could do what she did when confronting the threats of the Sannyasi (p. 32). It would be physically impossible for a young Bengali girl of the *Bhadralog* class to carry a sick man on her shoulders for miles and miles over hilly tracts as she did (p. 33). It was only possible for a girl who had the physical training of gipsy-life with its sports and plays. No Bengali maiden could ride as she did on the memorable night of her flight (pp. 23-24).

Her love for **Nader Chand** knew no bounds. It is true, that though a prince he had reduced himself to the condition of a *fakir* for her sake and wandered about in forests, heedless of dangers and of pangs of hunger and thirst for many a day. But **Mahua** was no less miserable within the confines of her mountain-home separated from her mate (pp. 19-20). Her sufferings were in no way less acute or tragic than those of her lord, though she was at her home and he a wanderer abroad, passing through the extreme freaks of our tropical climate.

Why did she not leave the custody of her parents and join **Nader Chand** at the outset, is a question which naturally arises in this case. That is, I suppose, due to her selfless love for our hero. However, strongly devoted to him, she had in the beginning no reason to trust in Nader Chand's constancy. Love for her might have been after all a passing fancy with the young lord. Had she encouraged him more than she had done, he would probably find himself irretrievably stranded in life, losing not only his social prestige but his great fortune as well, when the temporary fancy would have passed away, and there was every probability for this. On the bank of the Kangsa, she even advised the prince to return home, marry a beautiful girl and live a happy life (p. 23). It was only when Nader Chand was found to be a man of more solid calibre than ordinary lovers of youthful age that she cast her fate unreservedly with his, and followed him with the fidelity of a dog (p. 23).

Nader Chand yielded to his passion just like a straw resigning itself to the current. He was carried by his impulse and the good point about him was that the impulse was not a fleeting thing with him but a permanent incentive to all his actions. **Mahua's** passion for him was not a whit less, but her resourcefulness, tact and great presence of mind were everywhere in evidence for meeting the exigencies of a life so full of vicissitudes. This proves that as a heroine, she was superior to her mate, and the poet used him, as Dr. Kramrisch says, merely as a background for showing the greatness of **Mahua's** character by contrast.

Though she strikes us by her wildness as a mountain-girl, she nevertheless possessed in a pre-eminent degree the quieter virtues of domestic life that characterise the true Hindu wife. In this short Ballad the poet pictures her off and on in various artistic poses. We find her weeping alone when the prince wanted to eat rice which she could not get for him (Text, p. 31, ll. 13-14). We find her vowing the offer of two goats at the altar of a goddess for curing her lord when a fishbone had stuck into his throat (Text, p. 34). We find her again sitting by his side tenderly caressing him, when he had a headache (p. 34, ll. 9-12). When the prince goes to the market she whispers to his ears, her request to get for her a nose ornament (Text, p. 34, ll. 13-14). Thus in points of tenderness and domesticity she possesses all the grace and sweetness of a country-girl, but when faced with a trial that threatens to sever her from the lord of her heart, she is prepared to do anything; she is ready for murder, for suicide and for telling lies (p. 32, ll. 15-16). This trait in her character distinguishes her from the general run of our heroines, who while showing passive virtues, sometimes of an extraordinary kind, are found lacking in active resourcefulness, tact and will-force.

Though she fell in love at first sight (p. 7, l. 8), it was an appreciation of the qualities of her lover's noble heart that attracted her more than his handsome exterior, (p. 29, ll. 12-15).

When she had lost **Nader Chand** on the banks of the Kangsa, she had at first resolved to commit suicide, but latterly changed her mind as she had not yet tried her best for searching him out. We do not find her helplessly praying to God for a boon, when in danger, like most of the heroines of our classical poems. She trusted in her own action and until she had done her utmost by way of self-help, she would not leave the battlefield.

I have analysed her character at some length because, as I have already said, there are certain elements in her which we do not find in any of the female characters in the old Bengali poems, which more or less repeat the time-honoured story of Sita in their sketches of virtuous women. The female characters there though possessed of individual characteristics, which are striking, are modelled after the great heroine of the immortal epic.

Malua (Vol. I, p. 11; pp. 48-96) is a majestic and a more resplendent figure than Mahua, soaring in an atmosphere of unswerving fidelity, and she approaches the Hindu ideal of womanhood, not only in her devotion to her husband, who, though possessed of a loving nature, is a miserable weakling, but also in her tacit submission to the inscrutable ways of Providence and meek resignation to social tyranny. When a point of honour arises she is imperious. Read her glowing outburst of anger at the Kazi's offer in contrast with **Mahua's** stern silence and resoluteness in a similar situation. Malua's tragic end is lofty and spreads a halo of glory around her figure which looks like that of the goddess **Durga** at the time of its immersion in river, or of Sita, when she is carried off in the last scene by Mother Earth from this sublunary stage of ours. She is the type that is most admired in Hindu homes. Her constancy in love not only stood the test of all temptations and the severest stings of poverty but, that of abandonment by her husband which was the cruellest cut of all. She showed a genuine and real love for her co-wife, a rare quality even amongst Indian women, and committed suicide not for escaping the woes of her life which were "thick as leaves of Vallombrosa" but to save her husband from a perpetual scandal. At every stage her glorious life reminds us of **Sita**; in fact when **Chand Binode** was going to leave her for some time, she was fully conscious of the danger to which his absence would expose her and said things which have the ring of the very words that **Sita** said to Rama on the eve of her exile, though the poet evidently did not copy it from the Ramayana (Text, p. 74).

Kamala (Vol. I, Pt. II, pp. 113-162) and **Kajalrekha** (pp. 299-331) typify patience of the highest order. They both await the opportune moment for establishing their righteous cause. Exposed to danger of the gravest nature they do not fret or show the least mental agitation. That memorable scene of Kamala's offering her services to the queen-mother in her toilet room, with the beat of drums at the altar of Kali announcing the sacrifice of her beloved father and brother ringing in her ear, is a sublime instance of patience and self-control, unsurpassed by any episode described in our literature. We can conceive her match only in the all-forbearing **Kajalrekha**, apologising to the wicked bracelet-maiden on the eve of her departure from her husband's palace (p. 321), and perhaps in **Kanchanmala** too, when she gives up all claims upon her lord and like a statue sees without a sigh her triumphant co-wife quietly taking possession of her husband (Vol. II, Pt. II, p. 118). **Kamala's** speech before the court of the Raja to which we have already referred, with appeals full of pathetic emotion, making the whole case clear as daylight without any specific reference to the tyranny of the **Karkoon** but proving her points by documentary evidence alone aided by the words of witnesses, show the maidenly bashfulness and modesty of a Hindu girl of high caste on the one hand and her great intellectuality on the other. Though a perfect picture of maidenly shyness, she makes a confession of love before the court boldly like a **Desdemona**. Her plain but clever discourse on the occasion possesses the legal acumen and subtlety of the speech of **Portia**. When she describes her early life with its joys and happiness in her quiet home surrounded by mango and blackberry trees, with its reminiscences of the bathing-ghat from where the "eternal laughter of the waves" reverberates on the shore, the tender affection of her younger brother and the periodical religious festivities of the gay village-life, the appeal becomes irresistible and the reader, like her audience in the king's court, is moved to tears.

Kanchanmala (Vol. II, Pt. II, pp. 81-118) is another superb figure of the type of Malanchamala (Thakur Dadar Jhuli, by D. N. Mitra-Mazumdar). She proves that the true wife combines in her love the elements of affection of a mother, a sister and of a sweet companion of childhood. Raja **Dasaratha** in **Valmiki's** epic, gives this picture of a true wife while he recounts the good qualities of his devoted queen Kausalya. He says—"She is to me good and affectionate as a mother, dutiful and obedient as a servant and full of sweetness and confidence as a devoted friend" (Ramayana, Ayodhya Kanda). Just as the sea is the great reservoir into which the rivers fall, losing their individual names, even so does love, in its highest sphere, transcend all limitations, and there the paternal and brotherly affections and the nuptial love lose their special denominations and become merged in one felicitous emotion which is spiritual.

It is a point worth noticing that almost all the Ballads appeal most effectively and become highly impressive towards the end, which, in many cases, is tragic,—a feature in these Ballads not in conformity with the established canons of our classical poetics. The **Washerwoman's** love (Vol. II, Pt. II, pp. 3-28) has many touches of supreme appeal, her timid and modest approaches at the outset, showing the psychology of a country-girl painfully conscious of her low social status and of the ambitious nature of her love, the few days of exultant fulfilment of her cherished hopes, the pathos created by her desertion of home,—all these are no doubt very fine sketches, but sweet as she is throughout her brief career, she is nowhere so sweet as when courting death in the waters of the **Khorai.** There she prays to each turtle that flies above, to each tree that silently observes the tragic scene,—to the wind that seems by its doleful moanings to carry the news all around, —not to breathe out the report of her death, lest it should cause even a momentary sorrow to her lover, happy in the arms of the newly wedded princess (p. 28).

Kamala (Vol. II, Pt. II, pp. 211-230), the queen of **Durgapur,** was ordained to suffer death by an inscrutable stroke of fate. Her majestic, calm and resolute decision to die and her great love for her husband and child invest her towering figure with a charm which leaves a permanent impression on the reader. The frantic attempts of her husband to save her life, the supernatural dream that he dreamt in the distracted state of his mind, have many poetic suggestions, and the Ballad is one of the most beautiful productions of poetic art and fancy.

Madina (Vol. I, Pt. II, pp. 332-334) has been highly praised by Romain Rolland. As in the case of **Mahua** so also in Madina there are some features which are unique. No other poet in our literature has delineated nuptial love between a peasant and his wife with such fine touches and grace. Their love was essentially based on co-operation in daily life. They were companions every day, every hour of their life, helping each other in daily work. Through this co-operation, so finely sketched by the poet in minute details, their love grew strong as adamant. We get here glimpses of peasant life in Bengal, such as none but a peasant poet could give us. The periodical harvests stored in the granaries, the methods of transplantation then in vogue in the country, the different crops of the seasons and the routine-work in which one helped the other with affection and tenderness, are pictured in detail, and all these give the simple poetry and pathos of agricultural life in Bengal. One might suppose that this collaboration in work is altogether a prosaic affair without any romance fit for poetical treatment. But just look to another side of the sketch. When **Madina** was yet very young, **Dulal** was her constant companion. They caught a bird which both of them reared with utmost care. They planted a mango-tree which sprouted and grew under their fostering care. In hundreds of such little ways their romantic feeling had grown, and all this had taken place prior to marriage. Her heart was simple as that of a child. She was so confident of her husband's fidelity that she could not for a moment believe that he had divorced her though the letter of divorce was actually before her eyes. She thought it to be a mere trick which he was playing to test her confidence in him (p. 359). She prepared sweetmeats for him every day expecting his return. She would not let anybody throw a net into the pond lest the big fishes were caught in his absence. She kept the ripe fruits untouched on the boughs of trees, and prepared cakes which she preserved in a hanging rope-shelf and when these grew rotten she threw them away, shedding a drop of tear each time. But alas, the delusion could not for ever stay! When Dulal sent his son back with a cruel message, it was too severe a shock for her. There was now no room left to continue her heavenly faith in the false man, and she died of a broken heart. It was only a temporary weakness on the part of Dulal that had ruined the career of both. Love for his wife was deeply ingrained in his nature and yielding for a short while to worldly temptations he not only killed his wife but destroyed all the happiness of his own life. He could not measure the depth of his own nature at the outset, and that was his one great mistake in life. We can scarcely conceive of any account which is as touching as that of Dulal in remorse, given in the concluding canto of the Ballad.

These women of the Ballads have each such remarkable traits in her character, that it would be unfair not to refer to others like **Chandrabati,** the saintly daughter of the poet **Bangsi** (Vol. I, Pt. II, pp. 97-112), **Lila**, who possessed all the innocence and sweetness that we find in the budding flower (Vol. I, Pt. II, pp. 249-298), **Palanka** (Vol. I, Pt. II, pp. 3, 10-11, 36, 39-40), whom the poet Dwija Kanai with a few strokes of his brush raises to the dignity of a great character, **Manjurma** (Vol. III, Pt. I, pp. 9-20), who sang freely as the lark and cared not for the restrictions of society but flew like a lark in the illimitable regions of the sky, singing her joyous song—heedless of consequences,—**Bhelua** (Vol. III, Pt. I, pp. 64-106) and **Ayena Bibi** (Vol. III, Pt. I, pp. 116-161) two angelic women who stood the test of circumstances as severe as a fire-ordeal and proved to the world that they were true.

Are not these characters, the true models which have inspired us with the conception of the goddesses to whom we pay the tribute of our worship all round the year? It is **Chandrabati's** life which reflects the white heat and the mild effulgence of the figure of a **Saraswati**, whom we worship in February. It is Mahua, whose greatness and many-sided activities remind us of the ten-armed **Durga** worshipped in October. Malua is verily like our harvest goddess **Lakshmi**, worshipped in November. Constantly fed by the virtues of women whose lives burn like flames at our domestic altar, these deities of Bengal appear to us not merely as visions but as the very real and living figures whose prototypes we find moving about around us in our domestic environment. It is a pity that Miss Mayo saw only the bad side of our society. Even the great

Himalayas have grim cavities infested with poisonous worms and reptiles, but a poor judge is he who does not conceive the grandeur of that Prince of Mountains and confines his narrow vision to things low and ugly. Miss Mayo, I am sorry, deserves the unreserved censure of the Sanskrit poet "মক্ষিকা ব্রণমিচ্ছন্তি, মধুমিচ্ছন্তি ভ্রমরাঃ" (It is the bee that seeks honey whilst the fly is attracted by ulcers).

I will here quote an extract from a letter of Mr. Rothenstein, the distinguished painter and art-critic of England, about the women of the Bengali Ballads.

"Through every ballad moves that marvellous being,—exalted, grave, shy and passionate, reserved and bold,—and how nobly beautiful!—the Indian woman. She has remained unchanged through all the phases of Indian culture, religious and social. Her lovers carved her in stone and marble at Barhut, Sanchi and Amarabati, painted her, sinuous, radiant and bejewelled at Ajanta and Bagh, and delineated to honour her in thousands of humble studies in Jammu, Jaipur, Delhi and Agra, Muslim as well as Hindu, well into the nineteenth century. I am interested to find some among your Bengali Ballads date from middle of the last century. Indian art is unique in having preserved a robust primitive spirit throughout what in Europe were late and sophisticated periods, and I notice the same quality in the late literary examples you gave. No revival seems able to preserve the strength and directness of true Indian tradition which is still alive in your latest Ballads."

There is one phase in the character of the Bengali women which deserves a passing notice. We have often found in the Bengali women of the Ballads a martial temperament which may not be considered quite compatible with their traditional fragility and modesty. Mahua is no exception. We have already referred to this trait of their character in connection with **Sakhina** in the Ballad of **Firoze Khan** (Vol. II, Pt. II, pp. 392-433). The brilliant sketch of **Manicktara** (Vol. II, Pt. II, pp. 231-274) whose expertness in archery was really a marvel and who had, in the last canto of the incomplete Ballad, set out on a martial adventure, is another striking instance of the bravery and fitness of our women for heroic action in the battle-field. In some of the recensions of the Bengali **Mahabharat** there is a full canto devoted to the description of a fight of **Droupadi** in the field of Kurukshetra, and this canto, called "The **Droupadi Yuddha,**" seems to be a production of indigenous fancy, as I do not know of any Sanskritic source which contains such a grim episode. In some of the Ramayanic legends published in Bengal, **Sita** is described as fighting with the hydra-headed **Ravana** (*Dashaskandha Ravana Badh*). The above two instances are mere fictions, but Sakhina has a historical tradition, and the field of Kella-Tajpur, where she fought and died, still exists and attests to the truth of the tradition. In the Ballad of princess Mallika, the daughter of King Barun, of which a full account is to be found in my "Folk Literature of Bengal" (pp. 124-134) we find the story of a Hindu princess, invincible in war, and so formidable that her challenge to her suitors, on certain humiliating conditions in case of their defeat, was held in dread by all, and inspite of her angelic beauty and great accomplishments none had dared to respond to her call for a long time till she was overthrown by Hanif and converted to Islam. I have numerous Ballads with me, not yet published, containing sketches of these martial types of women. The fight of Hira Bibi, Muchha Bibi and Nur Bibi is evidently a historical fact. Chand, the redoubtable general of the Choudhuries, felt overawed by the superstitious belief that Kali had actually come to the field in the guise of these women (p. 301).

The history of Bengal furnishes examples of heroic women who could bravely meet the exigencies of a perilous situation to save their honour, and I beg to refer here to a historical episode that took place in Bengal during the reign of Aurangzeb. I take the following extract from the 'Narrative of the Government of Bengal' by Francis Gladwin (Ed. V, Feb. 1788, pp. 5-8).

"**Shova Singh,** the Zaminder of Chitwa Burda took up arms and was joined in his rebellion by **Rahim Khan,** an Afgan Chief.

"**Krisna Ram** the Zaminder of Burdwan, rashly opposing him with only a few troops, lost his life in the action .. .. **Jagat Roy,** the son of **Krisna Ram,** fled to Jehangeerpur, at the time the seat of Government. The daughter of the deceased **Krisna Ram,** Zaminder of Burdwan, a beautiful young woman had been taken prisoner at the plundering of that place. **Shova Singh** paid his addresses to her, but she received his proposal in horror and contempt. Finding all his felicitations in vain, he resolved to use force and for that purpose, got clandestinely into her apartment at night. Upon his attempt to ravish her, the heroine drew from under her garment a knife which she had concealed in hopes of finding an opportunity to gratify her revenge. With this weapon, she ripped up his belly."

The **Jahar Brata** which made hundreds of Rajput women offer their lives to fire when there was no other way to preserve their honour, was also practised in Bengal. The spot is still shown near **Ballal Dighi** in Bikrampur where the queens of **Ballal Sen II,** threw themselves into fire apprehending the approach of the Mahomedans. That spot is called **Pora Rajar Bari** or theburnt palace, the ashes of which are still to be found under-ground, though the embers which burnt the noble ladies grew cool centuries ago. There is no doubt that the number of **Satis** in Bengal increased at one time on account of a feeling of insecurity among Bengali women who had lost their husbands.

The power of our women to save themselves in the hour of peril, if required, by murderous action, is no imagined quality ascribed to them. Numerous instances have happened quite recently, where ladies killed the men who attempted to dishonour them. I have referred to a Ballad in this Introduction (Int., pp. lix-lx) in which a woman shot seven dacoits and a Chaukidar dead quite recently in a village in the district of Backergunj.

Women are called "Sakti" in this country. This ideal reaches its consummation in the conception of the Goddess **Kali**—the grim deity with a portruding tongue dripping the blood of the enemy, whose dissevered head she holds in one of her hands. With a garland made of the heads of the **Asurs** that she has killed, dangling on her breast, she looks terrible and savage, delighting in the funeral ground, followed by jackals and vultures and by her two grim attendants *Dakini* and *Jogini*. She is the goddess of destruction, riding the storm, with her wild dishevelled hair floating in the air and with her third eye on the forehead emitting fire. She wildly dances on the breast of her husband—the great god Shiva—who lies inert like a corpse under her feet. This goddess would naturally suggest a barbaric origin. It might be so. It is in all probability so. But the higher philosophy of the Hindus has given her a spiritual significance which deserves a passing notice, as it has a bearing on the martial temperament of her daughters in Bengal. She is the goddess of a country noted for its great hurricanes, storms and earthquakes, a country ravaged by famine and plague, where infant-mortality beats all records and women by hundreds courted death on the funeral pyres of their husbands even the other day. People see here the destructive agency of nature in too vivid and glaring a light to indulge merely in pleasant reveries about God's kindness and merciful attributes. The

Daughters of Kali.

deity of destruction is before their eyes and how can they ose sight of the naked truth that presents itself everywhere? They are not prepared to accept the theory of an Evil God by the side of a Gracious God, for their philosophy has taught them that all that they see around has sprung from one source. The evil of to-day is the good of to-morrow, and Nature in her evolutionary course is ever transmuting all phenomena into contrary forms and qualities,—the good and the bad being relative terms to denote the condition of things for the time being. But all comes from the same source;—darkness accentuates light; evil is a lesson and factor indispensable in the progressive stages of realisation of truth and has eventually a beneficent bearing on our moral and cultural progress. So it cannot proceed from an Evil God. **Kali**, the goddess, whatever origin she might bear, represents the conflicting elements of Universal Agency and harmonises the apparently discordant laws of evil and good. Her two hands threaten destruction, while the other two hands are raised up to bless and grant a boon. She symbolises the principle of destruction and preservation which we find simultaneously at work on all sides. If the law of Nature is transgressed there is no immunity, no escape, death is sure. But to the child who resigns itself to the mercy of the Mother, she is all tenderness. Ramprasad the great *sākta* poet sings: "Just as a child when beaten by its mother, cries 'O mother,' 'O mother,' and clings to her, so do I yearn for thy grace, O Divine Mother!" The conception of the terrible and the sublime, and of the kind and the merciful is typified in Kali's image, which in the process of Hindu spiritualisation has risen to a plane of grandeur in the place of its primitive barbaric terrorism. At every stage the Hindu Aryans have given an esoteric significance to the sketch drawn of her, and the women of Bengal have always approached her for being granted the sterner virtues of soul, instances of which are found in the Ballads and the history of our country.

Male Character.

My notes have already taken a considerable space but before I finish, I crave pardon from my readers for taking a glance at the principal male characters. The towering figure of **Kenaram** (Vol. I, Pt. II, pp. 182-226) and that of **Monsuir**, the **Coffin Stealer** (Vol. III, Pt. I, pp. 31-50) have many points of similarity. Kenaram roved in the wild tracts of *Jalliar Haor* in Eastern Mymensingh, delighting like a tiger in human blood,—one that had never touched a bed nor a good meal, not to speak of any luxury of life,—sleeping like a beast on the bare ground and living on the milk of wild buffaloes,—himself, the wildest of them in human shape. Hoarding money like a Jew and not spending a pice on himself or others, thoroughly unlettered but having a queer philosophy of his own to defend and justify his wickedness, Kenaram stands before us like the Archangel of Milton, tall as "Teneriffe or Atlas, unremoved: His stature reached the sky." (**"আসমানে জমীনে ঠেকে যখন হয় খাড়া"** Vol. I, Pt. II, p. 187). There is something in this wild man which reminds me of the Haunchback in Hugo's Notredame, though I cannot exactly find where the coincidence lies. It is perhaps the grim humour of his life which makes him so unique a figure in our literature. In the last canto where he becomes reformed, struck with remorse, the effect is dramatic. The sequel of a life so varied and wild in its course is shown with the masterly power of the gifted poetess **Chandrabati**, who had seen the giant with her own eyes. **Monsuir** was as great as **Kenaram** in vice, as latterly he became in saintliness. That superb scene in which he burst into expressions of spontaneous prayer in the house where he had committed robbery will leave an indelible impression upon the reader

(Vol. III, Pt. I, p. 49). **Garga** (Vol. I, Pt. II, pp. 249-298) is a complex character, as great in piety as in violent outbursts of his temper. He is a typical Brahmin of the old school. Sincere as sincerity's self, he could not brook anything that in the least degree smacked of unfairness. It was this sense of justice that led him to fight so vehemently in the cause of the poor orphan boy Kanka ousted from the Brahmin society. And though he was mistaken, it was this sense of justice that led him to conceive the horrible plan of murdering Kanka and even his own daughter. It was this sense of justice again that led him observe fast and vigil, seeking divine help, to ascertain the truth of the case, and, once convinced of Kanka's innocence, to make wild and desperate attempts to get back the young man whom he had lost by his own folly. In the Ayodhya Kanda of the Ramayana there is a significant line giving us a glimpse of the characters of saintly Brahmins. **Raja Dasaratha** was overwhelmed with a heart-rending grief that resulted in his death. The poet says that his condition was "উত্ক্রমনৃতম্ ঋষিং যথা" (like that of a Ṛshi who had spoken a lie). If an Indian saint ever told a lie, his repentance became unsupportable as death. Garga was a saint of this type. When he came to know that he had been made a tool in the hands of the conspirators against Kanka and his own daughter, his frantic remorse knew no bounds. Similar types of Brahmins were not rare in Bengal in her historical period. I will cite an example. When **Kumar Dutta,** a brother-in-law of king **Lakshman Sen** (1167 A.D.-1201 A.D.) was charged with attempts to ravish a woman named **Madhuri** of the Bania caste he was summoned by the Raja for answering the charges against him. But queen Ballava, the sister of the culprit suddenly appeared before the court in frantic rage and dragging Madhuri by her fore-lock, called her a public woman and a courtesan. The queen said: "Where is that judge, so impudent and foolish who will dare sit in judgment over my brother on the evidence of this harlot? " Like a boat facing a storm **Lakshman Sen** found himself staggered and stupefied by the attitude of his queen. The Justices of Peace could not speak a word for fear,—not even **Umapati Dhar** and **Halayudha,** the great dictators of public law. At this juncture **Gobardhan Acharya,** the chief minister, who verged on four score and had all along led the life of an ascetic, stepped forward and admonished the judges stricken with fear for allowing public justice to be tampered in that manner. His lips trembled in rage when he declared that the wicked queen who sided with her brother should be punished. He prophesied that ruin would befall the monarch who could tolerate such interference with justice in the public court. He said, " **Rampal** the king had an only son who was charged with ravishing a woman and she committed suicide after that affront to her honour. The monarch, his father, passed the sentence of death by impalement on his only son. Even up to now people sing songs of this noble act of the monarch; and you are disgracing his throne, O unworthy monarch! " He threw away his staff in a furious mood and with tears in his eyes, he ran towards the gate to leave the unholy city for ever. We find this interesting episode in " Shekh Subhodaya." Garga was a Brahmin of this type.

The musical fiddle of **Tona Barui** and his disciple Amir, the young merchant (Vol. III, Pt. 1, pp 95-96), recalls some of the most famous stories of classical antiquity,—that of **Orpheus** " Of delicate vein, whose music beasts and stones did follow",—of **Amphion,** Jove's son by Antelope, " Whose pipe gathered his flocks together when shadows fell." In the Indian tales examples are not lacking. We refer our readers to "The Romantic Tales from the Punjab" collected and edited by the Rev. Charles Swynnerton, F.S.A. There **Ranjah** in the tale of Hir and Ranjah, attracts men and women by the wonderful power of his lute and makes them transfixed to the spot like statues. But it is in the sketch of Mir Shikari that the power of music is shown as on a par with that of Orpheus. Charles Swynnerton remarks, " We think of Orpheus as he is often pictured in the domestic walls of Pompeii, sitting in woodland glades and enchanting all nature with the golden tones of his lyre. So too Mir Shikari is canopied by trees and seated upon rocks ravishing *the beasts and birds* with the dulcet music of his magic lute." (Int., xxxiv.)

Mir Shikari is certainly a beautiful creation of the poet's fancy. The tragic end of the buck which came near him, attracted by the sound of his lute, only to die by the arrow of his hand is full of pathos. The buck said, " Though I am dying, being shot by you, my last prayer is that you would play upon your lute once more before I die. I long again to hear that fatal music that has caused my death." But the beauty of the tale suffers a good deal owing to the circumstance that **Mir Shikari's** Muse was inspired by a greed for animal flesh which made him entice the beasts by music and then kill them by his arrows.

The Bengali Ballad, the **Herdsman Lover** (Vol. II, Pt. II, pp. 29-78) has many analogous points with the story of Hir and Ranjah. **Ranjah** tends buffaloes like the Bengali herdsman and though the latter does not gather his flocks by the charm of his flute as **Ranjah** does, he certainly allures his lady's mind by the infallible charm of his flute.

Bengal is specially the place for lute, fiddle and flute. In almost all the love-tales, the unfailing effect of music of the flute or the fiddle finds a place. The flute is the Bengali cowherd's only companion, solace and joy. The god that sways the hearts of the multitudes of this province is represented as a cowherd with a flute in his hand,—the flute whose music makes the current run against the tide and the trees bend low in still air.

When comparing Tona Barui with the musicians of the Ballads and legends of other countries, I should point out a difference. Though there is an element of poetical appeal in the legends of **Orpheus**, **Ranjah** and **Mir Shikari**, they do not possess the human interest of the sketches drawn of Tona Barui, Amir the merchant and of the Herdsman Lover. These characters are taken from life and are not merely legendary—beyond the boundaries of belief. There is an historical element which clings to these legends and makes the images vivid before our eyes. The homestead of **Tona Barui** still exists and his descendants still take pride in their ancestor who lived our in historical times.

4. *The Vaishnava Lyrics, the Ballads and the Classical Poems of Bengal.*

The Radha-Krisna cult in Bengal is of great antiquity; but formerly the legend was confined to the masses. Visnu was originally the Sun-god as we find him in the Vedas. He marched through the heavenly regions visiting by turn the different constellations, known as **Chitra, Vishakha, Radhá, Anuradha,** etc. But when in later times Krisna and Vishnu became the same God in popular belief, the whole paraphernalia of the Sun-God's legend in connection with his heavenly consorts was transferred to Krisna, the planets figuring as the **gopis** of Brindaban. Krisna thus dominated the field and became the hero of the whole solar legend. This must have taken place many centuries ago, as the names of Radha and Krisna are found mentioned together in the inscriptions and sacred writings of a very remote age.[1] Krisna is called Kanai in Bengali, and

The Radha Krisna cult.

[1] See Gatha Saptasati (1st century A.D., Chap. 1, Verse 89, the Panchantantra, 5th century A.D., Chap. I, p. 38 (Bcmbay Sanskrit series). The Vayu Puran (believed to be the earliest Puran) has this line রাধাবিলাসরসিকং কৃষ্ণাখ্যং পুরুষং পরং (Chap. 104, sloka 52.). In Paharpur, a stone-slab has been found containing a long roll illustrating Radha-Krishna *lila*. The slab cannot be later than 478 A.D, as has been proved by ineriptions.

Kanhu in popular **Prakrit**. I find that this latter name occurs in one of the oldest **Jatakas**—the 'Maha Ummaga Jataka' which is ascribed to the 7th century B.C., if not earlier. It says that the mother of the king **Sivi**, is named Jambubati, who was the beloved queen-consort of Vasudev,—the **Kanha** (Jatak stories, edited by E. B. Cowell, p. 216). Though in the Tantrik literature Radha is connected with a **Chakra** which is called **Radha Chakra** and a tantra exists in her name called the **Radha tantra**, the classical scriptures of the Hindus had given her but a hesitant reception in the pantheon of Hindu deities, till the 12th century, when Jaydev's lays made the whole air of India resonant with the tale of her sports and amours with Krisna.

I have mentioned in some of my previous works that the 10th and 11th centuries breathed a corrupt moral air throughout Eastern India, the evidences of which are supplied by nude figures in *bas relief* on the walls of some of the old temples of Bengal and markedly in those of Puri and Konarak. The onrush of this erotic taste in sculpture travelled so far as Central India and in the Khejuraha temples there the nude figures bear the stamp of the corrupt Uriya sculpture. Here in Bengal, in the lays of Jaydev, Vidyapati and Chandidas,—in the *Krisna dhamalis* and in the hymns to Siva-Parbati in copper-plate inscriptions, the same lax spirit is found pervading the works of art and literature belonging to those two centuries. This might have been due to a spirit of reaction against the stiff and puritanic standard of sexual ethics of the stoic Buddhist monk. But whatever cause we may assign to it, the corrupt sexual morals of the period have left their indelible stamp in Bengal not only on the contemporary literary works but also on her sculpture. The gross humour in matters pertaining to sexes which we find in some of the earliest popular songs known as **ashal** or **lal**, only shows the characteristic spirit of the age, accentuated by the doctrines promulgated by the vicious **Gurus** of the **tantrik** school. Some of these songs still linger in the backwoods of North Bengal and in Mymensingh.

Though the Shahajia community is now branded as sheltering immoral practices in the name of religion, it is these people who in their higher scriptures gave a lofty interpretation to sexual love. The sexual relation was idealised by the Shahajia creed. They declared without any hesitancy or fear that the highest goal of religion—the state of *beatitude*—is to be achieved by men and women loving one another in a spirit of true sacrifice and constancy. They even went so far as to declare that all other paths indicated by other religious faiths are the products of strained fancy and speculation, sexual love alone being real and natural,—"Shahaja" as they call it. They have their codes and rituals which require them absolutely to curb the instincts of flesh, and though one might take exception to the nocturnal meetings of the sexes which they organise for the culture of emotion, the crystal-like transparence and purity of their creed are in evidence in their higher literature. I am not however, at present concerned with the details of the mystic Shahajia cult, but I must emphasize the fact stated by Chandidas in the 14th century, that in his time every youthful man and woman aspired to practise Shahajia love.

The Sahajias.

The heroes of the Ballads lived in an atmosphere of this higher emotional plane, but they had nothing to do with the Shahajia propaganda. The lovers described in the Ballads, true to the emotional nature of the Bengalis, were drawn by the sweet attractions of sexual feeling of a Platonic form, which, in point of gallantry beat all records of knight-errantry, and in the spirit of renunciation shows a roll of golden deeds no way less striking than those of the great martyrs of the world.

The female characters of the Ballads should not be mistaken for Shahajias ; for their love did not proceed from any doctrine promulgated by any sect. If they climbed the highest summits in the field of emotion it was Nature that led them to such heights. They owed no fealty to any religion or creed but followed their own instincts which were true and constant. These characters, women more particularly, filled the atmosphere of Bengal with the fragrant breath of their pure and unsophisticated feeling and created a phraseology of tender emotion which the Shahajias and Vaisnavas adopted in their love poems with some added grace and refinement of their own. I gave numerous illustrations of such set-expressions from the Ballads and the Vaisnava lyrics in my General Introduction to Vol. II, Pt. I (pp. xix-xxi). Oftentimes the very lines seem to be identical, at others the phrases of a Ballad and of a Vaisnav *pada* seem to be the echoes from the same voice.[1] When we find the same idea couched in a language

[1] Numerous extracts have been quoted by me in my Introduction to the Second volume to show the striking similarity in language between the love passages contained in the Vaisnava lyrics and the Ballads. There are many more which we have come across. For instance here is a *pada* of Chandi Das : "

" ধিক রহু জীবনে পরাধীন দেহ। তাহার অধিক দুঃখ পরবশ লেহ ॥
পাপ কপালে বিধি এমত লিখিল। সুধার সায়ের মোর গরল হইল ॥
অমিয়া বলিয়া যদি ডুব দিলু তায়। গরল ভরিঞা কেন উচালে হিয়ায় ॥
শীতল বলিয়া যদি পাষাণ করি কোলে। পীরিতি অনল তাপে পাষাণ যে গলে ॥
ছায়া দেখি বসি যদি তরুলতা বনে। জ্বলিয়া উঠয়ে তরু লতা পাতা সনে ॥
যমুনার জলে জাঞা যদি দিএ ঝাপ। পরাণ জুড়াবে কি অধিক উঠে তাপ ॥
চণ্ডীদাস কহে দৈব গতি নাহি জান। দারুণ পীরিতি ইবে দহিবে পরাণ ॥"

(M. S. No. 298, Pada No. 26, Calcutta University Library of old MSS.). In Bhelua (Vol. II, Text, p. 179) we come across such lines—

"গাছের তলায় আলাম ছায়া পাইবার আশে। পত্র ছেইদ্যা রৌদ্র লাগে আপন কর্ম্মদোষে ॥
ঘরেতে পাতিলাম শয্যা নিদ্রার কারণ। সেই ঘরে লাগিল আগুন কপালে লিখন ॥

The same idea is conveyed in the following lines of Ayena Bibi (Vol. III, p. 256) :—

"যেই সে বিরথ্খের তলে যাই, আরে ছায়া পাওনের আশে রে।
পত্র চ্ছেদ্যা রৌদ্র লাগে দেখ কপালের দুষেরে ॥
দৈরাতে ডুবিতে গেলে দরিয়া শুকায়।
গায়ের না বাতাস লাগলে আর ভাল আগুন ঝিমায় ॥ "

a little different in each case, but with striking similarities, we cannot help coming to the conclusion that the Ballads caught the very words that were current in a hundred songs which have now faded away from this land leaving their echoes behind, whilst the Vaisnavas and the Shahajias exploited these rural resources and embellished them when using them in their lyrics. Like expert jewellers they showed their skill in workmanship while handling the diamonds obtained from their country's mine, whereas the rustic Ballad-mongers who had no scholarship or knowledge of Poetics used them in their pristine and somewhat crude form.

The rich phraseology in the field of emotional literature which our language possesses, is one of its greatest points of strength and this has been created by the sacrificing love of men and women in our country for ages. Mercantile people have developed a commercial language suited to the needs of their ever thriving trade ; there is a special language answering to administrative needs of peoples possessing political power. Our language, however, is so full of niceties in the field of tender feelings that a translator feels hampered at every step in his attempts to convey into other languages the correct imports of indigenous words, on this point. Such words are in exuberance in our country-dialect and this is the resource from which both the Vaisnavas and Ballad-makers reaped their golden harvests. We have given quite a large number of instances of these subtle forms that exist in our Literature in the Introduction to the Second volume (p. xxvii).

Then again in the Ballad of Manjurma (Vol. III, Pt. I, ll. 34-36) we have got these lines :—

"পীরিত যতন, পীরিত রতন রে, আরে ভালা পীরিত গলার হার।
পীরিত করিয়া যেজন মরেরে, আরে ভালা সফল জীবন তার॥"

which recalls a familiar and well-known passage of Chandidas.

Carefully reading the ballad of **Shyam Ray** given in this volume we cannot but be struck by the tender melody which breathes the air of Vaisnava poetry in this song without bearing any evidence of Vaisnava influence in it. The soft and subdued wailings of the Dom girl surrendering herself to **Shyam Ray**, doubting and fearing at every step but at last yielding to the irresistible passion, will recall the various situations in the love-episodes of Radha. This ballad, I must say, is a very wonderful one. The rich imageries it unfolds are culled from indigenous sources. The delicate situation of Radha engaged in household work, when Krisna calls her by the song of his flute, finds a parallel in that of the Dom girl described in many beautiful poses, while doing her evening duties at home or bathing in the river-ghat. There is a striking similarity of expressions used by Chandidas in his lyrical poems and those found in this Ballad. If the Ballad of the Washer-maiden (published in the Second volume) which in its earlier cantos is evidently analogous to this one, is more dramatic, that of **Shyam Ray** excels in lyrical wealth, though the poet shows a dramatic sense also of no mean order. Like a skilled hand that weaves a garland with the soft and gay petals of a flower, dropping the leaves and twigs, the poet strings the melo-dramatic incidents of his plot with all that is beautiful and fine, rejecting superfluous matter. In fact he skips over so many points that are stale and flat in the narrative that I at first thought that he made positive omissions or that the passages were missing which the ballad-collector could not get hold of. I wrote so in my preface to the Ballad. But reading it over again, I find that the superior aesthetic sense of the poet rejected all prosaic matter, retaining only those that have a lyrical or dramatic appeal, and leaving the gaps to be filled up by the intelligent reader, for which the poet has left ample suggestions.

In the Ballad of **Manjurma** again a few passages obviously recall the incidents of Radha's amours. Hassain sits at the bathing-ghat and calls **Manjurma** with the music of his flute, the irresistible appeal of which draws the poor girl from the call of her domestic duties. The very expressions have here the ring of Vaisnava lyrics. The Ballad-makers and the composers of the *Giti-kathas* had already prepared a soil for the emotional Vaisnavism to bud forth. Earth and heaven were brought nearer to each other by the self-dedication of the lovers, in whose eyes the beloved was as God incarnate. Though the Ballads we have found are not sufficiently old, there are proofs that Ballad-poetry existed in pre-Mahomedan times and they certainly left their charming vocabulary as a legacy to those that came after. True, the form of love described in the Ballads, was secular, but it certainly reached a height not greatly distant from the portals of spiritual bliss, visualised by Vaisnava masters. When Chaitanya pointed out with his raised hand the abode of beatitude, saying that the only beloved of man, his only friend, was God, the masses who had already received the culture of faith and devotion on the physical plane did not feel much difficulty in climbing to that spiritual height. A close study of the Ballads is essential for those who would like to study and analyse the causes that led to the development of Vaisnavism in Bengal.

I have already referred (in Vol. I, Pt. I, p. xxiii) to the fact that not only in the Vaisnava and Shahajia lyrics but even in other departments of our classical literature we find expressions and idioms strikingly analogous to those found in the Ballads.[1] The aphorisms of Dak and

[1] Numerous examples of this similarity have been shown in the Introduction to the Second volume. There are a few others to be found in the present collections also.

Khana, the Maynamati songs, the Chandi-mangal poems, the Bengali Ramayanas and other works have poetical lines which agree with the contexts of the Ballads almost *verbatim*. Is it not curious that in the interior of the district of Burdwan—in the villages of **Kogram, Kandra** and **Damunya,** where Lochandas, Jnanadas and Mukundaram lived,—in **Fulia,** the birthplace of Krittibas in the Nadia district,—in **Nannoor** of Birbhum from where Chandidas sang his immortal lays and in **Nilphamari** and other places of North Bengal whence Grierson and Bisweswar Bhattacharjya collected the Gupi Chandra songs not to speak of the Ballads, found in Mymensingh, Noakhali and Chittagong,—we find such a strange agreement in current expressions and terms of poetical phraseology, inspite of the fact that communication was so difficult in those days! The language of the works written in these different districts, as found in old manuscripts are full of provincialisms and local peculiarities. But inspite of them, the contexts often show an obvious analogy not only in spirit but in language too, though in the latter there are slight differences owing to the existence of some little dissimilarities in local dialects.

I believe that men and women of this vast province were linked together by a common ideal in the field of tender feelings under Buddhistic influence which accounts for the development of a common phraseology, used by the poets of different schools. But we feel that other potent causes must have been at work to produce such uniformly wide results.

Under the Hindu rule the masses indulged in festivities and amusements, naturally centering around themes which were the same in all provinces that formed one political unit. And we know that the Kingdom of **Gaur** even in the Pal and the Sen periods extended far beyond the present limits of Bengal. We have referred to the fact that the Manasha-mangal poems and the Gupi Chandra songs, which originated in Bengal, spread over a vast country comprising Bhagalpur, the Punjab, Orissa and even Bombay Presidency. These Bengali poems served as models from which the people of other parts of India copied, and hence quite naturally there are considerable points of agreement amongst the literatures of those two cults all over India. **Gaur** had at one time become the centre of fashion from which flowed the festive songs that were adopted by the peoples of many parts of India.

When **Gaur** was conquered by Mahomedans, the old tradition did not die out in a day. The Hindu capital still remained the centre of festive amusements. The whole province was not subdued at once. After the overthrow of Sen dynasty in Nadia the descendants of Lakshman Sen ruled as suzerains in Eastern Bengal till 1325 A.D., when Ballal II lost the day in his battle with Baba Adam by an unfortunate freak of fate. It was owing to a fatal mistake that the Sen dynasty lost their power and the chief members—the flowers of the family, perished in the flames of a fire kindled with their own hands.

From 1200-1325 A.D. the Hindus were in full power in East Bengal. The upper classes of Hindus, the best of them, resorted to various districts of Dacca, Jessore and Khulna still largely inhabited by the Kulins. The earliest and the best of the Bengali classics—such as Ramayana by Krittibas, Mahabharata by Sanjay, Manasha-mangal by Bejoy Gupta, Narayan Dev and Bangsidas were written in a Hindu atmosphere under Hindu inspiration. It is therefore very probable that the minstrels and rhapsodists of Eastern capitals, true to their ancient tradition, still mastered the field visiting all the important centres of the country for holding their musical performances. Though their field of activity was not now as wide as in olden times, it comprised the farthest boundaries of Bengal.

The ladies of noble families listened to the *Giti-kathas* in their natal rooms and whiled away their hours of lonely confinement, and though the Brahmin scholars looked on vernacular songs with contempt yet they furnished a perennial spring from which flowed the best festive amusements of the masses. Thus the Giti-kathas and Ballads had a large circulation over the vast province. The populace was kept in constant touch with the Hindu and Buddhist ideals of spiritual philosophy and renunciation in the capital towns. Hence these festive songs occasionally show the highest flight of spiritual philosophy in the conception of their great heroes and heroines, though the authors were generally void of a knowledge of letters. These were the days when Bengal was flooded with such wonderful tales as the Kanchanmala, the Sankhamala and the Malanchamala, published by Mr. Dakshinaranjan Mitra-Majumdar in his "Thakurdadar Jhuli" and Kajalrekha, Kanchanmala and Madhumala published in the First and Second volumes of Eastern Bengal Ballads. There are still hundreds of them interspersed with exquisite songs which have not yet seen the light but which like gems of purest ray serene lie hidden in the recesses of Bengali cottages. I have given a literal translation of the tale of Malanchamala, which is one of the best, if not the very best of these tales, in my Folk Literature of Bengal (pp. 267-322), the other three stories as already stated have been published in the First and Second volumes of this work.

The Ballads followed in the train of Rupa-kathas and Giti-kathas though most of the former are to be traced to a period not earlier than the 14th century. We find the Ballads more compact in shape than the other two classes of tales, and the metrical form in which they are couched has safeguarded their pristine beauty and charm, whilst the Rupa-kathas and Giti-kathas being mostly composed in prose have suffered considerably in the hands of singers, being mutilated in the course of their recitation from generation to generation. It is only in the songs which are found interspersed in the prose narratives, that we find the glorious poetry of the originals. For the songs are committed to memory and thus preserved from any substantial change. Some of the Rupa-kathas and Giti-kathas may be traced so far back as the 9th or 10th centuries A.D.

I think I have been able to establish the theory that the Bengali language in the different forms of its local dialects was given a homogeneity by the efforts of the minstrels and singers whose musical performances used to be called in requisition throughout the country, and this also accounts for the striking agreement in the poetical forms of expression which are so marked in old Bengali classical and popular compositions.

That most of the early Ballads have been lost to us may be proved by references found in many standard old Bengali poems. The Chaitanya Bhagabat (Anta Khanda) refers to the songs of Jogipal, Bhagipal and Mahipal of the Pal dynasty. It says that prior to the advent of Chaitanya, the whole country was madly fond of these Ballads. Unfortunately we have not been able to secure any of these. I have known men of culture and rank who informed me that in their childhood they had heard songs of Mahipala Raja. Pandit Kokileswar Bhattacharjya, M.A., Professor of Sanskrit in the Calcutta University, heard these songs as a child. But I have not been able to lay my hands on them. They surely contained some historical information, though probably mixed with legends, about this great king of the Pal dynasty. My pupil Mr. Mahammad Mansuriddin, B.A., has given me a small scrap from a Ballad in which the attempts of this monarch to ravish a beautiful country-girl named Lila, who had come to bathe in the celebrated Dighi, called the Mahipal Dighi after him, are described in the quaint and archaic country-dialect. We have got numerous references of Ballads composed in honour of many of the Hindu Rajas in classical Bengali works. I will notice them in the concluding chapter of this Introduction.

So this country was full of Ballads, Rupa-kathas and Giti-kathas sung by wandering minstrels who like the Mediæval rhpsodists of Europe singing the song of Aucassion and Nicolette, visited every part of a vast country and thus enriched our language with set forms of poetical expression so profusely found in later times in our Ballads, Classical works and in the Lyrics of Vaisnava song-masters.

5. *Notes on Language.*

Many peculiarities of Eastern Bengal dialects are in evidence in the Ballads comprised in this as in the preceding volumes. As no grammar of the Bengali language properly so called, has yet been written, the attempts of the writers of grammatical treatises in Bengal having been hitherto directed towards a slavish imitation of the works of Panini and Bopadev, the peculiarities of local dialects found in the Ballads should be noted for the use of our future grammarians and philologists. I jot down below some that have struck me.

(1) 'হ' is often found changed into 'অ'. Where a man of W. B. says 'হাঁ' (yes), his brother on the borders of the Padma will say 'অয়' (from 'হয়'). In these ballads we often find 'ইন্দু' for 'হিন্দু', 'আতি' for 'হাতী', 'এন' for 'হেন', 'অইয়া' for 'হইয়া', 'অইব' for 'হইব' and 'ময়াল' for 'মহাল'.

(2) 'ও' is often changed into 'উ' as in 'কুণা' for 'কোণা', 'কুরাণ' for 'কোরাণ', 'চুর' for 'চোর', 'ছুটু' and 'ছুড়ু' for 'ছোট', 'বুচকা' for 'বোচকা', 'জুখা' for 'জোখা' (জোখা as

লেখা জোখা), 'গুঁয়াইল' for 'গোঁয়াইল' (spent), 'যুল' for 'যোল', 'সুত' for 'সোত' (স্রোত), 'পরবুদ' for 'প্রবোধ', 'সুতুর' for 'সহোদর', 'সুনালী' for 'সোনালী', 'সুয়ার' for 'সোয়ার' (a rider), 'মুচ' for 'মোচ' (moustache), 'যুগ' for 'যোগ' (addition), 'কুল' for 'কোল' (lap), খুল (open) for 'খোল'.

(3) There are instances of 'উ' changing into 'ও' as in 'তোফান' for 'তুফান' (storm).

(4) 'ট' and 'ঠ' into 'ড' :—'ছুডু' for 'ছোট', 'কাডি for 'কাঠি' (stick), 'পাডা' for পাঁঠা (goat).

(5) 'ঢ' into 'ড' :—'ডুল' for 'ঢোল' (drum).

(6) 'ন' into 'ল' :—'লাড়া' for 'নাড়া'.

(7) 'স' and 'শ' very often take the form of 'হ' in E. B. dialects. The examples are so numerous that we need not quote too many of them. 'হেই' for 'সেই', 'হেওলা' for 'সেওলা', 'হাজি' for 'সাজি', 'হালা' for 'শালা', 'হুদু' for 'শুধু', 'হত' for 'শত' are very common.

There is a humorous story relating to the last form ('হত' for 'শত'). We have got a Sanskrit sloka which forbids the Westerners to accept blessings from a Brahmin scholar of Eastern Bengal. For the usual form of such a blessing would be 'শতায়ুস্ত্বং ভবিষ্যসি' (May you live for a hundred years), but the Eastern Pandit would say 'হতায়ু' for 'শতায়ু' ('হতায়ু cursed with a short life).

(8) In a few cases 'স' is used for 'হ' as 'সেন কালে' for 'হেন কালে', 'সাতী' for 'হাতী'.

Often a vowel is added to a word apparently without any reason, as in 'কৈন্যা' for 'কন্যা', 'বৈক্ষ' for 'বক্ষ', 'লৈক্ষ্য' for 'লক্ষ্য', 'সৈন্ধান' for 'সন্ধান', 'ঐঞ্চল' for 'অঞ্চল'. The introduction of the long vowel 'ঐ' is quite uncalled for in the above words. In some rare cases the vowel 'উ' is introduced in the same manner as in 'রাউখাল' for 'রাখাল'. In the word 'কয়বর' (for 'কবর') the vowel 'য়' is generally found placed between the first and the second letters. Sometimes letters are omitted. In 'মাজন' for 'মহাজন', the 'হ' disappears leaving the long vowel আ in its place. In 'মড়ল' for 'মোড়ল' the vowel 'ও' disappears and in 'থান' for 'স্থান', 'তন' for 'স্তন' there is an omission of 'স'.

The doubling of letters is another feature of Eastern dialects, as in 'হুক্কা' for 'হুকা', শিক্কা' for 'শিকা' (শিকে).

The idioms of E. B. differ in many places with those of W. B.

The first thing that strikes one on this point is the profuse use of the word লাগা as suffix to verbs in E. B. dialects. Take for instance খাওন লাগে, যাওন লাগে, করবার লাগছে, যাবার লাগছে, etc. In the places of the first two, the W. B. idiom would be খেতে হয়, যেতে হয় and those for the latter two forms would be simply কচ্ছে and যাচ্ছে in West. The verbal supplement লাগা was probably in vogue in Western dialects a few centuries ago, for we find it used in the old nursery songs ("লোটন লোটন পায়রাগুলি নাচ্‌তে লেগেছে"). It has not altogether vanished from colloquial dialect of W. B. Expressions such as 'সে করতে লেগে গেছে', 'সে উঠে পড়ে লেগেছে', are still in use but the idiom is not exactly like that current in the dialects of E. B. There is a special use of the word লাগা in W. B. When they say, বড্ড লেগেছে, লাগা means a hurt, a pain. The E. B. people do not use the word in that sense. They may say, ব্যথা লাগা, চোট লাগা, conveying the sense of pain or hurt, but the word লাগা alone does not carry such an import.

Another point of difference arises in the use of the different forms of দেওয়া by E. B. people, the idiom of W. B. people being in such cases the various verbal forms of ফেলা. The E. B. man would say বলে দিল, হেসে দিল, কেঁদে (কাইন্দা) দিল, etc., where his brother of the West would say বলে ফেল্লে, হেসে ফেল্লে, কেঁদে ফেল্লে, etc. The latter would add a form of দেওয়া to imply imperative mood, making it a suffix of the verb. Thus ডেকে দে, ফেলে দে, ছেড়ে দে, are idioms used by them where E. B. people would simply say ডাক্, ফ্যাল্, ছাড়্. Of course during the last century many changes have been effected in the idiomatic forms used by both the people owing to a far greater communication between the two provinces than ever existed before. I have cited examples from the dialect of backward villages, where we find forms of the older type unaffected by modern interchange of words and idioms.

That many Bengali words had originally a plural form will be proved by the remnants of old usages which still linger in them. In E. B. particularly such forms still exist to a considerable extent, as 'মুখা' for 'মুখ' (the word মুখা does not actually imply a face, but the model of it in burnt clay from which the faces of gods and goddesses are prepared by potters), 'বগা' for 'বক' ("শুক্‌না বিলে বগা চরে", Dak), 'কাগা' for 'কাক', 'চাঁদা' for 'চাঁদ', 'হাতা' for 'হাত' (হাতা means a handle of the shape of a hand for culinary purposes), 'ছাতা' for 'ছত্র', 'গান্ধা' for 'গন্ধপুষ্প' (a special kind of flower), 'মাথা' for 'মস্তক', 'পাতা' for 'পত্র', 'বুকা' for 'বক্ষ' (the word 'বুকা' means the middle part of a fish or of a fruit particularly a long gourd, when cut by a chopper easily traced from 'বক্ষ'), 'রাতা' for 'রক্ত'.

The words 'পাতা', 'রাতা', 'মাথা' may be taken as instances of the rule of the long vowel 'আ' being suffixed to the letters preceding the double letter of a word where there has been an omission of one of them. But the long vowel 'আ' of the last letter indicates the original idea of plurality.

The verbs 'যাব', 'খাব', etc., of W. B. take the forms of 'যামু', 'খামু', etc., in E. B., But instances of the latter are also now and then found in old classical works of W. B., showing that though originally these verbs in their different shapes were current in both the provinces, particular forms have become stereotyped in some localities in comparatively modern times.

6. *Suggestions for Corrections.*

Since the publication of the Eastern Bengal Ballads (Vol. I), I have received letters from a number of gentlemen of Mymensingh who have in a friendly spirit suggested some corrections to my notes as editor. These mainly relate to the meanings of the local words of the district used in the Ballads. I am conscious of my limitations in the matter and I heartily thank the gentlemen for their suggestions. I am, however, myself a man of Eastern Bengal, and have been working in the field of old literature of my country for nearly half a century. My knowledge of the dialects of Eastern Bengal is not only first hand, but is based on a comparative study, which, I presume to say, gives me a position of some advantage over those who have criticised me. Though I may not be able to accept all the suggestions, so kindly offered me, so far as those words are concerned which have a peculiar local use not to be found in the classics of other districts, I am prepared to accept the corrections after a discussion of each question on its own merits. I give below the corrections suggested with my remarks.

(1) Mr. **Surendra Kishore Chakravarti**, M.A., M.R.A.S. (Lond.), Professor of English, Anandamohan College, refers to the word বাজু (Vol. I, Introduction, p. liii) which I considered to have been derived from বর্জ্জিত (prohibited). Mr. Chakravarti argues on the authority of Todur Mull's Rent Roll of 1582 quoted by Galdwin and Blockman's History and Geography of Bengal, that the word is possibly derived from the Persian word বাজু— an arm, a wing. He says that the Persian word is again derived from the Sanskrit word বাহু, from which we have got the Bengali word বাজু, an ornament of the arm.

Whatever history the word may bear of its origin, there is no doubt that the current Bengali word বাজু (and hence বাজুদেশ) is considered to be a word of reproach. In the genealogical records of the Bengalis of higher castes, the word is always used in the sense of "forbidden" or "prohibited." The Kulins always speak with sneer about বাজুদেশ, and they imply by the term a place outside the recognised centres of respectable classes of a particular community. A man living in the বাজুদেশ, loses his *kulinism*. Hence the current meaning of the word when it is connected with দেশ, is degraded in sense. Moreover Mr. Chakravarti is not right in saying that the Persian word is derived from Sanskrit. There are common words in Persian and Sanskrit, derived from an earlier Indo-Iranian source.

(2) Referring to the date 1491 in connection with some incidents in Firoze Shaha's reign (Mymensingh Gitika, Vol. I, Part II, Introduction, p. 7), Mr. Chakravarti objects to it on the strength of some coins recently discovered, leading to the conclusion that Firoze Shaha ruled from 1486-1489. He does not give any particulars about these coins. According to his finding there is the difference of a year or so between his date and that given by me. I took the date from the History of Mymensingh by late Babu Kedarnath Bose,—an authoritative work on the history of the district. The matter however requires further historical investigations.

(3) The word খোলা (p. 45, l. 1, Mymensingh Gitika). Mr. Chakravarti says that the meaning of the word is probably "an open land near the homestead." This word is so common in all parts of Eastern Bengal and is so frequently used in conjunction with the word ক্ষেত that any meaning given merely by conjecture is out of place, so I see no reason to change my views.

(4) The word আইলা (loose) (p. 51, l. 10). The writer contends that the word is আউলা and not আইলা. In the face of the fact, however, that the word is found as আইলা in the Ballad obtained from his own district, I see no reason to accept the suggested change. In the part of Eastern Bengal, of which I am a native, the word is আইলা and not আউলা.

(5) শিস্থায় ভরা (p. 57, l. 2). Mr. Chakravarti says that the word should be ক্ষিস্থায় ভরা . He says that the word ক্ষিস্থা or thickened milk, is the term used in his district. In our part of the province, however, the word ক্ষিস্থা means a fruit of the species of cucumber. If in his part of the district it is ক্ষিস্থা, it is all right, but words are sometimes used in different forms in the different parts of the same district. So a uniform rule does not apply to all cases.

(6) চই (p. 57, l. 4). If the word means vegetable-food of a particular kind and also a certain kind of cake, the latter would be more relevant.

(7) বউগড়া (p. 67, l. 11). Mr. Chakravarti refers to a particular ceremony observed by the women-folk of his district, when the bride first enters her father-in-law's home. This ceremony is called বউগড়া . Not only Mr. Chakravarti but also a few other critics of my book have given the same interpretation to the word. It is a word peculiar to Mymensingh. So my meaning (বউগড়া = বউসকল) is evidently incorrect.

(8) ঝাণ্ডাগাড়ি (p. 73, l. 14). The word ঝাণ্ডা means a flag. ঝাণ্ডাগাড়ি means the planting of a flag-post as a sign of possession. I wrote that the word meant planting of a post and omitted 'flag' which was understood and implied as a matter of course. Mr. Chakravarti makes the meaning clearer.

(9) ফুইদ or হুইদ (p. 76, l. 8). Mr. Chakravarti is right in holding that it means "To ask." The word is derived from "শুধান".

(10) নীয়ড়ে (p. 113, l. 4). The meaning জন্য (for) suggested by him may be more relevant to the context. But I cannot accept this meaning as the word is nowhere used in that sense. It is a very common word n Bengali literature and nowhere is it used for জন্য. It always means "near" নিকটে. Here also the meaning নিকটে would not be inappropriate or irrelevant.

(11) কাছলা (p. 123, l. 11). I think Mr. Chakravarti is right in holding that it means "A big earthen pot." I thought it meant a napkin. This meaning I gave on the strength of what Mr. Suresh Ch. Dhar said. He was formerly my assistant and himself a native of the Eastern Mymensingh whence the Ballad was collected.

(12) উষ্টা (p. 128, l. 12). Mr. Chakravarti says that its meaning is "a kick"; whereas I said that it meant a slap. I did so on Mr. Dhar's authority and I think I was right. The sense "kick" would be quite inappropriate here.

(13) কারশা (p. 149, l. 10). Mr. Chakravarti suggests its meaning to be খেরো. But for obvious reasons I cannot accept it.

(14) রায়ত বিলাত (p. 158, l. 20). Mr. Chakravarti suggests its meaning to be 'dependents.' But he is not supported by any authority that I know of. The word বিলাত বাকী is very common in the account-books of shop-keepers. They imply by it arrears from "outside people." I think the meaning "England" which the word "বিলাত" now bears is to be traced to its original sense of "outsiders."

(15) চুপা (p. 160, l. 14). I left the word with a query, as I could not know its meaning. Mr. Chakravarti says that it means a gold or silver ornament shaped like a flower with some holes in it. He further says that the word is now out of use. Is his meaning then a mere guess? What is his authority?

(16) ছিকর (p. 184, l. 13)—"Burnt earth." I think this meaning is right.

(17) হালি ধান (p. 160, l. 7). Mr. Chakravarti says that its meaning is "seed paddy." But হালি is apparently a distortion of শালী, and শালীধান is a very common expression. If, however, the word has a local meaning, he may be right.

(18) ছিটা ছড়া (p. 315. l. 22). According to Mr. Chakravarti the meaning is "The sprinkling of cowdung mixed

with water.'' He is quite wrong here and if he carefully consults the context he will surely be convinced that my meaning is right.

(19) ইতে (p. 361, l. 14). It is contended that ইতে is an abbreviated form of 'ইহাতে'. But were it the case, the form would have been ইথে which is frequently found in our old literature. The word হিতে বিপরীত is so common and the word ইতে is so often found in these very Ballads used in the place of হিতে that I am sure I am right.

Mr. **Mahim Ch. Dutta Choudhari,** B.A., Rector, Anjuman High School, Netrakona, has drawn attention to the following words and offered some suggestions for correction.

Mr. Dutta Choudhari says that the words in the printed Ballads do not always exactly conform to the local pronunciation. I quite agree with him in this respect. The Ballad-collectors, inspite of my instructions to the contrary, did not give the colloquial forms of words always, not being able to avoid the influence of written Bengali. I do not, however, agree with Mr. Dutta Choudhari on every point of detail as local pronunciations vary in different parts of Mymensingh. He has referred to the following words :—

(1) 'আচিল', 'সুদুর', 'কুট্টা', 'আঁন্দাইর', 'বান্যায়', 'শিওরা', 'বইসা', 'কান্দের কলসী', 'কান্দা মরে', 'জলে দিছ দেউ.'' These, according to him, should be as follows, respectively :—'আছিল', 'সুদর', 'কইত্যা', 'আন্ধাইর', 'শিয়রে', 'কাঁখের কলসী', 'কাইন্দা মরে', 'জলে দিছ ঢেউ.' 'কান্দের', 'শিওরা' and 'দেউ' are evidently printing mistakes and I am sure that the words 'আচিল' and 'সুদুর' are pronounced as such at least in some parts of Mymensingh.

(2) 'ভানুশ্বর' (Vol. I, Part 2, p. **1**, l. 1) certainly means the Sun-God. In my notes I have mentioned this as an alternative meaning.

(3) 'পশর' (p. 5) means আলো, ফর্সা ; but I hold that the word was originally derived from প্রসার and see no reason

to change my views, as it may be traced to "extension of sun's rays."

(4) 'রাও চণ্ডালের হার' (p. 7). I think my meaning is right. 'রাও' and 'রায়' are corruptions of রাজ. If the word would come from রাহু, it would be রাউ and not রাও.

(5) 'শান' (p. 10). The word implies both brick and stone in popular language of Eastern Bengal. It evidently bears a closer relation to the word পাষাণ.

(6) 'উড়ের ধন' (p. 15). Mr. Dutta Choudhari contends that 'উড়' means নিকট (near). উরস is a Sanskrit word and means বক্ষ—(breast). The phrase বুকের ধন is very familiar. I am afraid my critic is not correct here.

(7) 'দফা' (p. 24). I accept the correction suggested. The word means দল (band) and not a 'stable' as I supposed. But is the word 'দফা' still current in the dialects of Mymensingh and in the sense suggested, or is it a mere guess? If latter be the case I would feel a hesitancy in accepting the suggestion.

(8) বাণ্যা (p. 27). The word means "Bania" and hence a goldsmith according to Mr. Dutta Choudhari. The word বানি however means wages of a goldsmith in popular dialect. I think both the meanings are applicable. Mr. Dutta Choudhari's suggestion seems better.

(9) 'আকাল মাকাল' (p. 29). Mr. Dutta Choudhari derives the words from কাল ও মহাকাল, the names of the two serpents on the head of the god 'Siva.'

(10) 'তাত' (p. 34) is said to be an abbreviation of তাহাতে. Quite likely.

(11) 'দিনের সন্ধ্যাবেলা' (p. 35). Mr. Dutta Choudhari supposes the word সন্ধ্যা to mean 'close,' 'end.' This is quite unwarrantable. The word everywhere means evening. 'দিনের সন্ধ্যাবেলা' means 'evening of the day.' He supports his queer view by citing 'জীবন সন্ধ্যা' (literally 'evening of life'). But there the word is used in figurative sense.

With reference to words নাগান্ত (p. 41), সলাভ্য (p. 41),

উভে (p. 43), etc., he gives meanings at a guess. We want meanings in current use. Everyone may give a catalogue of his conjectures. We are not interested in them.

(12) 'ষরু শস্য'. He corrects the meaning that I have given of ষরু as being derived from সরিষা (mustard). Mr. Dutta Choudhari and several other people of Mymensingh are unanimous in remarking that ষরু শস্য is a very common word in the place and always mean 'agricultural products of all kinds.' So my meaning is wrong.

(13) '[illegible]' (p. 59) I thought it to mean 'ঘটক' (a match-maker). Dutta Choudhari says the word not only means a match-maker but also other classes of men as artisans, labourers, etc. Quite so. But my object was not to write a vocabulary while giving meanings, and I confined myself to the context only.

With regard to the words 'মন্দান্না' (p. 42), 'তুইন' (p. 113) he supposes that the suffix 'ন' is not a separate letter, it is an integral part of the whole word, the meaning of which does not change by the letter being used as suffix. With regard to 'তুইন' he contends that it is a contemptuous form of 'তুমি' ; but 'তুই' itself is contemptuous ; and the suffix 'ন' would be quite superficial if it were used to imply contempt. I believe this 'ন' is derived from 'না' and used to give stress on the word of which it has become the suffix. The usual significance of 'না' throughout the country is to imply a negative sense. But in these Ballads we so frequently find the latter used in an affirmative sense that we have no doubt, this 'ন' in মন্দান্না and তুইন bears the same import as we find in other places. Curiously this use in the affirmative sense is not altogether extinct in other parts of Bengal. We have cited examples in our Introduction to Vol. I, Pt. I, p. lxii). This 'না' is still used as a sign for both interrogative and affirmative, and does not always imply negation.

(14) নিয়ড়ে (p. 113). Like Mr. Chakravarti the present

critic also commits a blunder by supposing that the word means 'জন্য' and not 'নিকটে', and I need scarcely repeat that the word is found so profusely in our old literature always in the sense of নিকটে (with which it is so analogous in its form), that there is no room for guess here.

(15) 'খামারিয়া জমি' (p. 114). The phrase evidently means 'land fit for agriculture.' It is in use in every part of Bengal. But Mr. Dutta Choudhari contends that it means 'plot of land which has not been leased to any tenant.' I do not know if it is the local meaning confined to a particular place.

(16) 'ভূনুনা' (p. 167). Choudhari says that it means the cage of a bird prepared with split bamboos. I think he is right.

(17) কেরুয়াল (p. 199). I derived the word from কাণ্ডার (helm). The word is found used in this sense in many old Bengali poems. "কাঁধে কেরুয়াল করি হাসয়ে মুরারি" (শ্রীকৃষ্ণমঙ্গল by মালাধর বসু, Saka 1395, corresponding to 1473 A. D.). If it had meant an oar, it would not have been placed on shoulders of the boat-man at the time of plying the boat. That it is derived from কাণ্ডার is self-evident. If it means an oar in the local dialect of Mymensingh, it has certainly deviated from its original import ; and instances of such confusion in meanings of words when they are accepted as loans from a different province are not rare. The word কেরুয়াল is derived from কাঁড়াল and both the forms are in evidence. By the law of 'ল' changing into 'র' it is easy to trace the word from কাণ্ডার.

(18) চুটিয়াচুটী (p. 244). According to Mr. Dutta Choudhari it is a particular class of birds which are locally called চুটিয়া ময়না.

(19) হানা (p. 272). Mr. Choudhari objects to the meaning I gave of the word, *viz.*, 'to destroy,' 'to hurt,' 'to attack,' and 'হানা দিল' he interprets as 'began to come.' But I am not prepared to accept this meaning.

It is a very common phrase all over Bengal and I think I am right in sticking to the sense.

(20) 'পাছাড়ি' (p. 318). Mr. Choudhari says it means a sari worn by women through the middle of which runs a striped line like a border (পাছা-পাড়). Here he is quite wrong. পাছাড়ি is frequently found in old Bengali literature and means a coarse cotton sari (বিনে বান্দী নাহি পিন্ধে পাটের পাছাড়ি—Maynamati songs).

Babu **Amulya Charan Chakravarti** (P. O. Joyka, Kamaratia, Dist. Mymensingh) has offered some suggestions. He says 'জালিয়ার হাওর' is not in the South-East of Kishoregunj, it is the 'বড় হাওর' that is so ; জালিয়ার হাওর is in the North-East of Kishoregunj. His suggestions seem to me to be generally very fair. I note them below :—

(1) জুইতের ঘর (Vol. I, Pt. II, p. 7, l. 15). I supposed that the word meant ' a house of good fashion ' but it has a local meaning. Mr. Chakravarti says that it locally means a Bungalow. He has drawn a picture of the house implied by the word from which I find it to be the familiar type of a house of old school, which at one time was extensively in fashion. It is a house or temple with curvilinear roofings of which Furgusson gives the credit of invention to Bengalees. This sort of house used to serve the purpose of a parlour in Mymensingh till half a century ago. In olden times it used to be built with bricks, but the জুইতের ঘর though it retains its traditional form is generally made with straw and bamboos.

(2) কামলা (p. 62, l. 11). I find from what Mr. Chakravarti writes that the word is not confined to the meaning " day-labourer " as I supposed. In Eastern Mymensingh it also implies " artisans who are noted for their fine workmanship."

(3) ঝাপেঝুপে (p. 62, l. 11). ঝাপ according to him means the lower part of a thatch or hedge. But in our

part of the country (Dacca), the word means a thatched door.

(4) তিন আবা দিয়া (p. 63, last line). I meant "To create a sound by mildly striking the lips with one's palms, three times." It is an expression often found in the Vaisnava padas used in this sense in connection with the games and sports of the boys. But Mr. Chakravarti while agreeing with me on this point says that in the present case my meaning is quite wrong and that তিন আবা দিয়া is a sort of painting on the ground by means of powdered rice and water made by women for the reception of the new bride. He has shown the sort of painting by a drawing in his letter. It is a familiar rite observed during marriage ceremonies in the district and in the present case the meaning is as clear as anything. I think I must accept his meaning.

(5) সরাইয়ের পথে (p. 61, l. 12). The word সরাই means a hotel and I gave the meaning "The way at the vicinity of a hotel." But I learn from Mr. Chakravarti that the word has a local meaning. সরাই means প্রশস্ত (broad).

(6) কাছ্‌লা (p. 123, l. 11). He says that my meaning 'napkin' is wrong. The word means an earthen pot. I have already referred to this meaning of the word given by another gentleman.

(7) বাগুনি (p. 127, l. 2), according to him is a tigress, a corruption of বাঘিনী.

He corrects the meanings of বউগড়া (p. 67, l. 11), বান্ধা (p. 27, l. 7), জুলুঙ্গা (p. 167, l. 17), হালিধান (p. 186, l. 7) as others have done, in agreement with Messrs. S. N. Chakravarti and Dutta Choudhari.

(8) কাগমালা (p. 268, l. 20). I explained it as শিকা (a hanging rope-shelf). This I did at a guess. But he says that it means a post of bamboos over which there is a circular holder made of split bamboos for keeping plates

and cooking pots in the kitchen. He is, I think, right as the word is purely local.

Mr. **Dhananjay Bhattacharjya**, M.A., Professor of Cooch-Behar College, corrects the meanings of the words বউ ঘড়া and জুইতের ঘর, given by me on the lines of the other critics, so it is not necessary to repeat his arguments here. With regard to the word পাণখিল (text, p. 104), I thought it to be an abbreviation of পাণখিলি—the familiar manipulation of the betel leaf into a triangular shape with nut, lime and other ingredients inside. But Mr. Bhattacharjya says that in Mymensingh it means a special rite observed by women before the bridal ceremony. Though betel leaf and spices are important factors in the rite known as পাণখিল, the word implies many things more, from the *alipana* painting in the courtyard and placing of the vermilion box in an auspicious can down to the singing of bridal songs by women, recital of metrical poems relating to nuptial devotion and playing different kinds of musical instruments prior to wedding. All these are implied in the পাণখিল ceremony, and sometimes it requires full five hours to go through it.

I have had a long correspondence with Mr. **Jatindranath Majumdar**, B.L., Pleader and Zemindar of Mymensingh, about the date of Bangsidas, the great poet of the **Manasha** cult of the district. Bangsidas figures in the Ballad of Kenaram as one of its chief characters, sketched by his daughter Chandravati—the author of the Ballads of Malua and Kenaram (Vol. I, Pt. II, pp. 41-96 and pp. 182-226) whose unfortunate life has been so pathetically described in the Ballad named after her composed by the poet Nayanchand.

In the edition of Manasha-mangal written by Bangsidas with the help of his gifted daughter, and published and edited by late Ramnath Chakravarti, we find the date of the composition of the poem given by the poet himself ; it is Saka 1497 or 1575 A.D. Mr. Majumdar's contention is that the work was a much later composition. In order to prove this he marshals out an array of arguments which shows a great painstaking zeal on his part to arrive at the truth. I refer to one of his arguments. He says that the dates given by scholarly manipulations of words, all denoting mathematical figures, should be read from the left side—অঙ্কস্য বামা গতি. But here we find the contrary to be the case. It is not likely that a scholar like Bangsidas should transgress the canon in vogue in this matter. This, I beg to say, is not a correct view of the point. In vernacular poems, even great Sanskrit scholars do not always follow that rule. The great Bharat Chandra himself gave the date in the colophon of one of his poems as সনেরুদ্র চৌগুণা which is to be read from the right and not from the left side. Khelaram wrote a Dharmamangal poem in 1527 A.D., and in the colophon, he gave the date in the following verses :—"ভুবন শাকে বায়ু মাসে শরের বাহন। খেলারাম করিলেন গ্রন্থ আরম্ভণ।" (Banga-Bhasa-o-Sahitya, p. 400) which is to be read from the right side and yields the result Saka 1449 (1527 A.D.).

Similarly in the translation of Kashikhanda, compiled under the auspices of Maharaja Joynarayan Ghosal, by many learned Pandits, the date is put as Saka 1714 (1792 A.D.), to be read from the right side. Even in Sanskrit poems the rule অঙ্কস্য বামা গতি is not always observed. In the well-known Sanskrit work Ballalcharit, we find an example of a breach of this canon. In the Sabhar inscriptions relating to Raja Harish Chandra discovered by the late Pandit Amritananda Gupta and published in the Dacca Review, some years ago, the date given is to be read from the right. So the arguments of Mr. Majumdar on this point does not hold water. But I need not give here the gist of the whole correspondence, as his contention, that the book was written much later is based on a wrong arithmetical calculation, so obvious that it will make his whole logic crumble down like a house of cards, as soon as it is pointed out to him. I am sure, he will at once accept the date of the colophon and not brand it as an interpolation. According to his calculation,—chiefly based on the genealogical records of the family of Bangsidas,—the poet lived 300 years ago, that is to say about the year 1627. He says, "If we follow the date given in the colophon (Saka 1497) we find that the book was composed 450 years ago." This he considers impossible, arguing on the strength of a variety of reasons based on the facts of contemporary history and leading to the conclusion that Bangsidas could not have flourished earlier than Isha Khan. But where does he find that Bangsi lived 452 years ago? According to the colophon, Bangsi lived about Saka 1497. It is now Saka 1849, so he lived 352 years ago. The date of the colophon is 1575 A.D. and his date is 1627 A.D. So the difference is only of 52 and not of 152 years as he has erroneously supposed. The date in the colophon does not show that the poet lived at an age earlier than that of Isha Khan. Isha Khan fought with Mansingh in 1593 and Bangsidas wrote his Manasha-mangal in 1575, so they were contemporaries. I would not have taken so much space in pointing out a simple error in arithmetical calculation but the side-issues raised by Mr. Majumdar are important and a discussion was necessary for obvious reasons.

He further says that the account given by Chandravati of her father's poverty is not correct, for the family is rich now and they have a landed property which goes by Bangsidas's name in the Collectorate records. His descendants were and are still rich and influential in the country. These rich descendants would not naturally like to hear that their great ancestor was so poor that "his straw-roof profusely leaked during the rains." It may be a question of prestige with some of his descendants and I am afraid Mr. Majumdar was probably led by the views of interested parties in discrediting the simple account given by Chandravati. As regards Bangsidas it is quite possible that in his later life, as his fame spread over the country, he got some landed property. It is not also unlikely that the property in question was named after him in his honour by one of his descendants. But whatever the cause may be, we cannot disbelieve the story given by Chandravati. She had no reason to refer to her father's poverty, if he was not actually poor. Everyone reading the account would be impressed by her simple narration of facts and her childlike sincerity. The description she has given of her father, is so graphic that we feel it to be true in its detail. It is consistent with the traditional pride of ascetic life of the saintly Brahmins of that age and there was no reason on the part of his daughter to be ashamed of his poverty. He spurned the offer of unlimited wealth from the robbers, because it was earned by the murder of innocent men. This account, far from lowering him in our estimation, adds a superb grandeur to his personality. The picture of Kenaram has the stamp of real history in it taken from life by a direct witness and I do not see how he could be a copy of Narada, there being hardly any analogous point between the episodes of Valmiki and Kenaram excepting the fact that both were reformed by the influence of piety.

The autobiographical notice given by Bangsidas is interesting. I quote below the genealogy of the family drawn up to now :

" বংশী বীজ পূর্ব্বে গোসাঁই চক্রপাণি।
ভূত ভবিষ্যত আদি ত্রিকাল যে জ্ঞানী ॥
রাঢ় হ'তে আসিলেন লোহিত্যের পাশ।
হাজারদি পাতুয়ারী গ্রামেতে নিবাস ॥

সম্বন্ধ করিলেন রত্নাবতী ঠাকুরাণী ।
তান পুত্র কালিদাস হৈলা মহাজ্ঞানী ॥
তান পুত্র পুরুষোত্তম প্রাজ্ঞ মহাশয় ।
এক প্রজাপতি বলি সর্ব্বলোকে কয় ॥
কুলেশীলে গরিষ্ঠ সম্পদ অতিশয় ।
হৃদয়ানন্দ হ'ল তাহার তনয় ॥
তান পুত্র যাদবানন্দ সুধী অতিশয় ।
দ্বিজবংশী জন্মিলেক তাহার তনয় ॥
দেবগুরু প্রসাদে হৈল দিব্য জ্ঞান ।
পদবন্ধে রচিলেক পদ্মার পুরাণ ॥
পদ্মাপুরাণ কথা শুন এক চিতে ।
বিস্তারি' কহিব আদি পাঁচালির মতে ॥
যদি বা অশুদ্ধ হয় দেশভাষা মতে ।
বিজ্ঞজন লইবেন পুরিয়া পশ্চাতে ॥
পুরাণ রচিতে মোর কবিত্বের আশ ।
চন্দ্র ধরিতে যেন শিশুর প্রয়াস ॥
জলধির বামে ত ভুবন মাঝে দ্বার ।
শকে রচে দ্বিজবংশী পুরাণ পদ্মার ॥ "

The Genealogical table of the family :

1. Chakrapani
2. Kalidas
3. Purushottam
4. Hridayananda
5. Jadabananda (married Anjana) — Raghunath
6. Bangsidas
7. Sriballav — Rajiblochan — Chandravati
8. Janakiballav
9. Ramballav
10. Gobinda
11. Nilkanta
12. Dwarikanath
13. Jatindra
14. Harendra

7. *Stray Notes.*

Every Mahomedan, however low his position may be, has an instinctive desire to contribute something to local history, and in this respect he shows a great contrast with his Hindu neighbour. As soon as a Hindu becomes a Mahomedan convert, he becomes conscious of the disorganised condition of the older society, participating in a sense of vigorous unity, characteristic of the followers of Islam. He commences to take pride in the glories achieved by Mahomedan arms on their mission of world-conquest and considers himself an integral part of the whole Mahomedan community. There is hardly any such conscious feeling in a Christian convert. Inspite of all outward professions of brotherhood made by the followers of Christ, he feels that he is outside the pale of the society of the heaven-born—the Whites.

Short printed Ballads recording local incidents.

The Hindus are quite apathetic to the incidents that transpire around, whereas even the most petty affairs of this mundane world are taken seriously by the Mahomedans. This interest is clearly in evidence in hundreds of short Ballads which issue forth from the Press, every year in Bengal, composed by Mahomedan peasantry. It may interest our readers to know something of the great activities of the Mahomedans of the rural villages in the field of local history. It is the country bards amongst the Mahomedans, generally illiterate, who have composed and preserved the historical Ballads about Dewan Isha Khan, Dewan Manwoor Khan, Dewans Alal and Dulal, Dewan Firoze Khan and other chiefs of Bengal. But not only this, no incident however insignificant is allowed to pass unnoticed by Mahomedan peasantry. When anything transpires to cause a little thrill in the popular mind, it is at once translated into a short

Ballad which the ploughman and the cultivator sing in chorus after their day's work in the field. These Ballads are at once printed and sold at a price, generally ranging between half an anna and two annas per copy. It will amuse our readers to know of the subject-matters of some of these Ballads.

In one of these Hamid Ali recounts the glories of one Yakub Ali, a village landlord of Chittagong "resplendent as the God Indra." In another, the writer laments over the death of Golmani, the boatman, who perished in the high seas by a freak of gale. The religious belief of these Ballad-makers, as indeed of the whole Mahomedan peasantry, is a curious medley of irreconcilable elements. Golmani, the Mahomedan boatman, when facing the storm, laments in this way:—"বিপাকে ফেলিল মোরে চৈতন্য গোঁসাই" (Lord Chaitanya has thrown me into this peril). Another Ballad describes the vicissitudes in the life of one Golok Bahardar, the captain of a number of ships, as to how he lost his fortune on the 15th of Paus, on his return home from a sea voyage. The author gives an account in another short Ballad as to how Manohari, sister of one Bangsiram in the village of Jaynagore in Chittagong, left the custody of her husband owing to his persistent maltreatment and took a second mate. Haradayal Baidya sat as a judge in this case.

There are historical Ballads such as *Habar Yuddher Katha*, describing the Burmese War, as the sequel of which Raja Thebaw was dethroned and exiled. The Chittagong Mahomedan peasant keeps himself in touch with the affairs of Moslem interest abroad, and no wonder therefore, that we find a somewhat long Ballad on the achievements of Kamal Pasha. We have published in this volume a Ballad of considerable length describing "The Fight at Manipur" by Mokbul Ahammed. There are many Ballads on the storms that blew over the Bay, destroying villages and causing floods during the last half-a-century. "In Amshakuli"—a village in Chittagong—says one Ballad-monger, "hundreds of people died but it was a great fortune that our redoubted Latu Pandit survived." Another Ballad describing a storm regrets the loss of a quilt belonging to an old woman, familiarly called 'Golair Ma' who shivered in cold as she was suffering from chronic bronchitis. The poet refers to the one tooth, the only one that she had, which she displayed in all its ugliness when lamenting the loss of the quilt. One Ballad describes the valorous deeds of a woman who single-handed killed seven robbers and also a Chaukidar. This Ballad is surely based on facts. I will give here the substance of this interesting song. The Ballad is called সাতজন ডাকাতের কবিতা (a poem about seven robbers). The author, Mokbul Ahammed, published the Ballad from the Saraswati Press, Chittagong. It gives an account of a burglary attempted by seven robbers resulting in their death in a village within the police station of Amtali in the district of Bakargunj :

A certain rich man of the village, popularly called, Matbar Shahib, had two wives. One evening seven robbers came in a 'Pansi' boat, resolved to commit robbery in the house during his absence. Two of them, disguised as ordinary men, paid a visit to the house and said that they were friends of Matbar Shahib. One of the ladies received the guests kindly and the other went to the river-side with a pitcher for bringing water in the evening. She was surprised to see a large 'Pansi' boat moored on the bank, and overheard the conversation of the five dacoits in the boat from which she perceived their foul intention. She forthwith returned home and standing on a terrace of the first floor cried aloud to the two robbers that they were perfectly free to take away whatever they liked from the ground floor, but they must not attempt to come to the first floor. They paid little heed to her request and were going to assault the ladies and seize the keys that they had with them. One of the ladies bolted the door of the room in which the two men were, from outside, so that they were made captives. In the meantime the five robbers, anxious at the delay of their comrades, came in a body to the house. The ladies taking a secure position on the roof of the first floor exclaimed that if they would not abscond from the place immediately they would be fired at, without delay. Both the women were equipped with fire-arms. The dacoits began to abuse them and commenced hostile operations. They removed the bolt of the door and made their friends free. The ladies without delay fired at them and killed all the seven men. At the report of the guns a large number of people gathered at the house headed by the village Choukidar. When the Chowkidar wanted to enter the house, the ladies said, "We do not know you, you may be a dacoit in disguise. So go away from here and come in the morning. If you attempt to come up we will fire at you." The Choukidar, heedless of the threat, was about to ascend the steps whereupon one of the ladies fired at him and he fell dead on the spot. This created a great consternation and the Sub-Inspector of Police appeared on the scene. The ladies held out the same threat to him and said, "Who knows that you are not a dacoit in disguise ?" The Sub-Inspector reported the matter to the District Superintendent of Police who was a European. The same threat was held out to him by the ladies who said that it was quite possible that a dacoit might assume the guise of a European. The D.S.P. called for the father of the ladies who lived in the same village. With a Hooka in his hand the old man came to visit his daughters, upon which the ladies opened the door and received him. The ladies were charged with eight murders, including that of the Choukidar, who was a Government servant. But the District Judge of Bakargunj realised the position of the ladies and discharged them. They were moreover given a reward of two hundred rupees for their bravery.

These Ballads comprise a great variety of subjects. Here is an interesting account of a tiger-hunt. It is written by one Channu Mia and published in 1265 Maghi, by Abdul Rob from the Chittagong Saraswati Press.

The Ballad gives an account of a tiger who was warming himself on the sandy bank of a river near Halisahar and was at first mistaken for a cow by the villagers. They assembled to watch him closely and were frightened to see that it was a tiger. The animal ran towards the river and swam at ease helped by the tide. He came near the city of Kattali. The hunters of the village Bhaluadighi gathered there with their bows and guns but the tiger in the meantime again swam across the current and came to Selimpur where the people mistook him for a boar. The Ballad goes on describing how at Mirjanabad the Hindus and the Mahomedans resolved to kill the animal and three of them closely pursued him at the risk of their lives. The tiger at once leaped into a boat and stood with uplifted paws without heeding the crowd, whereupon they took him for a disciple of the Pir. At the next moment he swiftly got over to the land and disappeared in the neighbouring hill.

Thus we see that from higher subjects possessing a world-wide historical interest down to the pettiest local incidents which stir up the fancy of the rustics, there is no subject that these village-poets do not touch. I have with me 83 of such Ballads which I read with the interest and pleasure of a man who goes through a newspaper report.

The facts of a case are at times found mixed up with legends, but generally speaking they are true narratives occasionally enlivened by a touch of rural humour. They have neither any poetical value nor any literary grace. They are current gossips put in a metrical form. Their plainness and unassuming style are their only qualifications. But they may supply a page of a country's history, being records of contemporary events carrying the interest of the moment. It is really regrettable that our learned literary bodies and associations have no knowledge of this rural literature of Bengal which has been growing like mushrooms in every part of the country year after year. There are rustic poets who have achieved their literary celebrity over a vast agricultural area, so that, when they publish a short Ballad of this kind, it sells by thousands amongst the peasant population, and several editions come out in the course of two or three years. Our literary bodies seldom know anything about them. The peasantry of the E. B. districts, particularly of Mymensingh, Chittagong, Noakhali and Dacca have quite a praiseworthy record in this field.

The word Pali.

We cannot say from what time exactly the Ballads or *Pālā gāns* as they are called in the country-side, became so popular. The Hindus used to give a poetic interest to their science and literature by putting every matter in a metrical form to be sung or recited in a sing-song voice, in order to effectively popularise them. We have found even mathematical formulæ couched in a poetical form—and it is no wonder that historical matters assumed a poetical garb for popular singing. From the time of the Jatakas, the historical tales mixed with legends were often-times recited and sung, being composed in verse. My friend Revd. Siddhartha, M.A., an eminent Sinhalese scholar in Pali, tells me that the word "Pali" sometimes meant the poetical passages given in a prose narrative. In the Panchatantra we find the prose tales interspersed with *Slokas, i.e.,* Sanskrit verses. So that both amongst the Buddhists and the Hindus the poetical forms in prose narratives were a current fashion from a very early period of history.

Now curiously we find that poetical portions in prose narratives known as Rupa-kathas and Giti-kathas are called *Pali* by the rustic people. The Buddhists, as I have just said, also called them so. When a minstrel or a story-teller recited a tale he sang some verses at intervals, lending an effective interest to his performance. This word '*Pali*' in the Buddhist literature has that technical meaning which corresponds exactly with what is given by the Bengali populace to the word in respect of their Rupa-kathas and Ballads. Hence is it not quite natural to suppose that these kinds of popular songs are to be traced to that ancient period when the Buddhists were in power and the popular dialects got a recognition from the intelligentsia of the country?

After the decadence of the Buddhist power, the vernaculars of India fell into disfavour, for a time, being looked down upon by the Brahmins as *patois.* The revivalists of Brahminism, not only hated the vernaculars but also all historical subjects. As a rule their point of view was that only the deeds of the immortals should be sung and praised. History, which recounts human acts and their glory, is not worth studying. Such accounts are full of reports of petty squabbles, party-politics, victories and defeats, which while pandering to the vanity and interests of a particular people create a heart-burning in others. So the Brahmins declared that the pursuit of a history of mortals should be abandoned in preference to that of the immortals, which cleanses the soul and helps its ascent to a higher plane. In this way within a few centuries of Brahminic revival, whatever remained of Indian history was allowed to run into oblivion, and the Ballads, the Rupa-kathas, the Giti-kathas which related the tales of human affairs grew out of favour. They were supplanted by the supernatural tales of Dhruva and Prahlad, proclaiming the glory of devotion, and the Pauranic stories which gave the pre-historic accounts of men and gods living together and showing their marvellous feats of arms or of wisdom not only as neighbours but even as relations.

I therefore consider that this wonderful folk-literature of Bengal—in which the glory of action and not of religious devotion,—that of renunciation in the cause of secular love and not asceticism for seeking divine favour,—the best attributes and qualities of human heart and intellect, and no element of divine grace,—the entire dependence on self-help and not on the divine,—form the fountain and spring from which the peotic inspiration flows in such crystal-like transparence free from all mysticism in it,—is to be traced from the literature of the Buddhists, and that the word 'Pali' by which the rustic people of Eastern Bengal imply the verse-portion of a narrative is a direct indent from the early Buddhist times, being the same expression that was once used by the Buddhists in regard to the metrical portions of their tales.

A reference is found in many Ballads included in this volume, specially in that of the fight at Manipur, where incidentally the deeds of men performing heroic feats in their fight with tigers and other wild animals are on record. An account has been given in the preface of the Hati Kheda, illustrating the wonderful courage of the 'Dal Shikaris.' The Historian of Manipur refers to the fact that Tikendrajit had killed no less that 2,000 tigers with his own hands during his short span of life which extended to 32 years only. This may seem more or less hyperbolic and doubtful. But the hill-men lead a strange sort of life, which living

Man's contact with animals.

as we do in towns, feel hardly inclined to credit. The hill-man is the neighbour of wild animals and frequently comes in contact with his foes. There is no other alternative left to these men, passionately fond of their mountainous homes as they are, than to face the wild animals and be engaged in hand to hand fight with them at various stages of their chequered life. I refer to the following passage from an article by B. C. Allan on the wild tribes of Assam, recently published in the London "Times" and quoted by the "Statesman" in its issue of February 5, 1928.

"In the west (of Assam) are the Garos, who live in tiny hamlets in jungle-covered hills where elephants and man-eating tigers are so numerous that men have taken to sleeping like birds in the trees. They have huts on the ground which they occupy during the day but at night they mount little houses of bamboo built in the branches of a tree, stout enough to resist the attacks of a wild elephant." It is no wonder that living as they do, in an environment of such perilous risks, they become hardy, adventurous and well skilled in fighting with a tiger or a wild bear who pays his frequent visitations to the hamlets of men, with a greed for flesh or for the products of gardens made by them.

The Ballads in our stock.

Besides the Ballads published in these three volumes, there are many others that we have secured mostly by the help of our Ballad-collectors. We have got a number of short Ballads composed by the Bhats of Baniya Chang in Sylhet. They are not exactly like the Ballads of the rustic people. There is evidently a classic element in them—the Bhats were a class of Brahmins, who had made it the avocation of their lives to transform the reports of all stirring local events into the form of Ballads immediately after their occurrence and who wander about the country singing them. In the Bhat songs, we very often find hymns to Hindu gods and goddesses and philosophical reflections in the style of scriptural writings. The metre adopted by them is moreover peculiar and not on the lines of rural Ballads. This metre is a medley of *tripadi* and *payar*, and when sung in chorus shows an abrupt rise and fall in voice which though it hardly produces any melody—seldom sinks into hum-drum or jarring music. The Ballads of Rajkumar Babu of Kirttipasha in Bakargunj and of Kirttinasha which swallowed the palatial city of Rajnagar in the district of Dacca are the most popular of those composed by the Bhats. They are about two centuries old. I have also secured two Ballads from the districts of Burdwan and Birbhum of this kind. We have got a number of Hindu Ballads, the most interesting of which are those on Madan Mohan of Visnupur and on the floods of Damodar which took place at various periods during the last century. They are not at all like the Bhat songs, excepting for the fact that they are characterised by their obvious Hindu element. From East Bengal we are having a quite considerable supply of Ballads and Rupakathas, sometimes full of exquisite poetic and artistic merit. Leaving those that are of indifferent merit, if we confine ourselves only to really beautiful and interesting ones, there will be sufficient scope and material for anothor three volumes of the size of this book, if the services of the Ballad-collectors are retained for a few years more. The country is full of Ballads, not only on love-topics, full of exquisite poetry, but also on historical subjects. Everything the Bengali took an interest in, he turned into a song and thus all matters were popularised amongst the illiterate masses. We have not yet been able to secure (1) the Ballad of Dharmapal (8th century A.D.) about whom I find the following lines in the Kalimpur inscription : "গোপৈঃ সীম্নি বনেচরৈর্ব্বনভুবি গ্রামোপকণ্ঠে জনৈঃ ক্রীড়দ্ভিঃ প্রতিচত্বরং শিশুগণৈঃ প্রত্যাপণং মানপৈঃ লীলাবেশ্মনি পঞ্জরোদর-শুকৈরুদ্গীতমাত্মস্তবং যস্যাকর্ণয়তস্ত্রপা-বিবলিতা-নম্রং সদৈবাননং" (He—Raja Dharmapal—

always bashfully turns aside and bows down his face on hearing his praises sung by cowherds in the rural localities, by wanderers in the forests, by sportive children in village-paths, by merchants and traders in every market-place and by birds in cages taught by their masters in their pleasure-houses), (2) that of Rajyapal (10th century A.D.) whose great and beneficent works were once praised in songs throughout the country as mentioned in the Bangaḍa Inscription of Mahipal, (3, 4, 5), those of Yogipal, Bhogipal and Mahipal, of which reference is found in the classical Bengali work, the Chaitanya-Bhagabat (1573 A.D.) in this couplet :—
"যোগীপাল ভোগীপাল মহীপাল গীত। ইহা শুনিতে যে লোক আনন্দিত."
Referring to the Ballads of these three monarchs of the Pal dynasty, the author Brindaban Das says that before the advent of Chaitanya, these songs were a source of great amusement to the people. We have not been able to lay our hands on (6) the Ballads of Rampal (11th century) who sentenced his only son to death for having ravished a woman, forming the theme of popular songs to which the Sanskrit work Shekha Shubhodaya alludes, and (7) that of Dhanya Manikya[1] of Tipperah (1578 A.D.) who brought musicians to teach songs and dance from Tirhut (Darbhanga) to his capital,—(8) of his chief queen Kamala Devi,[2] the Bengali songs in praise of whom the Raja could not at first understand having known only the Tipperah language in his boyhood, (9) and of Amar Manikya[3] (1579 A. D.) referred to in the Raja Mala or a Chronicle of the Rajas of Tipperah. These Ballads which no doubt once existed and of which parts at least may be still recovered, should be vigorously searched. The Ballad of Shamsher-Gazi[4] has been found out and published by Maulavi Lutfur

[1] P. 122 of Raja Mala, published at the Bir Jantra on the 28th Chaitra, 1311 B. E.

[2] P. 92.

[3] P. 117.

[4] Died 1752.

Khabir of Tipperah. It is a mine of historical information about which I have written at some length in my Folk Literature of Bengal (pp. 136-152). I am convinced that the Ballad of Mahipal is still sung in the district of Rangpur. I have already referred to the fact that my friend, Pandit Kokileswar Bhattacharjya, M.A., Professor of the Calcutta University, heard this ballad sung in this district when he was a school boy. And late Mr. Pransankar Chaudhuri of Taota in the district of Dacca, owner of extensive landed property at Rangpur, also informed me that he had heard the Ballad sung by some of his ryots. This Ballad, he said, was a long one ; it took the village-rhapsodists full three nights to sing the whole piece.

All these are no doubt important. For inspite of their being mixed up with legends and rustic fancy as usually they are, they generally furnish us with historical material of considerable importance. We have arranged for a regular and systematic hunt for these. Unless we shall have exhausted the rural resources of our country for materials to build up the social and political history of Bengal, it will afford us no satisfaction by merely relying on the information supplied by inscriptions and the meagre records left by Moslem historians about the period of Hindu rule. It is the people who with their natural insight into what is truly great and noble in human affairs, appreciate and record, inspite of all crudeness and inaccuracies, the really great traits of human character. The Ballads of a country show the strong points and the peculiar qualities and graces in the character of a particular people, and those who discard this raw material, confining their attention only to the broken letter of an inscription or the faded carvings on some bricks, and pursue the frivolous and the worthless, in the name of scientific enquiries, are no better than those schoolmen who in the mediæval age wrote controversial volumes on such topics as

"How many fairies can dance on the point of a needle?" With all respect for these scientific scholars hunting after the day or month of a particular year or some such trifle with the dogged zeal of an Arctic explorer, unnecessarily turning petty things into momentous problems, and with many apologies for my bluntness, I would prefer the study of a rural Ballad to the survey of monuments of scholarship of such antiquarian researchers.

ILLUSTRATIONS.

The pictures given in this volume have all been drawn by Mr. Biswapati Choudhuri, M.A., excepting the frontispiece, the one of Rangamala and Rajendra Chaudhuri, printed in tri-colour, which I owe to the artist Mr. Satishchandra Sinha.

The photographs have been secured at great pains from the distant villages of Noakhali and Chittagong by our indefatigable Ballad-collector, Mr. Asutosh Choudhuri.

Munaf Kazi's pond (p. 100) bears the name of that redoubtable Daniel who disposed of the suit brought by Amir the merchant against Bhola, the abductor of his wife. The Kazi had named this pond after him and the bank still contains the relics of his house. The neighbourhood of the pond is called 'Kazir Para' or the ward of the Kazi. It is situated at the village of Soronipara, under the Police Station Double Muring in the district of Chittagong.

The pond of Bhelua (p. 105) is the memorial of the unfortunate girl Bhelua, dug where the home of Bhola stood by the order of her husband Amir, in order to appease his great vengeance which did not cease even after he had killed him and destroyed his palatial buildings. It is close to the Pahartali station on the A. B. Railway. The visitors are often reminded of many a tale current in the air about the poor girl, as they observe the transparent calm of the water of the pond reflecting the dark blue trees on the bank.

The pictures of elephant-capture (pp. 111, 129) were taken from the actual scene of 'Hati-Kheda' during some past years.

The cannon (p. 239) belonged to Rajendranarayan Chaudhuri. It is broken in part and measures 20″×18″. The great earthen wall which surrounded Rajendranarayan's palace has been in recent years cut down in part by enterprising peasants for agricultural purposes. The cannon was recovered from underground when they were levelling down the mound. It is in the village of Sindurkayit in Pargana Babupur in the District of Noakhali.

Rajendranarayan Chaudhuri's pond (p. 239).—This pond belonged, as its name implies, to Rajendranarayan Chaudhuri and is also near his old palace at the village of Sindurkayit in Babupur. The large tree on its bank is called there "Achin Briksha" or the unknown tree. It is said that the head of the unfortunate Rangamala was kept hanging on one of its boughs.

The relics of the fort (p. 239), which should be more properly described as a big earthen wall, indicates the secure position of Rajendranarayan Chaudhuri's palace. It was once a huge construction.

Rangamala's pond (p. 279).—It lies about three miles from Rajendranarayan Chaudhuri's palace: the space once occupied by this great pond may be still traced, though a great part of it has been filled up and converted into agricultural fields. The pond, as will be seen from the text, was dug at the cost of Rajendranarayan by the Burmese leader Rama Magh. The unfortunate events connected with the construction of this pond are fully related in the context. It was this pond which caused the tragic end of poor Rangamala. It is said that on the bank of this very pond, the head of the girl was cut off by Chand Bhandari.

The 'Ballad-singer and his Party appended to the book.—This picture was sent me last year by Munshi Jasimuddin, one of our Ballad-collectors.

The four specimens of workmanship on paper, were obtained from Chittagong, from the women-folk of the district. These were executed by the great-grand-mothers of the present generation of adult women and must therefore be between 70 and 80 years old. It will be remembered that in the Ballad of Kajalrekha (Vol. I, pt. 1) an elaborate reference has been made to the culture of fine arts by the women of Bengal. These are very imperfect specimens but their work, 3 to 4 hundred years old, are simply superb. I have got a "Kantha" (a cotton-bedding) on which the Radhakrishna lila has been given as an embroidery work by a Mahomedan woman which is 200 years old and very fine. But the older specimens are still better though I have not been able to secure the best ones.

DINESHCHANDRA SEN

7, BISHWAKOSH LANE,
BAGBAZAR, CALCUTTA.
May, 1928.

A Ballad-singer and his party.

THE BALLAD OF MANJURMĀ

PREFACE TO 'MANJURMĀ.'

The ballad of Manjurmā is evidently written by a Mahomedan, though I do not find the name of the poet anywhere in the colophon. The characters are all Mahomedan, but the whole poem is closely permeated by Hindu thought, showing beyond doubt that a catholic spirit of assimilation of mutual ideas and a warm sympathy subsisted between the Hindus and the Moslems when this ballad was composed. The poet refers to the holiness of the Ganges (Canto VI, l. 32) though he is not the only Mahomedan to do so. The Sanskrit hymns composed by Daraf Khan in honour of the Ganges are well known in the country. The poet of the present ballad not only speaks of the holy river in terms of respect, but also refers to the sanctity of the *tulasi* leaves (Canto VI, l. 36). Kanai, our beloved cow-herd, was the symbol of love even with the Mahomedans, as we find it in old Bengali literature. Numerous Moslem poets wrote about Radha-Krishna love in the sixteenth and the seventeenth centuries, such as Nasir Mahomed, Syed Martuza, Fakir Habib, Shal Beg, Kabir, Sheik Lal, Sheik Faten, Sheik Bhikan, Akbar Saha, Syed Alwāl, etc. And we are not, therefore, surprised by the respectful reference made in this poem to our pastoral god of Love. But is it not rather strange that the Moslem poet should pay his respectful compliments to *Durga Dasabhuja* ? (Canto VI, l. 34.) In the country-side, however, there are many Mahomedans who still sing songs in honour of Kali. And I knew a minstrel, named Gōl Mahmud, who had organised a band of singers in the district of Tipperah and made it his avocation of life to sing songs of his own composition in praise of Kali. The exquisite song composed by him, beginning with the line "উনমত্তা ছিন্নমস্তা এ রমণী কার" still rings in my ears, though I heard it more than forty years ago. I have got with me some old Bengali manuscripts of the poems of the Manasacult in the hand-writing of Mahomedan copyists. In Eastern Bengal, there are professional Moslem singers who sing songs of Manasa Devi.

The two great communities of Bengal—the Hindus and the Moslems—once thus joined their hands with each other in their festive ceremonies, apparently participating in their mutual beliefs without losing regard for their respective creeds. At Chhatarpur in Central India, I found Hindus organising regular bands to take part in the Mohurrum ceremony. Many Mahomedan Mosques were there founded and are still maintained by Hindu Rajas. Our Bengali literature is full of references to this happy state of fusion of ideas and of mutual participation in the festive joys of one another.

In the face of all these evidences what should I say of the present bitter feelings that are rending the very heart of India ? We have already fallen low in the scale of national progress and if the two sections do not unite, the extirpation of the rank and file of Indians will be the inevitable result in no distant future. The glorious people who had fought on the plains of Kurukshetra, the invincible Jadus who had assembled in the shrine of Pravash were exterminated by communal and family-dissensions in pre-historic days, and the same scene will be enacted in this Gangetic valley of ours—our ruin would be far more accentuated now by the circumstance that we have been enfeebled and have degenerated a hundred times more than in those days of India's glory.

The happy age when peace in communal matters was gaining ground in the past is infallibly reflected in these ballads which form a valuable record, not only illuminating pages of our obscure social history but also indicating the lines to be pursued by us for bringing about union and peace again in this vast country inhabited by people professing diverse religions.

This ballad, though short, is full of unique interest. It obviously presents some points of difference from those composed by the Hindus. Though no one would believe that every woman is chaste and blameless in Hindu homes, yet the Hindu conception of feminine ideal is very guarded and scarcely allows of the portraiture of a lawful wife in love with another man. The Vaisnava songs have a special sanctity attached to them by the allegory of spiritual love, and hence they should not be brought to bear on our present topic. But rarely in our vast secular literature of the past is there an instance of a woman bound in lawful wedlock, running astray. The Hindu poets did not like to depict what seemed abhorrent to them from their own ethical point of view. The air of our literature is assuredly stiff and puritanic on this point.

But nevertheless we cannot blame the moral standard of other peoples who view matters from a different standpoint. The Mahomedan community—its literature and ethics—are permeated by a spirit of far greater freedom. They have been exponents of liberty, and from the very outset have warred against traditional customs and orthodoxy. We find this ballad composed by a Mahomedan, made pleasing to us by a rush of fresh air, breathing freedom from orthodox notions of sexual love. A Hindu writer of those days could never have portrayed Manjurmā, doing full justice to her as the Moslem poet has done. The former would have sulked in anger at the thought of a wife running away from the lawful custody of her husband. He would have poured forth volleys of anger at her conduct, condemned her by quoting verses from holy scriptures and by bringing in an array of typical ideals of Hindu women like Sita and Savitri by way of contrast. Theology and traditional faith would blind him to the glaring fact that she was a mere child and that the marriage was inhuman to the extreme from a commonsense view of matters. He would completely ignore another fact which would appeal to all people except the Hindus of the old school that in matrimony woman had the power of choice equally with man, and no one, however strongly equipped with the sanction of social authority, had the right to wreck another's life.

The chief merit of the short ballad consists in the author's doing evenhanded justice to all parties. He creates a pathetic interest for the girl by describing her sorrows with which every right-minded man should have sympathy. He condemns the snake-charmer for marrying this pretty girl, laying stress on the incongruity of the situation in the most striking manner. But nevertheless he makes our heart beat in sympathy for poor Manir's sorrows, so pathetically described in the last part of the ballad. Though we condemn him for the wrong course he adopted, yet he is not altogether shut out from our compassion. A wild man was he—this snake-charmer. He had all along shunned women as he held the sex to be treacherous. Yet at last he fell into the trap and was wrecked by the snares of a woman whom he had loved so dearly. Providence had thrown her in his way—anyhow she was not there by his own seeking. It was a saintly feeling of compassion that had made him take her charge, fallen as she was in an utterly destitute condition. His subsequent career was chalked out for him by Fate, and while charging him with indiscretion in not thinking about the girl from the point of view of her natural feelings, we cannot charge the man with cruelty or as doing anything from an evil motive. The poet has compared him to a devil—to loathsome dung—but nevertheless has given such fine touches to his aesthetic feelings that towards the end we feel our heart moved to extreme pity for him. This shows the great power of the poet as an artist. Grimly pessimistic, the snake-charmer has a lovely feature in his character—his childlike faith in the innocence and purity, verging on worship, of Manjurmā. She was practising all along the characteristic tricks and cunning of her sex on her doting husband. But his romantic love founded on implicit trust in her character raises him far above the level of weak and sordid attachment of a henpecked husband so strongly condemned by Tennyson in Guinevere :—

> " I hold that man the worst of public foes
> Who either for his own or children's sake
> To save his blood from scandal lets the wife
> Whom he knows false abide and rule the house."

Bold and free is the utterance of the poet when he says that one who has loved has really lived. A life not ennobled by love is stale and flat (Canto V, ll. 34-36).

This compliment to love he pays in the case of a wife who has been untrue. It shows that he has transcended the limits of social tradition and seen matters from a higher standpoint. At the same time, while calling Manir a devil (Canto III, l. 32) the poet does not condemn him to a place in hell where a devil should go, but in the last line of his poem, he has confidently stated that the miserable man, the inhuman monster, who, tottering and trembling in his path to the grave, wrecked the life of an innocent girl for seeking his own comforts, is nevertheless entitled to a place in heaven because of his great love.

There is no verbosity in the tale and the poet draws freely from the atmosphere of Vaisnava phraseology with which the very air of Bengal was charged in his time. But this point I reserve for fuller treatment in my General Introduction.

The language, though occasionally coarse, is fully expressive, and brevity gives the ballad a unique interest. There is no theology, no propagandism in it. The poet like a true child of nature has warbled sweetly this song of love. I am sure I have marred the original beauty of the poem in my translation. But no apology, I trust, is needed from a foreigner writing in English, if he fails to reproduce the original charm of a Bengali song.

From the language of the poem, it seems to be a production of the sixteenth century. Mr. Nagendra Chandra De, who supplied it, refers to the local tradition that the story was founded on fact. This song was at one time very popular in Mymensingh. It was latterly given up obviously because of the opposition of the purists who considered its tone to be unhealthy, and for a long time he could not secure more than a few scraps of this beautiful ballad. A persistent and dogged search has, however, ultimately succeeded in recovering it.

DINESH CHANDRA SEN

Manjurmā

(1)

A wonderfully clever man was this Manir—the snake-charmer who lived in the village of Kanir Bari.

Cases of snake-bite, given up as hopeless by doctors, he cured by exorcisings, incantations and by the power of his mystic touch.

Adept was he in *Gaḍura* lore and when he sprinkled holy water from his magic basket *pala* on the body of his patient, reciting mystic words, the man long given up for dead, would stand up and walk. And his fame went on increasing all the more as he charged no fee but offered his gratuitous service to all.

Should any one out of gratitude offer him a meal or good drink, he would not touch it ; nor would he accept even a betel or betelnut from any of his patients. Saint-like he did his benefaction, free of charge, not accepting a *cowrie* in return.

Cases came to him of snake-bite where poison had vitiated a patient's system for many long months; but such was the power of the healer that he who had come to him, borne in a litter, went away on foot, a full and healthy man.

Even when he failed to cure a man, Manir would make his power felt some way or other : for the patient, totally benumbed, would at least utter a few words before he expired.

Infallible were his charms and to this every patient bore testimony. In this world, canopied by a sky of limitless expanse, many charmers lived, but none dared match his lance with Manir of Kanir Bari.

A celibate was he and lived alone, having no wife or children. So deep-rooted was his prejudice against women that not one of them he believed to be true. He abhorred even to look at one of the fair sex. (Ll. 1-18.)

(2)

One Jamiladdi, a Fakir, poor, decrepit and homeless, lived on the sea-coast in a miserable cot with a little daughter—left by his dead wife as her last token on earth. Unlucky was the baby in losing her mother in infancy. But the bereaved Fakir stayed in the cot day and night with the child, shedding tears and nursing her with care. One day, the Fakir, while strolling by the bank of the Ganges, was bitten by a venomous snake. Quick like lightning, the venom spread from foot to brain and the Fakir, though a strong man, fell down on the ground senseless. Kith and kin he had none to share his misfortune. So for a time he lay alone on the bank of the Ganges.

Some friends came up at last and carried him to his house. Hundreds of snake-charmers and healers of the country-side flocked to the spot at the report; they applied all their charms and skill to bring him round.

A long application of their healing art—the rubbing of the body and the blowing over it with their breath,—the uttering of incantations and *mantras*—all failed, till the healers sat down exhausted hanging down their head in shame.

At this crisis they remembered Manir, the most famous of them all, and five of them forthwith went to his house and brought him thither in haste.

First of all did Manir try to exorcise the evil spirit by means of a sieve sanctified by *mantras*. Then did he try his magic basket and many incantations and charms acquired from the *Gaḍura* lore. Closely attending his patient he sat for hours together and applied all his charms, till he exhausted all his skill.

How strange it was—the man who had never failed before could not show any success in this case. The Fakir was doomed to die and who could stand against the decree of Fate? The venom of the reptile slowly spread over the system and eventually the Fakir succumbed to it.

He is dead—he is relieved, but woe to the little child, forlorn and helpless! The Fakir's death was a death-blow to her as well. Who would now save the orphan from the dangers that lay ahead? There she lay a helpless orphan, crying, beautiful as the full moon fallen on the earth. And though spectators there were in plenty to cry "alas! alas!" none came forward to feed or nurse her.

Alas! How many are there in this world to show active sympathy to one fallen in distress! The world is self-seeking. Oh my friends, none cares for the sorrows of others!

For a time they pitied her all, but it was mere lip-sympathy. Not one stayed but all went their way at last, and the fairy-like little thing lay weeping alone.

All went away, but not Manir. He could not bear the sight of the little thing in distress. It was still a baby, subsisting on milk. Manir thought for a moment and speedily decided his course. He took up the girl in his arms and came straight to his home.

A rare man with a heart full of love for all was Manir,—the snake-charmer. As he had none in his home, neither wife nor child, this girl became his only care and he doted on her in his lonely home. A sympathetic and kind soul like Manir is rare on earth. He nursed her with affectionate care.

As we said before, he had no trust in womankind. "Treacherous are they all," he thought. Hence he lived a bachelor, not wishing to bring one from the wicked sex to rule his house. Pessimistic and full of bitterness, he did not even cast his glance at any woman. He had a mosque at his house where he allowed no woman to come. If ever a woman crossed his path, he returned home, stopping his intended trip, for the sight of a woman he took as auguring ill for his purpose. (Ll. 1-48.)

(3)

Youth has dawned on her and often did she look askance at the way-side impelled by desire for a companion, natural to her age.

Neatly did she perform her household duties, cooking meals for Manir and doing everything that he needed. He now enjoyed the comforts of home to which he had been heretofore a stranger, and in his lonely house he thus thought of the girl and of himself.

"Three-fourths of life have I passed, and the heat and passion of youth are gone. I never married all this time. No child have I got to adorn my home. Declined as I am in the vale of years, there is none to do the nursings and the services that age requires. None will there be to look after me and cook my meals when I shall be disabled from doing so.

" I have always hated women, believing them to be wicked as a class. But my Manjurmā seems to be an exception. I have reared her up from infancy with affection and care. Night and day have I kept a close watch over her and observed her movements. She is chaste and pure, and to this I can swear.

" She has now attained her marriageable age. But how can I think of living at this lonely home, sending her away from here! Woe to me that I brought another man's daughter to my home and contracted affection for one who is nobody to me. But my affection has grown and there is no doubt of it. I have built the image of a god with my own hands, and is it all for throwing it away with my own hands?

" Womankind is untrustworthy and treacherous, save this Manjurmā of mine. The plant was nursed by me till it has grown into a blossoming and fruitful tree, and are the fruits to be given away to others?

" I do here resolve that to no other man shall I give my own Manjurmā. The bamboo plant that has sprouted forth of itself in my house will be employed for the purpose of the house. From infancy onwards I have brought her up and I will not give her now to another man. I will marry her myself and keep her in my home."

On one Friday of the waxing moon when the time was auspicious for marriage, Manir had his hands joined with hers, and the ceremony was gone through with due rites as laid down in the scriptures.

He had grown so old that he trembled while walking, but she, in the full bloom of youth, looked healthy and beautiful.

It was as though a charming fairy was by chance united with a devil, or a bud of lotus, glorious and bright thrown into a heap of dung.

She wept and thought, "How could I know that such a cruel thing was written on my luck? Like a tradesman's ship laden with cargo, sinking in the midstream am I lost in the depth of sorrow. Oh! this great calamity was hurled by Fate, all unsuspected, and sudden has been the blow."

The beautiful one thus cried incessantly, thinking of her condition. (Ll. 1-36.)

(4)

Hasan was a young man, handsome and accomplished—a fellow of decent taste who always cared for fashionable habits and attire. The youth passionately loved Manjurmā from his young days.

They were in love with each other, and being close neighbours, they often met in the village. Manjurmā thought the day lost if she did not see the youth, and the same was the case with her lover who pined away the live-long day, if he caught no glimpse of the young woman's face. Play-fellows they were even as children and kept company with each other in every little act they did.

When youth came, the feeling deepened, and privately they met, expressing their passion to each other, and no one knew of their secret love. Manjurmā had cherished the hope that she would have Hasan for her husband and a similar hope had lurked in the mind of Hasan too. They had often met in secret when there was none at home, and the girl and her lover spoke out their hopes and fears freely. No obstruction seemed to thwart them. So they had passed all their early life in a dreamy joy all undisturbed. It was strange—passing strange—that the old snake-charmer should at such a time take a fancy to marry her. Three-fourths of his life were gone and only one-fourth remained.

And yet the Fates had kept in store this great blow for her, smothering all her happiness. Manjurmā cried night and day, as she pondered over her miserable lot.

She cried and said, "None, alas, is there to extinguish the fire of my grief. How can I bear my lot. The fire smoulders and burns my body and mind. This human life is a rare blessing, but to me it has grown to be such an evil that the sooner I die, the better for me. My hopes are now all lost, and what good is there in dragging on this miserable existence? Often do I feel inclined to tie a pitcher round my neck and drown myself in yonder river. How often also do I wish to end my life with poison. The sight of a forest draws me and I wish to throw myself into the mouths of tigers and bears. And when I see the birds flying above, happy and free, fain would I wander with them in the sky, free from miseries of the earth.

"Unfortunate am I from my birth. I cannot open to others the secret pain of my heart. For him who is my dearest would I turn mad. None knows how deeply I feel for him. For his sake, I am ready at this moment to give my life up. My heart is laden with unsupportable grief when I see my beloved playing on his flute to beckon me, or sitting on the bathing-ghat to have a glimpse of my face. Oh, how tenderly does the sound of the flute appeal to my heart. What a heart-rending tale of grief is unfolded to me by the pathos of that music. As I hear his songs, my eyes glisten with tears. Dear is he to me as Kanu was to Radha. How cruel is Providence who has separated us in this way and brought about this dire sorrow.

"Nights pass as usual and I spend them weeping; days pass as usual and I spend them sighing.

"My mind is no more in the work of this home of ours. My whole soul yearns for a sight of him, and my eyes are ever strained to see his face to my heart's content.

"I sleep, hoping to dream of him. But alas! he does not appear even once in my dreams. It is the fear of scandal that is like a thorn in the path of my happiness.

"From my house I see him seated on the landing-ghat, shedding incessant tears. The grief of this I cannot bear. Like silent fire, it consumes my heart.

"Should any one ask the real wish of my mind, frankly I would tell him that I would like to leave this land for ever and live with him in the depths of jungles, giving up the society of men and all that is honourable in their eyes." (Ll. 1-50.)

(5)

One day Manir was called to attend a case of snake-bite far away. It was a journey of three days from his home. This was a good opportunity and Manjurmā went to the landing-ghat to let know her lover by signs her heart's secret wish.

That evening he had resolved to put an end to his life, if he could not have a sight of Manjurmā. His eyes were swollen with tears.

He had come as usual and looked around with thirsty eyes. He saw everything there as before save the lovely face for a sight of which his eager eyes roamed on all sides.

He became hopeless and desperate, not seeing her come and jumped into the river to drown himself.

Just at that moment did the fair damsel arrive at the spot and dragging him by her tender arms brought him to the bank. His life was thus saved. Clasping

" Dragging him by her tender arms, brought him to the bank." P. 16.

each other by their arms they returned home, happy beyond measure.

Evening had passed away and Manjurmā brought her lover to her home. With soft care and a hundred ways of love she made him sit on a cushion. She offered him fine *chira*, sweet cakes, and cooked curries of different sorts, sparing no pains to make them of good flavour and taste. It was, as it were, with the blood of her heart that she made these preparations and offered them to her lover. She completely captured his mind by a thousand ways in which women are adept.

They spent the night in pleasant conversation, and the night seemed to them to be full of the joys of paradise. Three days and nights they spent merrily and on the fourth they met again and discussed their points at full length. They finally resolved thus, "No more shall we live in this cursed land. Let us go to a distant, far distant place." In the deep hours of night, the lovers set out for countries unknown and strange. Their path lay through jungles and forests. Like birds they flew into regions not known to them,—as if a pair of parrots had cut off with their beaks the chain that had bound them to a cage. Rivers and canals offered no obstruction to them, determined as they were to go. They fled away with the swiftness of an arrow flung from the string of a bow.

Thirteen rivers they had crossed and seven seas, till they went far, far away. Her country she had abandoned for ever for the sake of one whom she loved above everything in the world.

Love, my friend, is better than gold. It should be the only object of care in the world. Love is dear as the necklace of one's breast. Even if one dies for the sake of love, that death should be more coveted than a dry and stale life. (Ll. 1-36.)

(6)

Manir had now returned home and he called aloud for his wife. Alas! where was Manjurmā then and who would give response to his call ?

He tried to open the door which was closed. Through the crevices in the mud walls he peeped but the house looked empty like a desolate plot of land. He neither saw her nor heard her voice. He forcibly opened the door and cried aloud at the top of his voice. When all search proved fruitless, he sat down and wept.

"Alas," said he, "where lay my enemy hidden all this time who has carried my Manjurmā away, attracted by her beauty and youth ? Alone I had left her in the house, quite unguarded. The wicked man found an opportunity to take her off. She was chaste and good and to this I can swear. With tender care I had brought her up. Never did I allow her to go to the public road, to the landing *ghat* or even to the house of my neighbours alone. With my eyes fixed on my idol did I help her to grow to womanhood. Oh the misfortune ! when did the wild tiger enter into my lonely house to carry her away ?

"Unhesitatingly can I assure all who would want to know that she is blameless, chaste and of a pure and sincere mind. The wicked man is to blame, who forcibly carried her off.

"Manjurmā was to me like the bright stars of my eyes—the crown and perfection of womankind. Dear as my lifeblood and the very soul of candour and fidelity was she.

"If it is ordained by Fate that I shall no more see her, this life of mine will not be worth living at all. Where is the jungle, where is that wild forest, into the recesses of which I shall enter seeking her ?"

Mad he turned in despair. And seeking her whom he loved with all his might he wandered about in forests and dales, towns and villages, asking those whom he met on the way: "Did any one of you see my Manjurmā?"

In the forests he asked of wild beasts and of the birds that sat on lofty trees, "Did any of you see her going by this path?"

He looked up and saw the sun blazing in the day and the moon spreading her beams in the night. To them he said, "Ye are the angels in charge of day and night. Have ye seen Manjurmā and can you point me out the path ?"

"Manjurmā, beloved as the dark paint Kajjal of my eyes —Manjurmā, holy as the stream of the Ganges—Manjurmā, dear as the ribs of my breast—Manjurmā, worshipped as the goddess Durga—sacred as the shrine of Kasi—pure as the *Tulasi* leaf dedicated to gods—Manjurmā to me was a coveted thing like the moon of the sky, and precious as the flag of victory carried by the gods.

"Be she in heaven, in this earth or in the nether worlds—be she in the abode of the gods or shades of giants, I shall seek her out at any cost, any sacrifice.

"I have sought for her in the depths of the forest, in the recesses of hills and mounts. Now shall I plunge into the depths of rivers and seas, to see if she is there."

Uttering these words, Manir the healer, ran fast to the bank of the neighbouring river and jumped headlong into the midstream.

He did not rise from his watery bed that day and indeed, never again. He had loved the girl and for her sake died, and it is sure that he found a place in heaven, because he had loved the lost one with all his soul.

(Ll. 1-48.)

COFFIN-STEALER

PREFACE TO COFFIN-STEALER

This is a ballad, which we have got from the illiterate peasantry of Chittagong in the primitive dialect of the district, breathing rural simplicity unadorned by any poetic tradition or art. The dialect is a form of old Prakrit and though the characters are all Mahomedan and the author himself and the minstrels who sing this song evidently belong to that community, there is no preponderance of Urdu words in it. The sprinkling of a few words of Arabic and Persian origin presents no difficulty whatever to the Hindu readers, as most of them have been assimilated into the Bengali language,—specially into the dialects of Eastern Bengal. The spirit of rural life that pervades the poem and the archaic Prakrit words in which the ballad is composed give to it a unique interest,—not only to the philologist but to those who have a literary turn of mind. Terse and brief are the descriptions, and the author's style is free from all attempts at ornamentation. The sketches are vivid and lifelike. Unlike the ballad of Nizam dacoit, to which the present poem bears a striking analogy in its subject-matter, there is much poetry in this ballad, and its naive simplicity is not marred by fantastic legends which we find in profusion in the other ballad. Like the ballad of Kenaram, it is enlivened by a touch of life. Kenaram, Nizam and Monshoor,—the chief characters of three of our ballads have certain undoubted points of affinity. Nizam's life, however, is pervaded by supernatural elements which keep it above human sympathy. Like the queen Maynamati and the Hārisiddhā, Nizam is a theological conception, a product of wild ultra-natural legend, which overpowers the masses with a mystical awe but never wins their reverence which a true saint claims from the simple peasantry. Nizam is reformed by a miracle, but not so Kenaram and Monshoor. Of course, Monshoor dreamt a dream, by reason of which there came a change over the spirit of his life. But the dream is certainly not anything miraculous. Kenaram and Monshoor were saved by the power of faith and real repentance for their sins. The account of their reformation shows the saving graces of trust in Divinity, and is full of a simple appeal that needs no theological comment to explain the extraordinary turn which their life latterly took.

In the life of Monshoor, reformation came all on a sudden, and in such a strange manner that the dramatic effect of the tale becomes almost overwhelming. He had already dug a hole into a rich man's mansion, opened a chest full of valuable articles, and was about to fly away with the booty,—when strangely came the falcon's cry indicative of the approach of the dawn. The morning prayer, the first *namaz*, must be offered. Whether he stole or committed robbery for earning his living, it mattered not, but he had taken the solemn vow of offering his *namaz* five times a day. This he could not avoid and he was practising it ever since he had dreamt the dream. The valuable booty was near him, but he forgot it altogether,—nay, forgot himself. The purple in the horizon, seen through the window, gave him the unfailing notice of the dawn, and the voices of the *mollas* were heard by the Dacoit from a neighbouring *masjid*, and to these, unconsciously and in automatic response, he joined his cry with all the force of his voice, "La Elaha Illallaha." The sudden cry made the landlord awake and the men of the Dacoit's party took to their heels. But he, roused to the sense of preserving his unalterable vow, heedless of the danger that lay before him, and of the dire loss of the riches that had almost come to his hands,—loudly uttered the holy name of Allah and said his *namaz*. The scene is supremely dramatic. The last scene in which the Fakir comes to visit the grave of Ayera Bibi and disappears like a phantom after having paid his respects to it, accentuates the great effect of his noble renunciation.

The ballad has a good many passages of great poetic beauty. The march of the palanquin carrying the bride through a moon-lit night where the moonbeams looked like handfuls of white buds of *bela* thrown by some one from above on the earth, is described in a charming and picturesque language. The verses run in limpid course describing the graceful motion of the palanquin and the sorrows of the girl-wife just parted from her parents. (Canto III, Ll. 1-10.)

Monshoor was not altogether without some noble instincts in him. If he had inherited the wicked elements of one who had fathered him,—the terrible physical features of Ludhagazi and the grim factors of his wicked character,—there certainly ran in his veins the blood of a virtuous maiden,—the victim of a demon's lust. The quiet grace of his mother who died a tragic death like a martyr must have lain deep in his nature as a latent force, helping the development of his spiritual nature at an opportune moment in such a strange manner. Something of a martyr's patience in his nature is displayed by the manner in which he bore the assaults of the people on his person without uttering a word. Is it not strange that in spite of his great physical strength, our hero of a hundred fights did not show the least inclination to retaliate, nor even to make an attempt to escape from his critical position ? From that time forward his virtuous nature was showing signs of budding forth and his great patience in suffering was an index to his coming transformation. (Canto VI, Ll. 86-96.)

With elegant poetical passages interspersed in his narration,—pregnant with a deep religious meaning—the history of a sinner's psychological evolution has been told by the rustic poet in a masterly way. The descriptions of the hills and the forest-shades—of the adventurous life of the traders, and the hilly people—possess a great interest.

Babu Asutosh Choudhury, our Ballad-collector, got this ballad from three men :—

(1) Shekandar Gayen of the village Haidgaon ; Police-Station Patiah.

(2) Alwar Rahim, popularly known as Allia Andha, of the village Dhoral, Police-Station Boalkhali.

(3) Tazu Pagla—Char-chaktail Police-Station, Kotowali.

Asu Babu obtained only a few parts of this poem from Nos. 2 and 3. By far the most important portion of the ballad was secured by him from Shekandar Gayen. Shekandar is a professional rhapsodist. He was once in jail, being convicted of theft. But his present career is marked by marvellous spiritual zeal. When he explains a religious subject, the masses listen to him with rapt attention and take him very nearly for a saint. When Asu Babu sought his help in the field of ballad, he was taken by Shekandar for a spy from the Excise Department. But gradually his fears were dispelled and Asu Babu's real mission was latterly made clear to him. At this stage, Shekandar opened to him his whole heart and rendered to him a cordial help. He has composed some songs describing his sufferings in the jail. One of which runs thus :—

"Woe to me! my gracious God has become ungracious. The sufferings of prison-life are hard to bear. Immat Ali and Golab Habi are my bitter enemies. Owing to their intrigue, my innocent hands are bound in chain."

When Asu Babu had the present ballad recited by Shekandar Gayen, he perceived that 'the stealer of coffin' had some elements in his nature which appealed to this minstrel most. He sang it with his whole heart and in a manner which stirred up strange emotions in the hearts of his audience. Much stress has been laid in the ballad on the earnestness with which Monshoor said his *namaz.* Shekandar daily says it as many times, as the hero of his tale, if not more. As he recites the holy formulæ he strikes his head against the ground out of a feeling of profound devotion, so forcibly that a portion of his fore-locks has formed into a knot.

Babu Asutosh Choudhury gives the following further account of Shekandar,—" At the house of one Nibaran Chandra Sutradhar in the village Parigram under the Police-station of Patia, I heard Shekandar sing this remarkable ballad continuously for eight hours in the night. About four hundred men of the peasant-class had assembled there. The performance was held in a square plot of land having four bamboo-poles on its sides. At the tops of the poles, four kerosene lamps were burning like torches. The whole atmosphere was covered with a dense smoke issuing from these lamps. In the lurid light of these kerosene lamps, the minstrel's figure appeared half-hid in smoke. He had a striped turban on his head. A sort of *toga* hang from his shoulder down to his feet, with the badge of a crescent moon fixed in one of its sides. In one hand he held a '*chamara*' to drive away the flies and insects drawn by the lamps, and in another hand he had a pair of cymbals which he played, producing a jingling sound. A drummer sat behind him and a few singers sang the chorus. The voice of Shekandar rose far above that of others and the audience listened to him with rapt attention. Towards the north of this court, an iron post, with an iron ring of the shape of the crescent moon over it, was planted making a picturesque show. The stick was called the '*Asha.*' [1]

[1] Some Mahomedans contend that the word '*Asha*' implying a Fakir's staff is derived from an Arabic word. But we have got the word "*Ashara jasthi*" in Kadambari, denoting an ascetic's staff.—Ed.

Beneath the ring a few garlands of flowers hang in several folds. When Shekandar was singing, at times he touched the '*Asha*' with his head as a mark of respect. On the ground lay a can filled with rice and other things. These were meant as '*Shinni*' or offerings to the Gazi. Hindus and Mahomedans still offer the '*Shinni*' in honour of the Gazi. But the time has changed. The Mollas have issued a '*Fatwa*' branding all classes of songs as '*Haram*,' with quotations from religious texts. So it is certain that this class of songs will no more be sung in the country-side."

It should be stated here that the Mahomedans used to sing the song of Gazi all over Bengal, specially in the localities near the Sundarbans. The fight of the Gazi with Dakshin Roy, the god of the tigers, forms the subject of this Gazi-song. Many Hindu writers composed the song of Dakshin Roy and amongst these the Rai-mangal of Krishnaram, an inhabitant of the village Nimta, should be prominently noticed. The Mahomedan writers have called it "the Gazir gān" and in their versions the Gazi gets victory over Dakshin Roy. Some of these songs have been published by the peasantry composed in the rural dialects of Eastern Bengal. Truth and legend have mixed fantastically in this curious song of the Gazi, but we are not at present concerned with it. The Gazi-song became so popular that many ballads sung by the Mahomedan minstrels, though their subject-matter is altogether different, are included within the Gazi-songs. The reason is that the minstrels whose chief subject was this fight of the Gazi became so closely associated with this song that latterly whatever they sang fell under the category of the main subject and were denominated as Gazi-song. It is not therefore strange that this ballad of Monshoor, the dacoit, is called as such by the village-peasantry.

Of the two other singers who helped Asu Babu, Alwar Rahim's version is very imperfect. He recites only a small portion of the metrical verses of this song, giving the gist of the major part of the ballad in prose, as his memory frequently fails him.

Tazu Pagla, as his name indicates, is a crazy fellow, who sings this ballad quite well in the lucid intervals of his disease, but when he gets a relapse while reciting the song, as he sometimes does, his song becomes an incoherent tale "full of sound and fury, signifying nothing."

The scene of Monshoor's activities lay in the hilly tracts of Chittagong. Chintapur of the ballad is situated on the banks of the Kurmai which is a branch of the Karnafulli. The village is within the jurisdiction of the Police-station Rangunia. The name of Chintapur has now slightly been altered. It is now called "Dakshin Nichintapur." The native village of Ludha, father of Monshoor, is Gazaligram, now known as Gazalia, which is not far off from Chintapur. Asu Babu in course of his trip to recover the ballad paid a visit to all these places. The river 'Thega' mentioned in the ballad is another branch of the Karnafulli. The paddy fields on the bank of the Thega in a locality named Dum-dummia-para (Canto I, Ll. 24-28) are still famous for their bumper crops ; and the forest near this river is a reserved tract of the Government.

Chittagong was formerly named as "Harmad's Mulluck." The Harmads or the Portuguese (from Armada) once played an important part in this hilly district. In the 16th century Mukundaram referred to the great dread in which these Harmads, the Portuguese pirates, were held by enterprising traders who made sea-voyages in the Bay of Bengal. On the west of the district, the pirates, principally the Portuguese, were greatly feared, and the dense forests inhabited by the Kukis, the Murangs and the hilly tribes were no less dreaded. With a view to save the country from the capricious attacks of these wild hill-tribes, the Hindu kings of Gour had at one time had recourse to sending the Hazaris of the Punjab to go to these mountainous regions and settle there. Large endowments of land were made to them for keeping in control the non-Aryan tribes. These Hazaris who came principally from the Punjab and partly from Allahabad still dwell in large numbers in Chittagong and are popularly called "Hazari-Khottas." Hazari means leader of a thousand soldiers. They now own extensive lands in Chittagong. During the decadence of the power of the Mahomedan Nawabs of Murshidabad, the Hazaris revolted, trying to throw off the yoke of dependence. The Nawab found it necessary to send a large troop under Mahasingha to quell this rebellion. He brought to Murshidabad eight chiefs of the Hazaris bound in chain and they were all thrown into the Bhagirathi to meet a watery grave. It is probable that during the latter part of Moslem administration, when a sort of anarchy prevailed in the district, the notorious dacoit Monshoor with his band of robbers carried on his depredations throughout the country. The ballad in its original shape must have been composed in that case about the middle of the 18th century.[1]

DINESH CHANDRA SEN

[1] Babu Asutosh Choudhury supplied me with some of the materials of this preface.—Ed.

Coffin-stealer

Preliminary Hymns

Obcisance to my learned audience. I pay my respects to my elders and compliments to my juniors. I admit my shortcomings. Many an error I may commit, but kindly bear with me till I finish my song. I see around me old people, men and women, from whom I expect an indulgent treatment as their children would do. Every one cannot tell a tale relevantly, nor can one expect everything fine and faultless. I entreat you, therefore, my friends, to pardon me if you discover in my composition anything inelegant or faulty. I have not studied music as a science, so I may not keep time while singing. I think I have said all that is necessary. No further preliminary will be needed. I pray to God that He may help me, and I begin my humble song here. (Ll. 1-10.)

(1) Cheuṅa, the Fairy of the Hill Tracts.

In the eastern limits of the fair district of Chittagong, there is a great hill, where beasts of all kinds rove in wilderness. The jungle is dense and in its impenetrable depths tigers, leopards, elephants and wild buffaloes have made their favourite resort. The farther east one goes, the higher are the peaks that one's eyes meet. These peaks seem to touch the very sky.

In the heart of this forest dwell the hilly people of Arakan, the Pankhowas, the Murangs and the wild Kukis in a perfect state of nudity. These wild people wander about the forest like the very buffaloes and tigers. If they happen to meet any person of Chittagong or of the lower valley they stab him without mercy. The Jummas and the Chakmas live upon their favourite food '*jamkuchi*' they construct two-storied houses with bamboos, and in these heights made of bamboos which they call '*machang*' they live with a sense of security and ease. In the valleys at the foot of the hills the land is so fertile that the earth seems to yield gold. Rich harvests of various kinds of paddy, cotton-plants, the luscious fruits called '*marfa*' and '*chinars*' grow on the soil, and the wild people come down with these products to the markets in the down-countries where the people of the valley flock to purchase them. (Ll. 1-16.)

(2) The Trader in Love.

There was a man in the hilly regions named Ludhagazi who traded in bamboos and straws. It was a prosperous business that Ludha conducted with the help of two boat-men. They once came to one of the bends of the Karnafulli, popularly called 'Kaincha,' and marching upstream crossed the canal of 'Thagerkul.' Thence they proceeded to a village of Chittagong called Dum-dumma where they purchased a good quantity of rice and cotton. They had constructed their kitchen on bamboos and made themselves happy with food cooked thereon. The whole of the day they spent by hawking in the village path. In the vicinity of the canal, there was a small settlement of the Jummas. For a few days the Gazi moored his boat near the landing-ghat of the canal in that locality.

Ludhagazi was attracted one day by a strange spectacle. A maiden was going to the paddy field. Her appearance was striking. She wore a dark coloured *khami*[1] and her eyes cast sidelong glances as she walked. The gold ear-rings dangled on both sides of her moon-like face enhancing its beauty and grace. It seemed that two pomegranate fruits were about to burst at her breasts, and a golden string

[1] *Khama* is evidently a distortion of the famous *Khouma* cloth.

added charm to her lovely neck. The garland of flowers round her chignon moved in a wavy dance, touched by the playful breeze. She was smiling all along, though alone, evidently at some sweet thought natural to youth, and that smile was so sweet that one could pay his whole life for its price. Her father was Gurādhan, a local merchant, and her name was Cheuna-pari. The girl was engaged in fieldwork on the bank of the Thega ; and Ludhagazi, seated on the bamboo structure, gazed wonderingly at her. As often as he beheld her, his heart beat quickly. (Ll. 1-26.)

(3) The Tiger and his Prey.

O my audience, listen to what transpired next. The girl came to the canal for a bath. The evening was near, and streaks of the sun's rays were still sparkling as crown on the tops of the trees. The Gazi came down from his bamboo-seat and approached the girl. There was no talk, no preliminary action, but all on a sudden, from behind her back, he clasped her with his arm tightly. Struck with this sudden danger which came like a blow, Cheuna looked behind and screamed aloud. Ludha was quite up to the need of the moment and tied fast her mouth by his towel. His next action was to take up his pleasant burden on his shoulders. It was the old story of the deer caught by the tiger. Perfectly helpless, she shed tears without being able to cry aloud. (Ll. 1-12.)

(4) At the House of the Gazi.

The Gazi crossed the canal Thega and came to the Kaincha. The girl had exhausted her tears and lay unconscious in an utterly destitute state. They came now to the midstream of the wide Karnafulli. The water lay deep for a great expanse and the Gazi tried to console the distressed maiden by many a sweet word. She, however, listened not to the fair words of the devil and heedless of them bemoaned her lot. The tears that ran in streams from her eyes seemed to increase the volume of the water of the Kaincha. For four days they passed through the great river, and on the fifth, Ludha returned to his own village Gazali with the fair booty.

She took the vow of fasting, and the lovely colour of her cheeks faded day by day. She neither ate any food nor drank water. Her condition was verily like that of a deer put into an iron cage. (Ll. 1-12.)

(5) CHEUNA'S DEATH.

O my audience, hear what happened next. After a time it was observed that she was *enceinte*. Her own breath seemed to be poison to her and she felt a feverish excitement throughout her body. Her colour once bright as the *champak* flower now became dark and sooty; and there was no more any sign of beauty in her. The throes of child-birth completely overthrew her. She had not the strength to walk a few paces, and if she attempted to do so, she slipped her foot and fell down each time. The day of delivery drew near, and in fit time she gave birth to a son and immediately after lost her senses. Alas, she had suffered immensely, but could bear no more. It is a pity that she could not see her parents at the last moment. She died after the birth of a son, and Ludhagazi found himself really in great trouble with the unlucky child.

(Ll. 1-18.)

(6) THE SPOILED CHILD TURNED INTO A COFFIN-STEALER.

Like the cub of a ferocious leopard, the boy began to grow. The whole jungle tract of the east he roved about like a young vagabond that he was. They called him by the name of Monshoor. From infancy up, he became initiated into the life of wickedness. His colour was deep black and his eyes fiery red. Wherever he went, there was sure to be some fracas. Sometimes for the whole day he remained in the forests and at times came home. Nobody was there to look after or even enquire about the motherless child. A torn rag he wore round his waist and his body smelt the repelling smell of a buffalo. For the whole day he was seen to chew something and looked like a cow ruminating. When anybody saw him on the top of some tree, he was sure to mistake the lad for a monkey owing to his big jumps and dark colour. Nobody was there to feel compassion for this wild boy.

Now transpired another event to turn the fate of this lad. His father Ludha perceived one night that one of his cows in the pastures was seized by a tiger. He immediately ran to its rescue with a big club in his hand. The tiger became furious and leaving the cow seized Ludha, threw him down and drank his life-blood. Thus died Ludha, paying the penalty of his wicked acts in life.

Free from restraints, Monshoor's career became wilder day by day. He had no home, no provision and none to call him his own. He mixed with the wicked lads of the locality and soon became their leader. On the east of his native village lay some high peaks which abounded with bamboo-groves, fine canes called the *gallac*, and the species of straw named *ulu*. In this forest Monshoor wandered about day and night. The people of the locality considered him more like a tiger or a buffalo than man. His parents were dead and the father had not left him even a hut to live in. Jungle was his home, and he soon eked out a living,—one natural for such a wild youth,—dacoity. He became a confirmed robber in a short time. He felt no compunction when he murdered a man in cold blood. He often dug the plinth of a person's house and brought out by the hole, he made, large trunks and chests containing riches. But this was not all. He committed many more heinous crimes. He often dug out the graves of the dead and securing the coffins sold them in the market. Whenever he got a report of someone being buried, he stole into the grave by night and applied himself to digging it. He dug out in fact his path to hell by so doing. His eyes blazed like two suns and his voice roared like summer-clouds. He earned riches by his wicked trade and felt no pity for the innocent men he killed ; but lavishly did he distribute these riches amongst his comrades.

His fame spread far and wide. People took him for a devil and held him in dread. Some said Monshoor was fond of eating human flesh, especially that of corpses. Others said that no demon possessed the physical strength that he did. His party became large,—recruited from the vast tract of country at the foot of the eastern hills. So greatly was he dreaded that the young children crying and fretting, became at once silenced if they heard the name of Monshoor, the Coffin-stealer. (Ll. 1-44.)

(7) The Bridal Party.

The night was smiling with moonbeams and a palanquin was passing by the hillside. The moonbeams looked like handfuls of white *bela*-buds flung on the palanquin from above. Merrily did the palanquin pass by the side of the peak. Monshoor, the dacoit, perceived that the palanquin must belong to some bride just married. He pondered over the matter for some little time and then hid himself behind the screw-plants that grew by the side of the Kurmai canal. Merrily did the palanquin pass, eight carriers bore it. From within a sound of wail was heard. The new bride was crying in a low tone, remembering her mother and father, from whom she was just parted. She wept as she thought of her lovely younger brother. At times she was startled by the sound of the beetles, buzzing under the grasses. A mild southern breeze was waving the picturesque cloth that covered the palanquin. The moon shone in full resplendence so that night looked like day. Behind the screw-plants lay the dacoit silently like a tiger about to bound on his prey.

The palanquin bearers crossed the fordable stream of Kurmai in slow paces, and then they approached the grove of screw-plants. Suddenly like a tiger coming upon a flock of cattle did Monshoor jump upon the palanquin. There he gave out a loud yell. Some thought it was a wild buffalo, others mistook the sound for that of a tiger. The carriers left the place in all haste to save their lives. Monshoor Ali, now fully the master of the situation, opened the doors of the palanquin, with ease. The new bride cried out in fear saying, 'O my God.' Without any further ado, the robber snatched off the necklace from her breast. He took away also her nose-ornament, the '*nath*' and golden earrings. And then there was another jump and the dacoit disappeared into the dense forest.

The party of the bridegroom now came near the palanquin and were greatly moved by this mishap. They saw the young bride's nose bleeding. The blood soiled her rich garments. The party in deep sorrow came to the bridegroom's house. When they all saw the bride, the festive songs turned into bitter laments. (Ll. 1-32.)

(8) The Sad Tale and its Humour.

Chintapur is one of the most beautiful villages in the country. Many a house with two slanting roofs, and others with four, appeared in rows, giving the village an air of affluence. The lands on both sides of the canal Kurmai yielded golden harvest. The peasants used to get two seasons for sowing the seeds, so that in the course of a year they reaped double harvests. At intervals one's eyes were gladdened by the sight of the beautiful betel-plants. Azim's house looked particularly picturesque and beautiful on the bank of the Kurmai. He had five sea-going vessels—the *Sarangas*—moored on the bank. The whole village respected him as its leader. He carried the products of the soil to Kassalong and Maioni every year, and brought from those places purses filled with silver coins. He was in fact very clever in business. The Jumias and the Chakmas said that in the whole country, there was not another trader as honest as Azim. His first wife had died and at his fortieth year he had married again. The name of this lady was Ayera. I hope my audience will bear with me, if I take a little time in describing her beauty. Her face was so lovely that it fascinated even women, not to speak of men. When she smiled, her face became lit up with a flash. Her teeth were like a string of pearls. What shall I say about her hair ? They were as black as they were long and reached her very ankles. Her eye-brows were curved like the rainbow. Her limbs were fair and symmetrical and seemed to be soft as the *champa*-bud. When she walked, she looked like the bird Khanjan,—her gait was so playful. When she had attained her youth a halo seemed to emanate from her body diffusing love and light. Azim was rather declined in the vale of years. Possessing this youthful lady he felt himself happy beyond all measure. On the day of marriage, Ayerabibi had lost her nose-ornament and a little flesh from her ear with the earrings. When Azim affectionately touched her nose and ears, caressing her with all tenderness, the shy bride became overwhelmed with shame and hid her face into her husband's breast. Azim one day said, " Where are your earrings and nose-ornament?" She smiled with tears in her eyes and said, "On the day of my marriage a black leopard attacked me and seized the ornaments, and after this act, it fled to the Eastern hills."

Thus did husband and wife had many a merry conversation on a topic which had caused a deep wound in their minds in spite of all humorous references to it. The husband was deeply attached to the wife.

(Ll. 1-44.)

(9) The Parting.

December, the cold season, had already set in. Rice in the fields was ready for the reaper's scythe. Azim resolved to go abroad for trade. He was to go upstream by the Maioni. The mother wept as she tenderly held her son by the hand. "How long, dear son, will you remain away? You are like the staff to an old man. If I do not meet you for a second, my heart beats in anxiety."

The *Saranga* (boat) lay moored on the landing *ghat* while he bade farewell to her. Azim glanced at the face of his wife again and again. At last, he bade her adieu with these words.—"Life of my life art thou; I crave permission to go and stay abroad not more than three months. On the expiry of that time, I will meet thee once more, my love." Like a pigeon with broken wings Ayerabibi writhed in agony at parting with her lord. "I will not allow you to go away by any means," she said; "how can I live without you? I do not care for riches nor for all that you might bring by trade. My only joy is to be near you and satisfy my thirsty eyes by looking at your dear face night and day."

Azim said soothing words to his mother and wife, and having calmed them by sweet consolation, he started on his trading mission. As he proceeded towards the *ghât*, a fly was buzzing near his eye. Some one sneezed as he had just stepped out of his room. A snake was observed to pass from the right to the left. He saw also more ill omens; in the path lay a cow with horns broken, and a little child of a milkman was seen breaking his pitcher of curd. A fisherman was crying over his net which had got entangled with a wooden pole in the river. Three women were seen, searching lice from the hair of one another, and a fourth was observed going to the river *ghat* with an empty pitcher. Azim saw all these ill omens. He did not wish to divine the will of God. But having taken his repast prepared by his mother and chewing betels that his wife had offered him, merrily did he sing *'sari'* songs and steered his course up the Maioni. (Ll. 1-32.)

(10) THE SEQUEL.

The robber Monshoor was all along in the quest, and availing himself of the present opportunity, he paid a visit to the village Chintapur. He came to the house of an old woman and pleased her by calling her 'aunt.' "I am a Fakir," he said, "I want to put up with you for some time." He spoke many a sweet word and the old woman felt a real liking for him. He besides made a present of many edibles to the woman and held religious discussion with her now and then, to this effect—"O my aunt, I do not attach a pin's value to the things of the world. My mind is bent upon the happiness of after-life. You see that I always wander about the bank of the Kurmai. That is because I like to meditate upon the ways leading to Heaven and I am content with my life of a Fakir." Truth and untruth, facts and fiction, he mixed together in his prolific speeches. But his real object was to seize the prize that he had once let go,—the Lady Ayera, wife of Azim.

Some days passed in this way and the old woman was the more pleased with him as every day he provided fowl-curry at her dinner.

Now, my brethren, hear what took place on a particular day. It was the bathing time and the sun was just over the head. Ayerabibi had just finished her cooking, and being free, took a pitcher in her arms and went to the bathing *ghat*. She had put on a bodice of satin with a dazzling colour and through it glimpses of two pomegranate fruits could be seen inviting the bees. He observed this from some distance and his heart leaped out to have a touch.

She washed her fair limbs and plunged her head for a moment in the river. The lover, seated under a *hizal* tree, was watching her movement with close attention, "O, what a sight have I seen! I am fascinated. My mind is spell-bound. If I can ever meet her and win her love, it will be the crowning success of my life." The robber stretched his eyes to see her going home back with her pitcher, and when she was out of sight, he began to ponder over the course he was to adopt next.

She had just lighted her evening lamp. Her household work was all finished. April had just come in. She was perspiring in heat. Her mind was engrossed in the thought of her husband. The three months that he had fixed are now over. She was feeling the agony of separation. In the cornfields, far into the heart of forests, there wandered tigers, buffaloes and other ferocious beasts. She became deeply concerned, as she thought of her husband's adventure. She indulged in all kinds of fears, and when her grief was great she sang a *baramasi* song.

"Youth has just dawned on me and you, my love, cannot feel the longings of a woman's heart. The flowers have bloomed in our garden and the fragrance has spread far, and these cause me nothing but pain as you are away. You have dealt with me, O my lord, not like a lover but like a cruel enemy, consigning my heart, as you have done, to the fire of separation. This consumes me day and night. Parted from you I feel no pleasure in anything around me. You promised to return after three months. But now I see you played a trick on me. Over the full-blown flowers the bees hover with their little dark wings. They drink honey happily and from yonder branch of the tree the blackbird maddens me with its warbles. My room has a door on the east and the southern wind enters it without obstruction. How pleasant is this time and how happy I would be, if I could only see your sweet face now! Were I a flower, my love, and you my bee, how happy would have been our union. If you were here by my side now, I would have offered you a sweet betel and surrendered my youth absolutely to you and both of us would have been so happy. If ever you come back again, I will make a rope by my flowing tresses and bind your feet tenderly with them so that you would not be able to leave me again.''

With her reveries in this strain, she came to her bed. There were two couches close together and on one of them she slept. Then did she dream of her lord and was charmed by seeing his face though it was in her sleep. She breathed heavily, lost as she was in profound slumber and her breath sounded like that of a furnace mildly heated by the blacksmith. Outside, all was deep dark and the night had now advanced. At this hour did the robber Monshoor with a spade in his hand make a hole into the plinth of her house and enter it. Being in the room, he lighted a candle and on the couch he saw the beautiful damsel looking like a fairy. Her hair and clothes were all loose. For a few moments Monshoor kept staring at her without being able to move his eyes from that picture of the sleeping woman. Then did the wicked man take the candle close to her face and she awoke with a start, trembling. It was as if a spark of fire had fallen on a gunpowder magazine.

Monshoor said, "Hear me, O lady. I have turned a Fakir, giving up all worldly pleasure for your sweet sake. If my life is the firmament, you are like the full moon in it. Yield to me your youth, noble lady, and satisfy my great hunger for love."

She cried out in great rage, like a bomb bursting. She loudly called her neighbours. The robber had lost all his sense in the madness of his passion. He still stood like a statue, gazing at her with his thirsty eyes, unconscious of everything else. Men and women with and without arms came flocking to the spot. They caught hold of Monshoor and had him bound. Some kicked him, some gave blows with their fists. In fact, everyone of the crowd availed himself of the occasion to serve the guilty man with blows. Even weak men and children began to pull him by the hair, and there was none who did not play the hero by taking part in this general attack. The last thing they did was to bind his neck with a rope and pull him through the rough hilly path like a beast. They thus brought him into a deep forest, but the victim pretended to be a dead man and did not show the least sign of life. He lay inert and there was no breath in his nostrils. People, assembled there, hanged him by a rope on a tree.

It is a wonderful tale, my friends. When all people had dispersed, Monshoor Ali opened his eyes, and looking on all sides he perceived that there was none near him. Then did he slowly take off the rope from his neck and climbing down from the tree began to walk in slow paces. He was so thirsty that his very life seemed to run out. He reposed for some time in the shade of the trees and next proceeded towards a hill-fountain for allaying his thirst. (Ll. 1-100.)

(11) The Last Sleep.

Some time passed in this way and Ayerabibi had a most unhappy time of it. She fell a victim to remittent fever. Her youthful charms and her lovely face lost all their attraction. She was confined to bed, and when she attempted to sit for a while, she sank down all exhausted. Her anxieties like her fever slowly consumed her and not a day within a whole month had the fever any remission. Her sorrows she could not unfold to any one, nor could she bear them. She turned this side and that side on the bed restless, while tears dropped from her eyes secretly. Her head ached so severely that it seemed to burst. People who came to see her gave the unanimous verdict that death was in sight. It is the grave for which she had to be ready soon.

When her condition was so critical, Azim came to the landing *ghat* of the river in his large *Sarangi*. Frantically he entered his home and saw that the lady was breathing her last. Mollas and Khondkars were present there reciting texts from scriptures as their last service to the dying. Azim burst into a loud lament, saying "O my love, arise from your bed and speak to me. Long have I given you pain. How would it be possible for me to live without you? All my riches, my home, and goods are to me now without any value. It was at an unlucky moment that I had gone for voyage up the Mayani. The result has been that I have lost the best of my riches, more valuable than my life itself. How can I live in this world without you? Who would soothe me when suffering from stings of sorrows? Who will embrace me and assuage the pain of my heart? I have no desire to enjoy my riches without you. The big world is my home now and I do not know in what forest or depth of jungle I shall hide myself in order to suffer my sorrows alone Much have I earned by trade, but I have no desire to relish the fruits of my life's labour. I can no more think of relishing the sweet betel that grows by the bank of the Kurmai. Who will, after the day's work, look at me with a smile which has hitherto soothed all my pain? These two couches which are highly prized by me, reminding me of your sweet company, will remain now for ever vacant. It seems that my ribs have broken and my heart has ceased to beat.''

Azim lamented in this way for a long time and his eyes became swollen with tears. His friends and relations tried to console him saying, ''Life and death are in the hands of God, and one who lives in this world must be prepared for both weal and woe.''

Gradually, her breath ceased and she became a lifeless corpse. They made her lie on the bed with her face towards the west and recited holy texts after having washed her face with water. They bathed the body in hot water and sprinkled on it rose water and *attar*. They perfumed a new *sari* with camphor and made her wear it. Next did they cover her with a bodice and her face with a veil. Then the last prayers were said and they carried her on a litter to a maidan not far off. The neighbours, relations and friends were all present and she was buried in due form.

(Ll. 1-50.)

(12) Strange Experience.

The night was deep. It seemed that the pervading darkness was speaking through the sound of the beetle. The notorious rogue, the stealer of coffins, suddenly appeared at the maidan. None was there with him. He had a *khanta* and a spade in his hands to dig the grave. He had received a sound beating the other day and the pain of his chest had not yet abated. Yet so great was his attachment for the girl that he appeared there with an evil motive. When the grave was dug, he was surprised to see the dead woman all fresh, sleeping like a fairy. He stood and gazed at her for some time and then out of his old habit he caught hold of the bodice and pulled her cloth. It was quite an act of Providence, mysterious and inexplicable: the dead body moved all on a sudden and showed signs of life. He in a relentless spirit dragged her by her cloth but suddenly he was seized with lock-jaw. Like a bee hovering over a flower, still attracted by the woman, he began to walk round and round, losing all power of speech; and blood came out from his mouth in unceasing streams. He then lost his consciousness and fell rolling on the ground. A stupor seized his body and his eyes closed as if seeing the vision of death before him. He lost all sense of physical pain and remained inert for a time. In this strange sleep the dacoit dreamed a strange dream. It appeared to him that Ayerabibi left her grave and came near him. She waved her hand by way of blessing and said, "Oh Monshoor, think of the life that is coming; the pain of your heart will be removed. From to-day leave your wicked profession, say your usual prayers to God, the *namaz*, and observe fast and vigil as our religion bids us do."

In his dream, he unconsciously clasped his hands and mildly said, "How can I make provision for myself and my family, if I do not follow the avocation by which I have been earning my living all my life? If I die without food, who will say the *namaz*? What other profession can I adopt leaving the one in which I now trade?" Ayera seemed to say in reply, "One day you will be put to great trouble and then you will perceive the truth of what I have said. One day will repentance come to your mind, be sure. You may go on with your wicked trade. I do not request you to give it up. But promise to me that you will say the *namaz* five times a day without fail. No one is yours in the world. This world is untrue, people are mad after trinkets, but the only thing that is true is cared for by none. With the burden of the evil of a lifetime on your head you will have to walk your way to Hell. If it is impossible for you to leave your wicked profession, you must say your *namaz* five times a day."

Even in his sleep he nodded his head in assent and said, "I promise to you, noble lady, that five times a day I will say my *namaz* without fail." Ayerabibi disappeared after this and the dacoit lay unconscious on the ground. (Ll. 1-46.)

(13) Reformation.

The falcon made its grim sound. Monshoor came back to his senses, at the approach of the dawn. Slowly did his dream come to his recollection, and looking near him he saw the dead body of Ayerabibi lying open on the grave. He rose up with haste and said the *namaz* due in the morning. That was his first act of the day. Then he covered the grave with earth and slowly returned to his house.

He became altogether a changed man. He scarcely spoke and remained always plunged in deep thought. Silently did the dacoit go to the neighbouring Masjid and say the *namaz* five times every day. Men of his party came to him every now and then but could not divine the cause of this change. Some said, "Since his last illness, he has lost his usual liveliness of spirit." Another remarked, "Not that. From the day he was beaten, he has lost his senses." They discussed the matter amongst themselves but none was satisfied with any of these surmises. One day they approached him and said, "Listen to us, Oh master, we are verging on starvation owing to your practically giving up the profession. You have so long provided for us with the care of a father. Now, we are really reduced to sore plights." Monshoor said, "My friends, be ready. To-night we must start on our usual mission of dacoity."

In the night they crossed the canal of the Kaincha and approached the mouth of the Ghillock. They saw a rich mansion and resolved to try their luck by entering that house. It was a night of the waning moon ; impenetrable darkness pervaded on all sides. They avoided the front gate and approached by the back-door. For a time they applied their ears to the wall in order to hear if the inmates of the house were still awake. There was, however, no sound and it was certain that everyone there was enjoying sound sleep. The robbers put their heads together for devising means to get into the house. Some of them remained concealed near the outer gate and others made a hole into the house by a Khunti. The leader Monshoor alone entered the house.

The master of the house and his beautiful wife lay asleep on a rich couch, over which a striped curtain was gently fluttering in the wind. Near their heads there lay a big iron safe. The robber-chief struck it with his hand now and then. The master and his wife were sleeping soundly and the sound did not seem to disturb them. Now did the robber bring out some keys from his bundle and with the help of one opened the safe. He found there heaps of gold, valuable ornaments,—eight sorts of them—and some shawls. He slowly brought out the rich contents of the safe and arranging them in proper order lay meditating for a while. At this moment the falcon with its scream indicated the dawn. All in haste did Monshoor rise up and saw through the window that there was no star in the sky, but the eastern horizon displayed a faint purple colour. The bird Kurgal was sounding, from a tree near by, its lay of the morning. The voice of the Mollas praying together was heard from the Masjid of the village. Losing all sense of his environment suddenly did Monshoor cry out, "La Elaha illallaha," joining his voice from that distance with that of the Mollas.

It seemed that the robber had practically lost all thought about his situation. He said his morning *namaz* owing to a habit that had now grown indispensable with him. Men of his party heard his voice and fled away in all haste. Then loudly did Monshoor say, "Allah ho Akbar." His voice roused the master of the house from sleep and he was surprised to see the strange spectacle. Monshoor had in the meantime finished his *namaz* and the lord of the house in strange bewilderment came near him and fell prostrate at his feet, saying, "Who are you, saint? Tell me and save me from my perplexity." Monshoor's voice did not tremble when he said, "In this world mine is the wicked profession of a dacoit. I earn my living by theft and dacoity. I have entered your house by a hole made by my Khunti in order to commit robbery."

The lord of the house said, "It is all false. You cannot do it. I pray to you to take me into the list of your disciples and I shall be a slave at your feet."

The master of the house after this short speech made a present of the great riches to Monshoor. Monshoor brought the wealth to his home and distributed it amongst his robbers. Then with the bag which a Fakir carries on his shoulders, he entered a deep jungle.

Many a month, many a year, passed and nobody heard again of this notorious coffin-stealer. At long intervals they saw a Fakir loudly offering his prayers to God and disappearing in a strange manner. Some said that they saw him in the great maidan paying his salutes to the grave of Ayerabibi. (Ll. 1-74.)

THE BALLAD OF BHELUA

Bhelua

PREFACE TO BHELUA.

In the second volume of Eastern Bengal Ballads we have included a ballad of Bhelua which, I should say here, is altogether different from the ballad of the same name going to be published now. Bhelua is the name of a heroine of more than one tale and the similarity of name should not confound our readers. The present ballad has nothing in common with those prevalent in the Eastern part of Mymensing and in Sylhet of which the heroine Bhelua seems to be a legendary rather than an historical figure. These ballads show us strange customs and manners in which the rules and canons that govern Hindu homes are more often honoured in breach than in observance and women are found indulging in a spirit of latitude, on which the influence of the Tibeto-Burman, the Koch and other hill-tribes is clearly marked. I have discussed these points in my preface to the ballad of Bhelua published in the second volume and I need not dwell on them again.

The ballad of Bhelua published here has a distinctly historical origin. We have altogether got four versions of it, three of which are printed. The first version was published by Hamidulla, which I mentioned in my *Banga-bhasa-o-Sahitya* in 1896. This poem is a bulky volume and the author in his eagerness to display his little learning has marred the simplicity of the original, and given us a hybrid tale consisting of some elements of the indigenous ballad, distorted by village pedantry and vulgarism which, not unoften, pass for wit in the eyes of the rustics. Nowhere else than in the printed editions of these ballads the truth of the saying, "a little learning is a dangerous thing" appears more forcibly. We dismiss the poem of Hamidulla with this observation.

The next tale told by Munshi Moazzemali was published at the Hamidia Press, Churihatta, Dacca, about the year 1920. It has attempted to preserve the simplicity of the original ballad, though in an abridged form. But wherever the village pedant touches a rustic song, his affectations and vulgarities are sure to be in evidence ; and though in this short poem such defects are much less than elsewhere, Munshi Moazzemali is not altogether free from the characteristic blemishes of a ballad-publisher. I will describe one of his attempts at humour. The young hero is going to take leave of his wife who does not wish to be left behind. When in a somewhat sour mood, contemplating the departure of her husband, she does not carry out his order to bring a little fire for smoking, her conduct irritates him and he gives her such a blow with the pipe of his hubble-bubble that she falls senseless on the ground. Taking advantage of her unconsciousness, he leaves her and goes on a sea voyage. These authors every now and then introduce episodes of this nature for displaying their humour. It is curious that such incongruities and perversion of wit are seldom found in the better class of the rural ballads. The unlettered peasants use a far greater art in handling the points of their narrative than these writers with a smattering of the Bengali alphabet.

The third version written by one Makbul Ahmed, an inhabitant of Nayapara, P. O. Gujra, in Chittagong was published at the *Noakhali Yantra*. It passed through a sixth edition about the year 1920. It is shorter than the poem of Munshi Moazzemali and has the characteristic defects of the printed recensions of an old ballad.

But the poem of Bhelua which is published here is a genuine old ballad, taken down by Babu Asutosh

Choudhury when recited by some old minstrels. It possesses the simple charm of a rural song and has none of those incongruities marked in the printed versions. Its descriptions are poetic and its situations quite dramatic. It is besides absolutely free from all irrelevant matter. The pathos created by the account of the love-lorn youth, playing on his charmed violin, which gives out the name of his lady-love as often as he applies the bow to its string, produces a singularly happy effect by its lyrical appeal. All that is true and beautiful in love becomes vivid in the sketch of the Fakir with the violin in his hand and tears in his eyes. Madness, fast, vigil and wanderings due to a most romantic form of love have been made remarkably effective towards the end of the poem. Wars, voyages on stormy seas, strategems of the wily, administration of the Kazi and the anarchical crimes of those days are so vividly brought out in this narration that the local historian wishing to find material for writing the social narrative of his province would find ample matter from these sketches. Here the poet's sense of humour is not at all blunted as we find it to be the case in printed versions. When the maidservant is commissioned to see that the young merchant's fingers are cut off, she creates a comic situation by her humorous report that the merchant has got no fingers in his hands (Canto VI, l. 32). The description of the old Kazi and his lust for the fair sex is another instance of the poet's power to create a scene of humour (Canto XVII, ll. 1-24). In a passage of remarkable beauty does Bhelua crave her husband to stay at home assuring him that she would sell her *baju, sapteswari har, hasuli, kankan, sonar dana*, earrings and other ornaments in order to be able to live in comfort with him (Canto IX, ll. 32-44). We need not doubt the sincerity of these women. Malua practically did what Bhelua showed herself willing to do (Vol. I, Pt. II, p. 75). The love of a Bengali wife is always in evidence in these ballads and shows the charm and the inducement that the Bengali husband has constantly to face, making him a home-staying individual. Another poetical scene which recalls a beautiful passage in the ballad of *Santi* (Vol. II, Pt. II, p. 127) captures our fancy by the reply given by Bhelua to the report of death of her husband. She nods her head to express her disbelief and says, "Had any evil befallen my lord, as this wicked man says, the red sign of luck on my forehead would have grown pale, my heart by its secret beatings would have conveyed to me the report before any information reached me from outside. My eyes would have felt a tremor indicating the evil" (Canto 12, ll. 75-80). The ballad is void of all superfluity and is told in one breath, causing no wearisomeness or monotony. Each page presents us with some sketch or other of an all-absorbing interest, not only dealing with relevant topics in regard to the incidents or characters described, but unravelling contemporary history and social condition. In this ballad alone we find the hero rising to as great a prominence as the heroine; nay, he wins our loving regard even more than the heroine by his extraordinary virtues. I shall here refer to one point that strikes me in regard to the course he took on hearing that his wife was dead. He dug the grave and found it containing the carcase of a black dog. Knowing this to be a foul play on the part of his sister, done with the knowledge of his parents, he abstained from taking any step by way of retaliation, but left home as an ascetic in grief. In western homes such acts of forbearance could not have been expected. The wrong inflicted by elders and those who are near and dear to us is suffered in silence in Hindu and Moslem homes in this country under the chastening influence of the joint-family system. The youth Amir loved his wife with all the might of his soul but he does not deserve the censure which his sister passed on him, of being a henpecked husband. His words, "My hand trembles as I lift to my lips the food not earned by me," and his resolve to live by his own earnings show that in spite of his tender feelings, he was full of masculine strength of character, and when (Canto XVI, ll. 45-46) his wife asked him to fly away with her from the clutches of the wicked Bhola, the same manliness of his character made him give the reply, "No, wife, I am not the son of a thief." All this clearly shows a towering character as great in the dignity of manhood as in the inherent emotional felicities of nature on which love stamped its own sweet and abiding seal.

This tale with all its poetical excellence is based on an historical event. We find traces of the historical side of the ballad from a book written in Persian named *Tarikhi-Hamidi* by Hamidulla Khan. The incidents of the tale are said to have taken place during the reign of Nasrat Shah, son of Hossain Shah (sixteenth century). In the Persian treatise we find the main facts of the story written in an abridged form. The '*Choṛ Sadagar*' (the thief Bhola who took away Bhelua) is prominently mentioned in the *Tarikhi-Hamidi* and the war between Amir and the abductor of his wife at the port of *Kattani* is fully described in it. I think the account given in this Persian work is entitled to credit. Babu Purnachandra Chaudhury has also written some notes on the history of this ballad. According to him, the events happened in the reign of Nasrat Shah. He, however, gives the name of Aḍaichand to the merchant called Manik Sadagar in this ballad. He also refers to the fact of a large pond known as *Bheluar Dighi* being excavated by Bhola under compulsion as a punishment for his abducting the girl. There is fundamentally very little difference in the history of the tale traced from all these different sources. But Purna Babu strains his imagination too far in his attempt to identify *Adaichand* (a name he got from some source unknown to us) with Chand, the redoubtable merchant of Ujani, who is, after all, a legendary character. Pursuing his fancy a step still further, he considers Bhelua to be none other than the mythical heroine Behula. This is gibberish ; for, while assigning the events to the reign of Nasrat Shah (16th century), he brings a mythological and pre-historic tale to bear upon the topics of an historical period.

The historical origin of the ballad is clearly proved by the geographical references in it which show that the incidents of the tale are confined to a particular locality in the district of Chittagong. All the ballads give the same references in regard to the dwelling places and whereabouts of the chief characters.

The port of Saflapur—the home of Amir, the merchant prince—still flourishes in the small island of Mohishkhali. At one time this port was in the hands of the Portugeuse, whose power decayed with the rise of Moslem supremacy in that place in the sixteenth century. The home of Bhelua's parents, *Telenyapur* is now known as *Telya Dwip*. It stands at the junction of the Sankha and the Bay within the Police station of Anwara. Bhola, the merchant, lived in the town of *Kattani* which is not far from the town of Chittagong. There the historic pond known as the *Bheluar Dighi* still exists, as a symbol of humiliated pride and rightly deserved punishment inflicted on the miscreant Bhola for his heinous deeds. Tona Barui, the musician, who could lull ferocious animals to sleep by the melodious sound of violin lived in Syednagar within the jurisdiction of the Police station Rangunia. A mound is still pointed out there as the spot where once lived the famous musician. A man named Ujir Ali, living in the locality, claims descent from Tona Barui. Near the pond *Bheluar Dighi* at Kattani is the historic spot where Kazi Munap used to hold his court. The hilly range of *Debang* mentioned in the ballad stretches from the junction of the Karnaphulli along the southern coasts of the Bay, and the *Kudali mura* with its head like a spade that gives it the name, overlooks the stream of the *Karnaphulli* at its base twenty miles from the town of Chittagong. A little to the north-east of this hill lies the dreaded whirlpool named *Kanakhali's pak* where the turbulent waters of the Karnaphulli move with terrible force and constantly revolve, creating a wild, circulating rush. The rivers mentioned in this ballad are the *Kachai* or the *Karnaphulli*, the *Sankha*, the *Sirmai* or the *Sreemaṭi* and the *Ichhamati*—all of them too well known in Chittagong to require more than a passing notice. There is mention of a village-stream which used to be called the *Khulshir Dhala*. It is now known as the *Tiger port*.

The whole of the district of Chittagong is full of historical associations of its favourite heroine Bhelua, and the geographical notes given above, materially substantiated by every ballad-writer, prove beyond doubt that the poem relates to an historical event over which the drop-scene has not yet fallen but which is cherished in loving memory by the rural people of the district down to the present day. Popular fancy is still at work, bringing out new recensions, giving new forms to the tale and the few printed versions and this one which never saw the light before are not the only poems consecrated to the holy name of Bhelua.

In some versions of this poem not yet printed there is a wild play of imagination which, I am glad to say, does not damage the simplicity of the present ballad. In one of them, Bhelua is made to pass through extraordinary ordeals for having lived for some time in the houses of Bhola the merchant and the old Kazi. She is made to undergo the fire ordeal, requiring her to be put within eighty maunds of cotton with the same quantity of clarified butter to act as combustible and then fire is set to it. In others ordeals by iron are introduced, not a whit less crude or ultra-natural than the fire ordeal. These ordeals are not novel features in the old literature of Bengal. We have such things in the account of the dowager queen Mayanamati and in those of Khullana and Behula. There is a class of ballads which deals with the supernatural legends of Tantrik and esoteric practices. The *Mayanamati* song is the typical ballad of that class, but the less ambitious peasants have always abided by the result of their own observations of nature, and the ballads of their composition are the gems of purest ray serene in the rural literature of Bengal.

Now I am going to give a short history as to how this ballad was collected by Babu Asutosh Choudhury of Chittagong.

Owing to the ballad being published in a distorted and abridged form by Munshi Mozzemali of Tipperah and Munshi Makbul of Chittagong, the older and the more genuine version in the indigenous dialect which the unlettered peasantry of Chittagong and adjacent localities used to sing in bygone times has grown scarce, the minstrels finding it by far an easy task to commit to memory from the printed versions which are available everywhere. But Asu Babu, whose zeal in the pursuit of ballads is unflagging, could not for obvious reasons be satisfied with these printed ballads. "Many a day," he writes to me, "have I sat by the side of the pond *Bheluar Dighi* near the Pahartali Station on the A. B. Ry., its crystal waters proving an irresistible fascination to my eyes. Men and women who came to fetch water from it told strange stories about Bhelua and the whole locality is full of romantic traditions about this ill-fated pair. Facts are often found mixed with fancy in these traditions but they all attest to the admiring love of the people for Bhelua which is deep-rooted in their mind. An old Mohammedan told me, 'Even now, dear sir, I can swear to you, people sometimes see in the depth of night a golden boat appearing from the pond with Amir and Bhelua seated on it embracing each other.'" Asu Babu got fragments of the original ballad from Jebal Hossein of the village Bagnan (P. S. Raujan) and from Ismail of Sambarghat. But these were so meagre that no connected story could be made out from them. "But," writes this indefatigable ballad-hunter, "I happened to learn that the whole ballad in its original form is known to an old minstrel of the village Pombra (P. S. Rangunia). I immediately started for Pombra and met this old man who seemed to me to be a remarkable person. He is seventy years old and his name is Omar. He is generally called Omar Vaidya or Omar the physician. He is a dentist of the old school and earns his living by quackery. Absolutely without any knowledge of letters, his memory at this old age is a wonderfully striking thing. Many ballads he can reproduce from memory from beginning to the end and he plays on a violin while singing them. It is difficult to say whether the violin or his voice is the sweeter. He lives in a wretched hut and he could not give his children and wife better things than glass bracelets,—so poor is he. But he has plated the ears of his violin with silver. Seated in his hut overlooking a hillock covered with rich green, he told me his life-story which is full of interest and is strangely pathetic. In his early years he had long hair and a girlish grace; he used to dance and sing in the party of some famous minstrel who sang the country ballads. His teacher in music, late Easin Ali, used to take him to the hills where the dancing boy enjoyed much favour with the Chakmas, the Kukis and other hill tribes. "On the 18th of October, 1926, I made him sing the ballad of Bhelua which he did from 6 P.M. to 12 A.M. of the next day incessantly. Occasionally his voice rose higher than the sound of his violin and the pathos created was so great that I could not restrain my tears at times. This ballad of Bhelua may verily be called a gift from the fountain of tears that Omar had made to flow. When he sang—'the Fakir played on his violin and as he played he shed incessant tears overflowing his cheeks' (Canto XV, ll. 16-20), it seemed that he himself resembled the hero of his tale."

This ballad is sung by Mohammedan women of lower classes as a bridal song and belongs to the class known in the country-side as *Hanhala* song. The word seems to be a corruption of the word *Sahala* (maidenly). The life of chaste women was considered formerly as a fit subject for ballads to be sung during marriage ceremonies.

I have already said that many versions of this tale were current in the country a few years ago. Sir George Grierson quotes a passage as a specimen of the Noakhali dialect in his linguistic survey of India, which is evidently taken from one of the versions of the ballad of Bhelua. I quote it below :—

"সেনকালে সাধু আমিররে সাধু দক্ষিণ ফাড়ে চায় ।
দক্ষিণ ফাড়ে যাইয়ারে আমির সাধু ডাইন বামে চায় ॥২॥
সেনখানে ভেলবা দেবীর ফুলের বাগানরে ফায় ।
ফুলের বাগানে যাইয়ারে সাধু চারিদিগেরে চায় ॥৪॥
ফুলবাগানেরে যাইয়ারে সাধু ভরমন্য করিল ।
সেইখানে এক ঘররে সাধু দেখিবারে ফাইল ॥৬॥
সেইঘরে দেখিরে সাধু অতি খুসী হৈল ।
সেই ঘরের মধ্যেরে আমির তখ্‌খন সাম্মাইল ॥৮॥
ঘরেতে সামাইরে আমির কোন কাম করিল ।
সোনার ফালঙ্গেরে আমির উড়িয়া বসিল ॥১০॥

বিছানার বালিসা ধরিরে আমির লাড়ি চাড়ি চায়।
মাণিক্যের হাররে ভেলবার দেখিবারে ফায় ॥১২॥
সেই হার লইয়ারে সাধু হাতে তুলি চায়।
হাতেতে লইয়ারে সাধু বুগেতে লাগায় ॥১৪॥"

The linguistic peculiarities of the dialect of Noakhali and Chittagong present many interesting forms. The letter 'স' often takes the form of 'হ' in East Bengal dialects. But the contrary of it is scarcely seen. Here, however, in 'সেনকালে' we find rather a rare instance of it. The profuse use of 'ফ' for 'প' and 'ড' for 'ট' is in evidence in this small passage as well as in the body of the text.

DINESH CHANDRA SEN

Bhelua

THE PORT OF SAFLAPUR.

I

The port of Saflapur is a picturesque town. On its west is to be heard the incessant roar of the sea. On the shore lie anchored ships and boats of various sizes and shapes, and the sailors and boatmen are frequently heard to sound their horn in the night. Hundreds of men are busy there—selling various goods in their shops and hundreds of purchasers crowd there for shopping. Hundreds of men are seen walking in the main roads, busy with their own occupation, not caring a bit for others. The country boats are innumerable. From foreign ports are pouring in, continuously, ships laden with cargo. They rush over the sea with great uproar, and with their sails unfurled in the sky.

The port belongs to a merchant Manik by name. His house is the abode of Fortune, abounding in riches. On the bank of a river stands his beautiful rest-house, where the merchant frequently spends his time enjoying the pleasant river-breeze. The house smiles with the light of chandeliers and lamps dispelling the darkness of night. The merchant enjoys landed properties, annually fetching him many lacs of rupees and many more are earned by his flourishing trade. He has a large retinue of soldiers and troops besides revenue-collectors and officers. Fakirs and poor men are daily fed sumptuously at his house and visitors high and low daily call on him to pay their respects.

Manik has a son resplendent as the moon. His name is Amir. An amiable disposition he has and a liberal and sincere mind. Skilled in fourteen arts is he, and a rare practical knowledge of worldly affairs he possesses. He has thoroughly mastered the Quoran and other sacred scriptures. Manik was right glad to have such a son whose reputation had spread far and near. With his wife, son, relations and dependents, the merchant was having a happy time of it for many years. (Ll.-1-28.)

II. Hunting Excursion.

April came and with it the gentle southern breeze. Amir expressed a desire to go abroad for hunting. He went to his mother and said, "To-morrow I must go for hunting in the morning. I want the ship 'Kaladhar.' Captain Goural Dhar is to accompany me. You should kindly secure me, dear mother, the consent of my father."

Mother.

"April is not safe for a journey by sea, my child. This month I cannot allow you to go by the rough sea. You are my only son, the only lamp of this house, prized as the black paint in a lady's eyes and dear as a rib of my breast art thou, my darling."

Amir.

"By my life, you must give me permission. The time is short. Make yourself firm. My business will now be to visit foreign lands for trade. I am not a farmer that I should be at home ploughing lands close by, nor am I the son of a fisherman that my work will be with the nets and fishing rods by some near canal or river. I am a trader by birth. A trader has no home other than the sea. Be up, mother. Do not detain me. I crave your permission without delay."

When the mother and the son were talking in this way, Manik, the merchant, came to the place. He heard their conversation and gave speedy orders for getting the ships ready.

The sailors and the captain became ready. Goural Dhar himself took charge of the helm. Sails of various colours and patterns, cords and ropes, anchors and bamboo poles, (*logis*) were carried to the ship. Provision that would last for half a year was stored. Arrows, bows, guns, gunpowder and bullets were taken in abundance.

The 'Kaladhar' ship was magnificent to look at. At the helm stood Goural Dhar himself. Manik the old merchant came to see the ship going and gave these directions.

"Steer the ship carefully keeping close to the coast as far as possible. If you apprehend high winds, steer the ship with care. I place my son, dearer to me than life itself, in your custody, Captain Goural Dhar." The father placed his hand on the son's head and blessed him a hundred times. Amir paid his respects and salaams to his father and then went on board the ship, ordering the captain to start with all speed.

The trumpet sounded, and "ply on" was the word heard on all sides. The anchor was carried to the ship and the sailors cried "Badar." Speedily did the ship march through the deep ; the southern wind was favourable and the sails were all unfurled. The ship plied her course with a graceful motion, and true to the master's word, the captain kept to the coast as far as possible.

Amir.

"Hear me, oh captain. We must go into the mid-stream if only to have a look at it. Do not like a coward continuously cling to the coast. Do not fear turn the helm and steer the ship across the mid-stream."

Gaural Dhar.

"Remember, young lord, the caution given by your father. I must take the course that is safe and I know my business well."

Being young in years, the merchant got angry at his words. He himself ran to the helm and turned it towards the mid-ocean. The ship went briskly on to the mid-sea. It is God's will, brethren. Human agencies are of no avail. In the mid-sea the ship lost its way. The rough winds blew, making a moaning sound and the crew could not ascertain if they were following the current or going against it. The sails were about to be rent. At one moment the ship seemed to rise so high over the waves as almost to touch the sky and at the next it went down and seemed to descend to the very bottom of the sea. The North and the South, the East and the West were all confused. The ship ran swiftly over the deep, and no one could say what direction it took. It was all whirl and confusion. The captain of the ship was stunned as if struck by thunder. Some cried for the help of Allah and others of Saint Feristha. In the illimitable deep the waves assumed a terrible shape. Some of the crew and sailors fell flat on their backs and others felt vomiting tendencies. Some tried to stand up and reeled and fell on their sides or backs. The roaring of the sea made Amir the young merchant tremble in fear. He cried out, "If we can reach the shore this time, I will pay a thousand Rupees to the Darga of Gazi Kali (saint). The sailors and *khalashies* raised an incessant cry of 'Badar.' But the stern helmsman Goural Dhar was unmoved. He held the helm firmly and thinking of God and His mercy, steered the ship towards the North. The ship flew like a bird and after a day the eyes of all were gladdened by the sight of land.

Amir.

"My brother Goural Dhar, you have certainly got angry at my rashness. Now I ask you to lay the anchor on the eastern side of the land that is in view. We shall land there and go hunting in the forests. I cannot see the land, it is so misty ; but it appears that we are near some hill which evidently abounds with beasts of prey."

Goural Dhar.

"Wait, my young lord, wait just for a day. It seems to me that we are near the hill called Debanga, but it is certainly not so near as it seems. It is at a considerable distance even now, and we shall have to walk a long way. Look at the red sun of the evening. It is sinking in the sea, painting the crests of the waves with its golden rays."

(Ll. 1-94.)

III

They cast anchor there and in the morning landed for hunting. The young merchant went forward and next came Goural Dhar. In front of them lay a beautiful garden of flowers. On the trees sat a number of pigeons. No one will, I am afraid, believe me, but still it is a fact that one of the pigeons recited the hymns of Kalma and the sacred scriptures. Struck with astonishment, Amir thought that he must by some means or other secure this wonderful pigeon which could recite *bayets* from the sacred Quoran. But the bird was very quick and evaded its pursuers each time by flying away from place to place.

Goural Dhar applied glue to each tree of the locality and bringing nets from the ship spread them over the garden. The young merchant lay concealed behind a tree, watching the pursuit. The bird was fatigued and attempted to fly away from the place. At this stage Amir aimed an arrow from his bow and struck the pigeon.

Near the garden in her rest-house sat Bhelua the beautiful one, and the bird, struck by the arrow and seized with terror, flew on to her breast in agonising pain.

The girl fondled the bird with care and wept saying, "Who is that enemy of mine that has struck my pet bird." She began to beat her breast, crying again and again, "Oh, my dear Hirani, oh, my pet one, who has struck you dear?" Hearing her lament, her maids all hastened to the spot. (Ll. 1-26.)

IV. Who was Bhelua ?

She was the only sister of seven brothers. So beautiful was she that she looked like a nymph of Indra's heaven. If one came to see her closely, she appeared like a statue made of gold. One of her many charms lay in her sidelong glances. The stars of her eyes were so lovely that they looked like bees sitting on full-blown lotuses. When she smiled, her face was lit up as though with heavenly light. Her curly hair touched her very ankles and her hands and feet were fine as though made by a sculptor's chisel. Her complexion was of the ripe banana fruit and the face bore the glow of moonlight and the purple of her lips reminded one of *bandhuli.* She had passed her twelfth year, but not yet her thirteenth. She lived in a *Jore mandir* house set apart in her father's palace for her. Her father Manohar was a rich merchant who had recently died, leaving seven sons. The town was called Telanya. The mother of Bhelua was a lucky woman who justly prided herself on her seven sons, all accomplished and handsome, and also on her daughter who was such a paragon of beauty. The mother held Bhelua dearer than life.

The city of Telanya was a small island surrounded on all sides by the sea. There the seven brothers had built magnificent houses. On the coast of the sea they had raised a tower two hundred and forty feet high. Bhelua went there every day and spent hours enjoying the sea breeze. On the west the waves of the sea were dancing eternally and Bhelua every day enjoyed the superb sight all alone.

At this moment of life when all was happiness and peace, suddenly came Amir the young merchant and killed her pet bird. The whole air rang with her lamentations. Tears dropped from her eyes incessantly. "Oh, my dear Hirani, oh my lovely bird, where hast thou gone leaving me and who is that rogue amongst men that has killed thee? May divine wrath overtake him and thunderbolt fall on his head," cried she and the agony of her heart gave her no rest.

When the brothers heard that Bhelua was grieving in that way, they hastened to the tower and asked her the cause of her sorrows.

Bhelua.

"This pet pigeon of mine, Hirani, has been shot dead by some cruel man. I have not been able to find out the wicked fellow."

The seven brothers were aflame with rage. They looked like a magazine set on fire. They made immediate enquiries and came to learn that a merchant from a foreign land had done the foul deed. (Ll. 1-46.)

V. Punishment.

They came to the sea-coast and saw the ship of Amir anchored there.

The Brothers.

"Who are you and why have you dared to kill our pigeon? You seem to be a downright thief or rather one whose business is to steal and rob in the localities where you cast anchor and land."

Goural Dhar, the captain of the ship stepped in and said,

"Hear me, brethren. You need not quarrel over this petty matter. We are prepared to give you proper compensation for the pigeon."

The seven brothers indignantly retorted, "You have no wealth with which you can pay for the pigeon." Amir, the merchant, came forward and said, "I care not a straw for your threat, vain fellows. The pigeon I have indeed killed. Do whatever lies in your power."

"Just see," replied the brothers, "what we can do. We will presently arrest you and send you to our prison."

The brothers ordered the ship *Kaladhar* to be dragged up to the coast.

Chorus.—Oh young merchant, your life is in danger.

From all sides soldiers and armed men came rushing and they bound the young merchant in chains.

In the prison they kept him, putting on his breast a piece of stone weighing seven maunds. He was in a sorry plight and it seemed that his ribs were about to break. The young man cried aloud in pain, saying,

"Oh my father, oh my mother, where are you now?" His sorrows were great. Tears fell from the eyes of the youth who had never shed tears before. The sight made fishes of the waters, the beasts of the forest and even the inanimate trees melt into tears. It seemed that the very stone on his breast melted in sympathy. "Oh my father, oh my mother," he cried again and again, "had you seen my condition, you would have drowned yourselves in a river. You would have turned this city of Telenya to a heap of ruins or sunk it in the sea."

The lament of the merchant drew the notice of Manai, the widowed mother of Bhelua. She was very old and with the help of a staff slowly came near the prison and began to listen to Amir's lamentations. She heard these words, "Oh, where is my father Manik, the merchant and where is Sonai my mother? Alas! you have no knowledge of what has happened to your dear son."

In slow steps did the old woman approach the young man who appeared like a handsome statue of gold rolling on the ground. She took pity on him and asked,

"Where is your home, young man, and who are your parents?"

Amir.

"My home is in the port of Shafla. My father Manik Sadagar is a well-known merchant there. My mother's name is Sonai. I came for hunting and here am I in this plight, as you see, with death staring me in the face."

When she heard this, the old woman burst into tears and said to her sons, "Take away the stone from my darling's breast. You are about to kill the son of my own sister."

The stone weighing seven maunds was removed and the old mother went direct to her sister's son and embraced him.

She said to her sons, "Not knowing who he is, you have thus punished him. I have a sister who was married to a merchant in the port of Shafla. My young sister, the constant companion of my childhood and dear as life to me, is Sonai, the mother of this boy, whom you have bound in fetters. See, dear sons, the beautiful colour of the lad has grown pale. The weight of the heavy stone has well nigh broken his ribs. Now you must procure him good medicated oil to be rubbed over his breast."

They were ashamed at the words of their mother and with clasped hands begged pardon of their relation. Right gladly they exchanged embraces with him and salaamed him, calling him their dear cousin. He was seated on a couch and a rich banquet was made ready for him. He was shown every kind of hospitality. (Ll. 1-72.)

VI.—Marriage.

Chorus.—Cry "Joy and Victory" now.

A maid came to Bhelua and gave her the information that the merchant who had killed the pigeon was arrested, bound in fetters and led into prison.

She was highly pleased at the news and said, "It is all right now and my wish, which must be carried out at once, is that the hand that shot my pet bird dead should be shorn of its fingers. You are to bring the fingers before me so that my grief for the loss of Hirani may be assuaged to some extent."

Now the mother spoke in private to her seven sons, "You are to attend seriously to what I am going to tell you now. The marriage of Bhelua should be immediately arranged. I and my sister are bound to each other by a vow that if she got a son and I a daughter, they should be married. I am not going to listen to any objection in this matter. God heard what we two sisters promised in His holy name and this must be carried out.''

Saying this, she looked at her sons wishing them to speak. The maid-servant sent by Bhelua overheard this part of the conversation.

Going to the outer rooms, she saw the handsome young man, looking glorious like the sun, seated on a couch. He was richly attired, wearing on his head a cap worth a thousand rupees. He wore a rich coat, made of the precious stuff of Cashmere (shawl).

He was robed in a fine *dhuti* and his shoes were rich Chinese. She was charmed with the handsome appearance of the young merchant and thought that Providence had graciously vouchsafed such a groom to Bhelua. They could not expect such a one for her even if they spent lacs of rupees.

She came to Bhelua and said, ''Surely, it must be a mistake of God. He has not given the young merchant any finger.'' So saying, she burst into a loud laughter. Bhelua was stupefied by the conduct of the servant and did not understand the meaning of her remark.

The seven brothers again called on the young merchant. They salaamed him and embraced him all tenderly.

The Brothers.

'' We caused you great pain by placing that stone on your breast. You must marry our dear sister Bhelua. This is the reward that we can offer you. My mother and yours are bound in promise for this marriage and the words of the two sisters were heard by the great Judge who sits overhead.''

Amir took a little time in thinking over the matter and at last consented to the proposal. The auspicious day and hour were fixed, when with due pomp and eclat the function was celebrated.

The bride and bridegroom gave mutual consent before the Kazi who made them recite proper verses from the sacred scriptures. After the verses were recited, the bride and the bridegroom were shown their room. The union was like that of the sun and the moon. Lovingly they met each other and were bound in sweet embrace. They spent their hours in happiness all the time. When the marriage was over, Amir made preparations for returning home.

The wives of the seven brothers now assembled to robe the bride and bedeck her with ornaments. They first combed her beautiful, curly hair and over it spread a net of pearl-strings. She was made to wear a *hansuli* around her neck and a necklace on her breast. She wore a nose-ornament and rings on her ears. On her arms she was made to wear *toraul torol* and on her wrists a pair of golden bracelets. Her hair was scented with sweet attar and on her head was placed a crown. She wore anklets on her feet. How wonderful did she look when she was fully decked! Thus robed and adorned with ornaments, she slowly advanced her steps and merrily did the ornaments make a jingling sound.

When bidding adieu, the mother wept and said, "Oh my son, my darling, I place the treasure of my heart in your custody. She is held dear by everyone and was the pet girl of the house. With great affection and tenderness have I brought her up all these years. You must take every care of her and if she does any wrong, you are to pardon her for her faults. Do not allow her to touch cow-dung,[1] for it will soil her clothes. Do not allow her to

[1] Every Bengali woman, high or low, has to handle the dung-pastes. They serve the purpose of soaps in washing the floors and compounds of houses, and are believed to be disinfectants. This custom is being given up in towns, but the dung is still considered indispensable in regard to *kancha* houses.

handle chilly in the kitchen ; it will cause her burns. Do not allow her to fetch water from the river ; it will give pain to her waist.

"Here do I place in your care the treasure of my heart. See that she enjoys every comfort regarding her daily meals."

Amir salaamed his mother-in-law Manai, and having boarded his ship with his beautiful bride, ordered the captain to set out for home. (Ll. 1-78.)

VII. A Typical Sister-in-law.

Amir had a sister named Bivala. Her body was a mere skeleton covered with skin. There was hardly any flesh in it. She was of a pale yellowish colour without any sign of blood. Her arms and legs were covered with profuse hair, just as we now and then see in the male sex. She was twenty years old, but curiously enough there was no sign of youth in her. She looked like a pomegranate tree that bore no fruit. Her eyes were long and sparkling. In a word Bivala did not possess a jot of the loveliness that usually belongs to the youth of her sex. She had a long face that looked like the cloudy sky of July and there was not a person in the whole world with whom she was on terms of amity and peace. Her words were bitter like the juice of *chirata* plants.[1] She used to give wicked interpretation to the simple utterances of others, and thus picked up quarrels. The servants of the house shook with fear when they had to approach Bivala. Her heart was full of gall, and her breath poisonous. Hence it is that no suitor came to seek her hands. Inspite of all these, she was a pet child of the house. The mother loved her, excusing her hundred faults and the father spoiled her by indulgence.

[1] *Gentiana cherayta.*

At this time a heavenly fairy seemed to come down, flying to the house of the merchant and it became radiant, as it were, with a heavenly light. The citizens of port Shafla whispered amongst themselves, "How lucky is the merchant Manik Dhar. His house now is lit up with golden moon-beams."

Amir's mother was right glad to get the beautiful daughter-in-law at her house. She remembered her sister Manai and the promise they had made to each other in childhood. The old merchant was happy beyond measure and so were the kinsmen and the neighbours. But a fire of jealousy was kindled in the mind of Bivala. If there be an unmarried sister-in-law in the house, the new wife can hardly expect to find peace of mind.

Some months passed in happiness, but evil befell young Amir through intriguing Bivala. In raptures of delight did he spend his days, caring not for the world or its concerns, when Bivala one day approached her mother and counselled her thus :

"The ships are lying moored on the river bank and they are getting rusty and rotten for want of use. The rowers and sailors are getting their pay every month without doing any work. My brother is a henpecked fool, pandering to the wishes of the new wife and cares not as to how the world is going on. This is the curse of marrying a beautiful wife. He passes his time like a woman within the confines of the house."

She went on buzzing like a fly, and the mother began slowly to realise the truth of what she said.

This is the way of the world, my friends. The son who yields himself to the fascination of his wife loses the favour of his parents.

Amir spent his time in pleasure in the company of his wife. Often did his parents and sister pass sneering remarks on his mode of life. Nor did this end here.

One day Amir's mother openly charged him in this way:

"Listen to me, lad. You are sunk in the lowest pit of pleasure, and have lost all sense of duty. The ships are lying moored on the river ghat and are being wasted for want of use. The rowers and sailors are receiving their pay every month without doing any work. You do not care to know where your ships are. Damaged and wasted are our goods in the store rooms attached to this house. If even an emperor does not seek to increase his income but spends from his treasury, it becomes exhausted in time. If a young man loses his head over the charms of a girl, know that it means the ruin of his fortune. You have compromised the honour and prestige of your noble house. You have ruined the commercial traditions of our family, sitting close by your wife and fondling her day and night in this way."

When Amir heard these words of his mother, he remained silent with downcast eyes, his mind was harrowed with stings of remorse and pain. He shed tears silently. Like one struck by thunder, he became stunned with grief and blood began to flow rapidly in his veins. He began to reflect thus, "This world is vain. Vain is the affection of parents. It was only a few days ago that my mother wept bitterly, thinking of separation from me, when I was about to go a short while for hunting, but to-day she charges me in this way. I feel as if my body is on fire. The stings of this insult I cannot bear."

Thinking for a time in this manner he came to the house of Captain Goural Dhar.

Amir.

"Hear me, my own Goural Dhar. We must immediately start from here and go to the city of Ujjain for trade.

The ship must be made ready by the morning of to-morrow. Call the rowers and sailors and make preparations."

(Ll. 1-72.)

VIII. Farewell.

Chorus.—Who is it that has roused me from sweet sleep, disturbing my dreams of Paradise ?

Bhelua was busy preparing meals for her husband. She filled a plate with ***khurma***, grapes and dates and mixed them with a very fine species of rice—the ***Dudhkamal***. She cooked ***khirsa*** with the milk of cocoanut applying some sugar to it. She sat near the threshold of the room with her preparations, waiting for Amir who duly came there in the evening. His eyes were swollen and he looked pale and morose. Bhelua wandered and cast her glances again and again at him in an inquisitive way.

Amir.

"I am not earning a pice. How long shall I spend time in this way ? You must be prepared for parting, my beautiful wife. If our saving be exhausted and we are rendered poor, everyone will cry woe unto us. Without riches one finds one's lot hard to bear. Such is the world. Be it mother or father or even one's beloved wife, no one cares for the man who earns not and leads his life idly. My mother's sneers and angry words and my sister's derision have become unbearable to me. I find it impossible to stay in the house. What can I say? I am the most unlucky of men—I have resolved to leave this city to-morrow morning. I will go to Ujjain for trade. Now, my dear wife, come up with a smile to bid me adieu."

When she heard these words of her husband, the plate of meals fell to the ground unheedingly from her hands.

She wept and said, "My senses run out at the thought of parting from you. I am your pet bird and how can I live without you? What is my fault that you wish to be so cruel? This house will be too hot for me, if you leave it. Prepared am I to go with my dear husband. Wherever you would go, I would be your companion and slave. Pray do not go alone, my beloved."

Amir.

"Where will you go, my dear? You are a young housewife. How can you dare a journey through the high seas where the roar of waves deafens one's ears. No, no, that cannot be. Wait patiently for a little time. I shall try to return home as early as good luck will allow it."

That night was a night of farewells. They lay bound in each other's arms in close embrace. The merchant gave her many sweet betels, and the night passed in conversation. In the morning, young Amir became bound for distant shores.

He came to the ghat and called aloud the sailors and rowers. Some of them uttered the name of Allah and others of Badar.[1] It was the month of January and the cold was very severe. The young merchant came on board the ship and ordered the captain to start. With the speed of lightning the ship marched on, piercing the very breast of the sea; the rowers rowed on and poor Bhelua caught the sound from her room.

A thick mist had covered the sky and the captain was at a loss to discover the way. For four days they thus

[1] Badar is a corruption of the word Bajra. In Bikrampur, the village Bajra Yogini is called Badar Yogini by the people. We have many instances of the kind. The word Bajra was used to indicate the Buddha, the Bajrāshan having been one of his favourite seats of Yoga. In Java we have the Bara Bahadur temple, evidently a corruption of the word Bara Bajra or the great Buddha. In later times, the Mahomedans associated "Badar" with the name of a Pir.

went on without knowing the direction they were taking, and on the expiry of the time the beautiful ship came to a landing ghat. The captain, unable to see things through mist, cried out to a man standing there, " What is the name of this port ? Whose jurisdiction is it ?"

The man in charge of the boat burst out into a loud laughter saying, "The sailors of Amir's ship have lost their head." Said he, " Goural Dhar, my expert captain, must know that this is your own port of Safla. You have returned to your own landing ghat."

The merchant looked closely on all sides and was greatly ashamed to discover that it was his own port where they had arrived again after four days, unable to know it owing to the mist (Ll. 1-52).

IX

At night slowly like a thief Amir went to his house and stealthily did he enter his own bed-room. The sorrows of Bhelua at parting with her dear husband pass all description. She had not touched any food these four days. She had wept the whole day and was now asleep in deep sorrow. She was dreaming a dream in which she saw her dear lord's face.

With some hesitancy and fear, lest it should attract the notice of others, Amir slowly knocked at the door. Once, twice, thrice did he call out but got no reply. But when he called a fourth time, she became awake, rubbed her eyes and sat up in her bed. Distinctly did she now catch the voice of her husband and quietly removed the bolt of the door. Maddened with joy, did Amir embrace her and felt restored to life like a fish that had been d[illegible]vn out to the bank and again flung into the water. They remained for a time locked in close embrace and from their eyes dropped incessant tears of joy. Bhelua threw herself into the bosom of her lord, and made it wet with her tears. She murmured, "I have known sorrows during these four long days that I cannot describe. A burning fire seemed to consume me day and night. I had no sleep in my eyes for these days. It was for the first time to-day after these long hours of sleepless pain that my eyes had closed a little. Severe is the headache that I am suffering from. It seemed to me that I would not be able to bear this life deserted by you."

Amir.

"Bear up with it a little while when I state my case. My parents are angry with me. How can I stay in this house facing their anger ? No right have I over my father's riches, and cursed will be my life if I cannot earn my own living. I hate to sit idle and enjoy my father's earnings. My hand shakes with disgust when I touch meals not earned by me."

At these words of her husband she fell at his feet and began to cry saying, "Do not go, Oh my lord, leaving me alone in this house. My *Baju* (an ornament for the arm) I will sell and live on its price for some time. Don't refuse my earnest request. My seven-stringed necklace (সপ্তছরির হার)[1] I will sell and the price will keep us going for some time more.

"Earnestly do I request you not to go to foreign lands to court dangers unknown. The string of golden beads (সোণার দানা) that adorns my neck, I shall sell for your sake and this will make us live in comfort for a little time more. Oh my beloved, oh jewel of my heart, do not go, I pray. For your sake shall I sell the golden bracelets (সোণার কঙ্কণ) of my hands and this will make us live in comfort for a further term. Oh my beloved, oh my dear one, you too, I know, are mad for love ;

[1] Mention of *Sapteshwari hār* we find in Kavi-kankan.

do not go, my *hansuli* (the garland of gold) and my ear-rings shall I sell for your sake and thus live in comfort for a little time more.

"Do not leave me, my love. My valuable Saḍi and my gold-embroidered *chaddar* shall I sell for you. This will maintain us for a further term.

"When all these sources will fail, I will beg from door to door and thus live together but, oh my dearest, do not talk of parting."

Amir.

"The night is drawing to a close. Have you got anything to offer me ; I am so hungry !"

She had fruits, *khorma* and nuts in the room with which she filled a plate and offered to her young lord. After taking his repast, the merchant went to bed.

From the Shimul tree, the osprey sounded its solemn note. Amir knew from this that the night was over. The eastern sky became aglow with purple light, and birds on the neighbouring trees sang their morning notes. The stars looked dim and faint like lamps with oil gone out. The happy night was thus gone. Bhelua lay unconscious in deep sleep. Amir was afraid that there had already been delay. So he hastened to the place where his ship lay anchored. He called aloud the sailors and within a few minutes the ship was let loose upon the waters of the deep.

Now hear what transpired next. The young merchant had gone away, leaving the doors of his room open. When he went away, Bhelua was in deep sleep and did not know of it.

In the morning Bivala rose from her bed and saw that the doors of her sister-in-law's room were kept open. Her mind had already been embittered by suspicion. Now grim doubts rent her mind. She tore off her own hair in great rage. There lay Bhelua like a nymph of heaven asleep in her bed. Bivala's brain was the devil's workshop. For a time she was at a loss to decide what to do. Sonai, the mother-in-law of Bhelua, came to the spot and saw that Bhelua was still sleeping, though it was high time to wake.

The crow from the roof of the house crowed and on her body had fallen the streaks of the morning sun. Her sweet dream was shattered, and Bhelua, with eyes still laden with sleep, awoke and was startled to find Bivala standing near her with a sour face.

Bivala.

" Oh, wicked woman, thou hast brought infamy on our house. I will tear off all your curly hair one by one. It is only four days that my brother has left home. Who was it that revelled here all night so that your sweet sleep has not broken so late in the morning to-day.

Bhelua bowed her head low and said weeping, " My husband came here last night. I can swear by the Quoran and the sacred scriptures that he alone is my lord. A second man I do not know."

The whole house was astir at this statement. They said in one voice. " How is it that your husband came? Only four days ago he set out for foreign lands."

Bhelua.

" I do not know anything except this that I have spoken the truth."

Nobody believed in her words. Some suggested that she should be subjected to some cruel punishments. Others said, " A pit should be dug out in a near place waist-deep and she must be thrown into it and bulldogs set on her."

Sonai, the mother-in-law, intervened at this stage and said, "Let her be treated as a servant of the house engaged to do menial work."

Chorus.—Oh ill luck !

As a menial of the house she worked night and day and had only two meals a day. The sister-in-law came to torment her with the weapon of her sharp tongue every time. The *baju* (ornament of her arm), the necklace, the flame-coloured *saḍi*, the bracelets, the *hansuli* (the golden ornament of the neck), the golden pendants of the ears were all taken away one by one.

In the morning she rose and cleared the dung of the cowshed. Then she set herself to dust the compound of the house. She cleansed the room and brought water from the river, covering her beautiful person as best as she could with torn cloths. One day Bivala ordered her to grind eight pounds of raw chilly. In deep anguish Bhelua shed tears but did the task all the same. Her hands got burnt with the stringent spice and her heart palpitated in great pain. Over and above all these, Bivala showered abuses on her.

She was scarcely given any meals worth the name. Night and day she wept. But when she was alone in her room, she sang the *baramashi* song to assuage the pain of parting from the lord of her heart. (Ll. 1-117.)

X. The Baramashi.

"The new year has come with April bringing fresh beauties of Nature. Alas ! where is the husband of my heart gone ! In my own home, I am as one homeless. There is none here whom I can call my own. Alas ! in what shores are you roaming and of what seas are you counting the waves when I am pining away for you here?

"In May the fruits are ripe. They hang from the boughs of trees. Who will, alas! fill the basket with mangoes and jacks to present them to me. Had I been a bird, oh my love, I would have gone flying to know your whereabouts.

"Now it is June. The clouds are pouring fresh waters on fields and rivers. Oh my love, a torn cloth I wear and that is wet with my tears. None is there to whom I may open my heart, and my grief is not such as can be told to others.

"In July, the peasants are busy sowing seeds near swamps and marshes. On such a day did you bid farewell to me, leaving the doors of the room open. That unfortunate day I can never forget when my sweet parrot cut the chain off its feet and fled from the cage.

"In August, the rays of the sun are piercing and more so are the words of my sister-in-law Bivala. I go to the landing ghat to fetch water and often do I cast my glances at the river fully swollen and strain my eyes in the hope of seeing my beloved come again.

"In September, the moon smiles bright in the sky. In my heart I perceive the tender call of love sweet like the sound of a flute. Oh my love, my colour once so fair has faded. There is none who cares for me. In my dreams I see you and my heart bursts in grief when I awake to find that it was a mere dream.

"In October, the milk within rice is thickened and takes the form of seeds. My mind yearns for you night and day. The flower of my youth will ere long fade; before it does so, will you not, my gay bee, pay me a visit?

"In November, the rice in the fields becomes ripe. Alas! where hast thou gone, oh my love, leaving one who was so dear to you. I am now a servant in the house and they do not give me sufficient food to appease my hunger. Grinding the stringent chillies, my hands have got-burns. Come, O lord, to see how miserable I am.

"In December, the biting cold is unbearable without you. Beautiful and warm blankets, their inside filled with warm cotton, I had in plenty. They have taken them all away and given me torn rags (*kanthās*) in their place.

"In January, the bitter cold attacks me with redoubled severity and causes the very tigers to howl in their wild homes. Need I say how miserably do I pass the month? I burn charcoals in my bed-room and thus warm myself a little. The inclemencies of the season may be put up with, but how can I bear the mental auguish which burns me like fire?

"In February, the southern wind blows, the cuckoo sings, causing me unbearable grief. Oh when will luck smile on me and you will come back to meet me?

"The year has drawn to a close and it is now March. Where and when may I find you is the one thought of my mind. To what shores, to what port, hast thou gone for trade? Who will tell me?" (Ll. 1-48.)

XI. On the River Bank.

One day Bhelua went in slow steps to the riverside for fetching water. She was all alone. She was weak as she had no meals that day. She walked through the village path. Her left eye felt a tremor and her breast beat in fear, indicating the approach of some danger unknown.

When she came to the landing ghat, she felt an uncontrollable fear and began to cry loudly, "Oh my love, by this stream have you gone to foreign land. Why did you not take me with you as I had prayed? I am weak and cannot bear the weight of this heavy pitcher filled with water. You left me in the custody of your mother and sister. Just see what plight they have put me to." She recollected the home of her childhood. Sister of seven brothers, she was seldom required to do any work. She used to put on a *chaddar* embroidered with gold. A hundred maid-servants there were to carry out her most trifling wishes. Now is she the servant of Divala—alas! how hard is her lot. Valuable couches she was accustomed to sleep on and now her lot is to live in a cowshed. Accustomed to scent herself with attar and other perfumes, now she has her body lying soiled with dust and mud. She used to live in the secure confines of the inner apartments where even the sun and the moon dared not have a peep at her face. Now, alas! it is her lot to come to the river ghat for taking water without a companion and through the public road!

"Oh my dear merchant, oh my love," cried she, "come and behold your dear wife, sent to the river ghat like a menial to fetch water."

She placed the pitcher on the bank and got down to bathe. Her luxuriant hair so profuse on her head was caught by the tide and it seemed to require some effort on her part to gather it together and free it from the hold of the strong current. When she rose, her hair fell to her feet and she remained standing in the sun for some time for drying it. (Ll. 1-32.)

XII. Bhola the Merchant.

Now I am going to describe Bhola, the merchant. He had travelled to the port of Masli Bandar. There he had filled his ship with cargo and was returning home.

He had journeyed by land, had crossed rivers and canals and was now near the port of Safla.

Chorus.—Your youth is passing in vain, oh maid.

Coming to the landing ghat, he cast his eyes on all sides, and spied a damsel of surpassing beauty who looked like a fairy descended on earth. "We all know that there is the moon in the sky without a peer, but how strange it is that we should find another shining on the riverside," thus reflected he.

Mad with a desire to secure the beautiful one, he discussed with his sailors as to how he could carry out his wicked end.

Who, alas! can fight with Fate ? Bhelua was forcibly carried off by Bhola.

The ship flew with the speed of lightning and unfortunate Bhelua lay stunned with grief at this new danger. She beat her head against the mast till it bled. She attempted to drown herself in the river but the rowers caught hold of her by force and prevented her from doing so.

Chorus.—O God, how unlucky is the girl!

"Oh pigeons that fly in the sky, travellers of the illimitable expanse are ye. Tell my love, if ye see him anywhere what has happened to me. Oh river flowing to distant lands, you may chance to meet my love. Tell him all about my sufferings. Oh waves who are in perpetual hurry to see new shores and are dancing in glee, tell him if you happen to meet him, that poor Bhelua will no more be allowed to seek his sweet embrace. Oh winds blowing in the south who visit the whole world in the twinkle of an eye, give an account of this miserable one, if you happen to meet him. Oh bad luck! why did I come to the river ghat ! The wicked Bhola has seized me finding me all alone."

Bhola, the merchant, approached her and said, "I am here, oh beautiful one, to tell you that I am going to take you to the city of Kattani. I am the master of a large property and have a house which is like a palace. I am going to marry you under the *Nika* system and I shall spare no pains to make your life happy. Like a flower bearing in its bosom a sweet treasure of honey, why should you live alone ? I will give you a couch of gold to rest on. Pray, do not waste your youth in vain but consent to my request and you will be the happiest of mortals."

She began to weep as she heard these words. "Alas ! Where is my beloved Amir gone, why did I not die before listening to these foul words?"

When Bhola heard her mention the name of Amir, he said, "Believe me, oh damsel, Amir died the other day in the port called Masli Bandar. We were all present at his funeral and he was buried in our presence. It is no use, sweet damsel, lamenting over him now. Come with me to my house, and you will find me just the man for you. Your slender body will be covered with gold ornaments. For your *chandrahār* (waist belt) I will spend a lakh of rupees. Fie, you are wearing a torn rag. I will give you a *nilāmbari* (blue-coloured *saḍi*) of the finest quality. You will have gold ornaments for your nose and ears, and your necklace will be a string of the largest pearls to be found in this side of the country. Your handsome figure has charmed me and you must note that I have known your real value as a jeweller knows the price of his jewel. Wealth, riches and all that I have I will offer you and I will cut off all connection with my other wives by divorce. But, should you like it, they will be your maid-servants, ministering to your comforts. When you will be at your meals, they will wash your hands. Your meals will consist of fine chickens, curry and first class rice called the *tulsimala*. In my inner apartments there is a smiling flower-garden where you and myself will delightfully ramble in mornings and evenings. On the second floor of my palace I have a rest-house to enjoy the breeze. There is a golden couch in that room, on which is spread a soft milk-white bed. We shall both be very happy there. You will prepare sweet betels and put them into my mouth. It is very well that the young merchant Amir is dead. You will find an infinitely better husband in me."

Bhelua did not set a *cowrie's* value to the words of this licentious wretch and began to reflect thus with her head bent low, "Had any evil befallen my lord, as this wicked man says, the red sign of luck on my forehead would have faded. My heart by its secret beatings would have known of it before any information from outside had reached me. My eyes would have felt a tremor indicating the evil."

She took her firm resolve, and cared not for what the result would be. When Bhola approached her again with his wicked proposal, her eyes wore the purple hue of anger and became like a flaming Java flower. She said, "A great mishap is awaiting thee, vile man, as thou hast dared carry me by force in this way. The evening lamp will no more burn in thy house. This is my curse and for immediate reward, here do I kick at thy wealth and all that thou hast to offer." Bhola retorted, "The bee does not leave a full-blown flower, because there are thorns. Know me to be such a bee maddened by your charms. You are now in my clutches and there is no escape this time."

One night when all were in profound slumber and the ship lay moored on the shore and only the snorings of the oarsmen were heard disturbing the general silence, did Bhola approach the cabin where Bhelua lay in her bed. He felt that tremor of heart which all sinners and criminals experience before doing a foul deed. The girl was indulging in wild thoughts; there was no sleep in her eyes.

She had perceived the wicked motive of Bhola. So when at such an hour of night she saw him standing near her, she was greatly frightened. She felt what the deer feels when caught by a tiger.

Bhola.

"Comply with my wishes, my love. Look but once at me with a smile and yield yourself to my loving embrace and I pray this to you on bended knees. Why should you be constantly under the shadow of a grief? Be rightly counselled and fulfil the earnest desire of my mind."

Saying this at the impulse of a passion that surged in his soul, he advanced towards Bhelua and tried to catch her by force. She retreated a little and tried to lull the wicked one into patience and hope by a device.

Bhelua.

"I will now open my mind to you and tell you the truth if you will wait a little while."

Bhola.

"Tell it, oh love, tell me what it is. I am dying with impatience. When will the golden hour of luck come to me and the moon of heaven be in my possession?"

Bhelua.

"How can I tell you now? You must first of all take a vow in the name of God turning to the West like a true Moslem that you will act as I will ask you. Then only can I frankly tell you all that is in my mind."

Bhola.

"Yes, I do hereby take the vow. Know me as your slave. I will carry out your command at all costs."

He took the holy name of God and looked expectantly at the damsel for her favour. Bhola was verily like a bull drawn with a rope in the nose by its master. Slowly she said now, "For six months you must not come to me. If you violate my wishes, know that I will commit suicide by drinking poison. There is no doubt of this. I will die if you apply force. During these months I will fulfil the vow of abstinence (*Iddat*) which it is incumbent on every Mohammedan girl to do on the death of her husband."

Like a snake under the touch of a charmer's wand, Bhola bent his head low, left the place, yielding to a wild train of thoughts. (Ll. 1-136.)

XIII. An Account of Amir.

In due course the merchant Amir came to the city of Ujjain and reaped large profits by his trade. In fact, he became master of lakhs. Fortune favoured him and by her smile the outlook of his trade took a glorious turn, so that if he touched a handful of ashes, it readily changed into gold.

The more he got, the more he coveted and in the course of his trade, visited Masli Bandar. Immense were his earnings and he made many valuable ornaments for Bhelua. His heart leaped in joy on account of his wonderful success in trade and he forgot for a time the sweet attractions of home.

Some months passed in this way. One night he dreamt a bad dream. His heart beat quick and he found no rest. He called Captain Goural Dhar to his presence and said "Be prepared at once; take what money will be wanted for preparations and start at once for Safla."

The ship was anchored off the shores of home. Slowly did the young merchant approach the house. Entering home, he saluted his parents. They did not say a word but their silent tears indicated some evil that had happened. At this moment came Bivala who said, you have returned now after full one year. The wicked Bhelua is no longer in our home. Marry a beautiful girl and be happy. Had Bhelua lived now, a great disaster it would have been to the family."

He could not understand anything, from this report and said, "Where is my beautiful Bhelua gone?" "Be cool-headed," answered Bivala, "it is only three days that she died."

Amir was, as it were, struck by thunder at the fell news. He trembled and was about to fall down.

Chorus.—Oh what an evil luck!

Amir.

"What shall I do with my riches? My trade and its success have no meaning for me now. Alas! where is my beautiful Bhelua gone? Wretch that I am, my eyes are still insatiate. I could not satisfy my thirsty eyes by feasting them on her to my heart's content. I cannot bear to live without her."

Lamenting in this way he made enquiries of Bivala, "Where is the grave of Bhelua?"

Bivala.

"On the seashore has she been buried."

He hastened to the spot and saw a new grave. There he rolled in the dust and began to weep bitterly.

"Oh my Bhelua," cried he, "come to my breast. Is the cold earth sweeter than my bosom. By my life, arise from this lowly bed, my beloved. If you will not, take me to you."

Lamenting in this way for a while, he began to dig the grave and to his great wonder he discovered the dead body of a black dog in it. (Ll. 1-54.)

XIV

He left his home, his riches and all, and turned a Fakir for love. His gold-embroidered cap with the setting of jewels in it, his silken robes, the *lungi*, his palatial house—all, all he abandoned and turned an ascetic. He wore a very ordinary coarse cloth. From his shoulders hung the beggar's wallet, and a torn cap he placed on his head. The mad Fakir wandered in unknown paths, lamenting bitterly.

Canals and rivers he crossed and came to a place called Chakria. There were many forests and small hills in that place. From there he travelled farther east and crossed the Sankha. Thence he came to the bank of the Kancha. "Oh my pet bird, where hast thou flown away," cried he again and again, and like one whose wits had completely run out, wandered through many unknown regions till he reached the river Kancha. There were no more any tears in his eyes. His head was unsteady. On a sudden impulse he leapt into the canal. It was the third day of the waxing moon and a high and strong current was running on account of the flow-tide. The mad man was carried headlong to the north. He crossed with great difficulty the whirlpools of the Karnaphully and reached the mouth of the Issamuti. He was pinched with severe cold and began to shiver. But his destiny would not allow him to stop. He marched towards a place called Rajanya. In the district of Rajanya there was the village Syed Nagar and in that place lived a musician named Tara Barui.

Tara Barui's power was wonderful. If he played on his violin, the river ran against the current, changing her course to listen to the sweet music. The wild tiger became tame, the deer forgot all about the trap laid for it, and the venomous snake bent low its uplifted hood at the sound.

Our young Fakir came to him and applied for being admitted as his pupil. He gave him an account of his distress and all that he had suffered.

Tara Barui.

"You have come to the right place. Music will afford you a solace which you will vainly seek elsewhere."

Tara Barui made a violin for his love-lorn pupil. The body of the instrument was made of Bailan wood. Its ears were made of fine Manpaban and the strings were prepared with the veins of *Dārās* snake. The bow was made of the wood of Narsha. The violin thus prepared was wonderful to look at. The accomplished artist's hand was so gifted that as soon as the bow was applied to the strings of the instrument, it gave out a sweet cry calling 'Bhelua,' 'Bhelua.'

Unmindful of hunger and thirst, and heedless of physical pain, from door to door the young Fakir wandered playing on his violin and as he did so, tears came forth unceasingly from his eyes. In storm and rain he wandered, his body all wet with showers. In the scorching rays of the sun, he wandered about, exposing himself to burning heat and in severe cold he walked with his body trembling like a banana-leaf. Thus travelling from place to place towards the west our Fakir came to a city called Faitabag. At the foot of the hills there was the pass called Khoolishir Dhala. On the west of this pass lay the beautiful city of Kattani adorned with many fine buildings and palaces. (Ll. 1-48.)

XV. In the House of Bhola.

The sun's rays sparkled on the crests of trees and the day was drawing to a close. At that hour of the day, Bhola who was profligacy incarnate came to the room of Bhelua. He had a sweet betel in his mouth and his beard was scented with *attar*. Slowly he entered the room and said, "Now your term is over. Six months have passed and you must remember your promise now."

Bhelua.

"I have known no peace of mind. You must excuse me, good merchant."

Bhola.

"It is not for you to seek pardon. I beg it at your hands. What good, my love, will you reap by playing deceit on me in this way ?"

Just at this moment, the young Fakir wearing a torn rag stood at the door outside and played on his violin which cried 'Bhelua,' 'Bhelua.'

The beautiful one was startled at the sound and Bhola said smiling, "I beg of you a humble boon. Make yourself merry. I have settled the date of marriage, it is to take place to-morrow by your kind consent." Just then was heard again the sweet sound "Bhelua" from the violin. The sound filled Bhelua's mind with a strange emotion, and she could find no rest.

Bhola.

"Now tell me, dear, if you agree. To-morrow you must recite the sacred word of scripture. The Kazi will be called in to minister to the function."

The mad Fakir was playing on his violin again and again. It seemed that some one was sweetly crying calling Bhelua by her name. She came out of the house and ascending the roof cast her glance on all sides.

A torn rag he wore and moving to and fro, played on his violin. His hair was brownish and his beard had grown long. He played on his violin, and as he played, he shed incessant tears.

Bhola stood behind Bhelua and said, "Now I wait for your answer. Give me the pleasing word of consent." Bhelua was listening to the music of violin, unmindful of everything else. The word that came unconsciously from her lips was "Wait." She was closely observing the Fakir and now she knew that it was none other than he. Her eyes were glistening with tears.

At the request of Bhelua, Bhola granted permission to the Fakir to occupy a room in the house. (Ll. 1-36.)

XVI

The Fakir took his meals and retired. He had no sleep in his eyes and no rest in his mind. At a deep hour of night, Bhelua mildly knocked at his door. There was no response. She thought that the Fakir had fallen asleep. She again gave a gentle stroke at the door and said in a whispering tone, "Open the door, my lord." The mad Fakir hurried to the door and they met. "Oh my merchant" cried Bhelua and bound him in her arms. Tears fell incessantly from both her eyes. Like pigeons they clung to each other locked in close embrace. Not a word escaped their mouths but their eyes shed copious tears. She was overpowered with an emotion inspired by extreme happiness and extreme sorrow, and with outstretched eyes lay gazing at the face of her husband.

“ Bhelua was listening to the music of violin.” P. 98.

A little abashed, Bhelua fell at his feet and saluted him. She gave a full account of herself, of all that she had suffered.

"In the depth of night you paid me a visit and left the doors of my room open without telling me anything. Your sister Bivala saw the doors of my bed-room open and spread a scandal which caused me great woes. Your mother and sister counselled by the neighbours had at first driven me from the house and on a second thought gave me a place there as a maid-servant. I cannot describe the oppressions to which I was subjected. I was sent to the river *ghat* to bring water all alone, and when returning home with my pitcher full, I was forcibly carried off by Bhola's men. I have been living at this wicked man's house, and all the time I have avoided him on one pretext or other. But it breaks my heart to tell you of my present situation. Friday next is the date fixed by Bhola for our marriage under the Nika system."

Amir.

"My mother and sister told me that you were dead. I dug the spot which they pointed out to me as your grave and found the corpse of a black dog in it. The world has since seemed to me as hell and hence I took the garb of a Fakir and have been wandering aimlessly throughout the country."

Bound in close embrace they passed the night in conversation, weeping as they talked. Bhelua said, "The night will be soon over. Let us fly away from this place at once."

Amir.

"I am the son of an honest man and not of a thief. I cannot agree to go away like a thief, stealing you as Bhola did."

The crows were crowing and the gay note of the cuckoo was heard. Bhelua did not contradict her husband and went away in a pensive mood.

XVII

The Kazi (Magistrate) of that town was an old man named Munaf. In the morning of the next day the Fakir filed a petition in his court.

He was seated on his *gadi,* leisurely smoking his winding pipe, and his constables and peons were assembled there, awaiting his orders. The Fakir salaamed him and stated his case as to how Bhola, the merchant, had forcibly carried his wife away. On reading the petition Kazi Munaf got angry and instantly issued a warrant for the arrest of Bhola.

The peons and constables carried out his orders and brought Bhola to the court. The Kazi threw a curl of smoke from his mouth at his face and said, "Is it a fact that you have forcibly brought the wife of this Fakir and are going to marry her to-day ?"

Bhola.

"It is a false charge. This Fakir is a mad fellow. What do I know about his wife? He is a very wicked man. On the plea of playing on the fiddle he visits the houses of people and seduces their wives if they are beautiful."

The Kazi was ninety years old and had only ten years to complete his centenary. He had not a single tooth in his gum, but still did not lack in sweet words to captivate a woman's heart. In his youth he was notorious for his licentiousness. He had outraged the honour of hundreds

Kazi Munaf's pond. P. 100.

of women. Now his bed lay, so to say, ready in the grave ; yet his nature had not improved a bit.

"Now I have secured a flower in full bloom and full of honey," thought the Kazi and then spoke out, "I order you, merchant Bhola, to bring the woman here at once. If you can prove that she is your wife, you will undoubtedly have her back and I will send the Fakir to prison for seven years."

Bhola went home, and instructed Bhelua as to what she should say; then she was carried to the court in a palanquin. When she came out, people were dazzled by her beauty. She looked like a flash of lightning, fallen on the earth. As he cast his glance at her, the Kazi's head was turned. He said, "Tell me, dear lady, without fear or shame, which of the two men that claim you is really your husband." Bhelua replied, "Pray, hear me, noble Kazi. This mad Fakir is the lord of my heart."

The Kazi got very angry with Bhola and drove him away from his presence. Then he called the Fakir and began to argue with him in this way: "You are not the fit man for this lady. This you must admit for the sake of truth. A dog cannot expect to be served with clarified butter. Now listen to me, you Fakir, that play on the violin. It is the bee that drinks honey from the flower. The worm lives on grass or leaf. So you too must look for what is suitable for you. You are not the proper person for Bhelua. If you take her to you, some one else will carry her off and you will come to vex me again. In this court there is a heavy pressure of work and I cannot attend to your complaints every day. Leave Bhelua with me. She will be happy here. I will give her a golden couch to sleep on and she will have proper meals and raiments."

The Fakir beat his breast in despair. Alas, the heart of Munaf Kazi was hard as stone. At a hint from the Kazi his constables and people forcibly drove the Fakir away.

Alas who can fight with luck ? Bhelua spent her time weeping at the house of the old Kazi. She did not take a morsel of food nor a drop of water at that house. She fell very ill and was confined to bed.

Meanwhile Amir arrived at the port of Safla and told his father his sad story with tearful eyes. The mother too heard everything and her heart was about to break in sorrow.

Manik, the merchant, ordered Captain Goural Dhar to prepare a navy of fourteen ships at once, saying, "My soldiers and *lathials* must go all and they must drown that small town of Kattani in the depth of the sea."

In the port the cry ran, "Get ready." The general of the army hurriedly prepared himself for the encounter. Some of the soldiers ran forward with long spears in their hands. The North-Western sepoys were conspicuous by their long moustaches. A part of the army had guns on their shoulders. From their waist-belts hang sharp swords covered under sheaths. The *lathials* were there with their long bamboo poles and *lathies.* Some took clubs huge as posts in their hands. There was no end of foot-soldiers. In all ten thousand sepoys marched to the field. Fourteen of the ships were ready on the shores at the command of Captain Goural Dhar.

The ship named *Forkan* went ahead ; it had in it a library of the Quoran and its commentaries. Next went the ship on board of which was the merchant himself. The third ship, the *Kalyan*, carried guns and cannon and the fourth, the *Kanchanmala*, had a store of ammunition of gun-powder and bullets. Then came the ship *Guadhar* on board of which were the splendid retinue and soldiers of Amir. The sixth ship *Hansanad* contained men armed with *lathies*. The North-Western sepoys were on board the ship *Syamal Sundar*. The ship *Hungar* (*lit*. the Shark) carried the instruments of war-music, the horns, the big drums and tabors. The ninth ship called the *Khaiapati* was filled with *lathies* made of bamboos called Keta Bairsha. The next ship *Rangmala* had in it big targets, swords and daggers. The ship *Hakchor* contained a store of food that would last for six months. The next one the *Aul Bāul* carried many tons of very fine rice and the *Hurmur* was filled with tanks containing drinkable water. The last of all *Lakshi Dhar* (*lit.* the abode of the goddess of fortune) was manned by Captain Goural Dhar himself. The fourteen ships marched with great uproar, and the drums and horns sounded a note of war which deafened the ear.

The soldiers raised the cry "Badar." The sea-fish and the shark fled away from the course followed by the ships. The winds blew and the sails, fully swollen, made a cracking sound. In three days they reached the port known as Kattani. On reaching the shores, they fired a cannon. It sounded like the thunder that comes out breaking the very bosom of the sky. (Ll. 1-114.)

XVIII. THE END.

The Kazi Munaf was frightened at the report he received and called at the house of Bhola. He said, "I have been put to great trouble on account of Bhelua. She is the very nymph of heaven and is in the bloom of youth. Old as I am, she has rejected all my overtures. She is in love with you. I should like to send her to you. Be happy with her."

Right glad was Bhola at these words of the Kazi. He thought that after all the girl had come round and been favourably inclined towards him. The Kazi said again, "She is very ill. During her illness, she speaks of nothing except you and wants to see you again and again." Just then was heard the thundering roar of the cannon from the sea-shore. The drums and the tabors raised a wildly confused sound.

The Kazi resumed the conversation : "I hear that Amir, the merchant, is coming to take Bhelua." At this report, Bhola wavered for a short time and then ordered his *lathials* and soldiers to be ready with arms. The constables and the peons of the Kazi also became prepared to face the situation. "Be ready to meet the enemy" was the cry that was heard throughout the town. The generals with daggers hanging from their waist-belts and targets in their hands assembled to defend the town of Kattani.

Thousands of soldiers now came to the battle-field and a hard contest set in. They struck the drums and tabors with long sticks, and the confused uproar of the soldiers engaged in the fight made even the earth tremble. The army of Amir came up with a dash and from their guns issued a volley of smoke, covering the whole sky with darkness.

The big cannon of Amir was fired and the bullets ran devastating the land. So dark it grew that one could not say if it was night or day. Many men of the city fell in the war and loud laments were heard from the cottages of the poor and the lowly. Some lost their hands, others their legs. Some again feigned to be dead and hid themselves amongst the slain. The sea itself began to tremble in great commotion. It looked as if the fair regions of God were all going to be drowned. For seven days the battle raged with great fury and on the eighth the combined armies of the Kazi and the merchant Bhola were completely defeated and they made a precipitous retreat.

A vigorous search was made for Bhola who was caught after some time. Amir passed the sentence of death on him. Goural Dhar slapped the Kazi on the cheeks. Already his life was almost extinct with fear and age. He rolled

"It is to be called after my wife's name—Bhelua's pond." P. 105.

on the ground in an unconscious state and then lay like one dead without sense or breath.

The young merchant called his soldiers and said, " You have now one thing to do. This wicked Bhola was my enemy ; though I have taken away his life, my thirst for vengeance is not yet appeased. I want to set up a memorial of Bhelua on the site of his home. Do you destroy his house, wiping away every sign of it and there on that unholy ground dig a big pond. It is to be called after my wife's name " Bhelua's pond."

After this, Amir went to the house of the Kazi to see Bhelua. (Ll. 1-56.)

XIX

Bhelua, we have already stated, had fallen ill at the house of the Kazi. She had been reduced to a skeleton and that bright complexion of her's had faded and become blackish. In deep dejection she had given up taking her meals and her head had gone wrong. At times she cried like a child and at others burst out into an unmeaning laughter. Often did she babble out an unconnected tale or sang a *baramashi* song. When Amir saw her, she had become stark mad.

In this condition she was brought on board the ship. Amir said, " Alas! for whom have I fought this hard battle? The bud has faded before it bloomed. Scarcely was the roof of the house completed when Providence has destroyed it by fire. Before water has sprung out, the pond dug by me has turned into a desert." He clasped the hands of Bhelua in deep affection, and tears flowed from his eyes, but Bhelua did not say a word. She only stared with an unmeaning gaze fixed on him.

The merchant returned to port Safla, having achieved victory in the war. There was a general illumination in the town by the order of his parents and a warm reception was accorded him by the citizens. Ladies of all descriptions, housewives, widows and neighbours came to the merchant's house ; some sang festive songs and others cried "Victory." The *nahabat* orchestra was played at the landing ghat and the whole place echoed to the sound of drums. People crowded at the landing step. The fourteen ships had returned, and one of them carried the dead body of Bhelua. On the sea shore a grave was dug out and Amir was seen wandering night and day near that spot. He had lost all appetite. Not a word did he utter to convey his mental anguish. Every drop of blood seemed to have flowed away from his heart and his eyes showed no sign of tears.

On the night of her burial, Amir saw seven fairies descending from heaven. They called aloud for Bhelua and he saw her rising from the grave and flying up to heaven in their company. (Ll. 1-30.)

" On the night of her burial. Amir saw seven fairies descending from heaven." P. 106-

THE BALLAD OF HATI KHEDA

OR

CAPTURE OF ELEPHANTS

PREFACE TO THE BALLAD OF HATI KHEDA OR ELEPHANT CAPTURE

In an address delivered by Mahamahopadhyaya Hara Prasad Sastri as President of the eighth session of the Bengali Literary Conference held at Burdwan in 1916, he referred to Bengali elephants as one of the chief glories of the province. He quoted chapter and verse from many scriptures to prove that the Bengalis were the first to bring these beasts under control, and found a system for treatment of their diseases known as "Hastyaurveda" which is traced to 4th century B.C., if not earlier. The author of this work Palakapya was a native of Eastern India and lived close by the river Louhitya (Brahmaputra) in a mountainous district which, after long centuries, has still retained its fame as the principal seat of elephants in Bengal. Abul Fazl wrote in the Ain-i-Akbari that the best types of elephants in the stall of the Great Moghul were those recruited from the hilly ranges through which the Brahmaputra passed. Palakapya, according to an ancient legend, was half man and half beast. His father was a Rishi named Sham Gayan, evidently an Aryan who lived in the mountainous regions from which the Brahmaputra flowed to the bay. The legend says that his mother was a she-elephant, no doubt a contemptuous designation given to a person of some non-Aryan tribe. We are familiar with such nomenclatures, given by Aryans to hill-people such as 'Banars' (monkeys), 'Nagas' (serpents), etc. M. Sastri says that the medicinal treatise compiled by Palakapya though written in Sanskrit bears in its phraseology and metre traces of the influence of a dialect which was non-Sanskritic. In the ballads on elephants, which we have secured, we have found mention of two Non-Aryan experts, Dhunchi and Mangla, whom we may take to be the descendants of a race of people who were the kinsmen of Palakapya on the mother's side, dwelling on the bank of the Louhitya. They have still retained their ancient proficiency in the art of capturing elephants and healing their diseases. Even in this age when scientific methods have undoubted approval and circulation all over the enlightened world, it is to be said to the credit of the *Kheda* system that Captain Caldwell and his colleagues who are trying to develop the method of elephant-capture have acknowledged the superiority of the Indians in the art; they are coming out to India to learn the secrets of the Kheda from the Indian hunters, some of whom were already employed by them to train their own people in Africa in elephant-capture. These elephant-capturers of India were the first to invent the *Kheda*, and after the lapse of many centuries, the superiority of their system is not only acknowledged but it is being adopted by scientific Europe.[1]

The exact geographical area of the lands where these animals are found is stated in the ballad itself. The hillocks lying to the east of Chittagong are linked with those of Tipperah, Manipur and Burma, forming a long mountainous range which may be said to trace their parentage from the great Himalayas on the north. This vast tract of hilly land covering thousands of square miles is the dwelling place of ferocious tigers, bears and rhinoceroses but principally of elephants. The natives of the country called Kiratas by Manu comprise various tribes such as Chakmas, Jummias and Maghs, who were at one time the best hunters in India, living as they did in the impenetrable jungles infested with those dangerous foes to human life. These hillmen had acquired the art of capturing the animals by ingenious crafts

[1] *Vide the Statesman* of the 8th May, 1927.

Capture of Elephants. P. 111.

which made their reputation spread far and wide over the whole of India. The Chittagong hunters successfully entrapped not only tigers and bears but even the dreaded rhinoceroses. Three methods were generally resorted to by these hunters for capturing elephants, *viz.*, (1) the *Kheda*, (2) the *Partal* and (3) the *Phanasi*.

The *Kheda.*—The word *Kheda* in Bengali seems to have been derived from *Khedan* "to drive." Wild elephants are driven by stratagems into an enclosure where they are imprisoned. These enclosures are called *Kheda*. This method of capturing them by leading them into the *Kheda* is still in vogue, and our present ballad deals with the enterprising adventure of a hunter named Golbadan who with the help of a Magh named Mangla drove more than a hundred elephants into a *Kheda* in the first part of the nineteenth century.

The *Partal* hunting is an ingenious method of capturing the male elephants when under sexual animation by setting tame female elephants to lead them into places where the *mahuts* or drivers can easily chain them or otherwise bring them under control. The wild male elephant in the rage of sexual feeling is called *Goondā* and the tame female elephants are called *Kunkis*; two or three *Kunkis* are set to entrap one *Goondā*.

The third method is *Phanasi* or hanging. It is an equally clever device. The tame female elephants are led into deep jungles where they contract friendship with female elephants of the forest. Two or three *Kunkis* sometimes bring with them one wild female elephant from the forest. The driver watches the fit time and throws a long rope in the form of a halter, which the wild animal following its habit, swings with its trunk to and fro, and the watchful driver seeks the opportune moment to put the rope by some clever device round the neck of the animal. The elephant is thus made to wear the halter of slavery for life.

The Jummias, the Chakmas and other hilly tribes have recourse to various other strange ways for hunting. A century ago there lived a tribe in Chittagong named *Dala-Shikari* who were expert hunters. *Dala* in Bengali means a large can. The root from which the word has been derived may be the same to which our familiar *thala* is traced. The *dala* hunter used to place a large *mashal* or torch on a big can and advance with it towards the wild jungles in dark nights ringing loudly a bell with one hand all the time. All unperceived under the shadow of the can, went forth another man with a sharp scimitar in his hand. The sound of the bell and the sight of the torch in the dark forest drew a number of tigers, bears and even rhinoceroses to the spot. The strong man with the scimitar in his hand suddenly came out and killed the animals. It is said that the *Dala* hunters often fell victims to snake-bite. This class of hunters is no longer to be found in Chittagong.

The hero of the present ballad Jamadar Golbadan constructed a Kheda in the valley of Garjana, so called after the trees of that name with which it abounds, and successfully carried on his adventure, capturing a large number of elephants. His son Ochhi Miah, who died only five or six years ago at the age of sixty, was an equally enterprising hunter. He is the hero of another ballad composed by Makbul Ahmed of the village Noapara (P. O. Gujra) in Chittagong. This ballad which was printed and published some years ago from the Sarasvati Press, Chittagong, gives a graphic account of the adventures of Ochhi Miah. We learn from it that Rai Nil-Kristo Kunda, a Zemindar of Chakbazar in Chittagong, defrayed the expenses of this raid on elephants and appointed Ochhi Miah as the leader of the party. Among this band of hunters, Choudhury Mafizulla is said to have been a very conspicuous man. They at first appointed five hundred coolies at Rupees ten each a month and equipped themselves with spears, guns and swords, taking ample provision of food-stuff with them. Sikdar Naher Ali was their guide in the jungly path. They fortunately met a Magh named Dhunchi who had an expert knowledge of all matters relating to wild animals of the neighbouring forests. They entered the deep forest. Surul Mia, the jamadar, Samas Mia and Abdur Razzaque were also on the alert. There were also other clever hunters with them such as Rahamali, Azgar Ali and Abdul Jalil. They kept the torches burning on the elevated points of the hilly land. The Magh Dhunchi Mia, appointed on a pay of Rupees twenty a month, selected the spot where the *Kheda* was to be constructed. It was a locality close to the fountain of Bhandaljuri in Banjalhalia. The number of elephants they caught was forty-five. The author gives an animated description of the capture of elephants :—how some of these animals died in their attempt to escape from the *Kheda* ; how the ever vigilant Magh Dhunchi was at last trampled to death under the feet of a wild elephant ; and above all, how the whole neighbourhood of the *Kheda*, formerly a waste land, suddenly turned into a city with brisk trade, all ablaze with innumerable lights in the camps and sheds, which made the nights bright as day. Many Europeans—the Commissioner, the Judge, the Magistrate, many Bengali Babus and Mohammedans had gone there to behold the grand spectacle. The ballad in its concluding lines gives an account of the sale of the elephants—the principal buyer being Maharaja Suryya Kanta Acharyya of Mymensing who purchased nearly the whole lot for Rupees forty thousand. The elephants were made to cross the Karnaphuli and the Kankhali and proceed towards the north to the *hât* of Garang from where they were taken to the palace of the Maharaja at Mymensing. The other ballad, which is published here for the first time, was composed by the illiterate peasantry of Chittagong about a hundred years ago. Who the author of the ballad was, cannot be traced, but Babu Asutosh Choudhury gathered parts of it from (1) Majbul Ahmed,

(2) Amir Hanza of Rajahat (P. O. Rangudia), (3) Makram Ali of Agartala, (4) Kuktá, a hill-man of the Jummia tribe, native of Chipsari, (5) Basu Ali of village Karaldanga and (6) Ali Khan of Chanatsao (P. O. Panchalash).

The great pains taken by Mr. Choudhury in collecting scraps from these sources, involving very difficult journey into the interior of the jungles, cannot be too highly praised. He visited the *Khedas* of Bengalhalia, Srimati and Mahiani and often passed a whole day without any food.

The *Kheda* of the present ballad was constructed within the jurisdiction of P. S. Ramu in Chittagong. Babu Asutosh Choudhury has sent me a map of Cox's Bazar sketched in 1914-16, which shows the exact position of the localities mentioned in the ballad. The peak Khamatang has been mentioned in the ballad as lying to the east of Garjania but it is really to the north-west of that hill. This, however, is no mistake. On enquiry it has been found that all the hills to the east of P. S. Ramu are popularly called by the general name of Garjani. These hills may be traced from a village called Chakmarkul. It is evident that Golbadan constructed his *Kheda* on the west of Khamatang mountain.

The ballad is full of life and animation. It is composed in rapid verses, all in brisk metres, so that one might fancy that he heard the very rattling sound of the weapons and implements carried by the hunters. The description is vivid and swift—without any superfluities. The interest that the peasantry felt in the enterprising hunt for elephants often involving a risk of life, lends its intense excitement to the audience of the song who feel their hearts throbbing as the verses are recited, describing the animated chase. The language in which the ballad is composed is of supreme interest to the philologist. Though evidently written by a Mohammedan, there is no obtrusive element of Persian or Urdu words. The ballad is composed in pure Bengali of Eastern Bengal in its original

Prakrit form. The country adages, the peculiarities of expression and a galaxy of indigenous idioms and phrases absolutely free from Sanskritic influence, showing their clearest affinity with Ardha Maghadic Prakrit—all combine to give this ballad a linguistic importance which will, I am sure, receive due appreciation from scholars.

This ballad was sent to me by Babu Asutosh Choudhury from Choudhury Para Lane, Tamakumandi, Chittagong, on the 3rd of April, 1927. It contains 438 lines, which I have divided into 10 cantos.

DINESHCHANDRA SEN

The Capture of Elephants

I

My obeisance to Allah and, next, my respectful salams to Nabi. At a great distance, the sky shines with the light of the sun and the moon. Innumerable stars, besides, wander about like wheels in the vast expanse. How wonderful is the hand that dug the great ocean, the flowing rivers, and constructed the great sandy banks. Wonderful is the hand that dug out earth and heaped it to form hills, and that pours rains from the sky with roaring sound. Wonderful is the skill with which the hands, the feet and the heads of men and animals are made, and strange is the art that conceals the tree in the seed and invests the tree with leaves. There is nothing that the Lord cannot do. He can at his will turn the sunny day into a dark night. At a bare signal from Him the monarch turns a fakir and a man of Satanic nature turns a saint. This life and this house with its accumulated riches are not of any real value. They are unsteady as is the water on the leaf of the *kachu* plant. The day is not far off, my friend, when the last breadth will be drawn and with it all will be over. Death with a wand in his hand stands waiting at the gate. Why should you, my friend, sorrow over this house (body) soon to be deserted. After death the day of judgment will come. Oh! Allah, oh Lord, forgive me for my sins. (Ll. 1-22.)

II

Oh! my friend, listen to the story as to how the elephants are captured. The tale is a wonderful one. No bigger animal lives in the world than the elephant. It is said that the young one of this animal lives in the womb of its mother for full eleven years before it is born. When the wild animal roars in the forests, tigers and bears are frightened and they fly away in alarm. At the time of the delivery of the young one, the mother strikes her head against hills so vehemently that they tremble. The legs of an elephant are like big pillars of a godown. If a man owing to his ill luck falls in the way of a wild elephant near a hill, the animal looks like the veritable death with a warrant in his hand. Its two large ears are verily like winnows, its two tusks are like two fully developed radishes in the month of January, and its trunk looks like the husking machine—*dheki*. It always walks with its head bent down. Considering its gigantic size, the eyes are too small and its stomach looks like a big trumpet. God is to be thanked that this large animal has two small eyes. What a danger would it have been if the mighty elephant could see its own vast self! (Ll. 1-16.)

III

In the depths of forest these elephants wander in large numbers. Men catch hold of them, constructing *Kheda* and by other means by dint of their intelligence. The footsteps of the beasts are to be seen in regular order and the hunter with a weapon in his hand pursues them to the hills where these bulky animals live and from where they come down to the valleys. I have heard accounts relating to these wild animals from old men and women of the countryside and I am going to relate them to you.

There is a hill on the east of Chittagong whose peak touches the very sky. There live the wild Kukis, the Murings and other wild tribes in happiness. On crossing the limits of the Kuki hill one comes to a dense forest where there are tall trees, bamboo groves and long reeds and straws of various species. This forest covers many a mile. There seems to be no end or limit to it. By day and night impenetrable darkness pervades this expansive region. If one starts on foot from one end of this forest, he may expect to reach the other in six months. Elephants have this characteristic that they always live together in large numbers and where they live there no bear or tiger is to be seen. No bird dares fly in the sky above the ground trodden upon by these huge dwellers of the forest. In the tanks of the locality where the elephants sport, no fish is to be found. The elephants out of sheer pleasure root out huge trees. What shall I say of this dismal and illimitable forest? For thousands of miles there are no other animals to be seen. On the south of this forest lies a place known as Ambaphalum. There dwell the elephant-hunters of the Burmese race, plying their trade with courage. On the north is the land known as Pohana Pari so called after the fairy-like Manipuri female dancers who dwell there, and on the east is a delightful spot where the white elphants drink water from the Irawady. (Ll. 1-24.)

IV

Once in the month of November when rice grew ripe in the breeze that blew in the pastoral fields, the roar of the elephants was heard from the tops of the hill Karal-dear. Colour disappeared from the faces of hillmen who apprehended the approach of these formidable destroyers of their harvests. The Jummas made their temporary sheds over bamboo platforms and the Bengalees retired into the very recesses of their forest houses. Those whose houses lay at the foot of the hills considered their lives to be in imminent danger every moment. The wild animals meantime destroyed their ripe paddy in the eastern swamps. The plough-men who had hoped to have a rich harvest of sugar-candy found the plants all eaten up. It was God's scourge they thought. Large tracts of lands which they had brought under the plough looked like a desert. Many of them found their smiling fields of brinjal and radish mercilessly smothered and others cried having lost their harvest of wheat. The wild animals not only destroyed the field products but also materially damaged their lands trampling them under their huge feet. There was an old woman named *Kaichanir Mā*. She lamented the loss of her kidney bean and the damage done to her fields. The peasants struck their heads with their hands and lamented that no provision was left there for the coming year, so the children and women would starve.

Chorus.

"Exposed to the rain and sunshine we ploughed the lands with care. These wild animals have destroyed all our hopes. We have no money, no house and we wear rags. The ornaments of our women have been mortgaged for purchase of agricultural implements and heavily indebted are we to the bankers. How can we expect to clear the debt ? Our granary is without rice. 'How shall I feed the little darling, twelve months old,' cried one. It is due to ill-luck that the wild elephants have ruined our prospects. God's anger has overtaken us surely."

The peasants began to lament in this way. The hill-tribes known as Jumma and Chakma fell into great distress. The cutters of bamboos and long grasses faced a severe trial. Near the slopes of the hill, the ways were deserted by men for fear of these wild beasts.

The tigers and the bears all fled away from the forest and the birds ceased to fly in the sky. The terrible animals then moved towards the south and pursuing the path at the foot of the hill came to a place named Dul Hajara near the Chumti hills. The men there by beat of drums announced the advent of this terrible scourge, from the eastern hills, dreaded as death. The report spread far and near causing consternation to all. But a few men secretly cherished the hope of capturing these wild animals by constructing *Kheda*.

The land adjoining the fountain Nalua, is salty and some people began to construct hedges on selected plots to be ultimately developed into *Kheda*. Some of the hunters made *Kheda* in Dul Hajara, others in the slopes of the Chumti hills. Near the rivers the Kactalang, the Subtalang and the Maini, elephant-hunters who were strangers there, wandered about to seize the animals. (Ll. 1-38.)

V

Far to the east of Kagbazar near the mouth of the canal Bagha Khali, there is a dense and impenetrable forest. Tall Garjan trees whose heads touch the sky are to be seen there, as if planted by divine hands in groves and it takes a person half a day to go round them. Besides the Garjan trees, there are Jarul and Gambhiras and canes called the Gallak. In this deep forest there, as we have already stated, is a particular spot which the hunters selected for constructing a *Kheda* on. There is a fountain of salty water and in the month of December the elephants flock in the neighbourhood of it. There is another fountain close by of which the water is sweet like the milk of the cocoanut. It is called the *mitha chhara* or the sweet spring, and on the south of it lies the country known as Roshang (Arakan) where robbers wander about and stab strangers if they find an opportunity.

Now, my friends, the tigers and the Maghs (the Burmese) have the same spirit and they belong to the same country. If the latter get in their hands crooked knives of their peculiar make, then woe betides the unfortunate wayfarers.

Close to the place of these Garjan trees once came great flocks of elephants. The deer, the *Gayal* and leopards of striped colour all fled away in fear. There were huge serpents in these hilly places, whose mouths gaped wide at the time of inhaling breath which blew like gale. It was so poisonous that animals fell dead as they inhaled it. The huge tails of these serpents lay on one side of the hill and the heads on another, so vast was their size. They swallowed goats and other animals and were called Ajagar or the swallower of goats. These animals understood that the huge elephants were coming and forthwith retreated into the big holes at the foot of the hills. The jackals remained in their recesses under ground and did not give forth their yells at the usual hours for fear.

In the month of January, the *jamadar* began those operations by which the elephants were to be captured. It is a wonderful tale which, I hope, my friends will bear with me when I relate.

Long ago, the Chittagong hunters of black colour came to these hills of Garjan trees. They wanted to construct a *Kheda* ; their leader was Golbadan Jamadar. This man was a great wrestler and possessed huge physical strength. He commanded the respect of the people of his community and was known for his sagacity and foresight. His fame had spread far and near as a great capturer of elephants. Even the bears and tigers of the forest, it is said, respected his presence and paid him salams.

In his front and behind him were fifty coolies of whom some were equipped with spears and others with guns. They were accompanied by a *choukidar* who was always on the alert and knew how to guard against danger. They took with them a large number of spades, axes, ropes and strong cords. They provided themselves with sufficient rice, chillies and oil. Thus equipped, they arrived at the slopes of Garjan trees. (Ll. 1-42.)

VI

It was the biting cold of January. They trembled as they advanced. Not a word emanated from their mouths and even the sound of their breath was not heard. They crossed small hillocks and mounts. They surmounted canals, rivers and many a slope in this way and when they reached a fountain, they cooked rice near it under the shade of some tree. Some of them suffered from pain all over their body for they had no rugs or warm clothes to protect them from cold. Some of them suffered from bowel complaints as a result of eating the Hilsa fish, stuffed with salt. Some became restless and regretted their coming to the strange land where death stared them in the face, and others reclining themselves on their bags and baggages began to think about their homes. One of them said, "Alas! we have dug our own graves and we are to blame for it. My little boy still suckles, so helpless is he. Who will protect him? Who will, alas, provide my family with food and repair the roofs of my straw-houses. Tempted by the prospect of capturing elephants in the *Kheda*, we have brought ruin upon ourselves. How happy was I when at home. I have pierced a spear into my own breast and with my own hands. The jack hangs far above on the bough and before getting it in my hands, I have besmeared my lips with oil."[1]

(Ll. 1-14.)

VII

There is a beautiful village in the country of the Chakmas named Chammankul. There live the Jummas and the Chakmas in small huts. They are a strange people,

[1] The Bengali adage is "গাছে কাঁঠাল গোঁফে তেল." When eating a jack-fruit, sometimes people put oil on their moustache to protect it from the sticky juice of the fruit. When one is too sure of success in any enterprise, but fails in the long run, people imply his foolishness by the adage which refers to his over-confidence. In the line in question the word 'lips' is used in the place of the 'moustache.'

their women are without Purdah and are void of any sense of shame; they move about freely without restraint. They wear a short Sari called Khema which is not long enough to cover their body, being only two and a half cubits long. They are not in the control of their parents or their brothers. They cover their breasts with a strip of cloth called Dhuija and do not care to hide their face with veils. These women of Jummas and Chakmas are absolutely free and select their own husbands without taking the consent of their parents. It is strange that women do not at all care or fear their men!

There was a general amongst these Chakmas named Mangla. He was a great man and his name was known all over the country. He had a large number of cows and buffaloes in his sheds and he possessed a vast plot of arable lands. His income from the sale of *gollak* canes alone amounted to a thousand rupees a year. He had grown very old and had no teeth in his gums; but still he liked to chew betel leaves, which he did with the help of his toothless gums. At the time when the incidents of our story occurred he was eighty years old.

Golbadan came to the house of this Chakma-general—Mangla. Mangla told him, "I know where the wild elephants live, for I have all my life wandered over the hills and I know well the paths in this jungly land. I advise you to stay at my house with your men. You will have plenty of rice grown in my own lands and there will be no want of vegetables in my gardens. The women of my house know how to prepare thickened curd, which, if squeezed, does not yield a drop of water. Live in this country-home of mine for a time and I assure you that you will have plenty of elephants as a reward for your enterprise at the time of returning home.

Golbadan was right glad at the words of Mangla, the Chakma leader, and had his temporary lodge there. With the old Chakma general they wandered about in the forest always thinking as to when elephants would come.

Nights and days passed in this way till a long time was over. There was no clue as to the locality of the elephants and Golbadan was greaty alarmed. "I have come to a great distance," thought he, "the losses involved in this journey will be ruinous. My creditor will seize my property, house and all and I shall have to live the cursed life of want hiding myself from others like a thief in my own country."

He was thinking in this strain, seated under the shadow of a tree when appeared to him an informer who said, "Take heart, my friend. In the near forest a large number of elephants is bathing." Instantly at the words of the man, Golbadan rose from his seat and accompanied by his Sirdar proceeded towards the spot. They walked slowly in great fear, so slowly that they did not hear the sound of their own footsteps and often did they hide themselves behind the trees for fear of being observed. Presently they saw a large number of elephants drinking water from the fountain and for a time Golbadan was at his wit's end to devise a plan for catching the animals. After sometime he came to a decision and explained his plan to the people of his party. They put their heads together and consulted about the scheme of Golbadan ; their next move was to proceed towards the hill named Itgarh. Next they went ahead of the fountain, near which they saw the signs of elephant's footsteps. These were fresh and there was no doubt that these elephants had come there just a little before. The Sirdar said, "No doubt the animals are here. We will anyhow catch them." Golbadan took heart at his encouraging words.

The coolies arrived there with the Chowkidar and the Sirdar. The latter gave orders, "Now advance, my friends, and cleverly catch hold of the animals."

Two peaks of hills appeared in the east and west, and in the south there was a delightful slope. On the north was a fountain; the stream was flowing but the water was not profuse. The small slope would measure about an acre. Near the fountain was a deep shade created by banana and other plants. They perceived that it was the banana plants that had attracted the wild beasts and that it was in the deep shade that they must have been lurking.

Then did the coolies go to the forest, cut down the huge trees and brought them to the slope. After this they planted the woods and made an enclosure with them. The huge trees were planted at the distance of a cubit from each. Each of these trees measured three cubits in circumference. They were planted deep in the underground and thus a regular fort was made and this in the countryside people called *Kheda*. Strong ropes were often used for binding tightly one pillar with another and huge blocks of wood were tied with the pillars crosswise. Though this fencing was strong enough they put a large number of wooden supports from behind, so that the pillars might not shake when pushed by violent force.

Golbadan said, " But I am not yet sure. Push, my brethren, these pillars and try their strength. It is not a child's play. Know that the ferocious and wild animals will apply their whole strength in pushing the pillars. So our *Kheda* should be a formidable one with power to resist."

On the north and south of the *Kheda* they prepared two doorways. Above them lay two huge doors made by wooden blocks tied with strong ropes and these were placed hundred cubits above the ground. They could be brought down or lifted up by means of a large pulley. The two doorways were made along the same line.

There was no knowing from which direction the elephants would come. Is it possible for men to make any guess as to the strange movements of these animals ? The Sirdar said, "Do not lose time, my friends. Just walk slowly and silently and gradually surround the animals. Some of you should proceed towards the north far beyond the Gajalia forests; and a little to the east of this place you will find a police outpost by the side of the Khuda-khali (canal). Those of you who would go to the south must come to the Dheba to scrutinise the place and see if there be any sign of the tread of elephants. A large number of men is to proceed towards the east. It is well known that it is the favourite place of the elephants. I request you to guard yourself against danger as you are going far off. I warn you, my friends, when you will have reached the eastern hills you need not go further up; there you have the prospect of meeting the animals but beyond that no search is necessary. (Ll. 1-94.)

VIII

The short day of winter comes to a close as if abruptly. When the party had reached the Garjania hills, darkness thickened on all sides. The enquirers hid themselves behind a tree and walked cautiously. If they caught the least sound, they retired into some safe recesses. It was a very dense forest and they tried to find some means to catch the elephants just like a fisherman who wanders about the bank of a river throwing his net here and there. Near the *Kheda* on the top of the hillock the Chowkidars kept watch; some of them had made a sort of house on the boughs of trees and intently looked around from that secure abode.

Those of the people who had gone to Khamanjmuda heard the sound of elephants in the bamboo groves. On hearing the sound they proceeded two miles more towards the east and there stopped. They had short scabbards fastened to their waists. They scarcely uttered a word. Their limbs were almost paralysed by the cold of January.

Many leaves had fallen on the ground in winter. They set fire to these. Their short scabbards they had fastened to their waists and they scarcely uttered a word. They warmed themselves by the fire produced by the leaves and woods. It was a dark night and the cold wind was blowing from the north. They had set fire to the forest on the tops of the hills. The tall bamboos now and then began to burst by the fire, and smoke issued from the bamboo groves as they were slowly burnt. The elephants as they heard the sound of the bursting of the bamboos were alarmed. They came a little to the east and evidently perceived that men were pursuing them. The fire on the top of the hills now became fully ablaze illuminating the sky. The elephants now took a northern course. They lifted up their trunks and ran without looking behind. They did not stop until they had reached the banks of the Khuda-khali. They assembled there and stayed.

In the meantime the hunters were already stationed there. Owing to the biting cold of January some of them were drawing their tobacco-pipe with all their force. The forest was impenetrable and the darkness no less so. Some of them had stretched their legs and were reposing in that attitude. Others were half asleep turning on their sides. Some were smoking while others snatched the pipes from their hands but there was a silence which nobody dared break. Just at the time they heard the rustling of leaves and their surprise was great when they heard the voice of the big animals. They immediately stood up all in haste and began to cry aloud in order to threaten them.

There was all confusion and every one raised an uproar. Some were sounding their horns. Others were striking split bamboos against one another which created a great sound. Some were shooting up rockets but in spite of all their sound and fury, each of them felt that it was a great moment of his life, involving a serious risk. The more devout of the party began to scream out their prayer (আজান); others began to ring a brazen bell with all force and a few shrieked as the *kukis* of the Tipperah hills use to do.

At the risk of their life and not at all caring for it, they devised various means by which eventually they succeeded in turning the elephants from the direction which they were following. When the animals turned their face eastward, they were alarmed at the sight of fire on the hills. The hunters drove them from both sides and they were obliged to take a southern direction. They broke with their tusks huge branches of the trees and hurried fast, while the hunters, remaining behind filled the sky with their loud clamours full of absurd abuses.

"Oh huge animals open your large ears and listen to our words. If you go astray, know that we will set fire and kill you all. Be all attention and listen to what we say. Do not take a zigzag course, that will be ruinous to you."

The elephants did not understand the clever device of the hunters. They approached the fountain and then proceeded towards the *Kheda*. As they went on their heads struck against tall trees and for a time they knelt down and looked forward with their small eyes. This is the characteristic of the elephants that they seldom turned from their course ; they followed one direction and never deviated from it. So whatever trees and plants fell in their way, they either broke with their tusks or trod down. Within the *Kheda* many bananas and plantains were planted. The fish cannot know the net spread for catching it. The elephant also could not understand the purpose of the vegetable plants grown there. They were all delighted at the prospect of a sumptuous feast, which was really a device to capture their whole race. Gradually

Capture of Elephants. P. 129.

large flocks of these animals came to the door-way of the Kheda over which and far above the ground the guards were watching all alert. These guards felt their heart palpitating and were breathless in fear. They were holding the cord of the pulley without making any sound. Gradually the elephants drew forth with their trunks the tender leaves and branches of the banana plants and after a time, they were found all within the Kheda.

The wild male elephants were clever and tried to turn back, but the guards all on a sudden let loose the cord of the pulley. The two door-ways were thus ingeniously closed and many elephants were made captives.

The East was lit up with a glow and it was understood that the night was coming to a close. Within the Kheda lay more than a hundred elephants made prisoners in this way. The hunters and the coolies all assembled there and guarded the enclosure on all sides. They had hundreds of torches in their hands, besides spears and arrows. They set fire to the hills. The wild elephants in great fright began to move wildly within the enclosure. Alas! they had no path by which they could make their exit. When they realised their situation they all screamed together in despair. Their voice made the very hills tremble, and it seemed as if a great flood was rushing in with a tremendous roar. In restless pain, they began to cry and the whole enclosure looked like the field of Karabala.

The wild elephants began to strike their heads against the Gazari posts. Alas! poor animals! they knew not the device to break the pulley. If with their trunks they would pull the machinery, the whole thing would give way in no time and the enclosure would break; but the foolish elephants did not pull but pushed the door-way further back with their heads. With their trunks, they could easily pull down huge trees but without doing the same in respect of the wooden poles of the enclosure, they simply pushed them by means of their head and the result was they were entrapped the more in the net. Like the bullock whose eyes are covered with a piece of cloth, so that it wanders in a circle round the oil-machine over again, the stupid animals repeated the same course of pushing without improving their situation a bit but making it worse each time. The guards were moving about on all sides of the Kheda and as soon as the elephants approached the enclosures they attacked them with their long spears. When unable to bear the pain, they pushed the enclosure again, the guards set fire to the rockets and threw them within. These bursting inside the Kheda caused a panic among the beasts who now helplessly shed showers of tears from their small eyes.

Then the hunters commenced their play with their fire-works. The rocket went high in the air and the তুবড়ী, another kind of firework, burst on the ground with great sound and light. The deafening roar of the fireworks made the animals stunned with fear; some of the hunters fired their guns and others threw bombs. In great fear the elephants kneeled down and then rolled on the earth.

The night slowly passed away and the sun like a red ball appeared in the eastern horizon. At the sight of daylight, the elephants began to jump. There was no trace of the plantain trees within the enclosure. They had trodden down the straws and the grass, which reduced to dust, flew up in the air. They then attacked one another and it was a terrible sight to behold the mad attempts of over a hundred elephants within that small compass. It seemed that the Kheda would not be strong enough to hold within it the ferocious animals.

The Jamadar Golbadan now felt the approach of a new danger and though it was severe cold, he began to perspire in fear. He became greatly alarmed and ordered his men to bring a fresh supply of hands from the village. "I want another five hundred strong young men. After the day will be over grim night will be approaching. It will be a terrible trial," he said. He ordered them to gather wood on all sides of the Kheda and heap them up for making a fire, if necessary. "I want," he said, "a thousand torches to be made with logs. These, you should take care to see, must not be wet but dry and combustible. When the night came and the hunters were feeling their eyelids heavy with sleep, they heard a great sound coming from the eastern *Mura*. The hunters advanced with torches in their hands and were alarmed to see that a large flock of elephants stood very near them. If they would approach a little nearer, there would be no hope of their lives. These wild elephants were slowly advancing towards the Kheda. The informers gave report to the Jamadar of the great danger that was near. Their very skin seemed to burst in fear and all of them trembled like banana leaves. Outside the Kheda there was a great uproar made by the wild elephants who were coming to meet their comrades within the Kheda. If these wild animals would break the fence of the enclosure, it would be all over with the hunters in no time. The Mahammadans began to offer their prayers loudly and the Hindus cried, "Jai Kali" (Victory to Kali); the Burmese recited, "Para" (Oh Lord!) and called on Niranjana to save them from the danger imminent.

At this juncture, the hunters again opened fire and threw bombs on all sides. They lighted hundreds of torches which made the dark night appear like day. They made a huge fire with the woods they had gathered. The flames rose high up in the air. The wild animals outside the Kheda took fright and fled away into the forest as fast as their heels could carry them.

(VIII)

Slowly and in great anxiety on the part of the hunters did four days pass. The elephants became totally exhausted within the Kheda. They were without food for all these days and their strength utterly failed them. When they tried to move, they could not do so but fell down on the earth rolling. The huge male elephant who had led the flock into the enclosure evidently showed his great disappointment and grief; for tears were seen streaming from both of his eyes. This *Goonda* elephant now bored the earth with his huge tusks and fell down and died.

Next the Jamadar brought ten tame elephants and made them enter the Kheda. It was a wonderful sight. Round the Kheda they constructed another enclosure. Within this outer Kheda rows of plantain trees were planted and a new door-way was made. This door-way was just enough for a single elephant to pass. When one elephant came out to the second enclosure, being attracted by the sight of the plantain trees, the door closed. Two tame elephants were set to escort the wild one that had come into the second Kheda. The wild one fed itself on the plantain leaves, heedless of anything else, and now listen, my friends, how this wild elephant was gradually tamed and bound.

Beneath the stomach of the tame elephant, lay a driver, covered with a linen, hiding himself as best as he could—careless of his life. At a signal from the driver, one of the tame elephants came forward and pressed the wild one with all its power. Another tame elephant then came in front and with its trunk pulled the wild one in a friendly way. Being pressed by the two elephants, the wild creature could neither move this way nor that. Those animals were sufficiently strong to hold in check the wild one, enfeebled by struggling and famished for four days. It was thus reduced to a state which made it impossible for it to move on any side. At this stage came the driver, thanks to his skill and bravery, down from his retreat under the stomach of a tame elephant and bound the two feet of the wild one. Thus the wild animals were captured one by one, and the success of the Kheda was achieved by the hunters.

Highly satisfied with the result of their enterprise, the hunters again assembled at the house of Mangla, the Magh. Thickened milk and curd of buffaloes were kept in readiness and they feasted on them. The fame of Golbadan now spread far and near. He had captured more than a hundred elephants whose price was over a lac of rupees.

AYANA BIBI

PREFACE TO THE BALLAD OF AYANA BIBI

The beginning of the ballads, like the precipitous path to the summit of a hill, is sometimes wearisome. Even in the best of the ballads we sometimes find the first cantos stale and monotonous. But gradually wending our way through tragic situations, we come in sight of really charming scenes of extraordinary poetic value. This is true of Kamalā, Madina and Mahishal Bandhu, the finest gems of this ballad-literature. The story-teller gradually reveals his power of weaving his plot so as to render it into a thing of beauty and art.

Ayana Bibi is one of such tales. The first few cantos are not only monotonous but even repelling. We have there the anxieties of the mother and the losses and crosses of the young merchant clumsily detailed in a rather diffuse story, not always relevant to the point. The incidents of the first part of this ballad look like wild plants which should have been uprooted or pruned by the gardener in order to make the whole thing a felicitous production of art.

But gradually the charming art of the poet comes into prominence with his exquisite skill in delineating the tender susceptibilities of the woman's heart, showing itself in its full bloom under severe trials. The Bengali women of the ballads have generally one striking characteristic. They are often as blythe as skylarks, singing their gay note of light humour when the smile of Fortune is on them. But when put to trial, they display the adamantine strength of their character and all the higher graces that adorn human nature.

We see Ayana for the first time in the house of her old father, full of maidenly shyness and grace—a lovely and tender woman facing a romantic situation which is a novel experience to her. The pain is, however, borne secretly. For a few years she enjoys the sweet sunshine of good fortune. How sweet are her words breathed in a whisper to her husband in which she asks him to bring her an ornament, a scented oil or a *Nilambari Sadi* from the market (VIII Ll. 1-12). He brings them with an exultant hope dreaming of the joy of seeing how beautiful she would look with these (VIII Ll. 8-10). This reminds us of a similar situation in Mahua, during the short-lived period of her nuptial happiness. The sunshine of Fortune enjoyed by Ayana Bibi for a little while is swallowed up by darkness for ever! Her tragic end is marked with a true dignity of unswerving love which does not flicker for a day inspite of the iniquitous treatment and unjust condemnation of her conduct by society and, the cruelest cut of all, her husband's succumbing to the social tyranny. When she comes back and sees her old home, the pathos created is even more appealing than that of Enoch Arden in his last hours of life, when he visits his own wife and children in the house of Philip, so touchingly described by Tennyson.

The woman never returns to seek the favour of the man who has taken another wife, abandoning her for ever. But her undecayed love ever burns without a flicker and she leaves such tender memories behind her as to produce their sure effect on her unfortunate husband and make the comforts of his newly wedded life bitter as wormwood to him. Like Dewan Dulal, he is driven mad by remorse and suffers for ever the pangs of his wrecked life.

Ayana is a charming vision of womanhood, and like Kanchanmala of the *Dhoparpat,* she becomes a towering figure towards the end of the story. We can never forget these women of Bengali ballads. Their sweetness, their great suffering and abiding love are virtues of which any nation could be proud. Hindu and Moslem women depicted in our ballads are equally noble in this respect and show their sisterhood in the conception of a common ideal which shows the glory of the country in which they are born, far above all communal narrowness.

The male type is decidedly lower and only serves as a background, in order to bring out conspicuously the whole wealth of feminine virtues by contrast. The character of Ujjal is a complex one. It should not be said that at any period of his life he lost his great love for his faithful wife. That he took another wife was not due to his falling under a fresh infatuation. The fault is not so much individual as racial. The Bengali loses his dignity, his honour and all sense of respect, when he stands on the brink of giving up his present easy life, not daring to encounter a change in his smooth course of life. Ujjal surely loved his wife as warmly as any husband did. He wandered for a time like a beggar in quest of Ayana Bibi and passed through unheard of hardships. But when his wife was unjustly condemned by society, he had not the boldness to stand by her and defy the authority of that most irrational hydra-headed monster—the community of which he was a member. From Khullana of the Chandi poems down to Malua of the ballad, wives have been banished times without number for no fault of theirs by the most irrational and ungracious society which instead of coming to the rescue in the hours of misfortune, as every other society does, has only helped their precipitous fall into the very worst pit of despair and misery. In the remote villages of Bengal many a Sita and Malua still weep their lot in silence, being given up by their kith and kin, because some one has touched them by force. If Ujjal had opposed the society he would have to give up his friends and suffer the hostility of his kith and kin, making his life at home unbearable. Neither a sense of justice nor what is higher than all other considerations, the love and sanctity of married life, could make him strong enough to stand by his wife in the hour of her perilous trial. Yet while we condemn him for this great drawback, we might take a compassionate view of his weakness. He was never an extraordinary man and we cannot expect from him any extraordinary sacrifice. Most men of the world succumb to considerations of personal comfort and easy life. This might make us feel a little sympathy for such persons as Ujjal, Chand Benod and Dewan Dulal, inspite of their weakness, though such weakness verges on villainy. The wrong they did was atoned for by their life-long remorse and suffering, and let us not be too hard upon these men who, after all, were not without a touch of higher emotion, and noble feelings.

The ballad of Ayana Bibi was collected by Chandrakumar De sometime in 1925.

DINESHCHANDRA SEN

Ayana Bibi

I

Mahmud Ujjal, a merchant, dwelt on the historic spot once occupied by the great merchant Chand. Listen, my friends, to the story of this Ujjal, the hero of my tale.

When a mere child his father died and he was brought up by the fostering care of his widowed mother. He had a sister who grew with him under the same affectionate care.

Their home stood at the city called the Narayan Khal; close along this place ran the lovely stream of Bheramana. The house was very beautiful to look at; its walls were built by split *khagra* plants artistically joined and the roof was made of fine *ulu* grass. They were joined by the thin herb known in the country-side as *sundhi-bet* so called from the sweet smell of the plant. The top of the house had decorations of pearls which reflected the rays of the sun and glittered all day long.

It was a crowded house, full of relations, kinsmen and retinue. Wealth and power, men and children had contributed to the glory of the joyous home of the merchant. The father of Ujjal died leaving this beautiful home for ever. The smiling house, so precious and dear to him, lay behind, when the master passed away before his time, with an insatiate desire.

However immense be your palace or great your power, ye mortals, do not place any hopes on them. The graveyard near the banks of the neighbouring river yawns with gaping mouth to receive you. Where do the great crowd go, after the dispersion of the market ? Men go away from this world like birds that fly away after temporary stay in night on the boughs of some trees. The big mansions, the temple compounds—are all left behind, and he who prided himself on these, never comes back to enquire about them, nor about his beloved wife and children. (Ll. 1-18.)

II

The widow felt her destitute condition and with wholehearted affection doted on the little child Ujjal and on her little daughter. A consolation came to her mind at the thought that when Ujjal would come of age, the long night of her misfortunes might come to an end, and she might once more be permitted to see the dawn of happiness. As the prop is to the blind man, this son and the daughter were to her, her hope and strength and the solace in her despair.

The boat drifting in the sea by the freak of wind seemed at last to be gladdened by the sight of the shore. The widow now found a resting place and consolation in her children. Two years rolled by and the son grew up little by little. When he was three years old, he was full of glee, smiling and playing. The mother's hopes waxed high as the lively boy increased in years and ever more did she look forward to the future in expectation.

Thus was added day unto day in hope and joy, till the young Ujjal reached the age of ten. The fond mother stored her little goods for meeting the exigencies of the coming years, and when her son had completed his sixteenth year, full of hope did she instruct him about his business. The house and the fertile lands around now engaged his attention. He purchased bullocks and took up farming and agriculture as his occupation.

In October, Ujjal cleared out the weeds and by the end of November he began to plough the lands. He got some work done by hired labourers, supervised their work and himself did a good deal not despising to take share in such work. In December the plants shot up and they looked promising, being planted in rows in five big plots of land. He watched the fields with great pains and when smitten with toil he returned home after his work every day with sweat dripping down to his feet, the kindly mother was sorry to see that her dear son still so tender in his years had to toil so hard. March was the harvest time and the hopeful youth with sharp scythe in hand went to his fields all lying on the borders of a swamp. He took some bullocks with him to carry the goods, and reaped the paddy that was ripe and returned home with it. The rice was husked and the chaff was cleared.

This first fruit of her son's labour the mother prized above everything else and bowed low meditating on the bounty of Saint Mādar whom she knew to be the giver of these gifts. She placed them next in her granary ; from the cart she took her first handful and reserved it for offering *sinni* to Pir Mādar. Now for the whole year the question of provision was solved and the mother's smile was now an index to her soul's contentment, showing how relieved she was from worry and indigence into which she had sunk since the death of her dear lord, for had not she spent many a day fasting, anxious to make provision for her children ? "May my son live long in happiness and health, and may he be strong as an iron rod to bear the stress of life," she prayed to God night and day, and she spread the upper part of her *sadi* filling it with rice, and promised *sinni* to the *pirs*, if her prayers were heard.

(Ll. 1-32.)

III

How wearisomely tedious is the long day of May, and how short is its night ! As soon as one shuts one's eyes in sleep it seems that one hears the steps of the Dawn.

The mango, the blackberry became ripe and the crows crew from the boughs of trees. How happily did the mother dress the sweet fruits for her son and when he ate, she sat near watching with eyes glistening with tears of joy. The long May at last came to an end ; the mother was sorry that she could not arrange for her son's marriage. In this month the birds build their blithe nests on the trees, and how glad would she be to give the lad a happy home with a bride, like these very birds who live with their mates. But May passed and she could not arrange the match. Then came June accompanied by the Queen of Seasons, the Rains. The incessant rains made the rivers and canals overflow. It was only the other day that the rivers were void of water and dry. To-day they are full, and the waves run tumultuously in a furious speed. This is the month when merchants go out to distant countries for trade. Look how the sails are flying and the boats rushing against the current favoured by the wind. Our merchant Ujjal wants to go with his cargo to foreign lands.

"You are busy with your household work, good mother, but stop for a moment, grant me permission to go out for trade," said he one day to the doting old lady.

In alarm the mother threw away the work she had taken in hand. How could she part with the jewel of her heart. "Do not," she said, "go to foreign lands ; be at home and earn your living from here. How can I bear to live without you ?" The young man drew pictures of his future prospects before his mother, but she was not tempted by them. All persuasion failed. He was, however, firm in his resolve and settled that he would set out the next day inspite of his mother's unwillingness.

A carpenter was called in and the planks of the ships were jointed by strong pins.[1] He struck them with a

[1] The Chittagong ships were built in such a way that the planks might be kept separated during the dry seasons, to be joined together again during the rains on the eve of a sea-voyage.

strong hammer to examine their condition and coloured them black with juice of mangostan. The roof, the covering and the upper horizontal timber were placed in their proper position. The ropes were made as strong as they could be.

The mother arose from her bed early in the morning, cooked meals for her son about to start for foreign lands. She sat near him when he ate. When the sun had not yet reached the mid-sky, it being eleven *dandas* after the dawn, he prepared for his voyage at the auspicious moment. The mother provided him with a good stock of *sali* rice and vowed to offer *sinni* to the *pirs* on his safe return. She stored fried *binni* rice in the store-room of the boat together with curd prepared at home with buffalo's milk and many other dainties besides.

She turned mad with grief in parting with him. After his departure her eyes showered tears like rains of June. She fell on the ground and cried losing all self-control. Alas! how can I describe the feelings of one who bears the child in her womb for ten months! Her affection is such as no one else can make even a distant approach to it.

When the banks of great rivers crumbled down by the force of the current during the rainy months, her heart beat in fears for her son gone to the high seas. When the flood was high, and the rivers chafed with their fierce whirlpools, the unfortunate mother walked to and fro by the river-side madly, and like a potter's wheel knew no rest. Ill at ease was she and could scarcely remain within the four walls of her house even for a few moments, but roamed where the current ran up-stream in high wind and the boats with sails unfurled made their way in great speed. There, she fancied that her son might be coming to meet her once more and assuage the pain of her heart. For six months not a day did her eyes become dry. Not receiving any message from her son, she passed all this time in the agony of her fears and anxieties. (Ll. 1-51.)

IV

Now my audience who have assembled here listen to what happened to the young merchant in his trading voyage. His boat bore him through the stream of Bheramana to the northern country. On the right was the bend of the river known as Shivar Bāk. The partner of the merchant Ujjal said, "Look here, young man. The last glimmer of evening is fading. This place is a notorious resort of thieves and robbers. It is not safe to ply our ships here." Other inmates of the boat likewise advised him to stay there at night. They said, "Let us not venture a journey through uninhabited tracts to-night." Here at this bend is a village close by. Let us stay here to-night. There was a big Hizal tree on the bank whose branches bent down to the water and the boat was bound to its trunk by ropes.

Ujjal went to the village for bringing a little fire. It was a sandy bank and the young merchant slowly proceeded towards a cottage where an old man was sitting alone. He was in a pensive mood and from the corner of his eyes, a few tears were glimmering in the setting sun. When he saw Ujjal, he called the youth and began to give an account of his life. He had no son, he said and had only a cousin who lived in the village. All his lands, his fields and gardens were swallowed by the greedy river near his hut. He was old and unfit for work and there was none to help him in his utter destitution.

"I take only a single meal a day, and I am afraid better days will never come to me! I have got a daughter," and as he touched this delicate point in his topics he could scarcely suppress a rush of feelings and his voice was choked. Controlling his feelings as best as he could he said, "She is to me what a prop is to a blind man, She is of

" She did not know what to do and was full of perplexity."   P, 147.

marriageable age, but where can I get a groom for her, absolutely helpless as I am? I shall go to the grave with this deep wound in my soul that I leave her entirely helpless." As he said this, he was overwhelmed with grief and could not say anything more. Here comes a change over the spirit of my tale.

The damsel Ayana had just stepped into the compound of the cottage with her pitcher full of water. She saw a stranger sitting there. Her cheeks reddened at the sight and she drew the flying ends of her *saḍi* closely round her body, and though she had apparently intended to enter the house, she felt a check as the stranger sat by in the compound; she did not know what to do and was full of perplexity. She had just stepped into youth and Ujjal thought that he had never seen a more handsome girl in his life. When he saw her eyes, he took his own eyes away, suppressing the desire to see them again. Her long hair almost reached her ankles and the charm of her person was scarcely hidden by her *saḍi*. At the sight of the maiden, the youth's mind felt a strange attraction. He had seen many a *champak* flower in his own village and he thought she was the prettiest of them all.

When introducing himself to the old man, he gave out the names of his parents and mentioned that of his native village also. At this account the old man said, "Your father and my humble self were fast friends, when we were quite young." He entreated the young man to pay a visit to him on his way back.

Now Ujjal wanted a little fire and the bashful maiden handed it to him in an earthen pot. While giving it, she cast her eyes on him and the four eyes met. The youth's soul was, as it were, sold for ever to the maiden at the first sight. He marched next day towards far East with thoughts never turned from the vision he had witnessed on that sandy bank. (Ll. 1-52.)

V

When doing her household work what was it that made dear Ayana shed tears ? Who is the thief that had stolen her treasure? When she was about to light the evening lamp, she stood like a statue forgetting what she was about to do. When she went to the river ghat, she forgot that it was for bathing that she had come there but stood gazing at the stream. If she saw a boat coming she fancied that perchance her lover might be returning in it. Why did the girl throw away the water from her pitcher and over again go to the landing ghat with the empty vessel? The bathing time was past, but she stood on the shore gazing on. Weak she had grown and a pallor marked her cheeks. No one understood the pang of her heart. Secret grief has no cure. A sore disease, a heavy debt and grim poverty—are evils which absorb one's mind and afford one no rest, but none of these is to be compared with the pangs of love felt in the first bloom of youth.

The ship of Ujjal, the merchant, went eastward, running against the current. The *manjhis* rowed it day and night and after having gone five bends, they set sail under a favourable wind, but this wind of the east was not good for health and the merchant felt feverish and was laid down,—his principal malady however was of the heart. When he closed his eyes, he saw before him the image of Ayana Bibi, and when he opened them again the same image haunted him still. In his dreams, in his wakeful state, Ayana Bibi became the sole object of his thought. The fever was more or less a pretext to lie down and follow the train of his thought undisturbed. After three months he visited the ports of eastern countries. For a time the transactions were of a doubtful character. At times he profited and at others he lost, but in the end he lost all that he had. The goods he had purchased with the savings of many years had to be given away for less than their cost price. His partner said that the merchant had not only lost his goods but his head also in the transactions. After six months, he was bound homeward.

There was that delightful spot under a large Hizal tree whose leaves rustled the livelong day as they touched the stream, which the merchant reached again and he ordered the ship to be moored there for the night. When it was dawn, the merchant expressed his desire to stop there for the day.

He went along the sandy bank to the cottage. It was empty. It looked like a cage from which the bird had flown away. The merchant wandered about enquiring about the inmates. He saw near the cot—a grave, and like a mad man anxiously asked the neighbours information about the old man. He learnt that the old man had died two months ago. The only sign of his existence that he had left in this world was the grave. In replies to his enquiries about Ayana Bibi, some said they knew nothing about her and others spread evil reports. He stayed there the next day also but his doubts were not cleared.

"O my partner, tell my mother, 'Your son Ujjal is not alive.' If she makes further enquiries tell her that her son has been drowned in the Great Eastern River. Tell her that Ujjal would never again visit his historic home on the site of Chand's palace."

Like a mad man Ujjal wandered about the villages and went from door to door begging alms. Some were kind enough and gave him a handful but others abused him. Some asked him, "Why have you turned a beggar at this youthful age?" Some people thought there was a reason for this, whilst others said there was none. From one village he went to another. When the young housewife was about to give him alms, the old mother-in-law came in and said, "No! no! you must not show your face to the youth." Some even openly said, "This lad is a love-lorn young man." The goldsmith knows his metal whether it is gold or trinket; so does one, who has one's own experience in love, know it in others.

Young Ujjal spent there days in begging but got almost nothing. (Ll. 1-66.)

VI

The evening was fading with its last glimmer in the village pathway. The young man was going from one village to another. The smoke issuing from the hearths darkened the bamboo groves. The crows and the cuckoos flew to their own nests and the village path could not be traced in darkness. Ujjal Mahmud thought of spending the night under a tree and then of going at daybreak a-begging as usual. Begging was really no question with him, nor hunger was it that drove him from place to place. Six long months he spent seeking his dear Ayana Bibi in this way. Matrons of the village houses sometimes took pity on him and offered him meals in the daytime but it was not infrequent that he passed his days without any meal whatever. (Ll. 1-11.)

VII

With the wallet in his hand, the young Fakir was crying for alms near the gateway, "Hurry up, good friends, give me alms."

A girl came out from the house with a plate full of alms. But as she looked at the youth, the plate fell down from her hands. When eyes met eyes, they were full of tears. Only once she had seen him but the impression could not be effaced in life. "I am not a beggar, dear girl, and you need not give me alms. It is for you that

I have taken this guise and been wandering from place to place. Six months have passed and weary am I. People of the world call me mad. It is not rice that I want, nor money. I want you, dearest. If you agree, I will go back to my home with you.

Ayana Bibi.

"I am in my uncle's house. My father is dead. For these six long months I have been spending my days, weeping and crying in vain. I am living here in the house of relations who are not close to me. Take me from here and I shall go with you wherever you may wish."

The union of lime and betel is a good thing. When eyes meet eyes, that is a happy meeting to be sure. But when heart is united with heart, that is perhaps the best of all unions. One who knows will surely say that love is the best thing in this world. Though a man may die for love, there is no reason to regret, for the best end of his life has been achieved. (Ll.1-22.)

[*Prose.*—The girl was about to be forcibly betrothed to a son of the uncle in whose house she was staying. Ujjal absconds with her and returns home and marries Ayana.]

VIII

Ujjal was going to the market. "What am I to bring for you, my beloved?" he asks.

"Bring for me a hair comb made of mica," she gently whispers.

Through a short way which cuts an angle with the main road, Ujjal went to the market. He had promised to bring a nose ornament for Ayana. It was called the *Nakbalāk*.

The young merchant was bound for the market again, for he had promised to give her a *saḍi* called the *asmantara* (starry sky).

Ujjal thought in this strain, "This *sāḍi* with flowery designs interwoven in it will fit her so nicely. She will wear it and go to bathe in the river with a pitcher of water. I will wait in the pathway for the pleasure of seeing how handsome she looks in her new *saḍi*."

Again the youth ran to the market. It was for bringing scented oil for Ayana Bibi.

As the evening lamp dispels the darkness of the house and brightens it, so this wife brought light and joy into the house. The mother and the sister were exceedingly pleased and the joy of Ujjal knew no bounds.

Now the youngman paid attention to the duties of his household. In December he made himself busy with the plants and in January he watered them. Ayana prepared curd with buffalo's milk and she offered it to her husband when he sat to eat. The mother had taken care to prepare fried *binni* rice and she served it too. Fatigued with field-work Ujjal returned home every day with sweat in his brows. Ayana with a fan stood near and gently fanned him. The cool water of the river offered by her renovated his energies in the scorching rays of the sun. Along with labourers he did very hard work every day in the field but there was a sweet smile in his face that indicated his inward joy, for he was ever more pleased that Ayana was now his own. Like unto a creeper bending at the gentle breeze, youth had given a modest grace to her gait. The sky-coloured *saḍi* that she wore gently moved in the air adding loveliness to her handsome figure. (Ll.1-37.)

IX

May drew to an end. The mangoes became ripe and hung from the boughs of trees. The work of the field was finished by this time. The new wife was overjoyed to dress the fruits and served them to her husband. The night was so joyful and short that the couple did not know how swiftly it passed away. "Don't leave the bed but rest dearest, a little while more, for the night has passed away so quickly that I have not tasted my full share of joy." (Ll.1-37.)

X

May passed away in this way. June looked like a water-nymph. The nymph paid visit from house to house with the clouds looking like her pitchers. Seated in the sky she poured water from them into the plains. The deep murmur of waters could be heard from rivers, ponds and swamps. Oh! whence has this overflow in its mad course suddenly come over the earth? The small pond, the fields are now all under water. Whence have come these high waves with foam in their mouth? The boats of the merchants with sails unfurled are seen rowing against the stream. The partner came to Ujjal and said, "Half of June is over. What are you doing my friend? The season for trade will soon pass away. If you do not earn when you have the vigour of youth, you will regret in old age."

Hearing these words of the partner, Ujjal called the carpenter to repair his ships.

The old planks were replaced by new ones and they were joined by iron plates. Sails were made of new clothes and he became ready to start from home.

Ujjal took leave of his mother and his sister and then went to Ayana Bibi and said, "O my Ayana, dear as life, grant me leave for six months. I am bound for a distant country for trade. My mother and sister are here. Live with them, awaiting my return with patience. My mother is a mother unto you and my sister is not a whit less your own sister. The good neighbours are kind to you and they are like your brothers and sisters. Be happy with them. After six months, if by God's grace and blessings of the saints, I am so lucky as to get my lost treasure again, I will once more be happy with you. For six months, I will be flying like a bird of the season in regions unknown. Don't think I shall forget for a moment my loving wife. Dear to me you are as my eye-balls.

Ayana

"Youth is not like gold, silver or any other metal of the kind ; if it breaks, it may be repaired. Youth once lost, can never be repaired again. Do not go, my love, during this short-lived youth.

"You see this flood of June. It knows no bounds, maddened by its inward joy, but when October will come, there will be no trace of the flood; it will subside. Such is youth. Stay my love, so long as youth lasts.

"A woman's youth is precious and short. It decays after its brief period of joy and once gone, it never returns. Do not go my love."

She lamented in this way but all in vain.

On Friday the merchant offered *sinni* at the mosques as a preliminary step before starting. On Saturday his boat left the shores of home. At the time of parting Ayana said weeping, "Swear by my life that when the clouds will roar in the sky, you will order the boatmen to cast anchors. When night will approach, the boats should not be rowed. Do not, for my sake, Oh my love, go to the regions inhabited by the barbarians, the Kookis and the Bhangars. Within six months, you must return home. Alas! what treasure will you get by trade! (better than the joy of my company which you reject!)

He went away leaving Ayana at home. (Ll. 1-73.)

The ballad is incomplete here. Evidently some passages are missing. The singer here narrates them in prose.

[Prose.—"The partner returned with the message that Ujjal was drowned in the river. The boat capsized, and many of the crew could not be traced. The survivors gave this information, so it could not be disbelieved. Ayana became maddened with grief. One night she left home without telling anything to the inmates of the house. She cried and wandered about in the depth of forests like one insane. She chanced to meet a kind-hearted man who took her to his house. His seven sons made a great search for Ujjal and at last found him out lying in a precarious condition on the shoal of a river,—completely broken down by six months' illness. Ayana returned home with her husband.

He gradually regained his strength and began to work in the field. At this stage the villagers raised a troublesome question. They said that Ayana was absent from home for six months. Nobody knew where she had gone. After much discussion on the point the decision of the community was that if Ujjal kept his wife at home, no member of the village would drink or eat with him. Weak as Ujjal was, he lost his wits at this juncture, and resolved to banish his wife to save himself from calumny. On the pretext of going out for trade with his wife, he came to the shoal of a river and leaving Ayana in the lonely place, went away. Thus abandoned by him she wandered about in an absolutely forlorn state. At this time a band of gypsies called the Kurunjias, visited the place."]

X

These Kurunjias were a strange people. They lived in boats and went from place to place for trade. Their men cooked meals and did household duties and their women went hawking in villages. They sold spice and other articles and wandered from one country to another. In fact it might be said that in twelve months they visited thirteen climes and got plenty of knowledge of life in the swamps and marshy slopes of Eastern countries. Their men were idlers who scarcely came out of the boats, but the women did trade and all their outdoor work. They rowed their boats night and day, and once happened to come to the shore where Ayana was wandering. They were looking out for fuel and chanced to meet the young woman there.

"Who are you, beautiful one, and what country do you come from? Why do you live in this jungly land all alone?" Said one of them.

"I have no home. I have been hit hard by Destiny. I have no parent, no brother. Like a weed drifting in a stream, I roam about driven by Destiny. Providence has sent me to this forest-land. So hard is my lot that if I happen to take shelter under a tree, the sun sends its scorching rays through the leaves and burns me. So hard is my lot that if I come to the river for drowning myself, the river dries up.

"I find no sharp weapon to kill myself with, no hole do I find to hide myself in the bosom of the earth."

"Come with me, dear one, you will be like my daughter. I shall be like your mother."

Thus did Ayana find a resting place and went from one country to another in the boat of the gypsies. But though the gypsies were willing to render her all help, they could not trace the place of her husband,—the historic seat of Chand the merchant. She took spices on her head for hawking as the gypsies did. Tears rolled down her cheeks, as she sold them in villages and towns. To every one whom she saw she put one and the same question, *viz.*,—"Will you tell me, where once stood the palace of Chand? Which is the path, which is the river that would lead me to that dear spot? Shall I go up the stream or down it to find the place?"

Some said, "We remember having heard of such a place." Others said that they knew nothing about it. For three years she sought the home of her husband to no purpose.

Once a herdsman who was leading a number of buffaloes gave the information, "Thirteen bends of the river from hence and you will find the spot once occupied by the princely house of Chand."

The sun had set. The housewives were lighting their lamps. She put the same query to them. The gypsies had moored their boats there at her request.

(Ll. 1-43.)

XI

In the morning she put on the dress of a Kurunjia woman. She put on a striped *saḍi* of jute tightly round her waist in the fashion of these gypsies, and her chignon she made high-topped. She wore a necklace of small Gunja beads, and on her head she carried a basket containing the little things of her trade. The Kurunjia women in a long row accompanied her and then she visited the village for selling these things.

Yes, it was that favoured spot, the historic town of Chand. The trees were standing as they did before. The crows and the parrots had built their nests as of old. But all hopes of home and hearth were lost to the girl now. With anxious steps full of hesitancy and doubt, she proceeded towards the place which had once been her home. Her heart throbbed, and in her tremor her feet faltered at every step.

Three years had passed and once again she was there. The houses were standing which once she called her own. She had come to see this home and the face of her dear husband after three long years. She gently wiped away the tears of her eyes with the flying end of her *saḍi*, but who was there to feel sympathy for the unfortunate one? At one end of the compound she saw the *mendi* plants she had herself planted, now grown to their full height. The house, the doors which she used to dust and clean with her own hands daily stood there as before. It was now like the nest of the bird *babui*, which it weaves with care but which gives it no shelter during the rains. The house and the dear things were all as before but the doors of her own home were shut for ever against Ayana. Mahmud Ujjal had married again and was happily spending his days with his new wife. He had shunned poor and unfortunate Ayana, as though she were his enemy. She saw her co-wife with a baby in her arms, healthy and bright. The mother was fondling the child in a sportive mood.

"How cruel is the fate of this unfortunate woman? Where is your home gone and the dear things you loved so well? Leaving all this, why have you turned a gypsy and are roaming vagrantly in the village? Whose daughter are you, oh girl? where is your home and who are your parents? By God, give us the answer. We have not seen you long, but no matter, it seems that you are the girl for whom we have been shedding tears night and day these long years." Thus said the mother-in-law and sister-in-law who wept at seeing Ayana, and her own eyes too streamed in tears as she heard them.

"I have no mother, no father. It is owing to my cruel Destiny that I have lost both of them. It is due to my bad luck again that I am a wandering beggar. But how is it that for me you should be weeping too? I cry because I see that you are so much like my dead mother. I am reminded of my childhood as I see you. If playing under the *khagara* plants, my body got soiled, my mother would gently brush away the dust with the skirt of her

"There is nobody to feel for me." P. 159.

sadi. If I cried, she would come running to me! Now I wander from place to place crying night and day but nobody comes to me with a word of sympathy. There was a time when if I lay on the ground for a little while, she would come and affectionately take me up in her arms. But just conceive my intense pain at the thought that there is nobody even to feel for me.''

Then she took up her articles, placed them in the basket and with tears that did not cease from flowing, gently wended her way back to the boat of the gypsies.

* * * *

''If it is really Ayana who came to see us, I should rather beg from door to door and live with her.

''If it is really Ayana who came to see us, I will leave this accurst society, so that I might live with her undisturbed.

'' If it is you, Ayana, who came to see us, do not go, do not leave us and go again to distant countries.

'' If it is you Ayana who came to us, I will rather go to a forest and live with you though branded and given up by society.''

When the mother-in-law cried in this way, Ayana threw behind her back the curly hair, all dishevelled, which she had bound into a knot; she took off the basket from her head, and cared not for it. Like a mad woman she ran into the boat of the gypsies.

'' Row the boat as swiftly as you can, it is the haunt of robbers;'' cried she, ''speed on, let us go to some other country.''

The gypsies raised a hue and cry and swiftly rowed their boats. The city of Chand was left behind and the boat flew off like an arrow into the mid-river.

''Alas, my home is gone, and lost are all my hopes. My own—my dearest—home has become another's. What happiness is now left to me that I should drag on this miserable existence ? There is not so much space in this house as would provide a corner for me. If the ties of love had not been broken thus, he could have realised what I have suffered.

"Oh ! the birds and beasts of this city hold your tongue. Do not breathe out the information that I have come here. Should he ask about me, tell him, 'She, your enemy, who caused you a lot of trouble is drowned in the river.'

"Be happy, my husband, with that beautiful baby in your arms. Be happy with your new wife. I, the unfortunate one, have seen your face stealthily and my best wishes have been fulfilled. I will not come again, and my only prayer now is that you may live in happiness. Beyond this I want nothing."

The current of the river in June flew like an arrow and the beautiful body of Ayana was seen floating on it. No father, no mother, no brother had she. So if she went to the strange land where she could not be traced, there was none to seek her out.

Chorus.—The merchant Ujjal cries for the lost one. The gentle breeze whispered to his ears the tragic tale, and the sky now and then spoke to him in the language of the clouds.

"Seeking you, O Ujjal, she the unfortunate one, had come. She was not a Kurunjia nor a gipsy. It was she, your unfortunate Ayana who had come to seek you. The bird had come to seek its own nest. Do not doubt but it was she—the same face, the same nose, the same handsome figure. It was to seek you that she had come. No one made a kind enquiry, no one asked her history. She came like a flash of lightning and like lightning she disappeared into darkness."

The merchant maddened with grief asked everybody whom he saw, "Where is my beautiful Ayana gone ? Which is the path that she has taken ?" He turned a fakir and wandered about from place to place. From village to village he went with the selfsame enquiry. He roamed from forest to forest with the same question on his lips.

The stars of the sky became dim losing their lustre. The flowers that had bloomed faded away and for the rest of his life Ujjal, the dear son of his mother, became a wanderer in foreign countries.

THE BALLAD OF KAMAL THE MERCHANT

PREFACE TO THE BALLAD OF KÁMAL THE MERCHANT.

The ballad of Kamal the merchant, is one of those tales of the cruel treatment, by a stepmother, of the sons of her co-wife with which every Bengali woman of the older generation was familiar. The story related in this ballad tallies in many points with that of Bijay-Basanta popularised by Kangal Harinath in his modern version of it published by Messrs. Gurudas Chatterjee & Sons, Calcutta. So popular was this version at one time that by the year 1913 it had passed through fourteen editions. I have dealt with this story at some length in my "Folk Literature of Bengal" published by the University of Calcutta (pp. 173-78).[1]

I have already referred to the fact of some of the Bengali ballads being rather irrelevant in their earlier cantos. It is said of our great poet Kalidas that while reading one of his masterpieces to a flower-woman who was his great admirer, the poet perceived that she was not quite pleased with the beginning,—upon which he remarked that his poem was like a noble mountain; the ascent was steep, requiring a good deal of patience on the part of a traveller who would resolve to scale its glorious summit. The same, I beg to repeat, is true of some of the finest of our ballads. Mahua, Chandravati, Bhabna, Dhopar Pat, Manjurma and a few others possess an all-absorbing interest from the very outset. But many of the rest are marred

[1] There are many printed versions of this story extant besides the one written by Harinath. I may name some of them : (1) "The Story of Shit-Basanta" by Golam Kader, published by Afazuddin Ahmed from 155/1, Musjidbari Street, Calcutta ; (2) "Shit Basanta," published by Dakshinaranjan Mazumdar in his Thakurmar Jhuli; (3)-Sharat-Basanta, published by Rev. Lal Behari De in his Folk Tales of Bengal. Kangal Harinath in his version changed the name of 'Shit' or 'Swet' into Bijay.

by the defect to which I have alluded, and the present ballad is one of this latter class. It has, however, a mediocre poetic value. The descriptions of the riches of the merchant and the virtues of his wife Surangini are stereotyped and commonplace. But from the time that she falls ill, the interest becomes unflagging. The pathos created by the misfortunes of the children and their unhappy nurse Maiphula is full of touching appeal. The *baramashi* which is one of the recurrent factors in all Bengali ballads, has some points of remarkable poetic merit; but as much of its charm lies in the unadorned beautiful language of the country, I do not think that it has been preserved in the English rendering. The sea voyage, another inevitable factor in our ballad literature, gives us some interesting information about old Bengali trade, and the account of the various religious rites performed by the housewife, found in this poem, unfolds the inner life of Hindu homes. The character of the nurse Maiphula is a bold conception and typifies the devotion and unfaltering love of a woman in an atmosphere of villainy and unrelenting cruelty. The rest including Surangini herself are traditional and commonplace.

In this ballad we come across a rare case in which a Hindu wife is guilty of adultery. Excepting in a very few instances in some Indian classics of almost pre-historic antiquity, the *Kathasaritsagar* and the *Panchatantra*, Hindu writers have seldom delineated an untrue wife. The story of Bijay-Basanta, popularly known in the countryside as Shit-Basanta, is the original from which the present ballad has been partly copied. In that story, however, the step-mother does all wicked things, not sparing the most heinous contrivances to kill the children, but she is not faithless to her husband. The present ballad-maker has introduced an innovation, repellent to Hindu taste and given the psychology of a married woman's heart in love with a stranger with considerable force, though she is by no means made the object of the reader's admiration. There is another ballad called Jiralani in which a Hindu wife is described as contriving the murder of her husband with the help of her lover. I have not been able to find out the names of the author of any of these ballads, but I shall not be surprised, if the authors are found out to be Muslims after all. A third one of this nature will be found in this volume. These three ballads out of hundreds that we have collected give portraitures of unfaithful wives, though none of these women is a prominent character in the ballads. We have found many Anna Kareninas in European literature. The Spanish ballads bristle with instances of disloyal wives, some of whom are glorified In Russian literature, we have perhaps the most abnormal and repelling types of such women. But the Hindu poets as a rule have abhorred to delineate infidelity on the part of heroines. We find in our literature intriguing women of the worst sort like Durvala and Manthara, but an unfaithful wife is a rarity.

The present ballad seems to have been a production of the Eighteenth century, when the ethical standard had fallen low. It was an age of love tales such as *Kamini-kumar and Chandrakanta* ; but that the court influence of Krishnanagar should have spread down to the peasants' cot seems somewhat strange, though the honest village-poet has used a good deal of caution in keeping his style above reproach, avoiding erotic situations. The language of this ballad is very fine with occasional poetic flashes.

This ballad was collected by Babu Asutosh Chaudhury from Chittagong on the 27th August 1925, from many men of the rustic villages of the district, principally from a washerman named Nabachandra who is absolutely unlettered. The city of Basantinagar described in the ballad is said to have been situated on the river Kaicha,

The Karnaphuli is called by that name by the villagers of that district. But I do not agree with Ashu Babu in believing the ballad to be an historical one. He has attempted in his correspondence with me to identify the villages mentioned in the ballad, with some of those small islands of which mention is found in the copper-plate inscriptions of Damodar Deb (Saka 1165) and those described in the Rajamala of Tipperah. I think his theory is strained too far.

As I have already stated, the story related in this ballad occurs so often in the nursery tales and folk songs of Bengal and it is so familiar throughout this province that we cannot believe it to have any historical origin. It is a folk tale, pure and simple. The ballad-maker has only retold a story told a hundred times before and after him, introducing some innovations and new features. Every singer who repeats an old song adds such things to his material.

The ballad of Kamal the merchant, contains 872 lines and I have divided it into 19 cantos.

Kamal the Merchant

(1)

On the banks of the river Kaicha stands a city named Basanti and here lived Kamal, the princely merchant. He was the master of a palatial house, a two-storied building, well-protected by walls on all sides. Around it were gardens, and the front-gate was grand beyond all description. In the outer compound was a large tank with well-built ghats of brick and mortar. Ships, sloops and shampans he had without number, and equally immense was the number of his cows which supplied him with milk for daily use. Who could again count the large number of goats, buffaloes and sheep that he owned? So immense were the hoards that he had gathered on his treasury that instead of counting them, he weighed his gold in scales as people weigh their paddy and rice. Then he was rich not only in his material wealth, but he was also particularly fortunate in his wife who was as devoted as she was handsome, and who, indeed, in beauty and character was verily like the harvest-goddess Lakshmi. The innumerable qualities of this exquisitely beautiful lady pass all description. It was a great pleasure with her to feed others, and she was like the goddess Annapurna herself, whose store of food never ran short. Surangini was, indeed, as good as a mother to her neighbours. The poor and the destitute had their meals at her house every day. Guests and Brahmins were always there and they also daily received the open-handed hospitality of the mistress of the house. Pious she was and of a noble and generous nature. She worshipped the gods and goddesses as prescribed in the Shastras, and it seemed that Lakshmi the goddess of luck particularly was constant in showering her bounties on the house, pleased with the devotion and piety of its mistress. In the summer month of April, Surangini propitiated the Tulasi plant by letting drops of water fall on it from a bored earthen pot. In the month of May, she worshipped the goddess Sashthi who presides over children's welfare and she worshipped the stars and the earth in the auspicious month of June. In July she continued her rites and in addition, had the sacred lore recited by Brahmin priests. Bhadrakali was worshipped in August, and September was the month specially dedicated to the goddess Durga. She ate the food on the first day of October cooked on the last day of September—an act of merit observed by the ladies of Bengali homes. In the month of November, she waited on holy hermits and the Moon-god claimed her attention in December. In January it was the Sun unto whom she rendered her devotions with offerings of red lotus, and in February came the swinging festival in which the union of Radha and Krishna was celebrated, the images being rocked to and fro. In March, the last month of the Bengali year, was the great god Shiva worshipped with due pomp and show. Thus passed twelve months in the observance of pious rites, and the good lady as a result of her manifold virtues was blessed with two sons. Chandmani and Suryamani were their names and they were, as it were, the light of the house and the soul of their parents. Chandmani was seven years old and beautiful to look at. He was the darling of his parents, and on his forehead were very bright lines which flashed and bespoke good fortune. In his horoscope it was written that he was destined to be a king. The younger son Suryamani was five years old, and he too was so handsome that he seemed more like a charming doll of gold than a human being of flesh and blood. The two brothers seemed, indeed, to be like the famous brothers Ram and Lakshman sung of in the Ramayana.

Servants and maids they had in plenty, and thanks to the management of Surangini, peace and happiness reigned supreme in every part of the house. She had a maid-servant named Maiphula. So trusted was she in the house that Chandmani and Suryamani treated her as one of the elders of the house and called her aunt. She had become a widow when a mere girl and now was she in the full bloom of youth. Kamal was the master of large pastures and fields, and had countless ploughmen and day-labourers who worked in his pastures night and day. There were other employees too, who did the household work and lived in his court. He had a clerk named Gobardhan loved and trusted by the merchant as his brother. Expert was he in his own clerical work and drew a pay of rupees thirty a month. He lodged and boarded at his master's house. Kamal plied a brisk shipping business and had besides a host of men doing work in his ships. His trading business fetched a large income every year. The two-storied building was packed full of relatives and dependants and his coffers were ever rich in gold. Wants he had none, but so rich was he indeed, that he scarcely touched silver but took his food from plates of gold. Destiny puts a moonshaped mark on the brow of those on whom she showers her bounties and our happy merchant was one of these men. (Ll. 1-62.)

(2)

It was the month of June. The rainy season had set in and the rivers were swollen with water. Canals and ponds too overflowed their banks, and the rivers and banks looked like one silvery sheet of water. Rain poured ceaselessly on the plains from the sky. On a dusky day of June Surangini approached her husband saying that she had contracted fever and cold, that her heart was weak and throbbed. She had a presentiment of approaching death and she had come there to bid farewell to him for good. She said further: "But I leave both my darlings with you and you must duly look after them. I feel as though I am plucking out my heart when I am going to leave the dear ones to your care." "Out with your nonsense," answered the merchant, "if you do not live, the world is all chaos and darkness to me. Cheer up, for you will soon get better. Why should you have such dark misgivings, my dear? Cast these gloomy thoughts aside and cheer yourself up." But alas! the merchant's hopes were idle. He knew not that Death shows no respect for rank or fortune but when one's term of life is over, the grim God is sure to come and claim his toll, irrespective of one's rank and pedigree. Our life is like a bird enclosed in a magic cage with an intricate machine working within. As the machine ceases to work on a certain day, the bird encaged within feels its period ended. Thus suddenly ends our journey in this earth in a mysterious way. It was so hard to hear, it was sad, extremely sad. A three days' fever was about to carry Surangini off and there arose a deep cry of agony from the house at this impending calamity. Before closing her eyes for ever, she clasped Maiphula by the hand and said, "Here do I leave both my darlings to you. When I am gone, there will be none for them to call mother. It will be your duty to look after them. In their hunger you will give them food and their thirst you will assuage with cool drinks. When they are in misery, it is for you to clasp them to your bosom with a mother's affection." Then she cast her eyes at her husband and gasped in pain, "Give me leave for I am passing away." "Alas, alas!" cried the merchant, "Is this to be my fate?" Surangini's voice had failed and she met her husband's query with tears. The merchant struck his forehead in an agony of grief and it was all over now. Life is a vain show. No one has any permanent holding here. All our ties and affections are like tales or pictures drawn by poets and painters—they are unreal fictions. Surangini's life slowly passed away. It was a pity that Death should have visited her when she was in the prime of life, enjoying its pleasures which fortune had showered in plenty. It is as if a cruel wind put out a lamp that had been shining resplendently in a house on a festive night.

Kamal broke into a ceaseless lament for Surangini and so did Chandmani and Suryamani. The merchant wept saying, "To whom have you left Chand and Surya, the darlings of your heart? Who will now raise their drooping hearts by affection and cheer? Since you are gone, my wealth is come to naught and so is all my business. Of what avail are they or my two-storied palace now to me?" He beat his head against the floor of the house and wept on. "This bed bestrewn with flowers on which you used to recline, lies empty now, and so is the house of which one day you were the shining light. Who will henceforth see to my comforts with the same affection taking care of this milk-white soft bed strewn over with flowers, fill my betel box with care and do those little things which have become great in my eyes owing to the love that inspired them?"

As the news of Surangini's death spread abroad, all the neighbours wept for the good lady. Maiphula, wild in her sorrow, rolled in the dust lamenting pitifully. The braids of her hair were unloosened. In her excess of grief she had no eye for this, and did not care to bind them. She who reigned in the merchant's home was gone, and he lay in a forlorn condition in an empty room. He wept so bitterly for his lost wife that it seemed as if the very leaves of trees were moved to pity and dropped down to the ground in grief. The funeral fire was soon extinguished but the embers of grief still blazed on, burning his soul night and day.

The last rites of Surangini were duly performed. A chariot of light seemed to take her off to heaven, pious lady that she was, and in this glorious transformation, the highest end of her life was achieved. Many pundits flocked to Basantinagar. They were given silver pitchers and also gold mohurs as *dakshina*. Brahmins and other respectable men were fed in large numbers, and innumerable also were the guests assembled from the merchant's own part of the country. The poor had a gala day and hundreds of vagrants whom nobody cared to invite were attracted by the noise and report spread in the countryside and they too had hearty meals in the merchant's house. (Ll.1-64.)

(3)

Now, listen, my friends, to the many calamities which visited the hapless merchant after the death of his beloved wife. A ship was lost in the dark waters of a distant land and it meant the ruin of a large capital. To add to this, the merchant sustained heavy losses in his trade. Such indeed, is the order of the day everywhere. Money, you must remember, is as fickle as the waters of a flow-tide current. It is quick to come and is as quick to go. Luck is like a machine. When it works, it works well ; but if it is out of order in any of its parts, everything goes wrong. Kamal had many employees and they now exploited their master's plight as best as they could.

One day Gobardhan came to the merchant and said, "Sir, if you do not marry now, you will come to grief afterwards." "What nonsense is it you say!" replied Kamal. "Supposing I am wedded to a second wife, the chances are that she will engross all my attention and who will then remain to feel for my darlings, Chandmani and Suryamani? My ship is lost and I am now hard hit by fate. A wreck of myself in every respect, I can no more return to my happy old days than can the two fragments of a broken earthen pitcher unite into one as before." "But don't you see," persisted Gobardhan, "your happy home is being ruined beyond hope? Don't you see that your prodigious business covering lakhs of rupees is breaking up? The remedy that we venture to suggest is that you should marry again and settle down. Every home worth the name should have its presiding mistress. Bring one to take charge of the house and then concentrate your mind in your work again. If you only give us the command, we can make necessary arrangement."

Thus did the neighbours drive the idea of marriage home into his head. Man's mind, I need hardly remind you, is as unstable as the waters on a Kachu leaf. If once stirred, it swings hither and thither and all its steadiness gives way. To return to our merchant, he thought over the proposal of marriage and though wavering for a time, at last gave his consent. As soon as it was known that Kamal had agreed, negotiations were set on foot on all sides. Gobardhan went to Dharmapur and there chose the daughter of Dharmamani as the bride. Sonai was her name and she was exquisitely beautiful to look at. To make a long story short, she was married off to merchant Kamal. But such was the freak of Fate that he could never win the affection of his newly wedded wife.

* * * *

The merchant was disconsolate with grief for his deceased wife and had, therefore, no heart to join in the frivolous enjoyments of youth. But Sonai was in the first bloom of youth, and maddened with desire for those pleasures for which her husband was no fit mate having grown too old. Her eyes cast anxious glances everywhere and she was always in smiles that bespoke her passionate heart. She was like a bark floating in the full-tide of youthful passion. The current ran in a wavy dance and the heart of Sonai was tossed about in it.

Some months passed off in this way and soon Kamal fell into bad days. Fortune is a very exacting mistress. She does not shower her blessings on a home where there is vice. The flippant unsteady nature of Sonai scared her away. Now the merchant's fabulous wealth was all gone. Ten sloops of his were on the waters, laden with paddy but they were visited by a tempest when about to start and were all lost. His wealth was gone and so were his honour and prestige. His cows died of smallpox and the stored up paddy in the granary was stolen by thieves,—that of the fields failing for excessive rise of water. Kamal's fortune was thus fast ebbing away.

Now let us return to Sonai. Gradually she contracted a passion for Gobardhan till her soul became maddened by it. He was a handsome person and though middle-aged, had lost nothing of his youthful spirit. He was of a cheerful disposition and had an ardent and passionate nature. He slowly reciprocated the attentions of the mistress of the house. It was his first love and he heeded not, therefore, the voice of discretion. In such a state it was no wonder that he gave his heart away to one who wanted him and was so beautiful. One day Sonai called away Gobardhan to a lonely place and said, "A word with you, please. I was very happy in my father's house and it is you who have brought me to this misery. Here there are thorns pricking me from all sides and how am I to bear them? My secret grief burns me like fire by day and night. It is a terrific fire that you have dropped me into. But you are not only indifferent but seem yourself to connive at my suffering. Here there is none whom I can call my own. How am I to allay the fire that is burning me?" Her eyes gave a charming glance as she spoke and it took the heart of Gobardhan captive then and there and easily did he appreciate the state of her feelings. He said nothing and went off. Sonai's next step was to write a letter to Gobardhan. She addressed him as her darling. The contents of the letter which fully revealed her heart ran as follows :—"Listen to me, my love. I am mad in my passion for you and may I entreat you to be sympathetically bent on one suffering so hard? I will rivet my soul to yours and make you mine own. This wretch of a husband is like a withered tree which is of use only as fuel. He cannot respond to the warmth of my heart and it is for you that I pine. Whatever I have, I am therefore, dedicating to you, my love. My virtue, my life, my soul, I commit to you all, for both by day and by night, I am writhing in the agony of unsatisfied love. I am restless with emotion. It is for you to soothe the pangs of my heart as fire is quenched only by water. Verily as does the bird pine for a drop of rain which will assuage its thirst, so do I pine for you day and night, my love. Like a fish out of water I writhe in my heart's agonies for you, my dearest. There is no remedy to my miseries. I can always give vent to my feelings sweetly as does a cuckoo express itself in songs, but I lack his wings to fly away where I like."

Retiring into a lonely place Gobardhan read this letter and his heart thrilled with emotion. He became mad for Sonai, and there was nothing strange in this. If one dangles a sour tamarind in the presence of another man, can the latter's mouth help watering? Gobardhan lost all feeling of gratitude for his master in his burning passion for the mistress of the house. He did not stay to consider what was right and what was wrong and was completely lost in love for Sonai. Some months passed away in this manner, and it was their look-out now to get rid of the thorn that was still in their way. (Ll. 1-106.)

(4)

One day Sonai said to Kamal with tears in her eyes, "Your business which was worth lakhs of rupees is now being totally ruined. Of what avail will it bo to keep indoors for all time and ponder over it day and night? The thing is you are an absentee master and your riches are being misappropriated by your own servants. My only care is as to what the two urchins will live on if things go on in this way. Our wealth and property are slipping off from our hands and if nothing remains, what will be our condition?" At this Kamal struck his forehead with his hand in despair and thought a good deal about the plight he was in. He then called Gobardhan and said to him, "Listen to me, Gobardhan. I want to go out on trade to-morrow. Just make arrangements to get my boats in readiness. Do call all the boatmen." And the merchant continued saying in tears, "My house and belongings I commit entirely to your charge. Do look after my two darlings. They have no mother and when I am gone, they will be orphans in the truest sense of the word." Then he said to Maiphula, the maid-servant, "I am going out for purposes of trade, the boys are to remain here under your care. Don't you fail to look after them."

He took leave of all his neighbours and then went into his boat. The crew now offered their prayers to Pir Badar and then took off the anchors. "On with the oars"—the order was announced by beat of drums and then the rowers set about rowing, and the voyage was begun. They rowed on for four bends and then reached the dark waters of the high seas. Here in the high seas of Sonai's love did Gobardhan plunge himself headlong. (Ll. 1-36.)

(5)

Listen, my friends, to the tale of woes that now befell the tender urchins Chandmani and Suryamani. It rends my heart to speak of the miseries which their hard-hearted stepmother inflicted on them. They had, indeed, a very hard time of it now, for if they addressed her as mother she turned a long sour face on them. If, pinched by hunger, they wanted food, her eyes grew crimson in anger, and cruel as she was, she would scold them severely. How alas, shall I describe their woes? They were served with stale and rotten rice and curry, till the two bright lads lost all their glow of health and loveliness. They wept bitterly and thought their wailings would move the very stones to tears, they could not move their hard-hearted stepmother to pity. Day and night they pined away in grief, remembering their parents. A fish need not be told where water lies ; it knows that by instinct ; so does a child pant for and seek the affection of a mother. No wonder therefore, that in the great anguish of their heart they felt a deep yearning for their dead mother. Their colour faded, and pale they grew as time passed. Unable to bear the sting of hunger, Chandmani approached his brother one day and said, "This is more than I can bear, brother. Better far it is to put an end to life. To a drug shop let us go and secure poison wherewith to end our miserable existence. Let us die together, as we have lived together, so that one may not survive the other to mourn his loss.

(Ll. 1-26.)

(6)

Now while asleep in a room at Kajalkata, Sonai dreamt a dream which set her thinking. The dream is outlined thus, "Chandmani and Suryamani had become kings by a freak of fortune and poor Gobardhan was about to be hanged, when Suryamani intervened and set him free." After this she called out Gobardhan and said, "So long as Chandmani and Suryamani are alive, I have no hope of happiness. Dearest, I have only one request to make to you and this is that you should manage to make away with them as soon as you might do so." Gobardhan agreed and set about devising means for the assassination of these boys, and then when a plan was thought out she called Maiphula to her and with tearful eyes disclosed all that weighed in her mind. She gave the maid a necklace, tied two gold mohurs to the skirt of her cloth and also presented her with a flame-coloured *sadi* of great value. Then she said to her, "From to-day we are fast friends and you will live here as the mistress and all other maids will wait on you and carry out your orders." Then she caressingly touched her cheeks and continued, "I will give you in marriage. You are in the first bloom of youth, as fresh as a flower full of honey, and many a bee will be eager to approach you. You will kindly pluck out the thorns pricking at my side. I will then build you a house to the south of the river. I will also bring you a lover after your heart, and then will your term of servitude end and you will verily be like the mistress of the house in all matters. Chandmani and Suryamani are sons of my co-wife and therefore, my enemies. If they live, I am doomed." Thus lamented Sonai and then whispered to Maiphula's ears, "Remove this thorn, say, you must." When Sonai had finished, tears stood in Maiphula's eyes, which she wiped away with the skirt of her cloth. At this Sonai perceived the maid-servant's affection for the children and with a view to test her heart baited her thus, "Chandmani and Suryamani are very dear to me. Though they have not been born of me, they are as good as my own children. I have none to call my own except these two darlings, and if they live, my funeral rites will be duly performed by them, so that I shall get water to quench my thirst after death. What I have said I have said only to test your heart and to see that they have no discomfort for want of food and drink. The merchant has thrown the whole burden of the family on my shoulder and gone abroad. So awfully pressed for time I am that I have no leisure to look after them and I do not know what they think about me. But let me tell you a fact here. When I sit to eat in the hours of noon, my food scarcely gets down my throat, thinking of these orphans entrusted to my care." Then in countless ways, she tried to bait the maid who, however, was clever enough to see through all her dodges. (Ll. 1-62.)

(7)

There lived a man in that village Manik Sardar by name. Of the lewd and wicked men of the locality he was verily the head and a finished master of evil ways. He dressed his hair in right good fashion and idly loitered about. He went from one pond to another with an angling rod in his hand. When housewives came to take water, he whistled to draw their notice and to captivate their hearts. Chaste women paid no heed to his whistling, but coquettes would show by their wily ways that they were willing to respond. He cared not for angling and got very small fishes but the bait he laid were not evidently for them. They were meant for women's hearts and when he could hook any of these, he thought his end achieved.

One day Gobardhan called Manik to the house of the merchant and having conferred with Sonai, appointed the rogue as the Durwan of the place. He had his meals both by day and by night at that house and the wily Sonai turned him into a plaything pandering to her wishes, as the charmer makes his snake dance at his wish. She selected Manik's quarters at a place quite near to Maiphula's and a rake that Manik was, he was right glad to live near the youthful woman who seemed to him like the moon dropped from the heaven into his hands.

Maiphula was in the full bloom of youth and Manik was so maddened with lust that he could not wait to court her favour by any slow and patient process requiring lapse of time. One night he slowly broke open the door of Maiphula's house and lighted a lamp to see things around. He found that the maid was in deep slumber with the two boys Chandmani and Suryamani lying by her side. Maiphula now woke up, surprised and annoyed by the sudden disturbance when Manik caught hold of both her hands. She looked like a snake which being trodden under foot raises its hood aloft and makes a terrific rush. Then when Manik fell at her feet she was all ablaze like dry cotton on fire, and addressing the miscreant who lay low at her feet, poured forth an indignant volley of words: "Strictly have I been observing the religious rites enjoined on a widow by our scriptures. I lead an ascetic life. I had my hair cut off when I went out to Gaya on pilgrimage. It is mere foolhardiness on your part to venture your wicked proposal here. I will now raise such a cry as will wake up the whole house. Hast thou not, O miscreant and low-born one, thy own mother and sister that you should thus tamper with feminine virtue?" Her lips quivered in anger as she spoke. But Manik picked up courage and answered undaunted, "Well, I know all about you and it is no good dodging me. Leave aside all thy mock-shows, thou seeming queen of virtue." "Off with thee," roared Maiphula and Chand and Surya woke up. It was now nearing daybreak. The eastern horizon was streaked with crimson, and the night was over. Muttering grim words of rage, the wicked one left the place at a slow pace. The rogue Manik thus tried to tempt Maiphula on many an occasion and she one day went to Sonai to whom she disclosed all his rascality. Sonai simpered a little and glanced archly at her as if she suspected her. Maiphula felt insulted and said, "I cannot tolerate all this. Do give me leave for I will no longer stay in such a house. I will husk paddy and earn an humble pittance, and rice-dust, and stale grain will be my sustenance. I am committing Chand and Suryamani to your care." So saying, the maid went out and the boys wept for her. She had not gone far when she began to reflect thus, "Let me go back. My heart yearns for the two dear boys. Before her death, their mother committed them to my hands. How can I make my heart hard like flint and go leaving them? Who will give them food and water when they are pinched with hunger and thirst? Whom will they look up to on waking from their sleep? Who again will treat them to seeds of bean—their favourite food in the morn?" She thus mused on many things and then went back to her old master's house, weeping. (Ll. 1-72.)

(8)

On that very day, Sonai privately called Manik in the evening and said, "Manik, though not born of the same mother, we are akin in mind and are therefore, as good as brother and sister. I will search out a beautiful bride for you and then brother and sister that we are, we shall live together in happiness in the same house." With these words she treated her new brother to betel leaf and then patted him on the back saying, "One thing you have to do for me, my dear brother." The redoubtable Manik then pondered over many things and folding his hands said, "There is nothing on earth which I cannot do for you at your order." Then said Sonai, "Do listen to me. If to-day you can contrive what I ask you to do, I will marry you to a bride of exceeding beauty. The two lads Chandmani and Suryamani are sons of my co-wife and most naturally, therefore, they are my enemies. If they live, I can have no happiness on the earth. Do remove these thorns from my side, my brother." So saying, Sonai put a sword into Manik's hand. "Do not stop, do not speak. Forthwith do end them once for all." At this bidding of Sonai, Manik posted off to the room where the two boys were lying on their beds. Slowly he entered that room and with the sword in hand he pondered a little. The two boys were dead asleep and Manik resolved to cut their heads off. With the suddenness of a flash of lightning, Maiphula held up the sword in Manik's hand. Tears were gushing from her eyes and her breasts were bare of cloth and her hair was dishevelled. The redoubtable rogue Manik now said slowly to her, "What makes you hold me back?" Maiphula answered, "Do kill me. You had a great longing for me and here I am to seal my love for you with my blood. Cut me off and then pluck out my heart. But spare these tender urchins and consider them as your own children." So saying the maid fell at his feet and beat her head against the ground in supplication. Chandmani and Suryamani now woke up, and the rascal Manik became a changed man. He said to Maiphula, "Listen to me, Maiphula. To-morrow morning Sonai will cut my head off."

Then they conferred together and bethought themselves of a plan. Maiphula brought a rope of *shan* thread with which she bound Manik tight. Then she placed him lying with his face upwards and placed on his chest a stone weighing full two maunds and a half. Then Maiphula went out with Chandmani and Suryamani. Many pools and canals they crossed and trudged on throughout the night, as a result of which they became footsore. The day broke and birds sang. They were now on the foot of a hill.

(Ll. 1-60.)

(9)

The eastern hills touched the horizon. The boys began to cry unable to bear the fatigue of the journey. Maiphula held Chandmani and Suryamani by the hand and slowly entered into the forest. The *shan* thorn pricked the feet of the boys. They walked wearily and could proceed no more. Tears streamed down the cheeks of Maiphula at this pitiable plight of her master's sons who lay down helpless under a Garjan tree. They had got severe headache and fever and restlessly tossed their heads in agony and pain in the shade of the tree. Alas! who would give them medicine or food and water? Bereft of everything they were, having only torn rags round their waists.

Maiphula then resolved that she would support the boys by begging. Then she approached them and touching their forehead with her hands, she was shocked at their high fever. " Had I not brought them here there would have been some chance of their life, but now I see there is none." She remembered their parents and was full of grief at the the ought. " Happy were they that they did not live to see this sight! There was a day when the boys were the darlings of the house and it is because their mother is dead that they have been reduced to this plight. On the eve of her death, she committed them to my care and fondly hoped that no evil would betide them. But really I have turned out to be a source of greater misery to them than even their step-mother. Woe unto me that they lie in this grim forest—it is all for me! When the merchant will come back and learn of this he will cut off my head before all. Of course, it is not death that I am afraid of. Let the boys survive and I will meet death cheerfully." Thus did Maiphula reflect within herself and wiped away her tears with the skirt of her cloth. " The dense forests," she continued reflecting, "are infested with tigers and wolves, and where am I to keep the sick children now? How am I to go a-begging leaving them here? I am now in a fix and what am I to do?"

Tears gushed from her eyes as confounded and stunned she lay there for a time reflecting on future. (Ll. 1-44.)

(10)

Then a sound reached her ears as of the cutting of trees. The maid rose up and went into the forest, following the sound. As she went, she often looked backwards at the two boys whom she was leaving behind. She trembled full of misgivings as to what might happen to them and it rent her heart to look at their misery. She had proceeded some way when she met a woodcutter. Maiphula addressed him as brother and said, " I implore you to grant me a favour. I have two sons who have been taken ill with fever and are now restless with pain under the shade of a Garjan tree. I seek shelter for myself and the children and I swear by Dharma (the God of Virtue) that I look upon you as my own brother in this distress and rely on your kindness." The woodcutter pondered over the request in his mind and seeing that the woman was very beautiful to look at, he agreed after a time saying, " Yes, bring both your boys and come to my house." " But you must help me," said Maiphula with folded hands, " and take one of my boys in your arms."

Then both of them repaired to the Garjan tree, when lo! to their surprise they found that the two boys were not there. To Maiphula it seemed to be a bolt from the blue; she dropped down to the ground and writhed in an agony of despair. The very hills seemed to quiver at her laments. The woodcutter was taken aback, and birds, beasts and snakes fled away at the shrill cry, and even the mighty tigers and bears took to their hills at the loud laments of the woman. She beat her breasts, tore her hair and was beside her senses. It rends one's heart to narrate what happened afterwards. Evening was drawing nigh, the sun was fast sinking down. Maiphula was lying unconscious and the woodcutter bore her home on his shoulders.

(Ll. 1-36.)

(11)

Let us now return to Sonai. She was in her room waiting for Manik. She had no news about Manik and of the two boys whose heads he was commissioned to cut off, and she felt very uneasy over this. She then sent Gobardhan to bring news about Manik. Gobardhan entered the room where the boys had lain and saw that Manik's hands and feet were all bound up and a heavy slab of stone was placed on his chest. Gobardhan unloosed his bonds and set him free. On coming to Sonai Manik said weeping, "As I entered the room I was beaten with a *lathi* on my hands and also on my head. The blow was so sudden and heavy that it seemed to be like a thunderbolt. I dropped down on the ground unconscious and when I regained my senses, a very strong man advanced and held me by the neck. He tightly bound up my hands and feet and placed on my chest a slab of stone weighing two maunds and a half. In such a plight I was more dead than alive, and every breath I took seemed to be my last. Last night I seemed to have been brought face to face with the God of Death."

When Sonai heard this she trembled in anger and muttered a few words resentfully. Hearing this strange story, Gobardhan went out in quest of Maiphula. He sent out spies to all places but nobody could bring any news about them. (Ll. 1-28.)

(12)

Now let us turn to Chandmani and Suryamani and attend to the tale of their woes. When Maiphula went away, the two brothers woke up and wept rolling on the ground. Said Chandmani, "Well, my brother, I am at the point of death in bitter thirst." Then they both went out in quest of water in the deep jungles and coming across a pool, drank its muddy water to their heart's content. They lost all sense of direction and could not find out their way back to the Garjan tree. Evening was drawing nigh and the sun was sinking down. The boys were bewildered and could not decide where to go. They wept in that forlorn state and even the birds and beasts joined their laments in sympathy.

* * * *

On the bank of that pool and under the shade of that tree, they sat weeping till they fell asleep. (Ll.1-28.)

(13)

There was a kingdom near the Southern hills and its king had died. This king left no issue and on his death, a cry of grief rang through the whole land. If there is no king reigning over a country it falls into disorder. There was a hard scramble and fight for the throne when the old Vizier called out to all saying, "Listen to me, inhabitants of this place. You will have to decide as to who will be king. You know gold and silver are debased if mixed with alloy of brass and copper, and honey is spoilt if adulterated with water, kingdoms are ruined if anarchy sets in. Of what avail is a pond if it has no water, or of what avail is a house whose roof has not been thatched ? So also a kingdom comes to no good, if bereft of a king. We shall all fall into chaos. But who will select the king? Let us go to the stable of elephants and decide there." The assembly agreed to the proposal of the Vizier and went to the stable where there was an old white elephant which was in the house for three long generations, revered almost like a household deity and was, therefore, fed with milk and plantain. The Vizier said that on the white elephant should rest the choice of selecting the king.

* * * *

With flower and sandals they bedecked the elephant and it walked on with raised trunk. Roaming through hills and jungles, it went out steadily towards the North.

The two boys were sleeping unconsciously in the shade of a tree and there the elephant came. It looked searchingly at Chandmani's face and finding that there was a mark of royalty on his forehead, raised him on his back. It rushed on with Chandmani who on waking began to cry in dread. The elephant arrived at the city and the people made him their king. But of what avail is a kingdom if there is no peace in mind? Does rich food like *polau* suit a man who is suffering from indigestion? Chand began to weep disconsolately. "Where," cried he, "is my brother Suryamani who was precious as a doll of gold to me?" The Vizier assured the new prince that men had been sent to all directions to seek him out. (Ll. 1-46.)

(14)

In the meantime a serious trouble had come about.

On finding no one by him, Suryamani began to cry. God had ordained great woes for him. He began to weep and was beside himself with grief. Tears gushed from his eyes in streams. Sometime after this he saw many bamboos, tied together, floating in the stream. On these were some men who were going home, the bamboos being the goods they had secured. These men saw the beautiful boy Suryamani who excited their pity and they took him along with them. The bamboos floated on, till they reached the royal *ghat* in the Southern country. It was a lovely *ghat*, off which many ships and sloops had cast anchor. The king of the South, the owner of the *ghat*, was a very strong ruler who severely punished those who did not regularly pay their custom duties. When all men reached that *ghat*, they stopped, and Suryamani was given some food and water.

A certain merchant in the high seas landed in an island where his ships had stranded. There he dreamt that unless a human being was sacrificed, the presiding deity of the seas would not be appeased, and the boat could not be brought into water again. Having dreamt this strange dream, the merchant went to the royal *ghat* and sat down there with a purse of thousand rupees, plunged in deep thought. The dealers in bamboos heard of the merchant's dream and forthwith resolved on selling Suryamani. And they did so for a thousand rupees. The merchant gladly came to his boat again, bedecked the boy with various ornaments and also fed him with many eatables. Just before the boy was immolated, he began to shiver and pant. It harrows one's heart to describe the doings of the merchant. He pushed the boy into the water. It was a night of new moon. The sky was overspread with darkness and the sea was chafing with stormy waves. The boy was set adrift in the salt water, one wave tossing him as high as the sky and another carrying him nearer and nearer to a sandy island—a long, long stretch of land where there was no habitation and where no direction could be traced. The current flew high and the ships of the merchant were once more afloat, marching homeward. (Ll. 1-44.)

(15)

Let us now follow the adventures of Suryamani.

In the island where he had been carried by the waves stood the house of a fisherwoman. She came across Suryamani and took him to herself. She saw that the little lad was stuffed full with salt water, but that his life was still lingering in him, and she tried to bring him to senses again by moving his hands and feet. She brought an earthen pitcher and into it she squeezed the boy with his face upwards. Then water oozed from face and nose and the stomach was lightened of its weight. The fisherwoman next bore the boy home on her shoulders. Such was the strange decree of fate. The boy had fallen into the sea but was restored to life. In this way the lad Suryamani found his way to the house of the fisherwoman. (Ll. 1-18.)

(16)

Chandmani was pining in ceaseless lament for his brother and his soldiers returned to say that Suryamani had been devoured by a wolf. As soon as the news reached the ears of the King Chandmani, he dropped down to the ground senseless, and for three days he went without food, weeping day and night for his brother. (Ll. 1-11.)

(17)

For twelve years Kamal the merchant roamed from one port to another, and then came back. Slowly the boats reached the aforesaid *ghat* and here was detained for a day or two for paying taxes and other custom duties.

Kamal was one day walking along a canal when he found a boy as lovely as a doll of gold in the house of a fisherwoman. He seemed to recognise the child and pondered within himself as to how he could find his way to that house. He was filled with misgivings and could not arrive at any definite conclusion. Alas! he did not know what had happened in his own house during his absence! He thought a good deal about his two sons and was troubled with many apprehensions. The officer in charge of the *ghat* now came and said that it was the order of the king not to let his boat off. The merchant said to him, "Do allow me to go out. I will give you a thousand rupees." One day, two days, three days passed and the new king now himself came on board his ship. The merchant was dazed at the sight. He seemed to be confounded by a dream and could not make out anything. The prince dropped down at his feet and called him father, thus soothing his heart. Then laying his head in the bosom of the merchant, he narrated the whole story in detail. The father then said in tears that Suryamani was alive and that he would soon bring him over to the palace. With these words, Kamal went off to the fisherwoman and said to her, "Where have you got this chubby boy from?"

It was a strange tale that he heard from the fisherwoman and tears came to his eyes as he listened. Suryamani fixed his gaze on the merchant and said in tears, "Alas, father, where is my brother, where is my aunt Maiphula and where again are our house and things? My brother had been in great misery which brought a high fever. I don't know what happened next." Kamal kissed him and taking him in his arms came to where the ships lay. The two brothers embraced each other and the merchant said to his men, "Hear, oh my rowers, I want to start for home to-day. My son is the king of this *ghat*. Do take off anchor and set out at once." With these words he struck his drum and gave the order for rowing. The helmsman laid his hands to the helm and set sail. The boat swung hither and thither and moved on like a show-thing. Three days they took in reaching Basantinagar and they signified their arrival by the firing of guns. Sonai and Gobardhan trembled in their hearts to see that the merchant had come back.

Kamal walked straight on to the inner apartments. He met Gobardhan on the way and asked him news about his two boys. "What can I tell you!" replied Gobardhan, "the two boys left their home together." The merchant now pulled him by the ears and asked him, "Where is Sonai? Bring her here at once." He roared out his command and the two-storied building trembled at the sound of his voice. He sulked in anger and his eyes grew crimson at the time. He then called all his soldiers and rowers and ordered them to arrest the rogue Gobardhan at once. Gobardhan did not say a word and some of the men caught hold of him by the neck and bound his hands and feet in chains. They pushed him by the neck and Sonai trembled to see the sad plight he was in. Kamal then gave orders saying, "Let their graves be dug and search out a mad dog to be set against them when half-buried. I will make them eat the hard fruit of their love."

At this time the two boys came there and had a look at the face of the stepmother. They then lowered their gaze and said not a word to her. They spoke to their father and entreated to spare their stepmother.

Kamal did not say anything and only called that bad woman near him. She shook in fear and was indeed more dead than alive. She only turned her eyes and cast a look at Gobardhan.

* * * *

Chandmani then said to his father, "Be calm and easy, father, and search out the maid Maiphula."

A long search was begun and a reward was announced in markets and bazaars with beat of drums, but all said that Maiphula was no longer alive. (Ll. 1-88.)

(18)

Chandmani now asked leave to go to his own country. An array of vessels was fitted out and Chandmani and Suryamani went smiling with their father. Kamal also took Sonai with them, her eyes streaming in tears.

As the boats reached the high seas, he took Sonai to himself and said, "Listen to me, Sonai. My heart has been broken to pieces. I had hoped a great deal from thee when I made thee my wife. But these hopes have proved false. Would that I had died with Surangini. In my old age thou hast sent murderous shafts at my heart and the fire of my anguish burns in high flames within my soul. If thou livest, there is no hope of happiness for me. Thou hast brought dishonour to the family and humbled the dignity of my sons."

So saying the merchant caught her by the hair and gave her a push. In the deep seas sank Sonai and the merchant himself wanted to rush into the waters, but he was held up by the sons who groaned in grief. The boats soon reached the royal ghat, and they went to their kingdom in the company of their father. (Ll. 1-24.)

(19)

The new king ruled his land with so much power that even the wild beasts, our enemies by nature, had to forget their malice for fear of him. Such was his prowess that even tigers and buffaloes roamed and grazed in the same field and were afraid of quarrelling. One day a crazed woman came there and narrated the story of how a foster-mother passed the twelve months of a year. It was a pathetic tale and it moved even stones to tears. One day the insane woman entered the inner apartments and wept while singing her sad tale, and at this the eyes of the prince glistened with tears. Suryamani rushed to clasp her in his embrace and addressed her as aunt Maiphula, at which all the assembled men were amazed. The knew -ing took his 'aunt' home, showing all his fondness for her. But she ate nothing nor did she speak a word. She only beat her forehead with both her hands and did not even stay there nor cared to listen to the words and entreaties of others. She went away weeping and singing her *baramashi*, the song of twelve months. Tears were her only treasure, for insane as she was, she was bereft of her sense.

Here ends the ballad of Kamal the merchant. (Ll. 1-20.)

SHYAM RAY

PREFACE TO SHYAM RAY.

About three years ago Babu Chandra Kumar De heard a few verses of this ballad sung by one Kailash Chandra De of the village Machhua in the Sub-Division of Kisoreganj. He took down the lines and felt interested in their simple pathos. Later on, he came in contact with two minstrels, who sang parts of this ballad,—Som of Sachhuni, Katghar and Adulla Dai of Mominpore. But though he had made a collection of some portions of the ballad from these three persons, it was very meagre and did not give him even a bare idea of the plot. He nevertheless felt from what he had secured that the ballad possessed the simple rural charm, characteristic of some of the best songs of this kind. In the month of Baisakh (May) of the Bengali year 1332, he happened to meet one Manmohan Sadhu living at the Malini Asram in the Sub-Division of Netrakona. This man was formerly an inhabitant of Khaliajuri. He had a note-book which contained a number of songs. But the fragments of Shyam Ray that could be secured from this note-book were yet insufficient. Lately, Babu Chandra Kumar paid a visit to that celebrated shrine of Mymensingh —the Gupta Brindaban. There lives one Kamal Das Bairagi whom Chandra Kumar describes as a veritable ocean of old ballads. This minstrel, whose avocation is to sing old ballads tuned to the music of the one-stringed instrument called the *Ektara*, supplied him with a very considerable part of the ballad of Shyam Ray, though it seems that the ballad has not been collected in its entirety even with this valuable help. One reading this ballad will apparently be struck with some omissions in it. Stray passages have been collected from different sources and these have not been strung together to make a consistent whole. There are some gaps to be met with in the descriptions, but still the collection as it stands, gives the entire story with some omission of details. The omissions might, however, be due to a high dramatic sense of the poet who did not consider it worth his while to give details of narrative but was content with giving suggestions, as regards the prosaic events, laying stress on purely lyrical elements of the story.

This ballad bears a close affinity to that of *Dhopar Pat* and the *Herdsman* published in the second volume of Eastern Bengal Ballads. The situations are often analogous and the pathos breathes the same air of rural simplicity. In its original the ballad supplies a rich treasure of indigenous imagery, very hard to be translated into English. The author does not give any classic similes. The country that he lived in with its picturesque landscape and humble occupations of the rural folk presented him with vivid pictures which he has delineated with great force and clearness. He has indulged in the imageries of his rural country sometimes to a fault. It seems that the poet was deeply plunged in his own sentiments and scarcely found time or humour to apply the poetic art for arranging his overflowing ideas in proper order. Such passages, irregular and unconnected as they are in the original, are likely to suffer greatly in translation, though in the original, the brilliancy of homely figures proves too absorbing to allow the reader to mind the defects in the arrangement of the incidents of the plot.

Like *Mahua* and the *Dhopar Pat* the situations described in this ballad are dramatic. The poet introduces the incidents of the plot without considering any prelude or introduction to be necessary, so that they sometimes look like unconnected scraps. But one reading the whole poem will find out the connexion and appreciate that the plot was very vivid in the mind of the poet and that he has been able to work it out with great pathos and poetic charm. The poet Nitai Chand mixes philosophy with poetry, and in the colophons, he sometimes discourses with a keen insight into the psychology of the characters who have loved and suffered. There is no rustic crudeness or quaintness in his philosophy. It takes us by surprise that a man who had evidently no education worth naming could have such deep penetration into the affairs of the sexes and could analyse them in such a subtle way. We know nothing as to who this Nitai Chand was. Only we know that he belonged to that famous nest of singing birds—Eastern Mymensing—and he pitched his note as high as the best of them did. If he cannot be ranked with Dwija Kanai, the poet of *Mahua*, it is probably because we have not been able to secure the poem in a consistent shape throughout and because of the fragmentary nature in which the tale has been woven. We are trying to recover a better version of this poem which, we hope, does exist in the shades of the big *Darakh* trees with which the rural district of Mymensingh abounds. The character of the *Dom* girl does not show any of the remarkable features that characterise Mahua. We have not liked her lamentations which are sometimes stereotyped and monotonous, but a wealth of lyrical thought often rising to dramatic heights pervades the poem, and it is this lyrical element which constitutes its chief excellence.

It will be interesting to note that many lines of this remarkable poem echo the verses of Chandidas and other Vaisnava poets. We have said in our Introduction to the Second Volume that many knotty problems as to the origin of Vaisnava lyrics are solved by a close study of these ballads. The ballad makers, it is obvious, did not owe anything to the Vaisnava poets and we beg to repeat that the whole atmosphere of Bengal being charged with gay notes of love, a phraseology rich in the expressions of sexual romance was already formed in the countryside. The Vaisnava poets and the ballad-makers both drew from the treasure-house of this phraseology.

The ballad evidently belongs to the older school and cannot be the production of a period later than the 14th century. There is no Moslem element in it, and love between a member of aristocracy and a low-born woman is the burden of the ballad, as we find it to be the case in the ballads of *Mahua* and *Dhobar Pat*. Chandidas himself loved a low-born woman. This was an age characterised by a bold departure from all social canons, which, the Sahajiyas indulged in, revelling in the æsthetic plane of higher love. The language reminds us of this particular epoch, which bears the stamp of the greatest of the Sahajiyas—Chandidas. Hence we are led to conjecture that the ballad in its original form probably belonged to the 14th century, if not earlier.

The ballad of *Shyam Ray* contains 397 lines and I have divided them into nine cantos.

DINESH CHANDRA SEN.

Shyam Ray

(1)

She was the wife of a *Dom*, and she came to the landing *ghat* with a pitcher in her arm. Shyam Ray seated in his pleasure-house beheld her through a window. She was rather of a short stature. Her long hair all loose was flowing in the air. The whole country she had maddened by the charm of her youthful look ; she had put on a coarse *sari* of jute, which played with the wind. No wonder that Shyam Ray became charmed by a sight of this young woman.

" If you would be mine, oh lovely girl, I would marry you. I would decorate your beautiful hair with golden pendants. A couch, a cushion and a fine mat I would give you for your use. How pleased with each other would we spend the whole night in amours. The coarse *sari* that you wear ill-becomes your lovely form. I would give you in its place a rich Nilambari *sari* to cover your charms. Is it fit that you should wear these glass-beads round your neck? Fain would I give you a necklace of large pearls. I would give you a pair of rich *Baju* to wear in your arms and a *Hāsuli* to wear on your breast. How gladly I shall myself adorn your eyes with the black paint Kajjal. If you were mine how happy both of us would be. A golden lamp fed by clarified butter (*ghee*) would I light in my room and for the whole night behold the graces of your lovely face, beautiful as the moon."

(Ll. 1-18.)

(2)

Chorus.—A helpless woman am I, dependent on others.

In the evening a maiden came from Shyam Ray with a message. She stood at the back-door.

The Dom Girl.

"I am a frail woman and my mother-in-law keeps a sharp watch over me. You have come in the evening, oh messenger. I have not yet lighted the lamp in my house and my husband will presently come with the goods of his trade.

"You ask about my condition—what shall I say? In the full month of August when lands are flooded with water, I find as if there is not a drop of water in the midstream of the Ganges. The holy river shows mere shoals and sands, instead of a flow of her sweet water.

"It is not now the bathing time, so that I cannot go to the river-side with the pitcher in my arm after emptying it, on the pretext of bathing. Neither am I a trader so that I could visit his house for a mere sight of him on the pretext of selling my goods. Were I a shepherd, oh lovely messenger! I would go and see him on the pretext of visiting the pastures. Were I a flower-woman, I would go on the pretext of selling garlands. If I were a washer-woman, I would go to fetch clothes from his house. Behold, oh messenger, the flowing tears of my eyes. They will tell him how sincerely I feel. Had I a trained parrot, I would have sent it to him with my love-message. Alas, I am not a pigeon which goes in darkness before the dawn to fetch its food. What pretext can I produce to go to his house? If I were a flower, I would have dropped into your hand from the bough to be taken to him as an offering of myself. If I were sweet camphor, I would have yielded my fragrance to the air to reach him; neither am I green cocoanut nor a pomegranate fruit, so that I could dissolve myself into juice to appease his thrist. If I were betel and betel-nut, I would shut myself in a small box and be an offering to him. If I were *Chua* and sandal, I would feel myself blessed by scenting his forehead with perfumes prepared of myself. Neither am I a banana or a cucumber, that I might cut myself into pieces and being served in a plate offer myself on his table. This youth of mine is neither a sweetmeat nor *polao*, to be presented on his table in dinner time. My youth is not the stream of the Ganges, so that I could be gathered into a cup to be offered to wash his feet. How happy would I be to be one of his numerous maid-servants to have the privilege of serving him. There is no way that I can plan to present myself as an offering to him. If I were a cuckoo of the forest, oh messenger, or a bee delighting in flowers, I would fly in the air and on the pretext of gathering honey I would have a sight of his face and satisfy myself."

Nitai Chand, the poet, takes the woman's brief and says in her strain :—" This youth is an essence culled from all the good things of the world but how sad it is when it comes to no use. Were I a flute, on the pretext of singing a tune, I would offer myself to his lips and be happy at the touch. I am helplessly dependent, a frail woman as I am. But were it possible, I would leave my husband and surrender my youth to my lover."

The Dom Girl.

" The lamp of the house is flickering, now leave me, oh messenger, and tell him that I cannot meet him to-day."

The Messenger.

"You are engaged in your household work, but put it off for a short time and listen to me. Shyam Ray has sent me to you for some purpose. Your lover, beautiful girl, is standing on the bank of the river, waiting for you. I have come, not being able to resist his appeal. He has grown mad for you and you cannot evade him by any means."

(Ll. 1-50.)

(3)

The Dom Girl.

Chorus.—Oh, Shyam Ray, oh my love, do not stand obstructing my way. I must quickly return home, filling my pitcher. It does not become you to distress me thus.

"Know that I am a woman of the *Dom* caste. Your status in society is high. Don't you know that a person so high as you becomes an outcast when he wishes to make love with one so low as I am. You are a full-blown flower of a rich man's garden and I shall be like a thorn unto your feet. If you really get what you wish, it will be a matter of public scandal in this life and through all time. You are the son of a Raja and I, a girl of the *Dom* caste. Why should you not launch your boat in oceans and seas but foolishly do so in a filthy pool whose water has run out? The son of a Raja, you are, my love, like the full moon. Why should you leave the glorious firmament and covet a lowly bed on the ground?

"There is no want of couches, cushions and golden beds in the palace, but this ground is hard. It will hurt your soft body. Neither is it the proper time for you to put me to such a trial. There are wicked eyes all around and who knows that some will not peep into our affairs.

"Dear, leave me alone, I pray. Do you ever expect to find a myrobalan as sweet as a mango or whey as good as curd? Dear, leave me alone, I pray.

"You are a right royal peacock. Why should you be attracted by the plumes of a *Bhairo*? Dear, leave me alone, I pray.

"Why should you, my beloved, leave pearls and stones and pick up *cowries*, or leaving a gold necklace, put in its place, a rope round your neck. Dear, leave me alone, I pray.

"A low-caste woman am I, a *Dom*, hated by all. Where is there a fool like my beloved, who would reject the water of a lake or a river but go in for that of a dirty well. Dear, leave me alone, I pray.

"You are willing to prefer a string of bones to a garland of large pearls and in the place of the scented red powder, *fag* and *kumkum*, you are going in for dust. Dear, leave me alone, I pray.

"Surely it is Providence that is trying your wits. Or how could it be possible that you would leave sandal and cover your body with ashes. Dear, leave me alone, I pray.

"A prince you are and I am a *Dom*. It seems that you want to get a supply of water by pressing a stone. Dear, leave me alone, I pray."

Shyam Ray.

"Though a *Dom*, you are exceedingly beautiful. I cannot give you up. You speak of scandal. For your dear sake, scandal will be like the precious black paint with which one adorns one's eyes. You say that wicked people will abuse me. It will not matter anything. This youth is not a handful of dust, that we might easily give up its joys. Nor is my love less valued than the consideration of caste. With you, my beloved, I will go to a strange land. I will leave home and all and be like an ascetic. My house will be under the shade of trees, and forests will be like my habitation. It will matter little, if I wear a string of bones in the place of my necklace of pearls. In exchange for all this, if I get one so prized as you, fain would I give up all scented perfumes and cover my body with ashes. What does it matter if I have to give up milk and curd? The fruits of forests will appease my hunger as well. For your sake, I will despise my rich costumes and put on a bark dress instead. You speak of couches and golden beds. They are of no value to me, I say. A lowly bed in the ground will give me a far greater joy. You have said of the water of seas and oceans. They are salty. Far sweeter is the water of a well. Let my scandal spread throughout the world. I will try to find if I can wring any sweet juice from stone."

Nitai Chand, the poet, says, "If love is real, a true man will appreciate it and place it on his head as a thing of the greatest value." (Ll. 1-48.)

(4)

The Dom Girl.

"Do not obstruct my path, my beloved, any more. Let me return home. I have not yet lighted the evening lamp in my house. The pitcher has not yet been filled up, and my mother-in-law is a tyrant, you know. She will not spare me. The evening is passing away and the village path is full of reptiles and worms. How shall I be able to return home? My husband the *Dom* will be away from home to-morrow for cutting bamboos————"

Shyam Ray.

"I will go to the landing *ghat* and fill the pitcher for you."

The Dom Girl.

"But you are a stranger. How can I wait alone for you?"

Shyam Ray.

"You are afraid of darkness. I will accompany you to your home."

The Dom Girl.

"But the enemies will find an opportunity to spread scandal."

Shyam Ray.

"Then let us fly away together. Be ready to leave this place."

The Dom Girl.

"Why should you subject yourself to the abuses of the people?"

Shyam Ray.

"I have got you in the path. I shall not leave you this time."

The Dom Girl.

"Is it becoming that a friable creeper should clasp a sandal plant?

"No need of all this, my beloved. I will go home alone. To-morrow will my husband go for cutting bamboos from distant groves. To-night have patience, and go to my home to-morrow. In my wretched cot shall I wait for you with my youth as an humble present to your noble self. Without the knowledge of my mother-in-law I will keep the backdoor open. I have given up all hopes of worldly happiness and courted misery to be the companion of my life. For the sake of your love, I have determined to treat my own people as strangers. My house to me is like a forest, and forest will be my home from this time. Prepared am I to set fire to my home and have its doors shut against me. For your sake, beloved, I have invited scandal to be my companion for life. But to a person who has tasted of the fruits of love, scandal and even death is nothing. That person's life is alone blessed in the world."

The Dom Girl.

"Near the backdoor of the house are you straying alone, my beloved, subjecting yourself to all this worry and trouble for my sake? You are the son of a king, but as fate would have it, you have come to steal in the house of a poor man. A wretched *Dom* that I am, where can I find couches and cushions for you? What can I offer you to lie on in this cot of mine. There are some coarse mats which are spread for you. You will have to give up your golden bed and couch for sleeping in this poor style. But should you feel pain in doing so, I will spread my long and flowing hair in the bed to make it easy for you. But afraid am I, since even a bed of flower seems rough to you, that my hair may be found stiff. What can I do, oh my beloved, to give you a little comfort ? But should you dislike the bed of hair that I will spread for you, my breast may be found soft to lodge you in. I will wash your feet, my beloved, with the tears of my eyes and wipe them with my hair, and the red sign of luck on my brow will serve to adorn your feet.

"I cannot light the lamp in my room. So I see nothing with my eyes. But I shall be able to feel your face, touching it with my hands. Wait, friend, a moment; bring your face close to mine and whisper to me what you may have to say. Come close to my breast and stay for a moment till I paint your sweet smile in the heart of my heart. A helpless woman that I am, whom shall I accuse excepting myself?

"Perhaps the night is coming to a close. You are sleepy, my beloved. But is not the cuckoo singing from the neighbouring tree, and are not the bees humming in our garden? Dawn is not far off? In distant swamps, my husband is engaged in cutting long reeds. Be pleased to come to my house to-morrow also, and I will gather all the flowers from our garden to present you a cup of honey and all that my youth can give will be for you."

(Ll. 1-55.)

(5)

The mother tried to dissuade him with her importunities and the brother and sister made a pathetic appeal, but Shyam Ray did not yield. He had grown mad for the *Dom* girl.

"Oh, my brother, take my word; I will bring for you a beautiful bride, she will be the very image of gold and I will have her married to you."

"No, my sister; no, my brother, why should you all urge in this way. If you will make your brother happy, get him married to the *Dom* girl."

"But how is it possible? Your society, your religion will not permit it. You will wreck your fortune, if you attempt to do it. Don't you know, dear brother, that a mere touch of the vile *Dom* woman will be enough to outcast you. Why should, you, brother, leave the public road when it is before you, and tread on a ground, full of dangerous holes. Being the right royal cobra, why should you like to turn a mean worm like the *Dhora*? You represent a noble house of which the insignia is a blooming flower. Why should you go in for dung? Being a bird of the noble species *Sua*, whose house is the sky, why should you be willing to make a nest on the ground?"

The mother tried her best and so did the brother and the sister. But how can a man bitten by a snake of deadly venom be saved?

Nitai Chand, the poet, says, "In vain do you, oh mother and brother, refer to religion and social injunctions. These are idle talks. If an alchemist touches poison his charm will turn it to nectar. It is not the high or the low status nor whether one is good or bad that weighs with the lover. From the very dust, you may find out a precious jewel, if you have got eyes of love to discern it. To a real lover, death and age are unmeaning. If the enemy cuts one's body, love repairs it." Nitai Chand says again, "If love be real, what harm if one is a *Dom*?"

Chand Ray seated in his Court.

The Messenger.

"Oh master Chand Ray, what are you doing, seated in your hall? Don't you know that your son has lost his wits for the sake of a *Dom* girl? Have you not heard that your son Shyam Ray is going to marry a *Dom* girl? The report has got in the air and is known to all."

Chand Ray burnt in rage and looked like a flaming fire. He employed some men who at his orders broke down the house of the *Dom* and had it thrown into the river.

(Ll. 1-30.)

(6)

The Dom Girl.

"Do not go to strange land, oh my beloved, in the garb of an ascetic. Your riches are immense, and noble is your mansion. Do not leave them. *I will leave the house and my native land.* But stay at your place and stay here as your mother's darling for ever. Call your brother once more, 'Oh sweet brother' and once more call your sister, 'Oh my sweet sister.' Be happy in your home. I was a poor thing that once gave you a little happiness and now its turn over, give me up and whether I live or die, I will be happy at the thought that you once loved me. Was I not like a little dust of your feet? Throw it away, dear, and never think of it again. Why should you leave your golden throne for the sake of a poor wooden seat which I may have to offer ? and why should you wander in the forest like an ascetic with a string of bones round your neck in the place of your gorgeous necklace bedecked with jewels ? You want to keep the mere knot, leaving the precious stone which it once contained ? Do not, my beloved, give up nectar and court poison. *Gorachana*, the precious perfumed medicine, should not be abandoned for an ordinary drug. You are thinking of gathering dust in the place of a basket of gold-coins. Why should you risk all that is dear for the sake of a *Dom* girl? You are going to give up a garland of flowers, wishing to put on a snake round your neck. For you do not know what you will have to suffer for this wretched *Dom* girl. In countries far and near yours will be a name of scandal for ever, and I feel that I shall be a thorn to pinch your feet evermore in the path of life. Give up, oh dear! your resolve to visit strange lands. Your mother will give you the choice of a bride from a hundred ladies far more beautiful than myself. You can have no idea, my beloved, as to the dangers you will have to face with myself as your companion. You cannot form an idea of it now, just like one who has a lamp in hand and tries to realise what darkness is. These dangers to me appear so obvious that it would be foolish to use arguments to prove them as it is foolish to try to see one's fingers with the help of a mirror when he can see them with open eyes."

(Ll. 1-27.)

(7)

Oh, my audience, now listen to the story of the Gaburias who live in a strange country. They are unmannerly as a class. If their king's eyes are attracted by a youthful woman he is sure to bring her to his harem and marry her by force. To him the woman that is handsome to-day becomes ugly to-morrow. He sports with the youth of women in a merciless way. Beautiful women whose charm has not as yet faded a bit, he abandons after favouring them for a day and hunts after new ones; and the glorious queen of to-day becomes the infamous menial of to-morrow. These people are all a set of scoundrels. Each of them observes the fashion of keeping a beard and has ten or twenty wives. In fact, they are more like the fabled Rakshasas than men.

Shyam Ray came to this strange country with the *Dom* girl. He took to the avocation of a *Dom* and began to cut long grasses and reeds from the neighbouring swamps and prepare baskets and fans with them which he sold in the local market.

The heat of April and May is unbearable and exposed to it Shyam Ray daily goes to the jungle for wood. The remorseful *Dom* girl laments at her home alone. "Son of a Raja, Oh my beloved, Oh my noble prince, it is ordained by Fate that you should be a grass-cutter and suffer all these for my cursed sake. How pained am I to see your bright complexion turn darkish? Whom shall I blame for this freak of fortune, but my wretched self. Like the full moon in the grip of dark Rahu dost thou look pale under my evil charm, my beloved. When your head perspires, you wipe them with your hair. How unfortunate am I to behold your condition? The Gaburias are a merciless people and it is thy hard lot to trade with them. Let us, my love, go from hence to some other land."

The Messenger.

"Listen to me, Oh Gabur Raja, a Dom girl has arrived at your city, whose beauty has the lustre of the moon and dazzles the eyes like a flash. Your Queens, Oh Raja, are scarcely fit to be her servants. In your city there is no match for her."

As soon as the Raja got this report, he at once brought the Dom girl to his harem and ordered that her man Shyam Ray should be impaled. They at once bound him hand and foot in fetters. (Ll. 1-38.)

(8)

In the Harem of the Gabur King.

The Dom Girl.

"Oh, king of Gabur, you must attend to what I am going to say. How foolish are you to expect love from a woman by physical force? The youth of a woman is not like a precious metal to be locked up in your treasury by force.

You want to taste the sweet fruits of love, but even a tree does not yield them, unless it is planted and watered duly for some months. I have not lived in your house for four or even two months. Do you really expect me to love you without your first taking recourse to those means by which love can be attained? First, try to win my heart by gentle ways, and then expect to enjoy. You are a Dhangar, a Gaburia by caste. You have never been fortunate enough to taste of the love of a true woman. You have heretofore sought pleasure and not love. Do you expect to wring out honey from a flower by tearing its petals ?"

The Raja was right glad to listen to this discourse though it was full of abuse. He wanted to taste of the sweets of true love and hence resolved to marry her. At the request of the *Dom* girl, the prince Shyam Ray, disguised as a *Dom*, was let off.

The marriage day was fixed. They began to play different kinds of instrumental music. Men and women gathered and began to dance together. They had built huge trumpets by means of buffalo's skin and the women began to dance round and round like potter's wheels. They had prepared large pipes with the horns of buffaloes which they sounded creating a great uproar. With the juice of the *Dewa* fruit they reddened their lips. Music set their whole town astir. Oh my sweet *Dom* girl, sleep quietly for this night. To-morrow you will have to marry the Gabur-Raja.

The Queen.

"You are a stranger, my dear girl, but I will give you an idea of what sort of a husband you will have in this Gabur-Raja, for I have been his Queen for these long years and can tell you all. He is a ruffian of the first water. If there be a little delay in the preparation of food or if the dinner gets cooled a little, he comes with a knife to cut the wife's nose and ears. Faults, however little,

"You have never tasted the love of a true woman." P. 216.

never find pardon at his hands. For very ordinary defects, he threatens to sell the wife in the near market. When offering betel, if the lime is a little less, then he tears by force the long flowing hair of his wife. If, perchance, by the freak of wind, the *sadi* gets loose, he inflicts blows repeatedly on her back by a cudgel. Are you really willing to court this man as your husband? Ordinary women who have a knowledge of the nature of my husband quake with fear, if he wants to shower his favours on them. But are you pleased that he will make you his queen?"

Like the clouds in the month of August melting in the sunshine to raindrops, the *Dom* girl, inspite of the agonies of her heart, broke into a pleasant smile at these words of the queen. Humorously did she say, "Well, my dear Gabur queen, if you can suffer all these and stay, why should I not partake a little of your good fortune and taste it? Let us both be his queens and live in terms of amity. Another thing I would do if you should agree,—let us cut him into two parts to be enjoyed by each of us separately. So we shall have nothing to grudge, but being satisfied with our respective shares, live happily in this country. But in sooth if Providence has given me half part of this kingdom without my seeking it, will it not be foolish on my part to give up the dear possession?"

The queen was alarmed at her words and began to cry aloud. She took great pains to convince the *Dom* girl of the cruelties of her husband. Then she said, "If you ask me why I live with such a husband, inspite of his cruelties, I should ask you to look at the worms which live on a corpse. They enter again and again into the corpse, though each time they are served with the rotten flesh ; the thing is that they are accustomed to a miserable life and cannot escape it."

The *Dom* girl said, "Listen to me, oh queen. I was all along joking with you. Don't you think for a moment that I shall be able to bear your great Raja even for a day.

I am seeking an opportunity to fly away from his clutches. Now hear what plan I have devised to effect my escape. The king has been very busy during these days to prepare very fine ornaments for me. The weavers have spun out the valuable *Paban-bahar Saḍi* for my bridal dress. Now I will give you all this. Cover your body with the *saḍi* and put on all the ornaments. Be like a coy bride and remain in a corner of the palace hiding your face with a veil. Meanwhile I will act the part of a menial; but do not give out the fact to any one else. In the confusion of the marriage-function, I will leave the house like a maid-servant, quite unnoticed by others. What a fun it will be, dear queen, when you will be called upon to marry the Gabur Raj again! (Ll. 1-59.)

(9)

After suffering all kinds of hardships, Shyam Ray returned home and learnt that at the wicked counsel of his own father, the Gabur Raj had contrived to seize the *Dom* girl and marry her. He took with him six hundred soldiers armed with long clubs. In all haste and burning with vengeance, he came to the country of the Gaburs. His soldiers destroyed the houses of the people there and threw the remains into the neighbouring stream. The long flowing beards of these people were used as ropes for binding head with head, and then being dragged together in a helpless state these heads were cut off. No way of escape they found and they cried for mercy which was not granted them. The Gabur Raj, the bridegroom, was arrested and impaled. The flowing waters of the river near the city became reddened with the blood of the Gabur people.

Shyam Ray.

"Oh, where is my handsome *Dom* girl gone at this crisis? Poison has spread all over my body. The cruel

Gaburs shot arrows tipped with poison and I am doomed to death. My father is responsible for all this. Whom should I accuse? That I leave this world is no pain to me, but that I leave you, my beloved, is a thought which pinches me at the hour of death. Alas! I am not destined to see your beautiful face at the last hour. For a day did I not enjoy your sweet company in peace! You will no longer, my love, spread your long flowing hair and make it a bed for me. No more will you persuade me by your sweet words not to give up our native country for your dear sake. That smile of yours which has maddened me all my life I am no more destined to see. Cruel Providence did not reserve you for my joy in this life. If you were a tree, I would snatch a quiet hour of rest and sitting by you open my whole heart to you. If in my next life, I become a bird, I should wish you to be my mate. Both of us in that case would fly in the illimitable space of air and sing to each other our lay of love. If on my death I turn into a stream, may you be its sweet water! If I become the bird *Suka*, I would wish you to be my *Sāri*. If I become a bee, you should be, my beloved, the female bee. But one thing I pray to Providence with all my heart at this hour of death, that He may not give me the human form again and curse me with all the sufferings of that life."

The beautiful girl lamented sitting near the dead body of her beloved, "You have left me, oh my lord! When my wishes have not yet been fulfilled your wicked father sent you to the land of the Gaburias by a contrivance. I dissuaded you with all my heart from leaving your own motherland but you did not listen to my counsel. Alas! How can I forget your love? Who is it that made the garden of flowers wither in my breast before it ceased to give fragrance? Sorry as ever for my sake, I did not see your sweet smile even once for these long days. You rejected the glorious throne of your ancestors for my sake, and ascetic-like, exposed yourself to all the hardships of forest-life. I can never forget that I am only a poor woman and that you were a handsome prince, the glory of your kingdom. Your lips are for ever shut, my beloved, but if they would open for a little while, I would ask you what message you had for me at the last hour.

"Awake, arise, my beloved, and do not deceive me. Why should you lie down on the hard ground and subject yourself to such pain? I will hold you in close embrace and fly away from the land of the cruel Gaburs. Don't you know, my beloved, that I have given up my little all for your sake and that there is none to whom I can go at this hour of distress? Alas! a single night I do not recollect that I passed in your company in peace. So long I knew you to be mine in all respects. You were the heart of my heart and the soul of my soul. You were the rib of my breast. Alas! who is it that cursed me and deprived me of my most precious possession? The Gaburias have killed you with poison. Just see that I take the same poison and follow you. My prayer to God is that in death as in life I may be united with you.........I have taken it; and now let me die in peace, placing my head at the feet of my beloved."

Says Nitaichand, "Death has come to you bereft of all terror, you true woman. You know it well that love makes one immortal. No one is born again after having loved with full soul. The heart joins the heart and the spirit the spirit and there is Eternal Union. The shackles of human frame being disjointed, no obstruction remains for that perfect union.

(Ll. 1-72.)

CHAUDHURI'S LARĀI

PREFACE TO CHAUDHURI'S LARĀI.

The song of Chaudhuri's fight is the most popular of the comparatively modern ballads sung by the Mahomedan peasantry of Noakhali. In the introductory hymns I find the name of one Bas Miah as the author of the *Sār Geeta*—the original ballad. He was a native of the village Asvadia in that district. The ballad is divided into seven cantos and there is, besides, a supplementary canto which describes the death of Chand Bhandari, the redoubtable general of Rajendra Chaudhuri. During the nineties of the last century one Mahommed Eunus of the village Kalipur (P. S. Sudharam) published only three cantos of this ballad. But it is even doubtful if these three cantos were composed by him. We have an earlier version composed by one Eakubali which tallies with the printed version so strikingly that we are inclined to believe that Md. Eunus's version is but a copy of it with some additions and alterations. The minstrels often appropriate to themselves the credit of the authorship of these poems by suppressing the names of the poets and putting in their own names in the colophons. I do not know if this colophon was tampered with in this way in the present case. In reply to the charges made in the case against Mohammed Eunus in the Noakhali court under Secs. 292-293, I. P. C., he admitted that he copied largely from the previous versions of the ballad.

The poem published here contains about 3,000 lines, including the supplement. The printed version which gives only three cantos is complete in about 1,300 lines. The incomplete printed version was evidently recast by the publisher and we miss in it much of its pristine grace and simplicity.

The places mentioned in the ballad are all to be found in the maps of the district published from the Office of the Surveyor General. Babupur had latterly become the seat of the more important branch of the Chaudhuris. Biswambhar Sur, the founder of the Chaudhuri family of Noakhali, originally settled at Kalyanpur. From this city its different branches had migrated to other places, among which Babupur latterly rose to importance. The names of other places mentioned in connexion with the incidents of the ballad are Bhagalpur, Chamrakhola, Gopalpur, Senbag, Pubbapur, Chitashi, Palla Naduo, Raipura, Bhawaniganja, Terbaji, Laxmipur, Lamarchar, Maijdia and Karimpur. The army recruited from various places in response to a call from Manwor Gazi to join an expedition against Rajendra Chaudhuri, are vividly described, their picturesque dresses and arms forming an amusing account. The army of Pubbapur came with long bamboo poles on their shoulders, those from Targa had in their hands sticks with barbed iron heads, the soldiers of Chitashi were armed with long spears, the Garos of Raipur were conspicuous by their long moustache and so on. Chand Bhandari, the general of Rajendra, used to wear a red jacket and though he was a hero of heroes, he was dwarfish in appearance (Bk. III, Sec. 4, ll. 23-26). Chandrakala, the Brahmin girl, dishonoured by Raj Chandra, belonged to the village of Maijdia. She was married to a Brahmin of Lamarchar and it will be interesting to know that the present ballad was collected by Babu Manoranjan Chaudhuri, M.A., who is a native of Lamarchar. I will later on subjoin a genealogy of the Chaudhuris, some of whom took an active part in the incidents described in the ballad, and I jot down here some incidental notes on other characters.

Rangamala, the heroine, was the daughter of Apta Nar and sister of Golap Nar. Swarupmala was the wife of one Kala Yogi. The rough handling of this woman by Raj

Chandra Chaudhuri and her heroic efforts, verging on the masculine, to rescue herself from the clutches of the tyrant, is described with considerable force, though in a somewhat vulgar style (Bk. IV, Sec. 2). The District Gazetteer of Noakhali says, "A feud among the owners (of Pargana Babupur) caused by the love affairs of one Raj Chandra who wanted to marry a dancing girl, is still celebrated in song as *Chaudhurir Larāi.*" It should, however, be stated here that Rangamala was not a dancing girl, though it is true that she belonged to the family of Nars who earned their living by song and dance. The feud did not arise because Raj Chandra wanted to marry this girl, as alleged in the Gazetteer. It would not be possible for him to marry her as she belonged to a depressed caste.

The cause of the quarrel was a misunderstanding between the uncle and his nephew which arose out of a foolish act done by Raj Chandra. He was over head and ears in love with Rangamala, and in conformity with her wishes issued invitation to people far and near to join a dinner-party to be given by her,—Raj Chandra, of course, bearing the cost himself. Invitation from Rangamala would be considered a direct insult to the gentry of the locality. But they did not dare resent it lest they incurred the displeasure of Raj Chandra by doing so. Raj Chandra wanted that he should invite his old uncle also, but Rangamala said that it would be not only a foolish but an extremely dangerous step. The uncle, already enraged at the intrigue of his nephew with a woman of low caste, would take it as a deliberate affront if he were served with an invitation to dinner from one of the low-caste vile women, who had dared to pervert the morals of his nephew. But the nephew's head was giddy with romantic ideas for the woman whose social status, he thought, would be improved by the presence of his uncle at her house on the occasion. He also considered that his uncle's affection for him was so great that his fault, if any, would be looked over in a spirit of generous indulgence, which he was always accustomed to receive from him. So Rangamala's dissuasions bore no fruit, and the unhappy letter of invitation reached the uncle in due course.

Rajendra Chaudhuri was certainly annoyed by the conduct of his nephew. But it was the instigation of Chand, his general, that made the case very much worse, leading to a catastrophe fraught with dire results. Chand came to the house of the Nars determined to take revenge on Rangamala, for wrecking the character of his master's nephew, and taxing his purse to the utmost by lavish expenditure incurred on her account. By a wily stratagem he made Raj Chandra leave the house of the Nars for a short time, and then like a tiger falling on a flock of lambs, attacked the poor Nars, not sparing the beautiful Rangamala herself. Inspite of her pathetic appeal, her head was cut off and brought to Babupur as a trophy. The result was a wild outburst of passion on the part of Raj Chandra who avowed revenge at any cost and sacrifice. He sought the help of Inga Chaudhuri, a local Mahomedan Zemindar, and attacked his uncle's palace with his help.

The first thing that strikes the reader of this long poem is its corrupt atmosphere altogether different from that to which the old rural ballads of Bengal belonged. During the decline of Mahomedan rule, the country had lost all touch with the ethical grace and the standard of morality of which we have got such vivid portraitures in most of the Eastern Bengal ballads. Vitiated morals and profligacies of all sorts were rampant in Bengal in the eighteenth century, and the atmosphere shewed a striking similarity with that which marked the period of English history on the overthrow of the Commonwealth. Here also in Bengal we find writers like Wycherley who set at defiance all established rules of purity, indulging in the delineation of unrestrained passion. Bharat Chandra was beaten in his own ground by the author of the Kamini Kumar and Chandra Kanta, and even the saintly Ramprasad could not resist the power of evil that pervaded the literary taste of the country. If he failed to make his Vidya-Sundar as successful as that of his great contemporary,—in erotic matters at least he did not prove himself a whit behind Bharat Chandra.

When the higher classes of people were given to a grossly immoral taste, it is no wonder that their ideas should be found filtering down to the rustics. The illiterate ballad-makers, however, had always adhered to a standard of purity and were never lavish in their expressions in the sexual field. Though, therefore, in this long poem of Chaudhuri's *larāi* the country-poet gives us sketches of profligacy and sexual wantonness, imbued with the spirit of the age, nowhere does he become obtrusively indecent in the manner of the great classic writers of the period. Inspite of this a perusal of the poem is sickening from the point of view of sexual purity, particularly so, as we are accustomed to the crystal-like transparence of ideas in the descriptions of the affairs between the sexes given by the village-bards of the old school. The hero of the tale—Raj Chandra—is a spoiled child of nature and goes Don Juan-like on his love-errands spurning all rules of discipline and right conduct. Seldom do we find in this ballad, the rhythm and the intrinsic poetical charm of the earlier ballads. The ballad, it is true, has a flow which does not cause weariness to the readers perusing it, but the unflagging interest of the poem rests on the power of the poet in narrating his tale, rather than on any poetic or aesthetic grace on his part. The verses are as clumsy as those of the Maynamati songs. But the poet is never verbose or incoherent. That is perhaps why there is a compactness in the framing of the story lending it an unfaltering interest. It is, after all, a vulgar poem though its language is guarded. The taste displayed in the poem is almost repellent by reason of its lack of all refinement.

We have said many things to prejudice our readers against the ballad, but still it is a very interesting poem which claims a place of importance in our collection. It gives rich details of the domestic, social, and political life of the Bengalis of the period. The sketches are all life-like and appear to us as if reflected in a mirror. The way in which the Zemindars of this time used to administer the country, their maltreatment of the ryots, their hunt after women celebrated for beauty or personal accomplishment, their outbursts of passion which chafed like a stormy sea on being crossed and were not appeased till they carried out their impulsive, rash and worst villainies,—give us, indeed, a true picture of the state of things, from which the English saved us at that critical juncture of our national life. I am sorry to say that some Mahomedan gentlemen of culture and position took me to task for publishing these ballads saying that I exposed the Mahomedan administration by doing so. Nothing could be more remote from my mind, nor do I believe that these unassuming and innocent country-bards were ever actuated by any communal motive. If they described the atrocities committed by some Kazis, they were as unsparing in dealing with some of the Hindu Rajas who oppressed the people. These rural poets recorded true facts about their local heroes and to ascribe any sinister or racial motives to their faithful compositions is, I must say , a gross instance of misapprehension and injustice. In the second volume of Eastern Bengal Ballads, the reader will find the atrocities done by Abu Raja, evidently a Hindu. His acts cast into shade the worst tyrannies of the Kazi who committed atrocities on Chand Benode in the ballad of Malua. The behaviour of the merchant Meghua is full of perfidious villainy and another tyrant Kengu Raja of Chittagong has been unsparingly condemned in the ballad of Maishal Bandhu. But all records are beaten by the villainies of Raj Chandra described in this ballad, who did not feel any scruple in violating by force the honour of a lady belonging to the Brahmin caste—nay, to the family of those who were his religious preceptors.

The ballad-makers should be reckoned as the true historians of the times. They have sung the glories of the woman-kind and given their well-deserved encomiums. But they have not shrunk from the task of holding to light the villainies and wickednesses of those placed in power. These rural people have not been swayed by any party feeling or political consideration. Far in the recesses of their village homes, living outside all influences of politics, these men have held torches to illuminate the history of their country in its true character, and I shall have no admiration for the man who will hesitate to give them their desert.

This ballad gives us glimpses of the domestic life of Hindus and Mahomedans as it was more than a century ago. It is a record which is valuable for its accuracy of narration and for the many interesting facts it has brought to light. The weak fury of the Brahmans at the molestation of one of their women by the autocratic hero of the tale, their protests and combination proving to be of not a straw's value, the insults heaped on Raj Chandra by his uncle's menials, the atrocious black-mailing of Ram Bhandari, the trusted servant and guide of Raj Chandra, the wily manœuvres of Symapriya for seduction of village-girls and the power wielded by Rama, the Magh leader of coolies,—have all a grim humour, showing the corruption and degraded ways into which our country had sunk in those days. The anxieties and suspicion of Chhamiraddi as regards the possibility of the valuable Chadar that he had got as a gift, being taken from him by force, the medical aid which Ram Bhandari, playing the part of a deceitful quack, rendered to his master when he had got a sprain in his foot, the ingenious and crafty way in which he gave an interpretation to Rangamala about the promise of his master to get a pond excavated in her father's name—all these savour of the atmosphere of wickedness and degradation of moral life which marked this period of the history of Bengal. It is true that there is a vulgar humour proving that the rustic poet could not paint high life owing to his ignorance, yet inspite of this, it becomes obvious that most of the sketches he has drawn are full of life and not merely visionary things of fancy.

The sixth canto has certainly some redeeming poetic value which should be praised. The deadly grapple of Chand Bhandari with three Mahomedan ladies becomes exceedingly interesting, and the interview between Inga Chaudhuri and his surviving nephew Manwor is full of pathos. The march of Manwor to Babupur, the scene of havoc and devastation which Chand had caused in the palace of the Gazis, the just indignation felt by Manwor at this tragical end of the hostile action of Rajendra's men, have been narrated with force and even poetical vigour.

Chaudhurir Larāi, though it is an historical account, has some legendary elements in it. Such for instance, is Chand Bhandari's interview and talk with the goddess Kali.

Rangamala, the heroine of the tale, as we have already said, belonged to the Nar or dancing caste. It is, as I have said, one of the lowest castes of the Hindu society. The avocation of men and women of this caste being singing and dancing, their morals are not always unimpeachable. Hence the love-affairs of Rangamala are neither strange, nor an index to the morals of the other castes of Hindu society. The father and brother not only connived at this affair but the former prided on his daughter, who could have a pond excavated in his name by contracting an illicit connexion with Raj Chandra Chaudhuri. Rangamala is certainly not a member of those classes in Hindu society who would accept a husband as an avowed object of worship, however unworthy he might be. A Brahmin girl, doing what she did, could never be excused by the Hindu society. But reviewing her character from a broad and liberal point of view, it must be admitted that there is nothing in her conduct that strikes us as deserving of reproach. She was a paragon of beauty, and her father and brother conspired to make her miserable by getting her married to the wretch of a hunchback for filthy lucre. It did not certainly require the help of sorcery, as alleged in the ballad, to make her attracted to a handsome young man like Raj Chandra. Nor can we censure her for kicking the hunchback out of her room, though she was bound in lawful wedlock with him. Marrriage-bonds lose all sanctity and obligation when a woman is forced to accept a groom by such mean considerations which actuated her father. Hence Rangamala appears to me, though not an ideal of perfection, yet a really lovable girl who is above reproach. It should be said to her credit that though Raj Chandra was faithless to her as he went hunting after Swarupmala, Ranga did not choose any other man but adhered to her love—her first and last as well! In a moment of great torture she had said to Chand Bhandari that should he spare her life, she would consent to be his mistress. But this was an utterance at a moment of a perilous crisis in her life, which should not be taken seriously.

The Chaudhuris of Noakhali belonged to a noble family that traces their descent from Adi Sur, the king of Bengal. But the genealogy supplied by a present descendant of the family does not justify this claim. None of the living members of the family is above twenty-seventh in descent from Adi Sur whereas many of them are only twenty-seventh from Adi Sur. Taking three generations to cover a century, as is usually done in such cases, we find eight to nine hundred years including Adi Sur, according to the table supplied by the Chaudhuri family. The descendants of the Brahmins and the Kayasthas—the contemporaries of that monarch—are thirty-eighth or even fortieth in descent from their ancestors. The period we arrive at by ordinarily adopted calculations brings us to the reign of Ballal Sen who flourished at least four centuries after Adi Sur.

The first man of the Chaudhuri family who settled in Noakhali was Bishwambhar Sur and about him the District Gazetteer says, "Bishwambhar Sur, ninth son of Raja Adi Sur, king of Mithila, returning through Noakhali from a pilgrimage to Chandranath in the Chittagong district, saw in a dream the goddess Barahi who promised him the sovereignty of the country if he would worship her and this led to the settlement."[1]

Adi Sur, according to the Gazetteer, was a king of Mithila and not of Bengal.

We should, under the circumstances, dismiss the previous portion of the genealogy as utterly unreliable, retaining one or two names preceding that of Biswambhar Sur. We give the following table which seems to us as the true record of the genealogy of the Chaudhuris :—

1. Harihar.
2. Kshapakar.
3. Biswambhar Sur.
4. Ganapati.
5. Surananda Khan.
6. Bidyananda Khan.
7. Bijay Thakurta.
8. Ram Bhadra Karna Sur.
9. Haridas.

[1] Bengal and Assam District Gazetteer, by I. E. Webster, Vol. IV, Noakhali, p. 15.

10. Kabi Kirtti Sur.
11. Raj Prasad Narayan Ray.
12. Mahesh Narayan Ray.
13. Uday Narayan Chaudhuri.

14. Pratap Narayan — Rajendra Narayan

15. Raj Chandra (the hero).

16. Rajmanikya Chaudhuri.

17. Kalikanta Chaudhuri.

18. Rajkumar and Sasthirkumar.

Jogendra

Another branch of the family descended from Kandarpa Sur, a brother of Kabi Kirtti Sur (No. 10) is shown in the following table :—

10. Kabi Kirtti Sur and Kandarpa Sur.

11. Krishna Ram.

12. Indra Narayan Chaudhuri

13. Narottam

14. Ram Ratan

15. Gopal Krishna

16. Nandakumar

17. Jatindra — 17. Bipra — 17. Amulya

The information about the ancestors of the present Chaudhuri family was surely supplied to the District Gazetteer by the Chaudhuris themselves, and they called their great ancestor a king of Mithila who, calculating the period covered by his descendants belonged to the 12th century.

Taking into account the historical information supplied in the District Gazetteer of Noakhali and by Babu Jatindrakumar Ray, we come to learn that "Pargana Babupur was formerly a part of Bhulua in Noakhali, which was taken possession of by one Babukhan, a Brahmin in the seventeenth century and named after him."

This was a period when the coasts of Bengal were ravaged by Portuguese and Magh pirates from Chittagong. "Many are the tales told of these fierce men and the whole country would tremble at the cry of "the Magh! the Magh!" that told of their approach." (The District Gazetteer, pp. 18-19.) But since the installation of Babukhan on the *gadi* as ruler of the Pargana, the oppression of the Portuguese and the Maghs seems to have greatly abated. The Pargana of Babupur is within the Police stations of Begamganj and Feni—its area 37,33 sq. miles, containing 35 estates—land-revenue Rs. 14,952. Babupur is the chief seat of the incidents of the ballad. That the Maghs were powerful there even in the middle of the Eighteenth century when the events described in the ballad took place is proved by the references given at some length of the Coolie-Sardar Ram Magh. He was a sturdy chief who did not bow down to any one in the world excepting his parents and the Chaudhuris of Babupur. Babukhan dying childless, his property passed into the hands of the Chaudhuris who had already established themselves as rulers of the district of Noakhali in the Twelfth century. Kabi Kirtti Sur, his son Prasad Narayan Chaudhuri and grandson Mahesh Narayan were the first of the family who occupied Babupur and established their power there during the latter part of the Seventeenth century. Rajendra Narayan, one of the principal characters of this ballad, was the great-grandson of the aforesaid Mahesh Narayan. And Raj Chandra, the hero, was a nephew of Rajendra Narayan, They flourished in the latter part of the Eighteenth Century.

The descendants of this once distinguished family have lost all share of their property, principally, as it appears to us, owing to the profligacy of some of its members. Babu Jatindrakumar Ray tells us that Rajendra Chaudhuri, uncle of the hero of the tale Raj Chandra, gave his share to his grandson on the daughter's side—Rajkishore. But this man ruined his property by his drunken habits and extravagance. The District Gazetteer says of Radhakrishna's descendants, proprietors of the Pargana Babupur, "they were profligate and once more the estate came under the hammer." Raj Chandra's lewdness, in all the various channels of its activity, forms the subject-matter of this ballad. The whole atmosphere of the moral life in the small localities bore the taint spread by the courts of big Rajas and Chiefs. Bengal of the Eighteenth century seems to have sunk low owing to anarchical movements on all sides caused by subversion of the Imperial power. In the printed edition of a part of this ballad already referred to, we find the following line written about Babukhan, the founder of the Pargana: "When Babukhan had the full vigour of youth, he had established a ward on the eastern side of a large pond attached to his palace, which was mainly inhabited by whores :—

"যখন সে বাবুরামের গায়ে বল ছিল
দীঘির পুর্ব্বপারে কত রেণ্ডি বসাইল।"

"The Chaudhuris had ten strongly built forts in the neighbourhood of Babupur and seventeen hundred guards were stationed at the front gate to keep watch over the palace by night.''—

'' দুই দিকে দুই কিল্লা দিল লড়াই করিবারে
সতের শ জাগিন্দার রাখে আগ-দরজার পরে ।''

(Printed Edition.)

The generals Ram Bhandari and Chand Bhandari were heroes of a hundred fights and the whole country was in dread of these Chaudhuris. But there were influential Mahomedan Zemindars in the district who sometimes proved more than a match for them. The power of Manwor, one of these Zemindars, may have been exaggerated by the composer of this ballad. But it is an historical fact that though Rajendra's general wanted to fight and teach a lesson to the interfering Moslem Chief, the lord of Babupur beat a retreat from the field, considering discretion to be the better part of valour. This flight is not only due to the fact that the great army of Manwor Gazi struck terror in his heart, but also that his own nephew became the ally of the Mahomedan and told him the secret about his army and resources. The tender relation between the nephew and the uncle, inspite of their strained feelings for a time, has been delineated with a fine touch of pathos and the reconciliation is sweet after the storm of hostility has passed away.

In these ballads of the old school written both by Hindus and Mahomedans, the catholic acceptance of objects of mutual worship and the respect paid to religious traditions by each other cannot but strike us, indicating the happy condition of amity and peace that existed between the two great sections of Bengal. The contrast strikes us all the more in view of the tension created of late by interested parties. The Moslem poet thus sings his hymns in the preliminaries :

"Let me first of all pay my tribute of respect to the image of Jagannath at Puri. There is no restriction observed there in regard to food, and cooked rice is sold there in the market. The *Pariahs* cook the food which Brahmins do not feel scruple in taking from their hands. People after taking cooked rice and fish do not wash their hands with water but wipe them on their heads......Further east let me sing a hymn in honour of Benares. The name of Hari is sung there in every house, and in the door-way one finds the sacred plant Tulasī everywhere. Formerly this plant was found on the mountains but the reverent Vaisnavas brought them to the plains for worship... In the south let me bow down to the golden city of Lanka and to the queen Mandodari, mother of Indrajit."

One might think that these hymns were composed by a Hindu. So strikingly the Moslems of old were imbued with the religious belief of their neighbours! Even now the singers of the glories of Manasa Devi and Goddess Kali are recruited from the Mahomedens, though the embers of communal strife are now burning down to ashes this beautiful and felicitous catholicity which had made village-life so pleasant to us in the days gone by. The Hindus in the up-country perform the Moharrum with no less ardour than the Mahomedans themselves.

In regard to the extracts which we have quoted above, we may note down some passing observations. The Mahomedan writer, evidently owing to his ignorance of Hindu practices, has committed some errors in his allusions to Benares and Puri. In Puri the people are not allowed to take fish within the temple-compound and in Benares the name of Hara rather than that of Hari is generally sung by the people as that holy city is the principal seat of the Saivas. Neither is the Tulasī regarded so highly there as the Bel leaves which are indispensable for the worship of Siva. The line—"ভাত মাছ

খাইলে তারা মুণ্ডে পুছে হাত" will recall the words of Bharat Chandra—"খাইয়া প্রসাদ ভাত. মাথায় মুছিব হাত." But the unlettered rustic poet did not get his inspiration from that eminent classic poet as will appear from his wrong allusion to fish. Such sentiments were in the atmosphere, and Bharat certainly got it from the current phraseology and embellished it when he put it in his poem.

Mohammed Eunus who claims the authorship of a portion of Chaudhuri's Larāi published by Rahim Bax Sardar from the Noakhali Hitaishi Press, was charged under Secs. 292-293, I. P. C., and punished by the Sadar Sub-Divisional Court of Noakhali. The book was found to contain many obscene passages and the publication was suppressed. I have often referred to the fact that the publishers of old ballads, generally speaking, introduce erotic elements not warranted by the original poems. In the present version which directly comes from the lips of a peasant, no such obscenity is to be found.

DINESH CHANDRA SEN.

Relics of a fort near Rajendra Narayan Choudhuri's palace in Babupur. P. 239.

Rajendra Narayan Choudhuri's pond at Sindur Kayit in Babupur. P. 229.

The broken cannon recovered from the fort. P. 239.

Chaudhuri's Larai.

Book I.

(I)

There was once a Raja of the name of Rajnarayan Chaudhuri who cut out jungles, founded a city and there built his palace. The city had fine gates in rows such as the front gate, the middle gate, etc. The Raja had constructed a beautiful Audience-hall in the city which they called Rajganj. He was one of the most powerful men in the locality and held in high esteem by all. Near the front gate of the city sixty pious souls (Bairāgis) recited scriptures, constantly offering benediction to the Raja and his people. Fond of amusements Rajnarayan had in his palace a compartment set apart for dancing women—excellent actresses all of them—and for dancing boys. The women wandered about diffusing light, humour and freshness which the Raja keenly appreciated. In his rest-house constructed in the middle of a tank he often enjoyed the company of gay women. (Ll. 1-11.)

(II)

[*Chorus.*—Alas ! Where and to whom can I disclose the secret of my heart? I have come to know of a precious jewel. How pleased would I be if I could secure it for myself !]

In the house of the Nars (*lit.* dancers, generally a class of people whose occupation is to beat drums and play on other musical instruments) at Talebpur there was once a great festivity. The hunchback Ramgaichya plodded his way thither to feast himself on fried rice. On the way, as ill luck would have it, he met the fair damsel Rangamala. He purposely kept himself at a distance and glanced at her closely. She was like a golden image from whom he could hardly take off his eyes. "Oh, good woman," he cried to a fellow passenger and said, "will you kindly tell me who this fair lady is ?" "Well Ramgaichya, I will tell you who she is. If you want to protect your honour and prestige, better be off and do not covet her. She belongs to the family of Apta Ram and a sister is she of Golap. They have given her the choice name of Rangamala."

When Ramgaichya heard this, he resolved, "If I should care for my life, I must try to secure her at any cost."

[*Chorus.*—Go first and put up your case before the mother of Shyama.]

Slowly did Ramgaichya walk up to his own home. He was all along in a pensive mood and then resolved to open his mind to his father Nachhi Ram. Accordingly he called on him and said, "Oh, my father, I intend to open my heart to you, and at the same time do not feel bold to do so." Nachhi Ram gave him a reassuring look, and said, "Do not fear, my son. Speakout, without any hesitancy."

"Hear me, my esteemed father. Be pleased to arrange my marriage with Rangamala. With a gay heart, you are to give me permission. She is a daughter of Apta Ram and sister of Golap. They have given her the choice name of Rangamala."

When the father heard this desire of his son, he took a broom in his hand and in great anger followed the hunchback saying, "You fool, you aspire to marry that girl who is the pet of the house!"

Thus pursued, the hunchback ran away and now and then looked behind to see if the father was still at his heels.

In great anger at this insult, Ramgaichya came to his father's house and swore in this way, "By my-life I swear that I will open my father's iron chest with the help of one of my numerous keys." As he resolved so he did. He succeeded in opening the big iron chest of Nachhi Ram with the help of one of his keys. On opening the chest the first thing that struck him was a purse containing a thousand rupees. Forthwith he took it in his hand and in great haste proceeded towards the house of Apta Ram.

Reaching the house of Apta Ram, he saw the maid-servant Durga, standing at the gate. He called her aloud and stated the urgency of the case.

[*Chorus*.—Oh my kind woman, do not be hard-hearted; I clasp your feet and submit my humble prayer.]

"Now hear me, my beautiful Durga. I offer you here rupees five hundred. This is only for taking betels (only a small sum for refreshments). I am going to propose my marriage with the lady. If you can help me in the matter, you will have a handsome reward. From others you may expect coins which they will give you counting with their hands, but from this hunchback you will have them measured in scales."

When the maidservant received this offer, she said, "Let me first go to the inner apartment and sound them."

Slowly did she proceed towards the inner apartment and met Apta Ram. She said, "Hurrah ! Comc close to me, Apta Ram, and see what I have to tell you about. Your luck has turned and there will be no end to your good fortune now."

Apta Ram.

"But, my good woman, here are my brows, the seat of fortune. If my luck has turned, how can my brows be intact in their place?"

Durga.

"Oh! no. It is not the forehead that has changed. Fortune has really smiled on you. I have got a bridegroom for your daughter, who has the highest social status. He has offered rupees five hundred merely for your taking betels. If you agree to the proposal, he will give you hoards."

When Apta Ram heard this, a smile played on his lips and he sweetly said, "Listen to me, my good woman. See my son Golap on this point. If you can secure his assent, mine will come as a matter of course. If he agrees, go and settle the marriage at once."

Durga Dasi called on Golap and said, "A bright star shines on your luck, dear lad. You will have a fortune in no time. A princely lad of the highest social status is suppliant for the hand of your sister. At the very outset, he has offered rupees five hundred for taking betels."

Golap said, "The question of money is of secondary importance. First I must know if he is worthy of being the husband of my beautiful sister Rangamala. Tell me if his colour is bright and if he is handsome."

When Durga heard the words of Golap, she began to think within herself: "It will be easy enough to satisfy their demands but what can I do to prevent the hump on his back from being seen?"

From there she went in slow steps to Ramgaichya and told him that the party had wished that he should be presently at their house.

In a high spirit of glee Ramgaichya went to Apta Ram's house, in the company of the maidservant.

[*Chorus.*—Who is there who has such a precious jewel for her husband like me?]

When he appeared at the house of Apta Ram, he wanted to see Golap Ray. Golap Ray came and was surprised to see Ramgaichya as the proposer. The hunchback had his body covered with ringworm. The very sight of the wretch was held inauspicious. His ribs had sunk low and his chest looked like a nut-shell. One would find a black owl hovering over his head in the air;[1] if one would look at the face of the hunchback.

A far greater consideration than all these weighed, however, with Golap Ray, and being unable to resist the temptation of money, he agreed to Ramgaichya's proposal and settled the date. (Ll. 1-112.)

(III)

[*Chorus.*—Who will go with me amongst you, oh! Braja Gopis? All are attracted by the sound of his flute. I am going to bring water from the Jumna.]

Admatara, Padmatara, Sonamala, Jaytara, Kalitara, Kanchanmala, Kalavati, Mugasashi and Rai (called *bet-tolani* for her skill in basket-making) are the names of some of those women who came forward to take part in the function of marriage. The mother of Rangamala brought the Gilla fruit, sandal and Chua for scenting the body of Rangamala. The maids surrounded her on all sides and in the midst of them stood Rangamala in the full height of her maidenly charms.

The maids helped her in her bridal bath and then took her near the altar where the hunchback was made to sit by her, and a Brahman priest was called to minister to the marriage function. The Brahman finished his Puja and recited the mantras suited to the occasion. Then came the moment when the bride and bridegroom had to look at each other's face. At a glance at the hunchback's face, sparks of fire emanated from the eyes of the bride. She burst into a fit of anger and looked like a bamboo-grove set on fire.

[1] An inauspicious sign foreboding a disaster.

"Did my brother lose his eyes and all power of judgment? He brought this wretch of a hunchback for me in preference to Rasik who is our close neighbour. It is my old father who is responsible for this foul deed. A mean greed of money drove away all his sense of right and wrong, and he chose this hunchback for my husband! Well, I will see how I may retaliate on this devil of a hunchback."

The marriage was, however, finished and the bridegroom took the bride to his house.

She stretched her body on a soft couch and the hunchback sat in a corner of it. Staying at a little distance from her he cast a stealthy glance at her wishing to observe how she looked. She at once kicked him out in great disgust, and afraid of encountering her again, the hunchback Ramgaichya took to his heels and breaking open the door of the house, he ran on to the street. From the day that Rangamala had seen him at close quarters, frightened by his hideous form she never agreed to put up with him.

Once Ramgaichya fled when his old father was pursuing him with a broom, and this story of his life was repeated. He fled this time to escape from the kicks of his beautiful bride. (Ll. 1-40.)

Book II.

(I)

[*First Chorus.*—I did not know that love would be a source of so much trouble to me. He for whom I have forsaken my social prestige, my property, my home and all, has abandoned me. Woe be to love!]

[*Second Chorus.*—If you will love, keep it secret. Let no one beside yourself know of it. Many a person died of broken heart by falling in love. Now, my audience, I am going to tell you how Rangamala fell in love.]

Near the gateway of Raj Chandra Chaudhūri's palatial building lived a Vaisnava woman named Syamapriya who maintained herself by begging. One day she went to a place called Ahladi. For the whole day she visited houses on right and left with the begging bowl in her hands. And it was only when four Dandas remained of the day, she came to the house of the Nars. She cried out for alms whereupon Rangamala called her from inside the house.

When her voice was heard, the maidservant Durga appeared before her near the temple of the house and with nine *buries* of cowries in a plate, she offered to give alms to Syamapriya. "Accept this," said she, "and with this the good wishes of Rangamala and Golap." Syamapriya felt pleased with the name of Rangamala and thought within herself: "Beautiful must be she whose name is so pleasant to hear. How can I have a sight of this maiden?"

She took out of her bag her cymbals and playing on them began to sing in musical concord with her instrument. The little children of the house of the Nars gathered there to hear her songs.

Song.

"Difficult it is to get a person after one's mind. If after all one is found who pleases the heart, that one alas! does not return love. Could I have one after my mind, I would have first conquered that one's heart. But such a one could never be found."

Sweet was her voice and the cymbals sounded merrily as she sang. The words and the rhymes could not be heard from a distance, but the voice with its tender appeal charmed the heart. Rangamala from within the house heard the song and asked her mother's permission to go near the gateway and listen to it closely. The mother said, "All along you have been within the four walls of your beautiful house—the *Jod Bangla*. Why should you feel a desire to-day to go near the outer gate?" The daughter, however, insisted on hearing the song and embracing her mother repeated her request, whereupon the mother took her near the gateway of the outer walls and asked her to stay there for a little while and hear the *Kirtan*. Rangamala said, "I will simply have a sight of her and return after staying a moment."

Now when Syamapriya saw her, she looked with intent eyes examining her from head to foot. Though a woman, she felt the overwhelming charm of her glorious beauty. Rangamala also was pleased with the appearance of the songstress and observing that she was fatigued, she fanned her waving the flying end of her sāḍi. This sympathetic treatment soothed her. So she said, "Your beauty charms my eyes, though I am a woman. I wonder who is the fortunate one who has got you for wife."

Rangamala said, "Thank you for your sympathy and kind query. I am the most miserable woman on the earth. The fire of my despair is burning my heart, and though inwardly consumed, I never open my heart to any one. Why have you, by your affectionate words, revived this fire with a redoubled force by a reference to my husband? My father felt no pity for me and losing his eyes and ears in the greed of money, he has married me to the wretched hunchback Ramgaichya. My brother Golap, hitherto full of kindness for me, unfortunately concurred with the wishes of my father. Close to my house is the worthy youth Rasik, but they did not care to join my hands with a really deserving bridegroom, but have destroyed my life, by choosing the hunchback for my husband. I now find that in the home of my parents no one has any feeling for me, since they have behaved as even my worst enemies would not.''

When Syamapriya heard this, her indignation knew no bounds. She burst out just as a bamboo-plant does when fire is put into one of its knots; but suppressing her feelings at the moment, she began to meditate on the step she should take to rescue Rangamala from her distressed condition. Suddenly an idea struck her —'' She is just the girl for Raj Chandra Chaudhuri. I am going to tell him about her. How nice it will be for her to enjoy herself in the beautiful Rest-house of the Chaudhuris. I am sure if I give a clue of this to Raj Chandra, I will have such reward that I shall not be in any need for the rest of my life.''

Thinking in this strain, she straightway left the house and did not disclose her intention to anybody.

(Ll. 1-92.)

(II)

[*Chorus.*—Full of satisfaction, she walks in a pleasant gait, the joy of Syamapriya's heart was manifest in her face.]

She came to the gateway of the palace of the Chaudhuris and began to think, '' The situation is difficult. I am not known to anybody here. How can I communicate my wishes to Raj Chandra? '' From a little distance she beheld that Rajendra and his nephew were holding the Durbar in the Audience-hall. An officer was explaining some papers to Raj Chandra and he reclining on his *Takia* (pillow) was seated at ease.

Full of presence of mind, she devised a way to introduce herself. She again took out the cymbals from behind and began to play on them. Its jingling sound attracted the notice of Raj Chandra and when he glanced at her, she made a sign to him with her eyes. Her eyes twinkled in such a way that Raj Chandra was not yet sure whether she signed to him for a private interwiew. But on a second thought, he perceived that it was a sign. He told his uncle that he was not feeling well and that he wanted to retire. Saying so, he came to his inner apartment. He wore a cloth with a golden border and from his shoulders hung a *Chadar* of rosy colour. His shoes were embroidered with jewels. Thus attired he approached Syamapriya. He said, "What is the reason, dear Syamapriya, that you have brought me here by a sign of your eyes?" Syamapriya sweetly said, "Listen to me with attention. I crave your Highness's permission to relate a story. I have beheld a spectacle at the house of the Nars which I can never forget, but Your Highness must reward me handsomely. I will give you love's treasure." Right glad at his heart, Raj Chandra caught Syamapriya in his arms. For he was so fond of forming new intimacies with the fair sex that he could run like a wild horse to fulfil his object, even if it were in the darkest of nights.

The tale was a simple one. Rangamala, the daughter of Apta Ram and sister of Golap, was the most unfortunate girl alive.

Raj Chandra said, "No need of further details. Just show me the way to the house of the Nars." Syamapriya said, "If I had given a clue of such a treasure to one who ploughs the fields with his own hand, even such a peasant would have given me four or five rupees at once as a reward." Raj Chandra was ashamed at the words of the Vaisnava woman and thrust his hand into his pocket to see what was there. He took in his hand a rupee and handed it over to the woman. She shrank a little and said, "Shame! Is it a fit gift for Your Highness to offer to me? Though I live by begging I have a lac of rupees in my chest and is it fair that you should treat me as a beggar?" Raj Chandra had nothing more in his pocket at the moment and really felt ashamed. He said, "My property is immense and so are my riches. Don't doubt me, I assure you, when through you, my object will be fulfilled, I will make you the owner of the Rajganj market." She smiled in derision and said, "*Baki* (credit) means *phaki* (deceit) : this is known to all. Many men have I seen who after having achieved their end have played false ; they latterly behaved in a way as if there had been never an acquaintance." Raj Chandra on hearing this took a piece of Chinese paper from his pocket and instantly drew a deed making endowment of a plot of land on which sixty families of Vaisnavas lived.

The woman was right glad at this gift and said, "You should come with me a few hours before sunset. Now I bid you farewell."

Raj Chandra went a few paces and then thought, "Easy it is to get information about beautiful women but difficult to win them for one's purpose. I have not asked Syamapriya if she knows of the art of charming women." When he was thinking in this strain, Syamapriya had gone a few steps and he ran in haste to overtake her. Turning her head back, she perceived the young landlord pursuing her and meeting him said, "Everything is arranged and you will presently have something to make you happy. What is the reason that you are running in haste evidently to have some further talk with me." Raj Chandra whispered to her ears, "I forgot to ask you one thing. Do you know the art of winning a woman's heart ?"

Syamapriya smiled wickedly and said, "Since I have learnt that art, seven times did I grow old and seven times did I become young again. If I put my charmed betel within the mouth of an old person, the ebbing blood will flow again (one's youth will revive)." Raj Chandra replied, "You must show me this wonderful effect of your charmed betel to confirm my faith in your words." Upon which she said, "Just bring me a handful of betel and nuts. If I get these, I can give immediate proof of the charm." Raj Chandra said, "No hurry. You may conveniently prove your point in the afternoon."

(Ll. 1-122.)

(III)

Saying so, he returned home. He took his meals and had his midday nap. When only four *dandas* remained for the sun to set he called Ram, the keeper of the stall, to his presence and ordered him to bring his waler. When the waler was brought, saddled and duly caparisoned, he at once rode upon it and started for the house of Kala, the betel-seller. The waler ran speedily in high spirit and at once came to the house of the betel-seller. The young landlord had the horse bound to the trunk of a mango tree and called Kala Barai (betel-seller). The man instantly appeared before him and when he beheld the lord of twenty-two parganas before his humble hut, he began to tremble in fear. With clasped hands, he delivered himself in this way, "People cannot have a sight of Your Highness's august personage even if they pay a thousand rupees as *Nazar*. How fortunate am I that I have the pleasure of seeing my lord at my humble hut!" Raj Chandra said, "I have come to you for one purpose. Just give me one *bira* of betels." The betel-seller did not seem to believe this and said, "Is it possible that for such a poor thing Your Highness has visited my doors? If you would have sent word through one of your meanest servants, I would have myself gone to your palace with cart-loads of betel."

"It is not that sort of betel that I want, my friend. I want that all the leaves of this *bira* should be the product of a single plant."

Then did the betel-seller believe in the words of Raj Chandra and asking him to wait entered his inner apartments. He asked his wife to get a *bira* of betels of very fine quality, all products from a single plant. She took pains to comply with the wishes of her husband and succeeded in securing the betels as desired.

Right glad was Raj Chandra to receive what he wanted and asked Kala what should be the price of his goods.

Kala Barai said, "It is a very small thing and I need not say anything about the price. Whatever your Highness will give me will be gladly accepted."

Raj Chandra thought for a moment as to what he should offer. He remembered that he was once put to shame by offering a rupee to Symapriya. After thinking a little over the point, he handed him five rupees and the betel-seller was greatly pleased with the price. (Ll. 1-48.)

(IV)

The services of Ram Bhandari were requisitioned again and he helped His Highness to get upon his horse. The rider was all in haste and the waler went along the way bending his neck in high pride. On his way, Ram Bhandari begged of the prince leave for a few minutes for a private business and being thus released from his duty, stealthily went to the house of Kala, the betel-seller, by a road in the east. He looked through the window of the house and saw Kala engaged in sounding the silver coins to examine if they were good.

He suddenly entered the house without waiting for permission and said, "Now, my betel-seller, you must repay the five rupees that His Highness has given you." He stared aghast at these words and said, "His Highness has just given me the money, why should I return?" Ram Bhandari replied, "He has given the five coins to-day only to get them back with interest in the shape of some blows to-morrow. Why should I come to your house if His Highness had not sent me for the money? Now readily consent to my order. If you object, instantly shall I have you bound to this *sal* tree and beat you with the sharp heels of my shoes." The betel-seller said, "No, I will not give the money," and as he said so, he drew the strings of his purse tightly. Ram Bhandari perceived that the purse was closed with five rupees inside. He instantly fell upon him and began to give him blows mercilessly. Many a blow did the betel-seller get in his back, as many on his neck and several on both his sides. The number of blows came up to nine *buries*. Not satisfied with this he caught hold of the bough of a tree and beat him with it.

Receiving the blows, Kala did not utter a word but many a time he bent himself low and clasped the feet of the man who assaulted him thus. The wife of the betel-seller saw all this from a distance and not being able to control her rage came up with a long bamboo pole for retaliation. Strong as Ram Bhandari was, it was easy for him to throw her down and drive her by catching hold of her flowing locks, and thus was the wife of the betel-seller removed from the battle-field.

When he saw no way out of his very deplorable situation, Kala was obliged to open the strings of his purse and return the five rupees that he had got. Seizing this money, Ram Bhandari came back to the youthful lord and when asked by him as to the cause of so much delay, he produced some plea which gave satisfaction to his master.

(V)

Then did Raj Chandra return to his house and visited the hut of the Vaisnava woman Syamapriya. He offered her the betels which she took in her hands and began to recite *mantras* on them for giving effect to her charm. She blew upon them with her breath, but the betels lay on the earth without moving, ever so little. Then did Raj Chandra say, "Now, sister, there is no efficacy in your charm. Yours is a mere vaunt. How can I put faith in your words? There was a time when you could charm young men with your youth and a charmed betel was hardly necessary. The lovers would fear your eyes reddened with anger but now an ebb-tide has come upon your youth. Your teeth have fallen and your cheeks have grown lank. The humour of your words is not appreciated now. And that smile on your lips which once charmed people has faded, so that those who prided on your friendship and sought your smile now pass by without noticing you and accost you as aunt, the epithet given to old women."

Greatly ashamed as she was at the words of the young Raja, she still continued to recite her *mantras* but the betels lay there as before without moving.

Then did she say in despair, "It is beyond my power, dear lord, to do anything with this betel, whereupon Raj Chandra said, "Give me the betels. I will charm them. Just see if you can resist the effect." Saying this he recited the name of Mother Kali and uttered the *mantras* himself.

Syamapriya snatched tho betels but got a shock and could not retain them in her hands. She admitted her defeat and acknowledged that he was a superior adept in the art. Then did she put in her bag the betels charmed by Raj Chandra himself. She took her meals as usual and slept a sleep full of anxieties. In the morning she arose and with the charmed betels went straight to the house of the Nars.

(Ll. 1-89.)

(VI)

She stood at the gateway and raised her voice, asking for alms. Rangamala heard the voice and ordered the maidservant Durga to give alms to the beggar.

Durga came with alms but was surprised to see that it was the same Vaisnava woman who had come the day before. She came back to Rangamala and said that the same Vaisnava woman had come again. Rangamala burnt with rage at this report and said, " Only yesterday she took alms from our house. This woman must be very greedy. She has come again to-day. Drive her off from this house." Durga was naturally bent on taking drastic steps in such cases and now the fire was put to flame by her mistress's words. She gathered together a number of maidservants and fell upon poor Syamapriya treating her to blows and kicks. Syamapriya in this critical situation had recourse to a device and exclaimed, " I have not come for alms. I have come on some other mission. Do not assault me so cruelly. Hear my story patiently. I had a sister whom I held dear as my life. Like two pigeons we lived together side by side in happiness. As ill luck would have it, she has left the world, leaving me alone. My heart longs for that affection which I used to get from my sister and I have been roaming like a mad woman in search of one who would be like her. Believe me, I have found in Rangamala some striking resemblance to my sister. My heart yearns for calling her sister. Will not she permit me to address her so? "

Hearing this the maidservants went to Rangamala and said, " It is not for alms that the Vaisnava woman has come. She had a sister whom she has lost and she has found in you some likeness of hers. She does not care for the company of Vaisnava men. She is longing for the sort of love she got from her sister, who is now dead and wants permission to address you as such."

When Rangamala heard the story she asked her maidservants to bring the Vaisnava woman to her.

Syamapriya was admitted into the room and a small wooden stool was pointed out to her and she sat there.

The stool cracked and broke down when she had taken her seat and this gave rise to laughter amongst the maid-servants. Rangamala caught hold of the woman by her hands, as she looked abashed and made her sit on her own couch. She was served with betel and tobacco. Syamapriya was full of hesitancy as to how she would introduce her subject. It was also a problem to her as to how she would make her take the betel charmed by Raj Chandra. But she had a ready wit and presence of mind and thus addressed Rangamala, " Now, Rangamala, I have got the liberty to call you my sister. I have taken your betel and tobacco. But what can I give you in return? If you would not take offence, I should like to offer you some betels that I have with me. From to-day, we two are bound by ties of sisterhood."

Rangamala without any ado stretched her hand and said, " Give me your betel." She took it and at once put it into her mouth and swallowed the charmed thing. Immediately the effect worked on her system and she asked Syamapriya to sit close by her. She said, " What is there in your betel I do not know, but on taking it I feel a strange tremor in my heart. I feel inclined to throw off my ornaments. My necklace of large pearls which I like so much does not please me. A strange feeling has overpowered me. Will you tell me what was in the betel? For reasons unknown to me, I feel a desire for a stranger named Chaudhuri."

Syamapriya said, " A poor woman I am and you are cutting a joke with me. Is it becoming of one whom I have called sister? You speak of a person named Chaudhuri. But I assure you I do not know any man of that name. Had I known him, I would have brought him here for your sake. It is a strange story that you have told me. I do not know where such a person lives nor anything else about him."

Rangamala said, " Strange! Your betel has taken effect. There is surely something in it." Syamapriya said in reply, " Your words are unreasonable. I shall swear that I am perfectly innocent. I have given you betels and called you sister, all for securing your good wishes and affection. Why should you accuse me in this way and give pain to my heart? I ask you one thing. Do you bathe in a pond or get water fetched at your house for the purpose ? Rangamala answered that it was her practice to bathe in water brought to her house by servants, whereupon the Vaisnava woman said, "I get betel and nuts by begging. They are certainly not of a superior quality. The nuts specially are strong and it may be that owing to your taking these nuts your head may have become giddy. It would do well for you if you bathe in a pond. If you take my advice, why not come to the pond Raghabshiar. It would cool your head." When Rangamala heard it, she went straight to her mother and asked permission to go to Raghabshiar. The mother looked at her with curiosity and said, " You have all along remained within the four walls of this house. What makes you to-day wish for going out and bathe in the pond? " Rangamala persisted in her request and would not listen to any objection. The mother was obliged to give her consent. She asked, " Whom would you take as companions?" Rangamala gave a list of the maidservants who were to accompany her. They were Adma, Padma, Saramala, Tara, Jaytara, Kalitara, Kalavati, Kanchanmala, Durga and others. "But," she said, " Syamapriya has called me sister. She too must go with me." The mother consented, the maidservants took with them *chua*, Sandal, Gilla fruit and other toilet-articles. Rangamala went ahead of them all and behind her Syamapriya proceeded in pleasant gait. Rangamala looked behind and saw that Syamapriya was dancing as she was following her, upon which she said, " But sister, how is it that though there is no occasion for it and neither any musical instrument to keep pace, you are dancing while walking on the public way?" Syamapriya whispered to her ears, "Ranga, you do not know that though I have grown old I cannot live without loving a man and this feeling of amour gives me such an impetus that I dance in joy." Ranga took offence at these words and her face reddened in anger. She called Durga Dasi and said, "This old hag should be taught a lesson." The maidservants of the house of the Nars were always eager to apply force, and they all gathered there with Durga at their head and began to beat Syamapriya. Leopard-like they jumped and fell upon the Vaisnava woman and treated her to blows. The blows they gave her were fourteen *buries*. Then they beat her with bamboo-sticks. Being assaulted in this way, she did not know what to do but as often as she received the blows, she clasped the feet of Rangamala and sought for pardon saying, "In an unguarded moment did I utter a wrong thing. It was merely for cutting a joke. Why should you take it so seriously? Show me a little compassion and ask the maidservants to desist from assaulting me in this way." Rangamala's heart melted in pity and she ordered the maidservants to cease.

They reached the pond and Syamapriya with Ranga's permission went to the other side of the pond and filled a small pitcher with water. Ranga in the meantime had descended into the water where Syamapriya poured the contents of her pitcher. This water was charmed by her. So when it came in touch with Rangamala who was pouring water over her head, the effect of it was instantly felt. She perceived a strange emotion in her heart and cried out, "Oh Syamapriya! this time there is no doubt of it. My mind for some unknown cause seeks a person named Chaudhuri." Syamapriya was enraged at her words, and said in a rude tone, "You talk light-heartedly with me in this way and if I am encouraged by your indulgence to cut a joke in response, you appoint your maid-servants to assault me mercilessly. I am frightened and would not like to speak freely with you." Rangamala embraced her affectionately saying, "I was wrong, dear sister, but after all I am your sister and can I not expect to have pardon from you?" The Vaisnava woman was right glad at her words and said endearingly, "I can tell you something which will interest you. I know a person named Raj Chandra. He is the son of a great landlord. If you wish, I can bring him to you." Ranga was pleased with her and entreated her to bring Raj Chandra to the landing ghat of the pond as soon as possible. (Ll. 1-150.)

(VII)

Now Syamapriya proceeded towards the house of Raj Chandra on this mission. But here I must change my topic and say something about Raj Chandra.

Raj Chandra one day said to Ram Bhandari, "That Vaisnava woman took a gift from me promising to bring me message from Rangamala, but since then she has not yet turned up. What is the matter with her? Has she played me false?" Ram said in a sulky tone, "These Vaisnava women are never to be trusted. They make large promises and then produce smooth excuses; they always practise deceit for earning money." The young lord asked Ram as to what should be done now. Ram wanted to go to know the reason and asked permission of his master for it.

He was a stalwart man. He clothed himself with a *dhoti* which measured forty yards. In majestic steps did he advance and come near the spot where the stone slab bearing inscriptions about Rusti Khan[1] lay and there as he

[1] Rusti Khan was the father of Paragal Khan, Governor of Chittagong, who had employed Kavindra Parameswar to translate the Mahabharat into Bengali.

cast his glance, he saw Syamapriya coming in slow steps. As soon as he saw her, he made a bound at her and catching hold of her by her forelocks, began to beat her. He said, "Thou witch, why hast thou taken money from my master and disappeared since, making false promises?" The woman angrily replied, "Who told you, you rogue, that I got money from your master?" At these words of the woman Ram became the more enraged and bound her hands with a rope and dragged her to his master's palace. From a distance Raj Chandra saw that his favourite servant was dealing blows on Syamapriya. He indicated his displeasure at this action and made a sign to Ram to desist, whereupon the servant fled in fear, and Syamapriya approaching the young lord began to cry. Raj Chandra soothed her by pleasant words and enquired how far she had succeeded in the mission entrusted to her. In great anger Syamapriya told him, "I have served many men and received rewards in gold and silver for my services, But woe to me, having served you, the reward that I have got in the shape of blows you have yourself seen with your eyes. I will have no more any connexion with you. Just look at me, the wicked fellow has taken away half of the hair from my head."

Raj Chandra was ashamed and said sweetly, "Do not mind what you have suffered. For my sake you should forgive and forget it. You will see that I will make you the mistress of this village in no time."

Gradually her anger abated and she told the whole story of Rangamala from the beginning to the end, and concluded by saying, "Be ready, my lord, and come at once with me to the landing *ghat* of Raghabshiar."

"Oh my good woman, will you tell me," said Raj Chandra, "how many men I am to take with me?" Syamapriya said, "What do you think you should do?" Upon which the young lord said, "Is it becoming that I should go without my soldiers?" Saying so, he touched the drum of the palace, beating it with a stick. Instantly a thousand soldiers assembled there. Syamapriya enjoyed the humour of it and said smiling, "You are acting foolishly. Where was it ever heard that a man went on a love mission with a thousand soldiers." Raj Chandra dismissed his men at these words of Syamapriya and ordered Ram to bring his white waler well caparisoned. The servant did as he was bid and Raj Chandra was pleased. He took Syamapriya on the back of the horse and asked his servant to bring for him his flute plated with gold. As he rode the horse, he played upon his flute and so sweet was the sound and so gallant-like did he look from the back of his waler that the women of the city stared at him with admiring eyes. Some thought how glorious he looked like the full moon and envied the woman who claimed him as husband. Others thought that he was fit to entice any number of women by his handsome appearance. (Ll. 1-79.)

(VIII)

From there the young lord rode in a jubilant spirit and came near the Raghabshiar. Ranga saw him with a sidelong glance and perceived that he was none other than Raj Chandra Chaudhuri himself. Abashed at her light clothings as she bathed, she plunged herself into the water. The maidservants surrounded her, so that she might escape observation. In the meantime Raj Chandra tied his waler to a bough of the mango tree near by, and asked Syamapriya to tell him as to who the woman was that stood in front. Syamapriya said that she was the mother of Rangamala. The landlord was enraged and said, "Return the reward I have given you. You have brought me to an old hag." Syamapriya said, "Why, my nephew, do you get angry without knowing anything? Certainly the woman is matronly but how glorious she looks inspite of her age. Just then imagine how beautiful her daughter would be."

Syamapriya then slowly came to the spot where Rangamala was and whispered to her ears, "You have hidden yourself in this way and the prince in great disappointment is returning home." At this word, Ranga stepped a little forward and separated herself from her gay companions. Now Raj Chandra had a full sight of her. She was, as it were, a lotus in full blossom in the pond and he gazed at her with steadfast eyes. Raj Chandra asked his comrade, "How can I have an opportunity of talking with her?" Syamapriya suggested that it would be well if he could pay some *Nazar* to Ranga's mother. He took a purse of a hundred silver coins from his pocket and offered it to the mother after having saluted her.

The elderly lady became ablaze with anger and said, "You are a stranger to me. How dare you offer me money at this landing *ghat* of the pond?" She threw away the purse in great rage.

The trusted servant Ram, when he saw that the woman spoke rudely to his master, came in great speed and seized her by her hands. He caught her hands with such force that her wrist was about to break. Ranga's mother cried in pain and was about to faint, when Ranga came up to the bank of the pond and said, "Release my mother from the hold of this man. You have come for some purpose. This is not the way to get it fulfilled. Behave well and I assure you that your expectations will be realised."

Ram Bhandari released Ranga's mother from his hold.

(Ll. 1-57.)

(IX)

Then did Rangamala approach the young lord and sweetly spoke to him, "What is the reason, oh prince, that you are here?" Raj Chandra said, "If you be graciously inclined, I shall be quite satisfied by being served with betels and betelnuts from your hands." She wickedly veiled her face on hearing these words and began to smile. She said, "You are a Sudra and I am a Nar. Will your caste allow you to take betels from my hands?"

The young lord addressed her quite gallantly and said, "If you agree to my request, dear Rangamala, you will be amply rewarded. I will have a spacious road constructed from your house to mine. Your brother Golap will ride the splendid waler of mine. Before your gateway I will have a large pond dug and dedicate it to your father. Thirty yards from your house, a *Nahavat* orchestra will be organised by me to please you night and day with their sweet music."

Ranga said, "Many a youth promises in this way at the first impulse of love. But after a time he forgets everything he uttered. I have known youths who clasp the feet and hands of their ladylove in order to win their hearts but after a time they pass by indifferently as if they are strangers. I can believe you if you swear by God that you will be constant. If I die you will cling to my memory to the last and fulfil the rites of cremation as ordained by the Sastras, gathering fuel, etc." The prince consented to do all that she wanted. He broke a branch from the near mango tree and swore touching it.

Then was Ranga pleased and she said, "Now I bid you farewell, my love. You are to come to my house at about mid-night. We shall meet and spend our time in sweet talk." The waler was brought by Ram, gaily caparisoned, and the prince rode upon it in pleasant humour, thinking all the time as to when the happy hour would come. (Ll. 1-33.)

(X)

When it was about mid-night, he asked Ram to accompany him. He wore a *dhuti* of the colour of gold and a *chadar* he cast upon his shoulders of the hue of rose. His beautiful slippers embroidered with jewels he wore and gaily rode upon the waler which Ram had brought in the meantime. Arriving at the house of the Nars he tied his horse to a branch of the mango tree near by and called Durga the maidservant. The lord of twenty-two districts was himself at the door. So without losing a moment, Durga brought the message to Ranga.

Ranga was in a pleasant humour and said indifferently, "Has he really come? Why should you be so busy over the matter? There is that old rotten mat. Spread it in a corner of our garden."

When the mat was spread the prince sat upon it in a moody spirit. Ram Bhandari was greatly enraged and said to his lord, "Your Highness has, indeed, got a splendid reception." Raj Chandra made the matter light and said, "Fortunate am I that I have got this mat. Any other man on a mission like mine would have blows as his reward. You do not know, Ram, that it is a thorny way that the lovers have to tread. One must suffer in the beginning and when gradually a woman's heart is won, the lover should expect proper treatment." Ram Bhandari was silenced by the arguments of his young master and quietly took his seat at a corner of the mat spread under some nut trees.

When it was mid-night Ranga began to think as to what she should do. She called the maidservant Durga and told her to bring to her room Raj Chandra Chaudhuri who was waiting in the garden.

With a heart beating with hope and fear Raj Chandra came to the room. The lady received him kindly and asked him to sit on her couch. With her own hands she served him with betel and tobacco. They were pleased with each other and began to talk merrily.

Rangamala opened her box and produced a packet of cards and asked Raj Chandra to play. He, however, said that the tradition in the country was that if a lover of two different castes play at cards in their first meeting, ill-luck seizes them. She belonged to the Nar family and he to the Sudra caste, so that card-play was ominous on the first night. Then Ranga threw away the packet of cards and began to play at dice. Time passed pleasantly. The young Raja and Ranga both won and lost, so that they were both in a pleasant humour over their play. The sequel was a number of kisses which Raj Chandra gave to the young lady who tried to evade them out of bashfulness. She then resigned herself to his embrace, and the love formed that day became strong like that of a creeper with a tree which cannot be separated unless cut with a saw.

When the night was over they both awoke and the young lord remembered his poor servant Ram Bhandari who had been left to his pitiable position on the mat during the night. He called him and wanted him to get ready for going home. Ram Bhandari was angry. He said sulkily, "You have, my lord, spent the night with your ladylove and left me to pass my time miserably in this wretched mat. Is it proper that people should be called to a place where there is no accommodation for them?"

Raj Chandra was ashamed at the words of his servant and promised that he would secure a fine woman from the countryside and get him married to her. So glad was Ram Bhandari at this promise that he forgot all his worry and sufferings of the night and opened the door and appeared before Raj Chandra with courtesy and submission. Raj Chandra offered him betel and tobacco with his own hands.

Ram Bhandari said, "It is high time now and we must return home." Raj Chandra glanced at Ranga and asked her permission to go home. Ranga said, "Your Highness should excuse me. Though you may think of going away I will not allow you to do so.'' Raj Chandra held her in his arms and affectionately said, "I have got lots of things to do at home. I crave your permission to go. Bid me adieu with a smile on your lips." Ranga smiled and gave her assent.

He rode on his horse and soon came to his palace. After his bath and meals, he came to the Durbar Hall and sat there as usual attending his daily work. His uncle seated at a little distance glanced at him with some suspicion. He said, "How is it, nephew, that you look pale to-day? You are a handsome man, but to-day it seems to me that you have been much fatigued.'' Raj Chandra said, "I have got cold and am not feeling well." The affectionate uncle asked him to retire into the inner apartments, since he was not keeping well.

III.

(1)

Uncle Rajendra had just finished his dinner and was pleasantly chewing a betel when information was brought by one of his officers, that the paddy of the fields in the locality inhabited by Karim had been eaten by worms. The leeches had attacked the cows and men died by hundreds owing to famine. It was not possible for the people of Karimpur to pay the revenue due to the State.

Rajendra called his nephew and explained the situation. The young prince was angry at the report and thought that the ryots were playing false and asked Ram Bhandari to get his waler ready. He was bound for Karimpur, to see things with his own eyes. He also asked his trusted servant to take with him a number of single and double-barrelled guns. It was a country full of game and the prince was willing to go a-hunting on his way.

The white waler ran on with speed and arrived at Karimpur. Raj Chandra saw a large number of birds flying above the tops of the forest-trees and hiding himself behind them took a double-barrelled gun in his hands and shot them till the wayside was strewn with the dead birds which Ram Bhandari was busily engaged in picking up. Here I must change my topics and relate an event that transpired at the time. (Ll. 1-29.)

(2)

She was a girl of the village Maijdia and was married to a family at Lamarchar. She had been in her father-in-law's place, and was just going to the house of her father for the first time after her marriage. She was carried in a palanquin borne by eight persons, and drums, cymbals and other musical instruments were being played on by the procession which escorted her. When the party had come to Karimpur the bearers felt fatigued and took down the palanquin under the cool shade of a tree and stayed there awhile for rest. At this time Raj Chandra appeared there all on a sudden and cried out, "Whose palanquin is this ?" The eight bearers said, "In the palanquin a girl of Maijdia is being carried to her father's house at Lamarchar." He was certainly a sane man but at this stage there came a fit of insanity on him and he said, "Well, bearers, will you please open the doors of the palanquin? I want to have a talk with the lady." The girl Chandrakala heard all this from inside and loudly gave order, "Raise the palanquin and do proceed in haste." Upon this the bearers took up the handles of the palanquin on their shoulders. Raj Chandra interfered and said haughtily, "Leave this palanquin, you cowards and be off, if you want to save your life." The bearers were not daunted but said, "How is it that you behave in this way ? A lady is going to her father's place. What right have you to order us in this way ? If you want to save yourself from being insulted, leave the spot at once."

Without caring to give any reply, Raj Chandra began to beat the eight bearers with the butt-end of his gun. They all fled in terror and Raj Chandra broke open the door of the palanquin with a kick. Then did he observe from a little distance the beautiful woman inside the palanquin, looking like a fairy. Chandrakala said, "You are a Sudra. I know, and I am a Brahmin. If you insult me, helpless as I am, woe will be unto you." But the young man whose head had got unsteady did not wait to listen to her threat or entreaties. He forcibly caught hold of her and insulted her. In great rage and sorrow the girl cursed him saying, "If I am born of Brahmin parents, I take this vow that I will get you outcasted from the community of the Sudras."

Like a statue did she stand near the palanquin and neither cried nor said a word. In the meantime the bearers had returned. She ordered them to go to Babupur with her at the house of the Chaudhuris.

(3)

The uncle Rajendra was holding his Durbar at the time and his officer Rajkishore was explaining to him some accounts from office books. At this time did Chandrakala come down from her palanquin and apply for an interview. Raja Rajendra heard the names of her parents and relations and recognised her. He ordered the palanquin-bearers to go straight into the inner apartments with her. When the palanquin was taken down in the inner apartment the female members of the palace all assembled there out of curiosity. Chandrakala came out and the old Rani asked her the reason of her coming there. She said weeping, "Oh queen-mother, have you no image of Kali in your temple to sacrifice wicked men at her altar? I was going to my father's place when in the forest Raj Chandra suddenly came and drove away my palanquin-bearers and insulted me, helpless and without a companion as I was."

The story was told briefly and with such pathos that the Rani was greatly ashamed and could not say anything for a time. Then she said, "I am grieved at what you have said, O Chandrakala. Men are not made perfect in the world. Every one has some flaw or other, and the world goes on, because there is forgiveness in it. Do forgive and forget. Take your bath and have meals here and when your fatigue will be over, go to your father's house." Chandrakala told her, "Raj Chandra takes meals at the hand of the Nars. So you have been all reduced to that status in society. You ask me to take my meals here, O fie!"

The mother felt herself insulted at this word and said, "Go back to your father's house. You need not tarry here." She then ordered the eight palanquin-bearers to take her away. (Ll. 1-96.)

(4)

So did she again resume her journey to Lamarchar and when she came near her father's house, her mother ran towards the palanquin in great joy but was shocked to see tears drop from her eyes. She said, "What is the matter with you, daughter, that you are crying? Your tears pierce my heart like an arrow."

Then did she relate her story with many a sigh and tear. The mother did not wait to hear it to the end but went and spoke to her husband all about it. The Brahmin trembled in rage when he heard this and called all the members of the Brahmin families residing in that locality. Two hundred men gathered there armed with swords, sticks and other country weapons. They all determined to attack Raj

Chandra and take revenge on him. There was however, a cool-headed Brahmin there who said, "You are like two hundred mice resolved to fight a cat. He is the lord of twenty-two districts and if you go there in this heroic attitude, your death will be inevitable at his hands. His general Chand is a man of indomitable strength. Alone he is fit to kill nine hundred men. His soldiers dressed in red jackets fiercely assault the enemies who die in no time at their hands."

When the Brahmins heard all these, they put their heads together devising means for retaliation. They at last came to the decision that fighting would do no good. "Let us all get him excommunicated from society. That will be his fit punishment." This was their decision. They sent message to all Brahmins not to administer to any religious function in the house of the Raja and waited for the opportunity for full retaliation when somebody would die in the Raja's family. No Brahmin would go to do the Sradh ceremony. The dead person would rot in hell for ever.

Thus they resolved to excommunicate the Raja and kept the matter closely secret. (Ll. 1-36.)

IV.

(1)

We shall here begin another topic. After having insulted Chandrakala, Raj Chandra wandered about hunting birds in the forests. One day he saw that no tank or pond was near. His thirst was great and so asked Ram Bhandari to get for him water from anywhere. Ram said, "There is the pond called the Sayardighi which is not very distant. Your Highness will find plenty of drinkable water." They went there in great speed and Ram prepared a cup with the leaves of banana plant and Raj Chandra drank to his fill. His fatigue was now gone, thirst being appeased and he took his seat on a side of the pond.

There lived a man named Chhamiraddi in the village close to the tank. He had heard that Raj Chandra had come out for hunting to that part of the country. He had also heard that if anybody gave him a clue to some beautiful woman, he rewarded him handsomely. Wishing to take advantage of the far-famed liberality of Raj Chandra, Chhamiraddi came to the side of the tank and clasping his hands before the young Prince remained standing in great humility. Raj Chandra asked him the reason of his coming. Chhamiraddi said, evidently with some hesitancy, that he knew of a woman of wonderful beauty but waited for permission of the master to give a full account of her. Raj Chandra, when he heard this, was maddened by the lust of securing a fresh prey and entreatingly asked Chhamir to tell him all about her. This Raj Chandra was such a man that if he got report of a new beauty, he would fast till he secured her ; he would not have a wink of sleep at night. Chhamir told him that the woman belonged to the Yogi caste, upon which Raj Chandra wanted him to show him the way to the Yogi's house without delay.

"I will show the way, but may I not expect some reward from Your Highness?" Raj Chandra had no money with him and began to think what he should do to meet the exigencies of the situation. He took his rose-coloured Chadar from his shoulder worth rupees five hundred and gave it to Chhamiraddi as his reward.

Right glad was he to receive the reward but thought that after he showed the young Raja the way to the Yogi's house, he might be deprived of the Chadar. The Raja might seize and take it back. He tore the Chadar into two pieces and when Raj Chandra asked him the reason of his strange action, he said, "I have got a son. I will give him half and keep the other for my own use." Raj Chandra was apparently satisfied with this explanation and said," All right, I have given it to you. You may use it in any way you like."

(Ll. 1-62.)

(2)

Chhamiraddi took the young lord to the house of the Yogi. The Yogi's wife had just come out with a copper-plate full of cotton thread. Raj Chandra approached her and signed her with a slight cough. She understood the hint and fled in terror and entered her room shutting its doors. Raj Chandra ascended the top of the house scaling the walls by means of Sal-pillars. In darkness he entered the room and with his hands stretched, he tried to find her out. He at last caught hold of her and then ensued a struggle. She was strong enough to keep him off for some time and in the course of fight Raj Chandra got hurt on one of his toes which had come in contact with a weaving machine. In the mean time Swarupmala, the Yogi-woman, made her escape and Raj Chandra began to call aloud for Rama who was waiting outside the house. On hearing his master's voice, he came into the room when Raj Chandra told him that in his struggle with the woman he had got a sprain in one of his feet. Ram Bhandari was delighted to hear this and thought that it was his due reward for his wicked action. The Prince asked him if he knew any medicine to cure his pain. Ram Bhandari said, "Yes, I know the remedy. I will give you the necessary medicine." Saying so, he entered the kitchen room of the Yogi. He took a little soot from the place and cut a leaf of the *Kachu* plant that grew outside the room. Then did he seek for a little salt. It was all dark and he got a hurt in his nose in his attempt to get the salt. Approaching his lord he said in a nasal sound, "In seeking a remedy for your pain, just see, the ridge of my nose is broken." Then did he hand him the remedy that he had secured. On applying it, Raj Chandra felt relieved a little and again went in trace of the Yogi-woman. Near the outer house had the Yogini concealed herself where the prince leaped over and caught her in a tight embrace. But the Yogini was a strong woman and having hustled Raj Chandra with force, shook him off a second time. Then did she swim across a ditch round her house and go to the other side. Raj Chandra was not daunted but followed her and caught her there. In the shade of some trees there did this rich youngster insult the helpless woman, but not satisfied by this he wished for revenge for the trouble that she had given him. He bound her hands with a rope and said, "You do not know who I am. I am the lord of twenty-two districts. You have shown me no respect. You will have your due punishment." Saying so he dragged her to the house and binding her tight to a pillar began to beat her with his shoes. (Ll. 1-67.)

(3)

Now let us turn to the topic of Chhamiraddi. This man was all along witnessing the events that had transpired. When he saw Swarupmala being beaten in that way, he at once went to the Rajgunge *hat* and there met Kala Yogi, the husband of Swarupmala. He acquainted him with the distresses into which his wife had fallen. Kala Yogi who belonged to the weaver caste and who was selling the clothes that he had made in the *hat*, left his business and at once came to his house. He saw that his wife was struggling hard to free herself from the clutches of the young Raja. He meditated in this way, "If I would now go to help my wife, I shall not be able to do so in any way. On the other hand, I myself shall be beaten by the young lord. So no use going there." He went at once to the house of the Chaudhuris and met uncle Rajendra who was at the time in his Durbar. He addressed him and said, "Why do you, my lord, maintain such a goat as your nephew Raj Chandra? Is there no image of Kali in your temple to have this beast sacrificed at her altar? All on a sudden he entered my house when I was away and beat my wife for no cause." When Rajendra Chaudhuri got this report, he hung down his head in shame at the Durbar where all his ministers and officers were present. He called Hanu Singh, Benu Singh, Mangal Singh and Durga Singh—four constables and ordered them to bring his nephew bound hand and foot from the house of the Yogi. (Ll. 1-36.)

(4)

When the four constables got this order they took with them strong lathis and gallantly twisted their moustaches. They came to the house of the Yogi and visited the young lord who left the woman for a little time and appearing before the constables said, "Well, Mangal Singh, what is the reason that you have come here?" Mangal Singh who was the head of the little group said with derision, "Our business is similar to that which has brought your lordship here." The young Raja was greatly annoyed with the men for speaking to him so vulgarly. He said, "You unmannerly rascals, you do not know how to talk with your master. I will knock down your teeth and teach you a lesson." The soldiers without much ado forcibly caught hold of him and binding his hands with a rope dragged him towards the palace.

When the Raja saw Raj Chandra brought in that condition his heart burst with compassion, but he outwardly expressed indignation and said, "How is it, Raj Chandra, that you are misbehaving yourself in this way? You have Phuleswari Rani for your wife. She is a paragon of beauty; but if for some reason or other you do not like her, you may marry any other fair-looking girl."

Raj Chandra said, "You have been, dear uncle, misinformed. This Kala Yogi has got a wonderful horse of white colour. I went to him to ask if he would sell it. Enraged at my request the Yogi fell upon me and assaulted me. Without hearing me, you have been doing me a great injustice." The uncle was again ashamed at these words, for really he had judged of the case without giving his nephew an opportunity to explain himself. He said, "All right, if you are sorry for not having a good horse, take a thousand rupees from our treasury and purchase a nice white horse from Pubbapur. I should be glad to see you ride that horse in this outer compound of our palace."

Raj Chandra gladly took the money, purchased a horse and came to his uncle with it. The old Chaudhuri was right glad to see it. (Ll. 1-45.)

IV.

(1)

Chorus.—My love, alas, has played a trick. He will not come. The flower with its honey will fade away and the bee will miss it, if it does not turn up in right time.

Rangamala was sorry that the young Chaudhuri did not come back for a long time. Her maid-servant Durga advised her to write a letter to him. She took a piece of Chinese paper and wrote a letter thus. At the beginning she wrote the name of Kali, and then went on, "People say lots of things when they wish to win the hearts of ladies. Their entreaties and supplications are so pathetically put that even a stone would melt at them, but after all this, when the lady has been captured, they become callous and they never think of her again. Will you explain to me why you have so cruelly forgotten me? You are a big man and I thought your love would increase my status and prestige in society but I find that everything has taken a contrary course in my case."

She entrusted the letter to her maid-servant. She dressed herself as a Vaisnava woman and arrived at the house of the Chaudhuris of Babupur. She saw the nephew and the uncle seated together at the Durbar and was thinking as to how she should deliver the letter. People thought that she was a Vaisnava mendicant and allowed her access. She stood near the Durbar and glancing at Raj Chandra moved the letter with her hand just to attract his attention. Understanding the sign, Raj Chandra took permission to leave the Durbar from his uncle on some pretext and going to the Southern part of the courtyard signed to the woman to come to him. Thus meeting him in a lonely place she said, "You are cruel, my lord, to forget all about poor Rangamala." Saying so she handed him the letter. Raj Chandra read its contents and dismissed the maid-servant. (Ll. 1-59.)

(2)

Raj Chandra next called Ram Bhandari and showing him the letter asked his advice as to what should be the pretext on which he would go to the house of the Nars. The servant said, "The charge of realising revenues from the locality in which the Nars live has been given you, my lord. The rent has fallen into arrears. You may seek permission from your uncle to go to that place for recovering the arrear-rent."

The young lord was well pleased with this advice and had no difficulty in getting permission from his uncle for going to the house of the Nars on this pretext. Rama brought him the white waler gaily caparisoned and riding it he at once came to the house of Rangamala. He entered the house and found her lying on a costly couch. She slowly approached her and touched her with his hands.

She in great rage threw his hands away. Raj Chandra sweetly spoke, "I was detained at my house for urgent work but now that I have come, I am not going to leave you again." Rangamala said, "Evil befalls the woman who believes in the honeyed words of a man. I was a fool to believe in your words and to be deluded thus." The young Chaudhuri said, "I will prove that you have not been duped. Tell me what you want. I am going to fulfil your desire, whatever it may be." Ranga with a smile of derision said, "Do not give me long promises again. You may recollect that when you first courted my love, you promised that you would get a pond excavated here and dedicate it to my father's name. Did you not also promise that a *Nahavat* orchestra you would construct about sixty yards in front of my house ?"

"Yes, I will do what I have promised ;" said Raj Chandra. "Can you give me a rope for measurement ? What would be the size of the pond you must tell me and show me the spot where the *dighi* is to be excavated."

Right glad at his words Ranga saw her father and said, "Give me a rope for measurement, papa." On being asked the reason, she said that she was going to have a tank excavated and dedicated to his name. The father was very glad and thought, "My daughter is doing what even a son is not often found now-a-days to do for the sake of his father."

With the rope supplied by her father she approached the Chaudhuri who asked her, "Please find where the pond is to be dug and show its size by measurement." Ranga with the rope in her hand measured the whole length of the spot to be covered by the pond. The Chaudhuri was astonished to see that the plot measured twenty-two and half *dronas*.[1] Ram Bandari said, "You have no wit

[1] 22½ *dronas* are nearly equal to 150 acres.

" Evil befalls the woman who believes the honeyed words of a man."

Chaudhuri's Larai.

in your head, my young lord. If such a big tank is to be excavated, your uncle will hang you." Then he gave him some advice to which Raj Chandra could not help agreeing. Ram Bhandari said to Ranga, "The size that you show is irregular. You must have a square pond which will be so nice. Give me the rope. I will show you the size which will be proportionate and regular. Being a woman, she could not understand the trick to which she was put and appreciated what the servant called a good size. The proposed pond would cover only two and half *dronas* (about 16½ acres). (Ll. 1-110.)

(3)

After arranging with Ranga and drawing the plan, he took leave of her and straightway made for the house of Rama Magh. He was the head of the Magh (Burmese) coolies and owned a great estate. He was so rich that he slept on a couch of gold and rested his feet on a silver footstool. When Raj Chandra came to his house, he lay on his golden couch and five beautiful Magh women were near him ministering to his wishes. He heard the call from outside, "Is Rama Magh in the house?" Rama Magh wondered at this call and wondered who could be so bold as to address him so familiarly. "It is my father and mother who used to call me thus and the only other man from whom I would tolerate such an address is the son of Babuchand." Thinking in this way he said to one of his maid-servants, "If you find any old man calling me so insultingly he must be impaled at once. If he is a mere child, he should be thrown into prison and if it is a young man, his head should be cut off."

The maid-servant went to carry out the order of her lord, but beholding Raj Chandra standing at the gate at once hurried to her master and said, "The whole city has thronged to your gate to see the son of Babuchand come here and you do not know it, pleasantly seated as you are on your golden couch."

He at once rose up and hurried to the gate to receive the young Chaudhuri and said, "Even if a man spends one thousand rupees as *Nazar*, he cannot easily have the honour of being granted an interview by Your Highness. What good luck for me that Your Lordship has yourself come to my humble house!" The young Chaudhuri briefly stated his object. He had come there to seek Rama Magh's help for having a pond dug. "Ah," cried the head-man of the Burmese, "if Your Lordship had sent a mere word, four or five thousand coolies would have at once gone to your doors. Is it necessary that for such a paltry business, Your Lordship would yourself call here?"

Raj Chandra said, "The matter is a private one and should be done in utmost secrecy."

Rama Magh struck his brazen drum with a stick and hundreds of men of his clan flocked there in response with spades in their hands.

With these men Raj Chandra came to Talebpur at the house of the Nars where the beautiful Ranga was waiting for him with eagerness. She had many delicacies prepared for him which were served to Raj Chandra and he after his bath relished them highly. Ranga said, "I have heard the name of Rama Magh many a time but never have had the pleasure of seeing him." (Ll. 1-62.)

(4)

The young Chaudhuri asked Rama Magh to come to the inner apartment. He was stalwart and looked like a hill. Ranga was frightened and said, "Dismiss the man. He has seen me and may take a fancy for me. To-day he has come to get a pond dug; to-morrow after having the work done he may come back and cutting your head off

Rangamala's pond. P. 279.

may seize and carry me as the Burmese pirates generally do." Raj Chandra smiled at her fears, "Set your heart at rest. I have extensive territories in the country of the Burmese. When they fail to give me rent, I pull hundreds of them by the ear and bring them to my place as if they were so many lambs."

Ranga nodded her head and said, "I cannot believe you, my lord, but I can do so if you can put a chain on the feet of this big man and keep him standing here as a prisoner." Raj Chandra said, "What a foolish idea! He has done no wrong. On what pretext shall I do so?"

Ram Bhandari came forward at this stage and said, "Many a foolish thing the lovers have to do. When she has once willed it, you must carry out her bidding. If the Magh Chief asks the reason of your strange conduct, Your Lordship may say, I do so because I cannot put any trust in you. You are so busy a man that you may leave the place without finishing the work. For this reason, you must agree to be my prisoner."

Rama Magh in a spirit of pleasant humour agreed to bear the rings on his feat. He said smiling, "Big ponds like *Hasusingh's dighi*, *Birsingh's dighi*, *Hoa Sagar*, *Jagannath's dighi* and *Kamala dighi* have I excavated. It is a small pond and it will take me no time in getting it dug. I am inclined to laugh at your fears. But I agree to your punishment."

Saying so he ordered his men to do the work quickly. They raised the cry of "Hurrah! Hurrah!" and with spade in hands applied all their force to dig the earth. (Ll. 1-25.)

(5)

When the work was thus being expedited, the young Chaudhuri asked Ranga if she had any other desire to have fulfilled. She gently reminded him of the promise for making the *Nahavat* orchestra. Raj Chandra ordered Nanda the artisan to build it. Then Ranga said, "You have fulfilled all my wishes. I have a little thing to ask you. I want now that the pond is ready that people high and low in this locality may be made to dine here one day."

Raj Chandra approved of his lady-love's desire and instantly sent letters of invitation to this effect, "Next Wednesday you are to come here to partake of a feast of *chida* to be given by Golap Ray on the occasion of his completing the excavation of a pond dedicated to his father's name. You are to come with your whole family without fail." He sent the letter to localities far and near, and they all complied with the request made in the letter and became ready to attend the function with due *Nazar* according to the means of each man.

Then did Raj Chandra make a request to Ranga in a tone of hesitancy, "Invitation must go to my uncle and aunt from Golap Ray. What do you say to this?" he asked.

In great fear Ranga showed her disapproval of this idea by a waive of her hand. "You must not," she said, "inform your uncle of this feast, not to speak of inviting him. The result will be disastrous."

But Raj Chandra did not pay any heed to her words. He drew out a piece of Chinese paper and wrote in the name of Golap Ray asking Rajendra Chaudhuri and his Rani to attend the function. Having written the letter, he ordered Rama to carry it to his uncle's palace, who with due humility expressed his unwillingness to do so. Twice did he dare disobey his master who got enraged and said, "If, again, you dare say 'no,' I will knock down your teeth, you stupid fellow."

At this reproach from his master with a sorrowful countenance he carried out his behest. Ranga perceived the unwillingness of the trusted servant and again implored the young Chaudhuri to desist from such a course. She said, "You are aware, My Lord, of the power of Chand, the general of your uncle. Attired in a small red jacket, this short-statured fellow is the very death to his enemies. When your uncle will read this letter, he will employ Chand to sever our heads at once. So do not, I pray thee, take this step." (Ll. 1-63.)

(6)

Raj Chandra paid no heed to her entreaties and signed Rama with the twinkle of his eyes to go home at once. Inspite of his unwillingness, with slow steps, he had to go to Babupur but he was always afraid of confronting the anger of Chand the general. When he approached the place he advanced a step and then receded a little, not venturing to come before the Raja. At last however, he came to the presence of Rajendra Chaudhuri and laying the letter near him at once took to his heels like a criminal. Wonderingly did the old Chaudhuri glance at him but he was already gone. He then opened the letter and read its contents. Quickly did the thrill of insult pass through his whole system and he struck his head saying, "Oh ! I am lost. My caste is gone; the wretched nephew has taken meals at the hands of the vile Nars and wants that I also should take share in this foul act of his." He called Chand his general for discussing the matter with him and said, "My wits are all gone, Chand. The fellow has done a deed which is a horror. He has lost his caste and destroyed my family-prestige and he has asked me to go to the house of the Nars to take meals there."

Chand said, "Why do you worry yourself over the matter? Give me orders ; I will go to the house of the Nars and with my sword cut off the heads of the damned Nars just as a woodman clears with his scythe the wild plants before felling a large tree."

"I see," said Rajendra Chaudhuri, "if you go there with your sword and arrows you will use them unsparingly, but whatever my nephew may have done, he is dear to me as the very rib of my heart. You may unwittingly hit him and if he dies, there is none in my family to do the *Sradh* ceremony after my death. You may go there but use your arrow with caution. Let not my nephew be hurt in any way."

(Ll. 1-38.)

(7)

With this order, Chand the general prepared himself for going to the house of the Nars. His body he covered with sixty yards of cloth and in each of his hands, he took a sharp spear. He was pleased with his dress and looked like the very son of the dreaded goddess Kali. Before he started, he made sacrifices at the altar of Kali. Rajendra Chaudhuri could not help feeling uneasy on his nephew's account as he glanced at his general ; for he looked like a veritable tiger bounding on a flock of lambs."

In the meantime Chand rode a white Waler named Santaran, but the animal could not bear his weight and fell down on the ground with his front legs stretched. He chose another noble horse from the stall but this one also proved no better. So in disgust he gave up the idea of riding and began to walk. A plan suggested itself to his head and he took off his dress of a warrior and disguised himself as a Vaisnava mendicant. In this dress he appeared at the village of Talebpur. He was going by the western side of the new pond and was interested to see a large number of Burmese coolies employed in digging it. Advancing a few paces, he saw only sixty yards from the gate of the house of the Nars the *Nahavat* orchestra playing a concord of music. A short way off, he saw a fine garden where birds and animals were sporting pleasantly and the bees humming near the flowers in full bloom. The pond looked transparent and beautiful and a pack of white geese was observed on the surface of waters swimming at ease. Near the house Gypsies were showing their magic-play and the dancing girls from the locality were brought there for showing their skill in dancing. Chand was surprised to see that the house had turned magnificent like the palace of a Raja. He resolved within himself, " If I am the true son of my parents, I will not allow the money of my masters to flow like water in these wretched people's house. I will kill them all and redden the water of the new pond with their blood. Somehow I must so contrive things as to make the young Chaudhuri leave this cursed spot and then they will all see that my retaliation will begin."

Disguised as he was like a Vaisnava mendicant he entered the inner apartment of the Nars' house and cried for alms. He observed with a sidelong glance that the young Chaudhuri was enjoying the company of Ranga seated on a beautiful couch. Ranga heeded not his loud call for alms. " Be blessed, dear people, I do not want alms," saying so Chand made for the city of his master and in the way threw off his disguise and dressed himself in his proper suit. (Ll. 1-61.)

(8)

He came to his master and related the story of his adventure. Nobody regretted the conduct of Raj Chandra more than his uncle. At the suggestion of his general, however, he wrote a reply to the invitation letter of Golap Ray in the following words: " What you have done, dear nephew, is all very well. My only regret is that you did not consult with me before taking the step. But be sure, when you have begun the ceremony, anyhow it must be completed. If you cannot do so with your own money, be sure my treasury will be open to help you. In the meantime come home at once, so that we may consult how to bring the matter to a satisfactory conclusion.'' He entrusted the letter to one of his constables Mongal Singh who duly went to the house of the Nars and handed the letter to Raj Chandra. The young lord was highly pleased with the letter and told Ranga that there was no reason whatsoever for her foolish fears. His uncle was a generous man and could not take matters ill as she had apprehended. '' He is sure to come and take meals here.''

Ranga said, '' My heart beats with fear as I think seriously about the motive that has inspired your uncle to write the letter. My apprehension is that they will not allow you to come back here. The letter is a mere trick and my heart is full of misgivings. I have been highly pleased with your company. Pray do not leave me. I will not be able to live without you.'' But Raj Chandra Chaudhuri was determined to go home in compliance with his uncle's request and prepared for the journey, whereupon she fell at his feet and implored him to stay. He also perceived that Ranga had bolted the door strongly so that he might not go. With a light smile on his lips, he kicked at the door which opened at the hard blow. Then he again rode on his white horse which flew like an arrow homewards. (Ll. 1-61.)

(9)

In the meantime Chand had already gone home. He saw Durga, the princess—sister of Raj Chandra—and said, '' Esteemed lady, your brother is on the high way to ruin. He has already taken meals at the hands of the miscreants, the Nars. You belong to the bright caste of Sudras and that family-prestige is about to break down. There is one way yet to save your brother from utter ruin. If you can do what I am going to request you, I may be of some help to you."

On the princess asking him as to what it was, Chand said that he had learnt a *mantra* by which water could be charmed. "If you can make your brother," said he, "take a sip from my cup, he will be above all danger." She readily agreed to the request and Chand prepared a cup of *sarbat*, mixing with it some little Bhang drug. She was, however, very clever and would not allow her brother to taste a thing the quality of which she had not herself experimented. So when Chand went away, she drank a few drops from the cup. She found that it was sweet and harmless. So her suspicion was removed and she stood at the gate of the inner apartment with the cup of *sarbat* in her hand. Some little while after, Raj Chandra came exhausted by riding the long distance and at the entrance of the inner apartment found the princess Durga with the cup in her hand. What is this, dear sister, he asked and Durga said that it was a cup of *sarbat* which she was about to drink. "I am tired by my journey in the sun. So give it to me and get another prepared for you." Saying so he hastily took the cup and at once swallowed the contents. As soon as he had taken it his head began to reel and his eyes grew red. He asked Durga, "What is it in the cup that makes me feel so uneasy?" Durga said "You cannot have faith in your own sister!" The drug *Bhang* in the meantime began to work and he fell into a sound sleep. Chand came to the princess and said, "Put him to bed. I am sure he will not wake till we have done our work." (Ll. 1-56.)

(10)

They helped the young lord to lie in a bed and Chand at once started for Talebpur. He met Rama Magh and could not control his rage. "This miscreant," he thought, "has helped the young Chaudhuri to excavate the tank which will be a standing disgrace to the family of the Chaudhuris." Thinking in this strain he began to kill the Burmese coolies right and left. Just as a tiger enters the shed of lambs, so did the general make a havoc on the poor coolies. Rama Magh stood there with his feet bound with rings and sulked in anger as he observed the ruthless destruction. He moved his legs with his mighty force and the rings cracked and broke down. With a mere spade in hand, he challenged the general to a fight. The arrows aimed by Chand were repelled by the spade which he dexterously moved in the air, and when in his turn, he gave Chand some blows with his spade, he made a deep cut in the flesh of his antagonist through his iron armour. Chand could not hold his own at this fight, and failing to hit his foe with his weapons he challenged him to a wrestling struggle. There also the general could do no better, for the Burmese Chief rose with great force as often as he was thrown down and at last throttled him in such a way that he made a precipitous retreat from the field. He went to the neighbouring forest and there offered his prayers to Kali in this strain: "Oh, divine mother, save me from the hands of this Burmese rogue and let me win the fight. I take the vow that I would sacrifice two goats at your altar." The goddess Kali said in a whisper to her favourite hero, "Both of you have worshipped me with the same devotion. How can I side with one against the other?" At these words of Kali, Chand said, "Just see mother, if you do not show me mercy, I am going to die in your presence. Here is this sword of mine, and I shall instantly cut off my head with it." Saying so, he aimed his great sword at himself. "Forbear, my son," said Kali, "I grant you the boon that you will win the fight to-day and kill the Burmese Chief." Saying so, she stimulated Chand with her divine energy and he at once ran towards the field and met his adversary. The fight was a stiff one this time but at the end Chand succeeded in striking off the head of the Burmese Chief. (Ll. 1-62.)

(11)

Overjoyed with the victory Chand took the name of Kali a thousand times, at one breath. He then proceeded towards the house of the Nars, and broke open the front and the middle gates. Rangamala was lying in a room with sixteen doors all shut from inside. He had to break open these with as many kicks and suddenly stood still at the sight of the beautiful Rangamala lying in her bed. It was as though the new moon had arisen.

Asleep or awake, but with her eyes closed, she feigned as if she was unconscious of the danger. He walked round the bed several times and saw her surprising beauty. But his stony heart had no touch of compassion. All on a sudden he slapped her on the cheek. She opened her eyes and said, "I will inform the young Chaudhuri of this insult that you have done me and you will have proper punishment for it."

Without caring to give any reply to her threat he had her hands bound with a rope and said, "Your beauty will not be able to save you. You are doomed to-day to death at my hands." Now with a torrent of tears in her eyes, she said, "It was the young Chaudhuri who enticed me to this dishonourable course. I am not at all to be blamed for it. Why should you kill me and deprive my mother of her only support? She would not be able to survive the shock."

Then did she say weeping, " If I could have a sight of the face of my sweet Raj Chandra at this moment, I would not feel the agonies of death. If I could hear his sweet words, it would have assuaged my pain of death." But the relentless general stood resolved to kill her and then she fell at his feet and said, " Do not kill me, dear general. I will be your servant and make you happy by fulfilling your wishes."

" But the old Chauduri's order is that you are to be killed," said Chand.

Golap Ray, Ranga's brother, saw from a little distance what was transpiring and came to her rescue. He attacked Chand with all his force but he was a mere boy and though at the first dash he had overthrown the veteran general, the latter regained his step and gave Golap such a kick that he was thrown away about twenty feet from where he had stood. Then did Chand bind both of them and asked them to be ready for death. Ranga said, " He is my younger brother. What good will you derive by killing him? Kill me if you will, but release my poor brother. You may feel that such assaults on a younger brother can be ill borne by his sister. My old mother will die of grief, if you will kill him. The affection of the mother knows no bounds. If the son dies at a great distance, before the news reaches others, by a secret law the mother comes to know of it first of all."

She lamented in this way and made all sorts of pathetic appeal, but these were of no avail. Chand cut off the heads of the sister and the brother at the same time.

The head of Golap Ray was raised on the top of a bamboo pole and placed in a conspicuous place to be observed by all. But he took care to hide the head of Ranga within a bundle of clothes, wishing to carry it to the old Chaudhuri. He also set fire to the houses of the Nars and after this

" The relentless general stood resolved to kill her." P. 288.

act of cruelty rode home and saluting Rajendra Chaudhuri brought out the head of Ranga and put it before him as a trophy. The old chief was very much moved by the sight of the head and said, "What a cruel thing have you done! How could you kill such a beautiful woman as Ranga? She is dead; it does not matter much. But my nephew will surely turn mad for grief. I never knew that she was so beautiful. If she had belonged to my caste, I would have paid a lac of Rupees at the altar of Kali for granting the boon of such an exquisite bride for my nephew. Even though she was a Nar I would have got her married to my nephew at any risk and would have expiated the guilt with sacred rites in order to keep up our social prestige. Listen to me, Chand. By this act you have set fire to our family peace. Raj Chandra will never pardon me for committing this inhuman act. I do not know what action he will take at the impulse of the moment, when he will come to know of it." (Ll. 1-102.)

(12)

Let us turn to Raj Chandra Chaudhuri. After the intoxication due to drugging was over, he came out to the outer apartment and at the gate-way saw Chand Bhandari with his garments all tinged with blood. On asking the reason of this he was informed by Chand that he had gone for hunting deer and the blood was of some animals of the species that he had killed. All on a sudden Raj Chandra glanced towards the village of Talebpur and saw the whole sky ablaze with fire in that direction. It took him no time to be certain that the fire was issuing forth from the house of the Nars. He localised it still more closely and perceived that it was the Rest-House in which he and Ranga used to reside, that was set on fire. He at once ran in the direction and jumped into the fire seeking Rangamala.

After some search he found the body from which the head had disappeared, lying in the courtyard. He searched for the head with great care but could not lay his hand on it. He then took a silent vow saying to himself, "By the name of God, I promise that ere long I will chop off the head of my uncle, and after killing the miscreant Chand set fire to the city of Babupur." His grief for Ranga was great and for a little while he cried like a child. (Ll. 1-32.)

(13)

Rajendra Chaudhuri knew that his nephew was approaching. He was quite sure that he would come home like a fire-brand inflamed with the worst passion. So he ordered his whole family to be removed from the palace. Chand complied with the order and was himself struck with no less a fear. All the inmates of the house thus fled away; but the youngest wife of Rajendra said that she was innocent and that Raj Chandra could have no reason to do any violence on her. Being satisfied with this belief she did not agree to go away from the palace. In the meantime Raj Chandra Chaudhuri came home like a mad man. The words that every now and then came forth from his lips were incoherent and all about his uncle. His eyes were red and his whole frame was trembling in great rage. Not finding him in the Durbar Hall, he entered the inner apartment. There too he found nobody. His young aunt was observed suckling a little baby on her lap. He flew towards her like a storm and dragging the child with force lifted it upwards to strike it down on the floor, whereupon the aunt caught hold of him and entreatingly implored of him to have mercy. "It is a baby. What good will you derive by killing the innocent thing?" At these words, Raj Chandra left the baby and began to inflict blow after blow on the poor woman. She was all along clasping his feet, craving for mercy. In mad fury, he left her there and again sought for his uncle whom he could find nowhere. At last despairing of getting him within his clutches, he set fire to the palace and when the big houses were ablaze, sat down tranquilly observing the wild scene.

From afar Rajendra Chaudhuri saw that his houses were burning. In great rage his general told him, "Give me order without delay. I will take proper retaliation and see how young Chaudhuri should be treated." "No, Chand, it is I that am at fault. I have first set fire to our family peace. Why should you make my nephew responsible for it? His great rage due to grief will soon cool down and then may we come to mutual understanding. Hasty action is not good." Chand was not apparently satisfied with this attitude of his master. He put on his martial dress and at once came to the palace. From behind, he inflicted some blows on Raj Chandra and disappeared quickly. The young Chaudhuri looked back and did not see anybody behind him. He thought that the place must have been haunted by evil spirits. He was struck with fear and left the place. He came to the house of Ram Bhandari and sought his advice as to what should be done at this juncture. Ram Bhandari advised him not to be in a hurry. "Let your uncle come and hold Durbar as usual. Then may we come to a settlement regarding this action that he has taken."

He took his advice and agreed to wait for some days. (Ll. 1-59.)

Book VI.

(1)

Raj Chandra asked Ram Bhandari after a while as to what should be done now as a considerable time had already elapsed. His trusted servant said, "Will it not be proper now to seek the advice of Inga Chaudhuri. He is more rich and influential than your uncle, and if Your Lordship be prepared to give him one fourth share of your property he will be right glad, I am sure, to recover the whole of your property from the clutches of your uncle for you." Raj Chandra Chaudhuri approved of this plan but said, "I am going to follow your counsel but I have presently to do something urgent. I am promise-bound to Ranga to cremate her and do the funeral obsequies if I survived her. Now I must first fulfil this promise of mine. So you should go to the Brahmins at Maijdia and bring some of them for doing the religious function." Ram carried out this order of his master and met Chandranath Thakur in that village. When he called him from outside, the Brahmin peeped through his window and saw that it was a soldier bearing the insignia of the Chaudhuri family. He remembered the vow that he and his people had taken of not ministering to any religious rites in the house of the Chaudhuris. So he fled away by the backdoor and his wife said that he was not at home. Ram was not the person to be duped in that way. His enquiring eyes soon perceived that the Brahmin was running away from the house. He followed his track and seizing him asked if he would accompany him to the house of his master immediately. Chandranath showed a heroic front and said in a loud voice, "No, never." As soon as the words were uttered, he was treated to some severe blows, and was forced to come to a quick settlement by agreeing to the order of the Chaudhuri. With his scriptures and implements of religious service he quietly followed the footsteps of Ram Bhandari. The performance of the cremation-ceremony and due religious rites in connexion with it followed as a matter of course and everything was quietly completed.

(Ll. 1-64.)

(2)

The next step that Raj Chandra Chaudhuri took was to pay a visit to Inga Chaudhuri. They came to the boat to cross a channel, but the water was so shallow that the boat was caught in the sands and would not move. They had to stop, and the Chaudhuri who had already given a reward of five rupees to the ferryman Madhab was impatient of the delay and ordered him to land them on the other side quickly. The poor man made a pathetic appeal, explaining the situation in which he was placed. Ram Bhandari came down and gave such a mighty push to the boat that it flew like an arrow and never rested till it had gone considerably ahead over the other bank and was again stranded. When they were about to go away, the ferryman imploringly said that he was placed in the same miserable plight as before. The boat was his only means of livelihood and it was not moving. Ram Bhandari gave it another push not so forcibly as before, which set it floating in the midstream.

The young Chaudhuri was kindly received. He told the Moslem chief all about his trouble. His uncle had ousted him from his rightful possession and monopolised his paternal property and was doing whatever he liked. "I shall give you one-fourth share of my whole property if you can help me in recovering mine." Bhelu, the younger brother of Inga Chaudhuri, advised him not to meddle in this matter. But Inga Chaudhuri seemed inclined t help the young man. Bhelu said, "You are not aware o. the heroism and strength of general Chand. Single-handed he can kill nine hundred men. Once I had called on the old Chaudhuri for getting a loan from him. Chand insulted me in such a way that I have not been able to forget the sting of insult though many years have passed. We need not take the risk of meeting him in battle for the sake of one who is nobody to us." Inga said, "You ought to hold your tongue when your elders speak. I must help the young Chaudhuri at any cost," and turning to Raj Chandra he continued, "Return home and ask Rajendra to give you your property. If he fails to comply with my request, he will have to face my anger." (Ll. 1-46.)

(3)

Now Raj Chandra returned home and arriving at the palace saw Rajendra holding the Durbar as usual with Chand seated near him. The young lord approached his uncle and said, "The property is mine. My father had earned it. You were nowhere at the time. My uncles Uday Chandra and Raj Kamal died and taking advantage of the situation you seized the whole property. You have so long deceived your nephew, depriving him of his rightful share, but now he will not bear this gross iniquity on your part any more. If necessary, I shall take up arms to recover what justly belongs to me."

Rajendra said nothing in reply but took a piece of Chinese paper and writing a deed thereon made a gift of seven-annas share to Raj Chandra. The general Chand sulkily observed this procedure of the old Chaudhuri and snatching the paper from his hands tore it to pieces. He said," So long as I live I shall not allow the grant of a *cowrie* to Raj Chandra. You know him well and yet you act so foolishly. If you give him any property, he will waste it in a day. He is a child. You know what is good for him and what is not ; and should not give him any scope for carrying out his wild ideas." But the old Chaudhuri did not listen to his well-considered advice, and caught hold of the hair of his head and gave him some sound blows saying," Indulgence has turned your wits, I see, you devil. It is our paternal property and I am giving my nephew his proper share. What business have you to interfere in my action?"

The general swallowed the insult and stood like a statue without uttering any word. (Ll. 1-44.)

(4)

We come back to Inga Chaudhuri. Raj Chandra was not happy at what he considered to be an iniquitous gift and wrote in detail to Inga Chaudhuri, who made preparations for war and asked Raj Chandra to see him again. He besides, wrote a letter to Rajendra Chaudhuri to this effect: "Raj Kamal and Uday Chandra are both of them dead. The whole property belongs to your nephew. But you have usurped the whole and Raj Chandra is now a beggar. If you do not give him his property, I will turn your city into a wild jungle."

Receiving the letter, the old Chaudhuri sought the advice of Chand who said," He has threatened us in this way. Leave the whole matter to me and see how I conduct the affair. Will it be proper for us to submit to him like lambs? Just write to him in this strain: 'You are a Mahomedan and I am a Hindu and the affairs are between uncle and nephew. Why should you come to interfere and break the friendship that has existed between us for a long time? I will certainly give my nephew his rightful share. It will be extremely unbecoming on our part to quarrel over a matter where your interference is unnecessary. I am coming to your place presently in order to dicuss the matter fully and satisfy you from all points of view.'"

The uncle wrote as the general dictated and Mangal Singh, the constable, was entrusted with the letter. When Inga Chaudhuri got the letter he said to his brother Bhelu," Rajendra Chaudhuri has been struck down with fear by my letter. I am the most influential man in this Southern valley. So it is not at all strange that he should seek my friendship. Of course, my object is to fight him out and recover the whole property for Raj Chandra. But in the meantime let the uncle come and we shall manage things under the mask of outward friendship." Bhelu approved of the plan and waited to see what turn matters would take. The date of interview was fixed and Inga Chaudhuri made great preparations for receiving Rajendra Chaudhuri. Many goats and sheep were killed and the palace of the Moslem Nawab was ready to receive the distinguished guest in every way.

(Ll. 1-90.)

(5)

Rajendra Chaudhuri starting from home reached the landing *ghat* of the river where Madhab, the ferryman, kept his boat ready to take the passengers to the other side of the river. On landing at the other side of the river Rajendra Chaudhuri was carried to Inga Chaudhuri's house by means of a palanquin borne by eight bearers. His Moslem host received him with all outward show of respect and gave him a good residential house to put up in. Rich banquet was served him at proper hours in which there was a plentiful supply of *Polao, Korma* and other dainties. Meat was, of course, the principal item of the menu. (Ll. 1-52.)

(6)

Now let us follow Chand the general, who, when his master was receiving attention from the Moslem Nawab, took the opportunity of surveying his city and the palace. He observed that the palace was surrounded by a strong and high wall which was impenetrable from outside. There was only one gate for entering the palace and around the walls was a large ditch which it was impossible to pass without previous arrangements and device. Chand was full of presence of mind and ready wit. Availing himself of the darkness of night, he put round his waist an apron and came down to the ditch. He carried a rope by which he measured the ditch while he was swimming across it and found that it was thirty yards in breadth.

Meantime Inga and Rajendra sat together to discuss the matter for which the latter had come to his capital. He agreed to give his nephew his proper share. " But," he said," I have come to your place. Does it not behove you to think of returning my visit ? Now tell me when I can expect you to visit my city." Inga smiled and said, " All right I will go to your place after a month from hence, but in the meantime I wish you should clearly demarcate the portion that belongs rightfully to your nephew." Rajendra agreed to this proposal and sought leave to return home. (Ll. 1-52.)

(7)

He came back and crossed the river with the help of Madhab, the ferryman, but Chand was busy carrying out some plan which he had concealed. He came to the house of one Bancharam Barai and asked him if he could prepare for him immediately a ladder thirty yards long. He promisd him a good reward for it. On being asked repeatedly as to what he meant to do with such a long ladder he took him into his confidence after much hesitancy and said, " I am going to wage war against Inga Chaudhuri and this ladder is to serve the purpose of a bridge by which I will cross the ditch which surrounds his palace. But if you breathe one word about this to anybody else, I warn you that you will be killed on the spot with your family and children. There is only one gate to enter his house. With this ladder I will make a second entrance, if really a war is waged."

Bancharam agreed to his request and promised privacy. Accompanied by Chand he went to the bamboo groves behind his house and went on cutting the big bamboos from the middle. Creepers and wild plants entangled the bamboos, so that Bancha was much fatigued by his attempt to drag the bamboos that he had cut down. Chand smiled as he observed his friend's trouble and at once dragged a number of the strongest of these from the grove with root and all, and got them ready for Bancha. He, however, was very much sorry that many of the bamboos which were not needed for the present purpose were uprooted. He told Chand that this bamboo grove was the chief means of his livelihood, but the bamboos being uprooted, there was no chance of new sprouts coming out from the roots. "Never mind, my dear Bancharam, I will win victory over Inga Chaudhuri and when returning home, I will reward you sufficiently to compensate for the loss."

Bancha was right glad at the prospect and began rapidly to do the work with his axe. (Ll. 1-91.)

(8)

At night the constant sound of the axe disturbed the sleep of his brother Ramdhan. He rose up and asked his sister-in-law (Bancha's wife), "What is this sound in the garden behind our house?" The sister-in-law said that an old mango tree lay rotten in the garden and Bancha was striking it with his hatchet. Ramdhan, belonging as he did to the Barai caste, famous for their cleverness, did not believe in this story, but on some pretext went to the garden and standing behind his brother said, "How is it, brother Bancharam, that you are constructing this monster ladder? What purpose would it serve?" Bancha said, "Be silent. Do not ask anything about the ladder. Better go home and sleep. What good will you derive by hearing about this ladder?" The younger brother insisted on being told as to why the ladder was being made. Bancha said, "If I tell you the reason, we are sure to meet with death." Ramdhan laughed and said, "Where was it ever heard that a man died for being told the reason of making a ladder?" He told Bancha that if he would not place a little confidence in his own brother, he would rather die there, so that there would be no one left to make a request to him again.

Bancha could not resist the appealing requests of his younger brother and said in confidence, after extracting all kinds of promises from him for privacy, that a war was imminent between Rajendra Chaudhuri and Inga Chaudhuri and the ladder was meant for crossing the ditch surrounding the latter's palace.

Ramdhan could not sleep for the rest of the night. He was a servant in the house of Inga Chaudhuri and thought that as a faithful servant who had tasted the salt of his master's house, it was his imperative duty to let him know of the danger that awaited him. He longed that the night might be over soon as he could not bear delay. When it dawned, he did not wait to take his meals but straightway ran to the city of Inga Chaudhuri. He interviewed him and said, "You are happily spending time heedless of the danger that is imminent. You have made friendship with Rajendra but that man under the pretext of outward friendship is planning your ruin. I have got a clue to this and have come to inform and warn you about the danger."

His tone and manner of speaking irritated Inga Chaudhuri. He said, "Being a little fellow, you speak of big things. You rascal, who deputed you to destroy my friendship with Rajendra Chaudhuri?" Saying so, he did not wait but took off his shoes and began to beat Ramdhan in great anger. Ramdhan in this distress began to cry saying, "You are a Raja and you are so unjust. I came to give you some information and the result is that you have beaten me. May God bless you but know that he who does not understand his own interests will have to regret in future." With words like these uttered with sobs and tears, Ramdhan became silent. (Ll. 1-86.)

(9)

Seven days after Chand came to the house of Bancharam and asked for the ladder. He was glad to see that it was ready. He carried it on his shoulders and coming home, he robed himself in his war dress, took a shield on his back and swords and spears in his hands. He went to Rajendra Chaudhuri, took leave of him and asked him to bless him, as he was bound for war. Rajendra raised his hand to bless the warrior, and he coming out from the palace looked like the favoured son of Kali with the sandal mark on his forehead. In one breath he recited the name of Kali a thousand times. Coming to the ferryghat, he did not find Madhab the ferryman there. He could brook no delay but swam across the river and in the depth of night he made a slaughter amongst the soldiers who guarded the palace. He had crossed the ditch and leapt over the walls that had hitherto been considered impregnable. A great tumult arose and Inga came out of his house to see what had happened. He espied Chand doing a great havoc amongst his soldiers but after a moment did not find him anywhere. He thought that the general of Rajendra Chaudhuri had fled away. He did not know that in the meantime the foe had made a second gateway behind his house by crossing the ditch. After a little time Inga found Chand again engaged in killing his men. Inga himself went and fought with Chand. It was like a fight between a lion and a tiger. Such a thing was never heard of. In the darkness nobody could see who were the people whom Chand was killing ruthlessly. If little children were found in his way, Chand caught hold of them and hurled them from above. His sword became sharp like a saw and numberless people fell at his hands which simultaneously waived a spear and a sword with the rapidity of lightning. Inga Chaudhuri could no longer hold his own. They began to fight with arrows from right to left. Chand moved like a flash so that his position could not be exactly known, and suddenly one of his arrows ran through the breast of Inga Chaudhuri, piercing it from one end to the other. "I am gone," cried the veteran chief as he fell down on the ground. Bhelu Chaudhuri, his younger brother, ran to attack the invincible foe who laughed a laugh of disdain and cried out "You, urchin, you have come to fight with me." And then with his sword cut off Bhelu's head in no time. Mohammed Rejah, the third brother, was observing the fight and the destruction made by Chand, and had recourse to flight, knowing for certain that there would be no good fighting with such a warrior. (Ll. 1-66.)

(10)

Hira Bibi, Muchha Bibi and Nur Bibi, the three Begams discussed amongst themselves as to what should be done at this crisis as they saw no way of escape. Each of them took a sword in her hand and came out of the house to join in combat with Chand. Hira Bibi's sword cut a deep wound in the body of the general after having broken a part of his armour made of steel. The three attacked simultaneously and so fiercely did they handle their weapons that Chand found himself in a really critical situation. The invincible general had now no recourse left to him but to beat a retreat. He came to the gateway and prayed to Kali the Goddess in great alarm. The deity appeared, being unable to resist the appeal from one favoured by her. She said, "What a beast are you that you fight with women! You have left virtue's path, and are fighting with the weaker sex; your ruin is inevitable. You have already achieved your end and do not proceed further. Now leave off this place and go home to-night. Evil will befall you if you go again to fight." The general stood with clasped hands before Kali and said, "It is a great shame that one favoured by you will bear such a disgrace at the hands of women. For to-night only grant me the boon of success and help me from the awkward situation." Kali was greatly vexed by these entreaties and left his presence without saying anything.

Now these three ladies having won victory began to seek where Chand had gone. The cruel man, daring not face the three women so resolutely bent, shot arrows from behind their back and one of these fell on the body of Hira Bibi. It was a poisoned arrow and the poison spread itself instantly through her system and she cried, "I am gone, dear sisters," and then fell down dead on the spot. The youngest of the three saw that the two brothers of her husband as well as her sister-in-law had fallen and that her husband had retired from the field; she thought that there was no reason why she should live after this disaster and with increased fury, with a sword in each of her hands, she inflicted severe blows on Chand by both the weapons. Chand was frightened and thought that the woman was probably Kali herself who had come to the field for the purpose of retaliation. He was struck with such a horror that he fled from the battle-field thinking that his object was practically achieved. He resolved that he would never return to the field to face a woman as his foe. (Ll. 1-52.)

Book VII.

(1)

We have to say something now about Mohammed Reja who had fled. Greatly distressed as he was, he resolved that he would go to seek shelter at the house of Monowar Gazi, a big Zamindar of the district and his own maternal uncle. In the meantime news spread everywhere about the destruction of Inga Chaudhuri's family, and Monowar Gazi heard a garbled report of it from a messenger. He at once started in a palanquin to enquire about his nephews. At a certain spot he made enquiries about Reja Mohammed who, he heard, was still living. As he proceeded, he heard that Mohammed Reja was not far off and after a little while he saw his nephew, pale and wearied, walking slowly on foot. The uncle came down from his palanquin and embraced the distressed man asking him, "Who is it, my darling, that has reduced you to this condition? Accustomed are you to lie on a couch of gold resting your feet on silver foot-stool and five beautiful maids softly stroke your feet for inducing easy sleep." Weeping all the while did Mohammed Reja speak about the tragedy that had occurred at their house, narrating how the two brothers and his sister-in-law had fallen in the field. He concluded by saying, "I ran away from home to meet you. Beyond what I have said I don't know anything." (Ll. 1-30.)

(2)

For a time Monowar Gazi could not say anything, his voice being choked with tears. His rage, however, was as great as his grief, and he looked like a bamboo plant set on fire. Mohammed Reja was taken into a palanquin and brought to Monowar Gazi's house. He was served with a rich banquet and an attire embroidered with gold was given him. Monowar Gazi next had a brazen drum beaten and at the sound a thousand soldiers at once arrived at his house. He then circulated a letter of invitation calling upon all his relations and allies to assemble there for the purpose of fighting the foe. The names of the places where this notice was sent were,—Bhagalpur, Chandra Khola, Gopalpur, Senbag, Pubbapur, Chitashi, Palla, Nadua, Raipura, Bhabaniganj, Terfai, Lakshmipur, Maijdia and Lamarchar.

On receipt of Monowar Gazi's letter, they all assembled at his city. The soldiers from Pubbapur had small clubs in their hands and the men of Chitashi came armed with their long spears. The soldiers from Rampur were characterised by their long moustaches. It was, indeed, a picturesque sight when these men of different localities assembled. In the centre of a plot of land, measuring two and half *dronas*, they planted a post with their war-flag on. The big drum of war was beaten and innumerable soldiers approached at the sound. About two thousand elephants were seen marching in procession which consisted of thousands of archers and foot-soldiers. The great elephant *Airavata* was seen in front of the procession, and on this noble animal Mohammed Reja Chaudhuri himself rode. The general chosen to lead this war was Siva Ram and the great army marched first towards the palace of Inga Chaudhuri. It was a grim sight that Monowar Gazi witnessed in the palace and its compound. Hundreds of corpses lay there and vultures were making a feast of these. He could scarcely suppress tears as he saw this scene. On entering the palace, he

Mohammed Reja and his army. P. 305.

saw Nur Bibi weeping in a greatly distressed condition. She gave a full account of the battle, shedding tears all the time. Ample provision was made for her comfort and she was given a large number of guards to protect her. The army then proceeded towards the river which separated the lands of the Chaudhuris. There with the help of the ferryman Madhab they crossed the river.

(Ll. 1-44.)

(3)

Information in the meantime was received by Rajendra Chaudhuri that Monowar Gazi and Mohammed Reja were coming to attack his palace and that Raj Chandra Chaudhuri had joined them. He decided to fly away and said, "Old as I am, it does not become me to fight at this stage of my life. What harm if Raj Chandra inherits his paternal property and sits on my *gadi?* It is surely his, and if he takes it there will be nothing wrong. For myself, I should like to turn an ascetic and leave the rest of my days in a forest. Still life should be preserved anyhow." Then he called Chand to his presence and asked his opinion. Chand said, "If you give me order, I do not fear. I am ready to fight with Monowar Gazi." But the old Chaudhuri replied, "Many a time have I fought with my enemies, but this time there is a misgiving in my heart and a presentiment boding disaster. Who will live and who will die nobody can say now. If I die, it does not matter much, for I am already old. But if my nephew Raj Chandra dies, there will be none to light the lamp in my house." Chand said, "What can I say to this? If you are so determined, I cannot disobey your order."

The whole family retired in precipitous haste, and on the way Rajendra Chaudhuri heard the sound of the war drum beaten by the enemy and he hastened to leave his jurisdiction. When Monowar Gazi came to the palace he saw neither men nor beasts in it. He had a placard raised at the front gate of the palace in which the name of Raj Chandra was inscribed. People learnt from this that Raj Chandra was now the owner of the whole property.

Monowar Gazi whose heart was burning in grief for his nephews ordered the drivers of elephants to seek out Rajendra from wherever he could be found. He promised them ample rewards. The drivers of elephants tried their level best to find out the flying Raja. The whole locality was covered with dust as the elephants with their huge legs beat the ground, driven by the *Mahuts*. But nowhere could any clue be found as to Rajendra's whereabouts.

(Ll. 1-54.)

(4)

Now let us change our topic and give an account of Raj Chandra. He approached Monowar Gazi and said, "Pardon us, Chaudhuri Sahib. My uncle has fled to some place which is quite unknown. No need of proclaiming war any more. I am now perfectly happy. You kindly do take possession of the *gadi* and sit in the Durbar Hall. For myself, I shall be quite content if you appoint me as a constable or a peon under you." When Monowar Gazi heard these words, he affectionately embraced Raj Chandra and said, "It is your father's property. It is for you to take possession of it. You need not feel sorry; just make yourself quite comfortable in your father's palace."

Raj Chandra at this stage could not suppress his feelings but cried out. He said, "I have sinned against my uncle in a hundred ways. It is due to my fault that all these unfortunate events have happened. My father was dead when I was a little child and my uncle nursed me with every care and affection. Had not my uncle done for me what he did at that time, my property would have gone to rack and ruin."

Then he implored the Gazi to forgive and forget. "You, my lord, intervene and bring about a reconciliation between me and my uncle. If you accede to my humble wishes in this respect, I will myself go and seek him out."

The Gazi said, "All right, I give you permission to go and bring your uncle here."

Raj Chandra proceeded towards the house and asked every man he met news about his uncle. Enquiring in this way he one day came to learn that Rajendra had concealed himself with his people in the forest of Karimpur.

Thither did Raj Chandra go in all haste and sought for the old man. (Ll. 1-32.)

(5)

Rajendra saw that his nephew was coming towards him like a mad man in a wild manner. He did not fear but at once ran to embrace him and said, "If you have come to kill me, nephew, I shall be glad to receive that sentence from you." But Raj Chandra could not say anything in reply. He only cried like a child and embraced him affectionately, calling him uncle. "It is I that have always given pain to your heart by disobeying your orders. From infancy up you have shown me every affection. I tell you, uncle, I no longer desire to have any property. Come with me and sit on the *gadi* as usual. The only thing that pains me is the recollection of the affront that the slave Chand has offered me at your order. We need not fight."

When Rajendra heard his nephew's words he called Chand to his presence. The hero came and fell at the feet of Raj Chandra Chaudhuri craving pardon with these words, "You are my master's son and my master as well. Whatever I may have done may you kindly pardon and once more take me into your confidence." With these words, he cried and showed his repentance by standing silent. Raj Chandra pardoned him and they all returned to their palace. Monowar Gazi had a long talk with Rajendra and they eventually came to a settlement. At Manohar Gazi's order Raj Chandra was placed on the *gadi* and the Moslem Chief asked Rajendra, "Do you agree to this arrangement?" Rajendra said, "I am perfectly satisfied. Let my nephew rule the country. For myself, I am going to the holy city of Benares to spend there the few remaining days that I may be permitted to live."

Let Muhammadans recite the name of Allah and Hindus that of Ram. Everybody's wishes have, I believe, been fulfilled. (Ll.1-42.)

SUPPLEMENT.

In one of the versions collected from obscure sources a few pages more are attached to this poem by way of supplementation. The account given therein is crude and I do not like to give a full translation of the episode described in it. I will, however, give a summary of it. The supplement refers to the tragic end met by Chand, the general of Rajendra Chaudhuri. It is said that the man, though born of a low caste, became very proud afterwards, and thought that all the successes achieved by his master were due to him, so that he was the real lord of the country. He one day came to the Durbar and haughtily tendered resignation to his master. There was, however, a belief lurking in his mind that Rajendra would not accept the resignation but would feel completely cowed down, as he considered the services of his general indispensable. But to his surprise and disappointment he saw that the old Chaudhuri accepted the resignation, without even asking him once to reconsider his resolution. Grumbling at this attitude of his master, he saw the Chief Rani Sonamala and expressed to her his indignation, cursing the family of the Chaudhuris and holding out some very insulting threats. The Rani was a woman of outstanding personality and did not brook this conduct in her servant. She had him turned out from the palace by force.

Chand did not long survive this insulting treatment. It is said that his great physical strength left him within a few days and that he had fainting fits during one of which he fell into a public drain without any power to rise from the filth in the midst of which he was rolling. His whole body was merged in the dirty and muddy pool and Rani Sonamala who happened to pass by the place at the time saw that two red-hot eyes were blazing from the drain, which appeared like fire. She was afraid that it was an apparition that she saw and hit her brazen pitcher at the eyes, and this was the fatal blow that ended what had remained of his life. (Ll. 1-72.)

GOPINI KIRTTAN

PREFACE TO GOPINI KIRTTAN.

Sula (an abbreviation of Skt. ' Sulakhana,' literally, one with lucky signs) was born at Thakurkona, a village in the Sub-Division of Netrakona in the District of Mymensingh about the year 1776. She was the daughter of one Ram Dev, a Namasudra, one of the depressed castes of Bengal. Her mother's name was Jaytara. Sula had two brothers, named Raba and Dukhia.

Music was once a favourite subject with the Hindu women in India. No woman was considered accomplished without a high proficiency in that science. Saraswati, the goddess of learning in the Hindu mythology, is represented as carrying a book in one hand and the musical instrument, the *bina*, in the other. Sanskrit poetics, enumerating the qualifications of a woman of the highest type, the *Padmini*, lay stress on "music and dance" as the two essential qualities that she should possess.

The downfall of Hindu supremacy was followed by a dark period in Indian history, when oppressions, the chief victims of which were women, became rampant. And no woman who had the reputation of beauty or any personal accomplishment in the Hindu community, however high her status might be, was considered free from the risk of being carried away by men in power. Many of the ballads show the ruthless ways of these men and their heart-rending oppressions of handsome women. History offers striking instances which corroborate the accounts furnished by the ballads. There were many noble women like Padmini, wife of Bhimsingh, throughout India who courted death, preferring *Jahar Brata* to dishonour, and the fate of Sonai and Malua were no solitary examples of this widespread brutal treatment of the softer sex. The Portuguese and the Burmese pirates also achieved notoriety by their ruthless cruelties which Bengal remembers with a thrill in her nursery songs and *rupa-kathas.*

What wonder that under these peculiar circumstances our women should give up music and fine arts generally! Cultivation of tender arts was sure to attract notice of the ruffians, and the Hindu society was obliged to subject the woman-kind to many of the restrictions that we find now. The peace which we are enjoying under the British rule has re-opened the portals of music to our ladies, though the present communal strife will be retarding the progressive culture of our women in the direction, if this state of affairs is allowed to go on unchecked.

Inspite of the restrictions imposed on the ladies of the upper grades, the lower classes have always enjoyed full liberty in respect of music and dance. The Vaishnava women publicly sing songs—nay, earn their livelihood by following this as their avocation. Half a century ago in the old Kavi parties we found men and women of the depressed castes singing and dancing together on festive occasions. Though owing to the morbidness of taste that characterised their amatory song and dance, these performances are no longer favoured by the more refined society.

Sula had a silvery voice which could be pitched to a high point in harmony with instrumental music and it was so sweet that it kept the audience spell-bound on the spot. When as a young girl, she sported with her young companions, it was she who played the part of the chief singer, singing bridal songs in the marriage of their dolls.

Her father was proud of her accomplishments and married her to a young man named Jay Hari, a talented young man noted for his handsome appearance. Ram Dev had desired to keep Jay Hari as a "*ghar-jamai*"[1] giving

[1] One brought up and permanently settled in the father-in-law's house.

him a share of his property equally with his sons. But young Jay Hari got disgusted with the world and fled away one night, and nobody could trace where he had gone. This mishap made Sula miserable for life. Though she was never known to be a handsome woman, yet she possessed a grace and loveliness which made her personality striking, and people liked her for her amiable nature.

She met her fate with a calm fortitude but never in her life gave up her shell-bracelets and the red sign of luck (সিন্দুর) or the practice of taking fish which are forbidden to widows. Not for a day in her long life did she give up the hope that her husband would return, and the few lines of her preliminary prayer (ll. 29-34) furnish us a striking evidence of how fondly she cherished the hope of seeing him once more. She did not for a day cease to pride in her husband though he had gone away forsaking her so cruelly, and her pathetic appeal expressed in the last line of her preliminary hymns wishing him to come to her at least for a few minutes before she died touches our heart by the sincerity of her devotion and the ardent love with which she cherished the memory of her dear lord.

When years rolled by and still the lord of her heart never returned, she prepared herself for meeting her misfortune with courage and patience. Possessed of a quick memory, she got by heart any song sung by stray singers on the wayside even when she heard it once, and thus her memory became a storehouse of songs, especially those relating to the gods of the Hindu mythology. So great was the devotional fervour with which she sang them, that people wept at their pathos and became full of admiration for her. In the countryside there was no want of her admirers and her society was sought for by the womenfolk of the noble houses of the locality.

After living with her brothers Raba and Dukhia till the death of her father, she came to the village of Chhatrasir and settled there at the house of a nephew (sister's son) of hers. Here she resolved to get some education. It was a bold step for a woman belonging to the Namasudra caste. There was, however, a school-master in the village, named Chhannu Nath, who was of a compassionate nature. He took pains to acquaint her with the mystery of letters. With her quick intelligence she picked up Bengali in a short time. She has paid her tribute of gratitude to Chhannu Nath in her preliminary verses (ll. 39-40). She could now read for herself the Bhagavat and other scriptures in Bengali, and as she read them, her mind found a solace which spirituality brings unto a distressed soul.

She began to compose songs herself and these are characterised by a simplicity and devotion, which soon gained for her a wide-spread fame in that locality. She gathered a band of singers round her, of whom she became the head, and she gradually achieved so great a fame that any festive ceremony in Netrakona and adjacent places, which could not engage the services of the reputed musician, was considered void of its principal attraction. In the houses of the landed aristocracy with which Eastern Mymensingh abounds she had gained an undisputed status, and ladies of high rank favoured her for her unique talents. One of these, the late Rani of Ghagra, made endowment of considerable lands to her in the village of Chhatrasir. She got profuse gifts of ornaments, valuable utensils and clothes on these festive occasions and the fee she charged for singing a *pālā* varied from Rupees ten to Rupees twenty-five per night.

Thus lived this remarkable woman till a good old age, dying about the year 1866.

It is not difficult for us to account for the great local fame which she had acquired in life as a singer and poetess.

Her poems are exquisitely sweet. They will remind one of the pathos and simple charm of Mrs. Hemans' songs. Simplicity is the characteristic of Sula's songs. There is no affectation, no effort in them and they flow with a natural and easy grace. There can be no doubt that she was inspired by great faith, and this spiritual trait, so prominent in all that she wrote, has invested her poetry with a singular charm, making her poems attractive to all pious Hindus who believe in Hindu mythology. Her musical voice lent a supreme interest to her compositions during her lifetime, and bereft of this element they have lost a good deal of the charm for which her songs were once so highly favoured.

Yet, living as we do in an atmosphere of high refinement and culture, we may read her songs with interest and pleasure and be still impressed with signs of piety and simple faith which pervade them.

It should be remembered that she does not belong to the school of Vaishnava poets known as *Padakartas* whose songs are of a surpassing quality and excellence. In Sula's account of Radha-Krishna love, there is no ornamentation, no artistic display and none of those intrinsic poetic suggestions, which reveal the mystic import of Vaishnava songs. Nor do we find evidence in her writings of that finished aesthetic taste which in the Vaishnava songs captures our hearts by the beauty and elegance of a highly artistic poetic language. It is in the genial flow of her thoughts, pure as crystal and full of appeal in their pathos, that we find her at her best. She has given the popular version of the early life of Krishna as described in the Bhagavat and other scriptures of the Vaishnavas. Her poems belong purely to ballad literature. They articulate rural thoughts in the rustic language of villagers and should not be taken as forming a part of classical Bengali or even of its cultured literature. We have got these poems from one belonging to a depressed class without any pretension to higner culture. Her sentiments are like the water of a village pond which allays the thirst of the rural people of a small locality. They do not, however, possess the vigour, the vastness of outlook of a river marching to the sea. Those who share in her faith fully believing without a question in the divinty of Krishna and in the holiness of His actions will appreciate her the most. But there is no suggestion in her verses, no solution of the perennial question of spiritual symbolism in her poems, which the *Padakartas* give us in the same field under the covert veneer of idealism, making their lyrical songs a part of world's higher poetry. The interest of Sula's poems may flag beyond a certain limit, and outsiders, unless their sympathy and love for the orient is great, may not relish the songs as we, the people of Bengal, would do.

Sula's poetry in our translation may be considered commonplace and crude. The purists may often find fault with her expressions. Where the Hindu mind with its hundred associations feels interest in topics of time-honoured religious traditions, the outsider may not be inclined to enter the inner shrine of her devotional feelings. Many things that create a storm in the mind of the orthodox Hindu may appear stale and flat to the purely literary reader. Yet our foreign readers will find in the poem a phase of Radha-Krishna love which is most popular in Bengal, even to-day.

The last episode in this poem where Radha stands redeemed in public estimation is undoubtedly the best in Sula's whole writings—Radha who forsakes her husband and surrenders herself absolutely to the wishes of the Lord, is abused by her kith and kin. The voice of scandal is the loudest and Krishna vindicates her character by a supernatural action. This is the episode. But even an outsider, reading between the lines, will discover the mystic philosophy underlying the incident.

Krishna is called by the Vaishnavas the *Lila-may*. I find no adequate English equivalent for this word. Take for instance a flower; God shows His marvellous design in its creation over which the poet, the artist, and the man of science will for ever ponder. Yet it is created for a day only. The merciless Maker destroys it after allowing it a brief life of joy. Why did He create and why did He destroy? The baby's face, the abode of all that is divine, becomes disfigured by disease. Yet what offence has it done to deserve it? "What a piece of work is man!" cries the poet. "How noble in reason! How infinite in faculty! In form and moving how express and admirable! In action how like an angel! The beauty of the world! The paragon of animals! and yet ..this quintessence of dust," is created and destroyed like a plaything by inscrutable Providence! Can ethical laws explain this ever-changing wheels of existence? The Vaishnavas call all this His *lila*. Like the child He is playing, making and breaking at His sweet will. If we invest Him with the wig of a judge dispensing his judgment in an even-handed way, the spiritual problem is not solved. A thousand inequities stare us in the face and how are we to account for them? Duty, Justice and all such words born of Ethics do not help us in the dilemma. Duty works within certain limitations; it is at best the servant's function. But the mother, and the true wife, are not impelled by duty, they are impelled by love. The ethical laws occupy a place inferior to those of love.

The judges sit in judgment over an innocent man and sometimes gives the order of capital punishment on him. What will the innocent man say to his God in his prayers? The Vaishnava will, placed in such a condition, say in the language of their greatest poet Chandidas: "I do not know what is good or what is bad. I even know not if I am a sinner or a saint—I have given myself up fully unto you—Play with me as you will. I know that there is no other way for me than to love, wait and learn."

The much-abused Radha was in this plight. She loved the Lord with her whole heart and He saved her from the great scandal which clouded her fair name by a marvel. Her humility which shows the spiritual wealth of her soul is striking in the episode. Those who vaunted of leading a moral life, shrank into a corner, and she who loved with her humble spirit full of lowly and child-like simplicity and resignation rose to the highest pinnacle of glory. This episode proves in a somewhat crude way that the ethical rules and an arrogant self-consciousness have not the saving grace which love alone claims in the spiritual world.

The lives of Christ and Krishna present many points of agreement and Growse and other scholars have dwelt on them. Even in the popular Vaishnavism one will be struck with analogies showing that Christianity and Vaishnavism have many undeniable points in common with one another. From Chandidas down to the latest Vaishnava lyrical writers, the poets have laid a great stress on the efficacy of the Holy name in the spiritual world. The hymns of the Vaishnavas will assuredly remind one of the psalms. We refer our readers to psalms 8, 1; 25, 11; 31, 3; 34, 3; 66, 2; 69, 30; 72, 17; 145, 1; 148, 5; 148, 13; 149, 3; 150, 4.

The songs of Solomon have passages which when translated would read like passages from the Vaishnava poets. I refer to one passage :—

"My beloved spake and said unto me: My fair one, rise up, my love, my fair one, come away. For lo, the winter is past, the rain is over and gone. The flowers appear on the earth, the time of the singing of birds is come and the voice of the turtle is heard in our land. The fig tree putteth her green figs and the vines with the tender grape give a good smell. Arise, my love, my fair one, and come away."

(Psalms, Chap. 2. 10-13.)

The religious dance of the Vaishnavas has a parallel in that of the Christians and the psalms have many a reference to the same. "Praise his name with timbrel and dance. Praise with stringed instruments and organs." (Psalm 150,4.) "Sing unto the Lord with thanksgiving; sing praise upon the harp unto our God." (Psalm 147, 7.) "Let them praise the name of the Lord." (Psalm 148, 5.) "Let them praise his name in the dance." (Psalm 149, 3.)

We have in the songs of Solomon (Ch. 4,9) such lines as "Thou hast ravished my heart with one of thine eyes" —"Behold thou art fair my love: Thou hast dove's eyes" (Chs. 1-15).

The lines "I looked on my right hand and beheld, but there was no man that would know me, refuge failed me; no man cared for my soul" (Psalm 142, 4) will remind one of Chandidas's "আমি ভাবিয়া দেখিলাম এ তিন ভুবনে আর মোর কেবা আছে। রাধা বলি কেহ, শুধাইতে নাই, আমি দাঁড়াব কাহার কাছে।" and the lines "Oh! that I had wings like a dove! For then would I fly away and be at rest" (Psalm 55, 6) will recall Vidyapati's "পাখি জাতি যদি হমু, etc." "All they that see me laugh me to scorn" (Psalm 22,7) will remind one of many passages of Chandidas, such as "কলঙ্কী বলিয়া বলে সবজনা, তাহাতে নাহিক দুখ, তোমার লাগিয়া কলঙ্কের হার গলায় পরিতে সুখ।" "Let the righteous smite me, it shall be a kindness and let him reproach me it shall be an excellent oil (Psalm 141, 5) re-echoes the sentiments of Chandidas, "গুরু পরিজন, বলে কুবচন, সে মোর চন্দন চুয়া, আমি কানু অনুরাগে, এ দেহ সঁপিনু তিল তুলসী দিয়া।"

In this poem of Sula though it is so simple and without pretensions to any religious propaganda, the reader will halt over many a line that will remind him of the psalms and of the Song of Songs.

DINESH CHANDRA SEN

Gopini Kirttan

First of all do I pay my humble respects to the feet of my *guru*. It was he who created in me a taste for the Holy Name which has since grown to be my only refuge in the world. Hard as stone was this mind of mine and it is now rendered joyous and soft as a flower garden. It is all owing to the Holy Name that he has given me. I am like a stiff and barren metal. Verily is my *guru* like a touch-stone. Whatever he touches with his hands transmutes itself into gold and becomes a thing of value.

To my teacher who took charge of my education next do I pay my humble salutations. Darkness covered me and unconscious of everything around, I lay like one void of sight. It was my teacher who imparted knowledge of things to me and opened my eyes, as it were, to this strange world of ours.

Next do I pay my worshipful respects to Vishnu with his two consorts Lakshmi (Goddess of Fortune) and Saraswati (Goddess of Learning). Here do I praise the great God Siva and his consort Parvati, residing in the Holy Mount, Kailas. I address a hymn to Maha Vishnu whose abode is in the milky sea—to Brahma, the Creator, Vishnu, the Preserver, and Shiva, the Destroyer of the Universe. With clasped hands do I pray to Gauri for her blessings. My tribute of respects I offer to the angels presiding over ten directions and to the darling son of Nanda, the Lord of cowherds.

Oh Saraswati, the goddess of learning, with joint hands do I offer my prayers to you. By your kindness have I ventured to approach this learned assembly to-day. With the flying end of my *sari* placed round my neck, here do I salute you, oh my audience! Bless me that I may please you by my song. May my rhymes elicit your gracious pardon, however poor and faulty they may be.

Next do I address my humble prayers to my husband. Oh my lord! I wish for your blessings with whole-hearted sincerity and devotion. Alas! Where is it that you have gone, to what distant lands, never to return to this unhappy home? But wherever you may be, I, your devoted wife, shall always take glory in being called thine. You are the true lord of my heart and may God keep my heart fixed to your feet for ever! I do not blame you. What has happened was ordained by luck over which no one can have a control. My only prayer—my only sweet hope of life is that before I die, I may see your face but once.

Now let me offer my tribute of loving respects to Radha and Krishna and to the sacred Vrinda groves. On these topics I am going to sing a song to-day.

Next to the gods, I should offer my prayers to the Vaishnava masters who are full of compassion for the world. You should bless me, oh Vaishnavas, assembled here, for I am a sinner who deserves your grace for her shortcomings.

Last of all, I bow to the feet of Chhannu Nath. It was he who with great pains taught me how to read and write. What do I know of composing a hymn or song? May God save me from the disgrace due to want of skill in rhyming. Oh, Thou the Lord of the Universe, I am a Chandal by birth, but thou art not void of sympathy even for one who is so low. This is the humble prayer of Sula that her heart may rest at Thy feet. (Ll. 1-44.)

THE BIRTH OF KRISHNA.

The planet Rohini was ascendant in the firmament at the hour. It was the eighth day of the waning moon, the hour and time were auspicious. At such a lucky moment did Krishna, the Lord of the Universe, come to this world of ours.

It was the month of September (Bhadra) and He the Lord was born of Daivaki in the prison of King Kamsa at the depth of night. The angels from Heaven showered flowers on the spot. The thirty millions of gods oppressed by Kamsa rejoiced at the Saviour's birth. He, the Lord of the Universe, was born in full glory in mortal shape and hundreds of Moons shone forth from the divine child.

When Daivaki saw the babe, she was struck by the divine effulgence issuing from it and cried out in sorrow, "Oh God, why hast thou given me such a child ?" Vasudeva, the father, said, "The child seems to me to be a divine thing. It is not human. As soon as Kamsa will see it, he will take it away and strike its head against a stone. Thus will the child be killed in our presence. I will instantly take it to the house of my friend Nanda Ghose secretly, so that the wicked Kamsa may not be aware of his birth."

Thus Vasudeva got out of the prison with the baby. Darkness prevailed in sky and in land, and there was no peace in his mind. The air was drizzling rain on all sides and often did he slip his feet on the wet slippery ground. He was seized with fear lest any one saw him going with the child. With great caution, collecting all his courage the anxious father went slowly on. He came near the banks of the Jumna. Drops of rain fell gently on the head of the child but the hydra-headed Ananta unfolded all his hoods like an umbrella and protected the child. Vasu was alarmed at the sight of the high waves. The other bank was so distant that he saw no trace of it. The water was deep and the darkness of the night made it terrible to look at. With Krishna—the master of the ferry,—leading men from this to the other world, Vasu was fearing as to how he would cross the Jumna,—how strange!

It was a wild scene. The deep black waters over which sat night like a curtain of grim clouds, appeared impassable and impenetrable. Despairing of crossing the river, he sat on the bank and began to muse. At this moment the black clouds roared and it seemed that all the gods of Heaven showered tears taking pity at this condition of Vasu. The winds blew on all sides swiftly and the flash of lightning now and then came to the rescue of the sorrowing father, showing him some rays of hope. In the quick lights he wonderingly observed a jackal walking across the river from one end to the other. The sight filled his mind with hope and courage, and he at once came down to the river. Vasu, to his great surprise, found that a shoal had been strangely formed on the bed of the Jumna. The divine child played a trick here by suddenly slipping out of his father's hand into the mid-river. He began to beat his head and cry aloud. At his sorrow the very sun and the moon hidden in the blue sky seemed to weep in the form of rain drops. "Oh, what a wretch am I!" said Vasu, "I have allowed such a treasure of mine to be lost in the waters." He sought for the child with his hands overstretched and how glad was he to find it once more! With the baby in his arms he came to the other bank. It was like a poor man getting great riches all on a sudden or like a blind man restored to his eyes, so overjoyed was Vasu in getting back the lost one. He looked at the face of the child again and again and it seemed that his happiness knew no bounds. In slow pace did he advance and at last reached the house of Nanda, the king of the milkmen of the Vrinda groves. He peeped into the room of Jasoda and found her sleeping with a baby by her side, a girl just born. He took the little girl, placing his own baby in its place and forthwith returned to the prison and showed it to the wicked Kamsa ever on watch, when he enquired as to what child had been born of Daivaki.

Vasu.

"Hear me, oh lord. This girl I have got, no male child."

Kamsa took the little girl and was about to dash its head against a stone. Just then the baby slipped out of his hands and flew off upwards with the swiftness of a bird and assuming the form of an angel, reproached Kamsa saying,

"Thou wicked Kamsa, thou dost not know what evil would befall thee in the near future. He who will kill thee is now growing at the palace of Nanda. Thou hast no power to kill me. I am going to my abode in Heaven."

Saying so, the baby, who was the goddess Durga herself, disappeared from view. Sula the poetess sings "Mayest thou, oh Goddess ! allow me a place at thy feet when my life will close." (Ll. 1-74.)

THE PASTURES.

Chorus.—Oh Krishna, come with us to the fields for tending the cows.

On one morning the cow-boys assembled at the house of Nanda, the king of the Vrinda groves.

They shouted, "Aba, Aba"—a word current amongst milkmen to turn the cows in the right direction. Sridam and

Sudam said, "Oh Krishna, be ready and come with us." Balaram himself sounded his horn and cried again and again, "Oh brother Krishna, come soon; do not tarry. You cannot expect us every day to wait on you and entreat you in this manner? Let us hurry to the pastures. You know it well that the cows do not move a bit if they do not hear the sound of your flute. Behold how eagerly are they waiting with uplifted ears for catching that sound."

When the familiar sound "Aba, Aba" was heard by Jasoda, she held her son close to her breast, and said, "I am not going to allow him to go to the fields to-day. Listen to me, my dear Sridam and Sudam, and oh my darling Balaram,—excuse me for this one day. I am not going to part with my son. People have five or seven or more children. But mine is only one, and the wicked Kamsa is his sworn enemy. All of you know it well."

Sridam and Sudam advanced a few steps and with eyes glistening with tears said, "You do not know, oh lady, what the effect of your cruel words is likely to be. If you do not let him go with us, we will die here. This is our vow. Do you think that it is merely for a fun or a whim that we want him to go with us? He is our very life and soul. If we meet death, it is he who restores us to life. This boy of yours is a charmer. He does wonderful things. We promise not to take him very far into the forest. Let him be ready, venerable queen. We assure you, we will keep a close watch over his movements."

The mother could not resist the appeal of the lads and began to robe her child with tears in her eyes. She said, "If you are determined to go to the pasture leaving your poor mother weeping at home, come, I will robe you suitably."

He was playing in the compound of the house. She gave him a hundred kisses and took him into her arms.

She cleaned his body and helped him to wear his *dhara*. On his neck she placed a garland of *nabagunja*. She decorated his head with the picturesque plumes of a peacock. The head-dress was placed slantingly and it added grace to his face. The cheeks and the nose of the gay lad were painted with *alaka* and *tilaka* signs. From his ears hung pearl-pendents and his eyes were decorated with the black paint *Kajjal*. He was made to wear a beautiful pair of anklets on his feet, and the waist-belt with jingling pendents made merry sound as he walked. In one hand he held the cow-boy's crook and in the other his flute. Though a prince, he was given a rope to bind the cows as that was the trade of his caste. He wore in his hands a pair of golden bracelets. On his arms the *baju* shone brightly and a golden locket adorned his breast. Some glass-beads and cowries with a crooked tiger's nail set in gold dangled on his breast.

Thus robed and decorated with ornaments the charming cowherd was again taken into his mother's arms and she shed tears incessantly at the thought of parting with him.

As a caution that no beast and no reptile of the woods would dare touch him in the forest, the mother mildly bit the little finger of Krishna with her teeth. In the flying end of the *dhara* did the doting mother tie a little store filled with thickened milk and butter. It would serve as refreshment when the child would be fatigued and hungry. From her left foot she took a little dust and placed it on the forehead of her son. With her spit she made a sign on his forehead to ward off any evil that might lurk in the forest. She then began to recite the infallible *raksha* mantra which would preserve him from all dangers.

By the time the cow-boys were all assembled there. "Now, revered lady, it is high time already. Give us our Krishna and make no more delay"—sings Sula, the poetess. (Ll. 1-28.)

The Mother's Request to the Lads

Chorus.—Do not, oh lads, take my Krishna far off into the forest.

"You are to tend the cows in the pastures near the city so that I may catch the sound of Krishna's flute, sitting in my room all the while ; oh Balaram, my darling, you must always be with him and keep watch that he may not leave you and go afar. He still sucks the mother's milk, so tender is he. When you will go, you are to keep him in the middle of the party. He must have some of you in front and some behind. The spies of the terrible Kaṁsa are always on your track. Any time they may put us to dangers from which there will be no rescue. You know well and I repeat it that not five, not seven sons have I. He is my only son. And yet do you persist in taking him to the forest every day infested with danger. He feels hungry at brief intervals and he will not taste any food except butter, cream and thickened milk. See, my dear lads, that my child may not be upset by hunger. It breaks my heart to think that he will perspire under the scorching rays of the sun. Take him under the cool shade of a big tree so that he may rest when the sun is up. The cows sometimes wildly run fast and go to forest-paths. Take my warning,—let him not pursue these animals. The sprouting grass often pierces the feet like thorns,—see that Krishna does not tread upon these; the wicked cows are there that come dashing with their horns and hurt those that fall in their way heedlessly and savagely ; protect Krishna from these wild animals. If he is fatigued and cannot walk, take him into your arms and pardon him if he is found doing wrong. Do not quarrel when playing in the pastures. Rather tell *me* all about his faults when you return home. Need I say that he is a fortune to his unfortunate mother vouchsafed by divine grace? These cows are a source of great trouble and dread to me, for it is for these that my loving child is taken away from me every day to wilderness beset with dangers. There is none to whom I can unfold the pain of my heart. Alas ! who is there to sympathise with me! I have got him by the boon granted me by the great god Siva and his consort Gouri. My heart throbs in fear when he is away. Rather should I like to see all the cows of King Nanda die one day in the pastures, relieving me of all anxieties for my son. Oh! Balaram, your mother Rohini knows how dear is Krishna to me, and what I have suffered for him all these years ; you are mere children, how can you know of it ?

"Now, my lads, return early. This is my earnest request."

Sula the poetess sings, " I will be awaiting the return of your child, keeping my eyes fixed to the way-side."

(Ll. 1-36.)

Play in Pastures.

Chorus.—There goes Krishna to the pastures playing on his flute.

With the herd goes Krishna to the pastures. The cowboys raise the cry, " Háré-réré," expressing the glee of their heart and go with him. In front of all is seen Balaram sounding his horn. Then follow Sridam and Sudam, merry fellows, dancing along the path. In front and behind, the cow-boys go in rows, and when the women of the Vrinda groves catch the sound of Krishna's flute, they raise the cry "Ulu! " "Ulu! " as blessings and good wishes for the lads. In a high spirit of joy Krishna marches towards the pastures with his companions; playing and singing in graceful steps, they all come to the bank of the Jumna, and take their seat under the cool shade of the Kadamba trees. They play various kinds of play and even when Krishna is beaten, some would say "He has gained the play" but a few would complain, " No, no, it is not true, he is beaten." One lad comes up to Sridam and says, "How can we play with Krishna? If he is beaten you will yet reward him as a victor. Why should he lord it over us in this way?"

Thus they played and quarrelled, and one day it so happened that the herds came to Kalidaha for drinking water. (Ll. 1-19.)

Krishna jumps into the Lake.

Chorus.—Lost is he in the great lake.

The monster reptile Kaliya lived in this lake. Its very breath was so poisonous that even a hill with all its trees would be burnt, if it caught the air breathed by the snake. It was known to everybody that one who would drink from the lake would be dead in no time. The birds that flew above the lake often caught the poison of the atmosphere and dropped dead below.

The cows were thirsty. So as they reached the lake, they drank from it to allay their thirst. The cow-boys engaged in play knew not the fate of their charge. When their play was over, they searched for the cows on all sides and Krishna was with them. After a fruitless and anxious search, they arrived at the bank of Kalidaha.

They saw the cows lying dead there and Krishna knew that death was due to the poisonous water they had drunk. There was a Kadamba[1] tree on the bank, and Krishna ascended it straight, his shadow falling on the dark waters.

The wicked snake was disturbed by the shadow and hurried to the spot in great rage to bite the daring lad who had ventured to come so near its abode.

[1] This solitary Kadamba tree survived the destruction caused by poison in that land, where there was no living being, nor any vegetation. The ancient tradition was that the bird Garura, while flying over the sky with ambrosia stolen from Indra's heaven, had sat for a little while on that tree to take rest. Hence it had become immortal.

"Why should he lord it over us in this way." P. 332.

" The Naga women, the wives of the great prince of snakes, assembled there." P. 333.

Right glad was Krishna to see the wicked one approaching him. He gave a big jump from the Kadamba tree and fell on the dark waters of the lake. He stood on the hood of the great snake and danced there to his heart's content. The virtues acquired by the snake in the various cycles of its past lives must have been great indeed, for it got without any pains Krishna's feet placed on its head, a privilege coveted by Brahma and other gods.

He stood on the hood of Kaliya and the report of this wonderful sight spread in the region of snakes. The Naga women, the wives of the great prince of snakes, assembled there to see their husband. When they saw the God of gods dancing on his head, they all bowed down to Him. They beheld Him with eyes fixed in devotion and sang hymns surrounding him. The dance of the Master Dancer in many a sportive way pleased them all and they were glad even at the defeat of their husband. The region under the waters thus breathed a gladsome air of spiritual content hitherto unknown to them. But the banks of Kalidaha were rent by the wild laments of the cow-boys who thought Krishna to be lost. Balaram was in wild despair and cried like a child.

Sula, the poetess sings, "Oh, Sridam and Sudam and other lads, do not cry. He the lad whose colour is lovely dark-blue, beloved of you all, will soon come up and join you."

(Ll. 1-38.)

The Laments of the Cowherds.

Chorus.—They all grieve over Krishna saying, "Where hast thou gone, O Krishna, leaving your dear companions—Sridam, Sudam and others?

"Where have you gone, oh Krishna, leaving all of us? Come and join us at once. Your mother has no child but you. See how Sridam and Sudam roll in the dust for grief."

Says Sudam : "Why did you jump into this poisonous

lake, oh Krishna, leaving us all so unkindly? How can I bear my life without you?"

Sridam.

"We cannot bear this calamity. Let us all assemble here and jump into the lake. The poor mother has her eyes fixed on the wayside. How can we return home without Krishna to show ourselves to the doting queen? A single treasure she had and none other. What should we give her in the place of the one lost? We have nothing to give her, not a word of consolation to offer. She cares not for anything else in the world save her Krishna. When she will get the report of this mishap, she is sure to strike her head against a stone and kill herself. The milkmen will all run mad in despair."

Some said, "Arise from the watery grave and tarry not." And others said, "May he be still living."

And all cried in the agonies of their great grief.

At this moment did Krishna ascend from the bottom of the lake to the view of his grieving companions. Their sorrows were all removed and they embraced one another in the overflowing joy of their heart. Krishna sprinkled a few drops of water over the dead cows and they were restored to life and once more played with their calves with uplifted tails. In a high jubilant spirit did the boys once more enter the pastures with their charges and began to play again as usual.

The poetess Sula sings, "I too wish to play with you even as the cow-boys did, and may you, O Krishna! be the lord of my heart." (Ll. 1-34.)

Return Home.

Chorus.—The cow-boys of Vrinda groves are returning home from the fields. They raise the gleeful sound "Hai, Hai" as they march on with the cows.

Balaram, the leader of the boys, now says, "The sun is setting, O my dear brother Krishna, let us now return home." Saying so, he sounded his horn and at the signal, the cows with their calves, all assembled there ready to start. The brown-coloured ones called Syamali and the white cows called Dhavali and a hundred others bleated as they marched with uplifted tails crying, "*hamba, hamba.*" At the head of all went Balaram, sounding his horn and the cows all followed his signal. Behind them went Krishna who marched in a dancing gait, ever playing on his flute. Then followed the other cow-boys with their gleeful voices crying, "Aba, Aba" and "Hai, Hai"—raising a confused noise which was heard from a distance. The women of the Vrinda groves with Jasoda and Rohini at their head were all awaiting their return with sacred grass and rice (to bless them) in their hands. They all sang "Ulu!" "Ulu!" indicating their joy. And the milkmen sounded their drums and other musical instruments in order to welcome their boys.

Krishna came to his house with the whole band and Jasoda the queen received him with all the warmth of her heart. She took him in her arms. She wiped away the sweat and dust from his face with the edge of her *sari*. She gave him a hundred kisses and blessings.

"These incidents of Krishna's life are all honeyed," sings Sula, the poetess. "Oh my mind, be merged in them and revel in them as long as you live." (Ll. 1-24.)

Krishna as a Ferry-man with thf Young Women of the Vrinda Groves.

Chorus.—Be quick, oh ferry-man, help us to land at Mathura on the other bank. We must sell our articles. It is already high time.

The life of Krishna presents so many lovable features that it can be compared only to a sea of which one sees no shore, no limit.

One day he became a ferry-man. The boat was a shattered one and the oars were all broken. He sat near the helm and played a hundred tricks. He was in the mid-stream of the Jumna with his broken boat. Who could guess what tricks he intended to play? The gay-headed Krishna had turned a ferry lad in order to fascinate the hearts of the milkmaids and play with them. At this time the Princess Radha, daughter of King Vrishabhanu, came to the landing ghat of the river. She saw the shattered boat with Krishna at the helm. With her maids Lalita and Bishakha she saw Krishna in that guise and began to laugh.

Bisakha called out, " Oh my young boat-man, new in your trade, will you help us to get to the other bank ? Bring your boat quickly. Do not delay. Radha, the princess, is with us."

As often as the princess beheld Krishna in the boat dressed like a boat-man, she smiled and stole a glance. She took off her veil every now and then on some pretext or other to catch a sight of the young boat-man.

Lalita.

" We must go quickly to the other side to sell our curd. So in all haste take us to the other side. You see we carry these pitchers which are full. The sun is up and we cannot bear the heat. How long are we to stand here waiting? "

Krishna.

" How can I carry you all in this broken boat of mine? I have heard it from old boat-men that you milkmaids are not at all of light weight. Add to the weight of your well-shaped fully blossomed round form, that of the goods you carry. If, by chance, my broken boat sinks in the mid-stream, my earnings will stop for ever."

The women became clamorous and all of them cried out in a confused voice, "You are a shameless fellow. Why have you become a ferry-man? Hundreds of men require the services of a ferry-man at this busy spot. How do you work with this broken boat? Why are you here?"

Krishna.

"You do not know the secret of my trade, my lovely maids. I take my passengers one by one. If you are really willing to go to the other side, bring your princess first. By her rank and accomplishments she deserves to be taken first."

The Maids.

"We are all ladies of respectable houses and have our social prestige. There will be scandal, if one of us go with you alone. We are nine, you see. We must go all together. Bring your boat to the *ghat*."

Krishna.

"All right, what objection can I have to agree to your request? I will comply with your wishes. But I must settle everything beforehand, so that I may not be charged with misleading you in future. Know that I shall not be to blame if the boat capsizes in the mid-stream. You will get drowned and I will lose my boat. This will come out of your obstinacy as a matter of course. Why should we take such a venture, my lovely friends?"

The Maids.

"If we get drowned, it is you who will be put to shame. People will say Krishna was at the helm and yet did the boat sink. The boat-man who can ply a broken boat is really an expert in his trade. Even a novice can ply a newly built boat. Oh sir, do not find fault with your boat. Say that you know nothing of your business."

Krishna.

"Then settle first what wages you are going to pay me. I shall next consider the point of taking you to the other side."

The Maids.

"Now help us, O young boat-man, to go to the other bank. We shall pay your wages when we shall sell our goods and return. Just see we have got no money with us at this moment."

Krishna.

"I want what you have with you."

The Maids.

"We have with us only pitchers of curd."

Krishna.

"Fie, who wants your curd? You are young lovely women and can repay with your love what you may want in coins."

The Maids.

"You wicked fellow, take care. You know that King Kaṁsa rules here. We shall have you punished severely for such impertinence. You are a daring fellow to talk in this way. We cannot bear it? Was it ever heard that a crow dared put its beak to the offerings to gods?"

Krishna.

"Sometimes it so happens, my friends, that even a mean crow tastes of sacred offerings."

The Maids.

"Take care, you mean fellow. You are taking undue liberty, heedless of your position as a ferry-man."

Krishna was ashamed and said, "Then mortgage to me, your ornaments, in lieu of my wages. For others, my rate is one anna per head, but from each of the milkmaids I will charge a gold ear-ring."

The maids smiled and said, "What you may want we will pay; but first take us to the other bank."

Then did Krishna bring the boat to the bank and one by one the nine damsels got up.

Krishna.

"Take care, maidens. By god, I say, if the boat sinks, you will not make me responsible for it. Place your goods near the prow and carefully sit behind. The boat leaks. You are to bale out water as I ply it."

Saying so, Krishna started the boat and the maidens cried out, "Ulu," "Ulu," praying for an auspicious trip. When the boat had come to the mid-stream, he steered the helm with such a force, that the milkmaids were frightened, and a plank was about to give way. They all raised a cry of alarm. The waves danced in fury on all sides and the boat now inclined to one side and now to the other by the force of the stream. Terror-struck the maids appealed to Krishna for saving them. Lalita and Bisakha, the most forward of them, said, "If the boat sinks, oh boat-man, all the world will proclaim your unworthiness."

Slowly did the boat approach the other bank and at last the milkmaids landed safe with Radha at their head. Krishna said, "Oh moon-faced Radha, O Princess, do not fail to pay my fee at the time of return. Do not play false with me. Here do I moor my boat and I will be waiting for you. I will take you to the other bank. Do not delay here."

Sula prays, "Do not fail, when my time will come to leave this world, to take me to the next, O my dear ferry-man."

(Ll. 1-104.)

Theft of Cream.

Chorus.—He who stole Radha's heart now steals cream from the milkmaids.

In order to satisfy the desire of Radha he steals cream at the house of Ayan Ghosh.

She goes to the landing *ghat* of the Jumna everyday and there she takes the best cream that she prepares at her house in order to entertain Krishna. Gradually it got publicity and Kutila, her sister-in-law, began to abuse her openly. From that time she could not take cream to the riverside and she was very sorry for not being able to offer it to Krishna. Jatila, the mother of Ayan Ghosh, kept all the cream of her store concealed in her house, so that Radha might not steal it for Krishna. In her store-room the old woman kept the delicious article securely in a rope-shelf hanging from a hook. Krishna came to know of it. He said to Radha, "Why should you be sorry for such a small thing? I will steal the cream from its place of concealment. Upon my life, I say, I will steal it anyhow to please you." Thus every day he stole and ate the cream from the store-room. He broke the pots, tore the rope-shelves and committed many mischiefs of this nature, escaping the utmost vigilance of Jatila and Kutila to detect the thief. One day the old woman saw Krishna taking to his heels after his adventurous theft, but being old, was too weak to follow and catch hold of him. She could not bear this sort of outrageous treatment any more. She struck her head with her hand and snapping her fingers said, " Vile being, die the death of a miscreant that you are. May you not live long. You are oppressing us every day. You will never be happy in life. If we could catch hold of you, we would burn your face."

Cursing him in this way, Jatila and Kutila felt greatly disappointed, being unable to take proper retaliation. Radha heard their abuses from the kitchen and smiled at their sound and fury.

One day Jatila, old as she was, went to Nanda Ghosh's palace with a staff in her hand in trembling steps. She began to complain to Jasoda about her son's conduct, and abused him.

Sula says, " No more, oh lady, do not abuse him. My heart can ill bear it." (Ll. 1-34.)

JATILA'S COMPLAINTS TO JASODA.

Chorus.—Oh, my darling Krishna, do not go to the houses of others to commit mischief there.

" Your Krishna, oh Queen, goes every day to our house and throws all things into disorder. Various are his evil deeds, and engaged in household work, as we are, we cannot keep watch over his doings. Taking advantage of this, he breaks the cream-pots, tears the rope-shelves and does a lot of mischief. We shut our doors from outside when we go to the river with my daughter-in-law. He enters the room. How he does so we cannot detect. He hides himself when we search for him, and all our attempts to get hold of him are baffled. If we happen by chance to detect him eating the cream, in reply to our abuses he turns back and looks at us with a wicked smile. Saying nothing he leaves the place quickly. Sometimes he raises his forefinger at us and says "Look here, this is a banana. Will you take it?" If, by the grace of mother Kali, we can catch him one day, we will make his head fall down from the trunk with a sharp knife. Not a moment is he to be found staying at home, so shameless is he. The whole day he wanders about in the public road; such a fine urchin have you brought forth! If we had such a child we would have delivered him over to death. Why does not the wicked fellow die and relieve us? I have spoken to you about his conduct times without number and, with clasped hands, I do so for the last time. Prohibit him to go to our house. You are the queen here. Milk, butter, curd and cream you have in plenty. Why should he steal these from the houses of others? If he does so again, his hands will be bound with a rope. It is a great relief to the public that you have got only one son. If you had half a dozen like him, the city would have gone to rack and ruin. How fine he looks with his dark complexion and purple lips! To you he may appear lovely and sweet but to us he looks like the very ghost that dwells in a myrobalan tree. The only training that he seems to have received is stealing things that belong to others. Is he not the shame of the community of milkmen?"

Sula, the poetess, with clasped hands, implores Jatila to desist, saying, "He whom you brand as thief is adored by Brahma, the Creator, and Vishnu, the Preserver of the Universe." (Ll. 1-36.)

Krishna is Bound.

Chorus.—You, spoilt child, come, I will bind you to-day.

Hearing the rude words of the old woman Jatila, full of bitterness, the queen felt greatly insulted and was highly incensed at her son. She took a stick in her hand and went pursuing the lad, who, when he saw his mother angry, took to his heels. He went a few paces ahead and though so near, Jasoda could not get hold of him. Alas, who can get hold of him, unless he allows himself to be caught? The queen had acquired innumerable virtues in her previous birth; hence she had got Him for her son. Who can understand the significance of these sports and tricks of Krishna ? A blind man cannot understand the quality of a looking glass. How strange that He at the very mention of whose Holy Name death flies away in fear, is flying away for fear of a milkwoman. Oh my sweet God, what charming things did you do in the lovely groves of Vrinda ! The milkwoman got you for her son and tenderly brought you up. At the very sight of Krishna the mind of the queen used to be filled with affection and she pardoned him as she saw his face. Though so dear, she gave him a stern look to-day and said menacingly, "Wait, I will surely bind your hands and feet to-day. You go to steal things belonging to others, and they pour forth a volley of abuse. What will the king, your father, say of the training you are receiving at home, when he comes to know of all this ? Is there any lack of cream or butter in my house ? You have more than enough, and yet you commit such mischief owing to the bad habit that you have contracted."

Saying so, she pursued him in all haste. It caused sweat to fall from her body, and Krishna, when he saw his mother really fatigued and worried was full of affection for her. He did no more run away but came and fell at her feet. The thief was thus caught. She got a rope and tightly bound his hands with it. When she was binding his tender hands with all her might, she secretly felt pain in her heart but yet continued doing so in a fit of anger. Krishna all the while tried to excite her pity, saying, " Do not, oh mother, bind me so hard. By my life I swear, I will no more do such a thing ; I feel pain. Do not bind so tightly." The queen did not listen to his appealing words but bound his hands with a rope which she tied to a husking machine, so that he might not escape.

Sula the poetess, sings, "Oh, good mother, for the sake of my life, do not cause him any more pain but release him straight." (Ll. 1-40.)

The Lament of Cowherds.

Chorus.—Oh Queen, be kind and set him free.

When the cowboys heard that Krishna was thus bound, they went to the spot. When they saw him in that plight they were, indeed, very sorry. Sridam and Sudam, Basudham, Subal and Balaram himself with his horn in hand assembled there. They found Krishna bound to a husking machine. Their eyes were full of tears at the sight. They all entreated the queen to set him free. Krishna was above all pain. Yet he pretended as if he was feeling pain. He began to cry before his comrades. The cowboys were all deeply touched. One of them said, " Look, queen-mother, his eyes are tearful. Even a stone would melt at the sight of that charming face flooded by tears. Is your heart made of stone? " Another cowboy indignantly said, " Many a mother have we seen but none so cruel as you. Why should you torture our brother in this way? " Another came forward with the words, " We all stand guarantee for his good conduct and give you our word—he will never steal again. Take off the ropes." One of them said, "Bind me in his place. I will bear this punishment with pleasure ; but do release him."

Still another said, "If you will cause him pain in this way in our presence, I warn you, mother Jasoda, we shall not be able to bear the sight any more. We may do something drastic and rash—may jump into the Jumna or do something like that."

Balaram said, "I charge you, queen, look at this plough of mine, I will destroy everything that I see before me."

Saying so, Balaram cast angry looks around and the other boys sat quietly in the compound and wept. Some of them clasped the queen's feet, who was touched by their sorrow. She was already full of affection for her darling and now could not resist this appeal from the cowherds and instantly set Krishna free.

One who listens to this tale of Krishna's release shall be released from all woes of the world.

Sula says, "Oh my audience, this song of the release of Krishna must not go unrewarded. I am entitled to the present of at least a cloth."[1]

She kissed her darling a hundred times and took him into her arms and wiped away the dust from his body. The cowboys expressed their joy by crying "Aba! Aba!" The boys looked like flowers bedecked with dews, as they smiled with tears still trickling down from their cheeks.

"Let us see, brother, if you have been hurt," they said and each examined his hands to find the mark of rope on them. When they saw the mark, they signified their sympathy and anger with cries of "Oh! oh!" Some blew their breath over the hurt in order to lessen his pain. (Ll. 1-52.)

[1] While the singers sing this episode of the early life of Krishna, a lovely boy attired like Krishna, his hands bound with a rope, sits on the lap of one who plays the part of Jasoda. The maids of the Vrinda groves approach her with a request to set Krishna free. But the main singer will not allow it until she receives some reward in the shape of clothes or ornaments.

Radha's Scandal removed.

Chorus.—Oh my wicked self, sing the name of Krishna. Your days are fast passing in vain.

Who can describe and rightly interpret the sports played by Krishna on the bank of the Jumna? They were not conceived in the Vedas or any other scriptures.

One day Krishna met Radha in her bower when she was with her maids there. Radha said, "Lord of the universe art thou, oh Krishna. But woe to me that resigning myself, as I have done, absolutely to your mercy, I have been still a subject of scandal. The inmates of the house and others abuse me day and night and how can I bear or prevent the tongue of scandal?

Krishna.

I fully realise your position. I give you my word, my love, this scandal I will remove in a short time. The maids were right glad at his words.

Some days passed and once the queen strolled about the courtyard with Krishna in her arms. The milkmaids assembled at her house and wanted to see the sweet dance of Krishna.

The Queen.

Dance, my child, I will give you the best of cream that I have prepared for you. But if you do not, wayward as you are, you will have none from me.

The queen and the women clapped their hands to keep time and the lovely boy began to dance. From the wrists of the ladies, the bracelets made a jingling sound as they clapped, in harmony with the pendants on the waist-belt of Krishna. The anklets rang merrily at his feet and "*jitang*!" "*jitang*!" was the sweet sound which was heard in harmonious concord. The ladies were pleased and said that there was nothing in the world so sweet as Krishna's dance.

He danced gracefully bending now on one side and then on the other with his yellow-coloured clothes waving in the air and the ladies all the while cried "Well done." Surrounded by women on all sides, merrily did Krishna dance with a ball of cream in his hand.

Suddenly Krishna recollected the promise he had made to Radha. As if exhausted by too much dancing he pretended to faint away and the queen cried, "What is it? Is he ill?" and took him in her arms. His heart was beating rapidly and they found him without breath, his mouth foaming, his eyes rolling upwards. He was profusely perspiring and gasping for breath with teeth clenched. Jasoda became greatly alarmed and began to cry. Rohini and other female members of the palace filled it with their loud lamentations. (Ll. 1-70.)

The General Lament.

Chorus.—Oh darling and treasure of our hearts! How can you depart for ever from your home leaving your mother!

It was like a blow of thunderbolt at a time when no cloud had indicated it. The maidens in their deep grief could not restrain their tears. Nanda Ghosh stood helpless benumbed by this misfortune, and Upananda was crying, "Alas! Alas!" Balaram in wild grief said, "Oh, my darling, what is it that has become of you?" Sridam, Sudam and other companions joined the note of lament saying, "Unbearable will our life be without you, oh Krishna. For whom shall we again pluck fruits from the Vrinda groves and busy ourselves gathering flowers to prepare garlands? Whom shall we make our Raja under the Kadamba tree, playing around him as his courtiers and ministers? Who will be our companion in tending the cows in the pastures on the banks of the Jumna? Who will charm our ears by playing on the flute? Whom shall we carry on our shoulders at play-time, delighted with the sweet burden? Alas! Who will protect us from the dangers that beset our forest-life in the Vrinda groves?"

Jasoda with tears overflowing her eyes said, "Oh, my darling, speak a few words if only to console Sridam and Sudam, maddened with grief."

The heart of Sula, the poetess is silently bursting in grief. (Ll. 1-22.)

THE ENTRANCR OF A PHYSICIAN INTO THE PALACE.

Chorus.—Oh physician, restore him to life.

The house of Nanda became a scene of wild grief. All people of the palace cried madly in deep affliction.

He, the god, knew many an art to bewilder His people. If He does not offer a solution Himself, who will unravel His mystery?

The god assumed the figure of a physician and came to the palace there. He lay in the arms of Jasoda senseless and apparently lifeless. But another manifestation of Him came to the palace assuming the figure of a physician. With a shattered umbrella in one hand and a stick in the other,—with a bag of medicine hanging from his shoulders, the physician came there saying in a low tone, "Oh, Hari! Oh, God!"

Jasoda.

If by the grace of Providence, you are here, oh physician, apply your medicine and bring my darling back to life. If he recovers through your kindness, nine lacs of cows that belong to our palace will be thine. Besides these, I will give you all my ornaments. King Nanda and his brother Upananda will give you further rewards.

At this moment Balaram came and fell at the feet of the physician and said, " Take my word, oh physician ; if he survives, this favourite horn of mine, prized above everything else, will I offer to you as present."

Sridam, Sudam and other companions of Krishna said, " We will seek the whole forest, and the fruits and flowers that we shall be able to gather with our utmost effort shall we offer all to your worship. The fruits of the cane plant, mangoes and other fruits with which our forest abounds shall we submit to your worship. Kindly restore him to life, and your reputation will spread throughout the world."

The physician said not a word to these appeals but slowly approached the unconscious Krishna and felt his pulse.

The Physician.

" Hear me, oh queen-mother. It is a very serious case. It generally turns fatal, the situation is critical, indeed !"

Jasoda clasped the feet of the physician and looked at his face in deep dismay.

The Physician.

" Never mind, do not despair. There is one remedy. I will suggest it. You must try to procure it."

Jasoda.

" Order us what we are to do. Through your blessing there is no want in this palace of ours. We shall be able to secure whatever you will command."

The Physician.

"Bring a new earthen pitcher. You are to make a thousand holes at its bottom. A chaste woman must be in attendance. I guarantee by the sacredness of my thread that if that chaste woman will go to the river and fill that charmed pitcher, not a drop will leak through its thousand holes. The water of the Jumna thus sanctified and charmed should be sprinkled over the body of the patient who will surely revive by this means. There is no other way that I know of to bring about his cure."

Jasoda brought an earthen pitcher and instructed by the physician made a thousand holes at the bottom of it.

Jasoda.

"Now I implore you, oh women assembled here, one of you should be ready to fetch water from the Jumna."

The women all looked embarrassed at this request and looked at one another, enquiring as to who should be ready. On some pretext or other they all tried to evade the situation. It was, indeed, a very difficult affair. One of them said, "If by chance a drop of water should fall from the vessel, our action would serve you no purpose and scandal would be the reward of our work. Who should like to play this game? We are not prepared to submit to this test of chastity."

Jasoda became alarmed at these words of the women. "Is the sacred Vrindaban void of chaste women?"—she thought.

The Physician.

"It is a shame that there is not one woman in this large city who is confident of the purity of her life."

At this reproach from the physician, the old mother of Ayan burst into a fit of rage and said, "Who are you, physician, and whence have you come to charge the women of this city in this way ? You are a coward to lay such a charge on us. I will show if there is a chaste woman here or not.''

When Jatila had said so, Jasoda felt her life revive at her words.

Jasoda.

"Here do I fall prostrate at your feet. Grant me this boon. Bring water from the Jumna and restore my child to life.''

Jatila.

" Yes, I will restore your child to life. But I warn you here ; tell him that he should not steal butter from my home again. Another thing I am going to tell you privately. Your wicked son has ruined the good name of our family. He plays on his flute day and night wandering about in the neighbourhood of our house and my daughter-in-law, the wicked one, becomes maddened by the sound.''

Jasoda.

" If he comes to life again by your kind help, I will throw his flute into the water. I will bind him to one of the pillars of our terrace, so that he will not be able to steal cream from your house again.''

The old woman felt relieved at this assurance. Slowly did she proceed towards the river ghat with a staff in her hand. She was to fetch water in that earthen vessel full of holes. Scarcely had she touched it when Kutila came forward and said, " Stop, you have grown old and unfit. Why should you go when your daughter is here? '' saying so, she snatched the vessel from her mother and proudly walked towards the river. A hundred people followed her to see the fun of it. They all stood in rows, surrounding Kutila, who, full of confidence, plunged the pitcher in water. When, however, having filled it with water, she raised it up in her hands, water began to fall in a stream from the holes. People assembled began to scoff at her, saying, "Look at the chaste woman." The physician smiled and said, "Now we have known that you did not remember your hidden sins when you made the venture." Overwhelmed with shame and disgrace Kutila stood there like a statue that had no life. Jasoda lamented saying, "What shall I do now?"

The old woman Jatila was enraged at this insult of her daughter and she took the pitcher in one of her hands and bending low with her staff in the other, slowly walked towards the ghat. Now also as before, people followed her to see what would come of her vaunts. The same thing occurred again. When the vessel was plunged in the water and carried up, not one hole was there that was shut but from all of these drops fell in incessant streams. People laughed as before, crying shame on her and the old woman hung down her head in shame and shrank into a corner to hide herself.

Now when the mother and the daughter failed in this way, other women who had reputation for chaste life dared not even look at the pitcher.

The Physician.

"Now hear me, queen-mother, I want a chaste woman in all haste. Krishna will die if there be any further delay."

Jasoda.

You have seen, my son, with your own eyes that old Jatila and her daughter Kutila have been put to shame at the attempt. They are reputed for their pure and religious life. Now no one will dare attempt it again. They have been all struck with fear. What can be done now to save my darling? You see the crisis. There is no help; I myself must go to bring water.''

Saying so she took up the pitcher in her arms.

The physician, none other than a manifestation of Krishna himself, thought, "How will the scandal of Radha be removed if mother goes to do the thing. Jasoda will assuredly be able to do it. There is no risk of her being exposed to shame."

The Physician.

"Hear me, mother Jasoda, you know the custom of the country and the injunction of the scriptures. Medicines administered by a mother's hand do not produce any good effect on a son. Rather they aggravate the disease tenfold. It has often been seen that a medicine taken from a mother's hands has killed a child. So you cannot go. Find out some other woman for the purpose.''

Jasoda.

"All are stricken with fear. Suggest yourself who will go now?"

The Physician.

"My mind says that there are chaste women in this holy city and the evidence of my mind is unfailing. Let me find out.''

Saying so, he paused for a moment and then said, "A woman named Radha of this city will be able to pass through the trial. She is the purest of the whole womankind, immaculate, chaste and perfectly faultless.

You cannot find out one like her in this world, not to speak of this small town. Call her here at once."

In all hurry Jasoda proceeded to bring Radha. Jatila like a tigress roared out, "Do not go, oh queen. Women of pure character like myself and my daughter have been put to shame and you are going to approach my daughter-in-law about whom there is such widespread scandal in Vrindaban. God alone knows how true to the very letter of the scriptures have we led our life. This wicked fellow has conspired to brand our good name in society by resorting to a fraud. He is now going to put our whole family to shame by advising you to bring my daughter-in-law here. A mean half-starved wretch that he is, his mission here seems to be to put a stigma on the whole society of milkmen."

Jasoda fell prostrate at the feet of Jatila and entreated her to give permission. She was in the greatest distress, she said, and wanted to try all possible means of saving her son. Jatila was moved by her importunities and sat silent without saying yes or no. Her silence was taken for permission and the queen went to bring Radha there as suggested by the physician.

Radha.

"In this city, mother, I am spotted as a bad woman. Why have you come to me?"

Jasoda.

"We need not spend time over the question. My Krishna will die, if you delay."

Saying so she caught hold of Radha's hands and inspite of her hesitancy, tenderly dragged her to the palace.

Jasoda.

"Now, physician, see if this woman will be found fit,"

The Physician.

" She is the crown, the perfection of womankind and will be able to do this marvellous feat."

Slowly did Radha wend her course to the river ghat, taking up the vessel which Jasoda showed her.

The Physician.

" But before she goes to face the trial, there is another thing which she must first attempt. Here, in the river ghat, I will make a bridge of hair. One who will be able to cross the Jumna by means of this bridge will be able to perform the next task, namely, that of carrying water in this pitcher full of holes. Let her first try to cross the river. Then if she succeeds, the next task may be attempted. No use of attempting the latter if she fails in the first.

The physician got a cluster of hairs and tied them with one another, till it was sufficiently long to cover the whole river. He made of it a bridge and spread it over the Jumna. Thus the bridge of hair was prepared. He pointed it out to Radha and said, " This will be your bridge. Cross the river by means of it. Take this pitcher in your arms. In the presence of all you are to cross the river now."

Radha was going to fetch water in that vessel with hundreds of holes. Thousands of people ran to see this great fun and the whole city stood breathless with curiosity to witness it on the bank of the river.

Says Sula the poetess, " Oh Radha, do not fear for a moment. Have confidence in Him to whom you have dedicated your life, your youth, in fact, all that you have in this world." (Ll. 1-186.)

Radha's Self-dedication.

Chorus.—Oh my God, preserve me at this perilous hour of trial.

With the pitcher in her arms, she cried, "Krishna, Krishna, oh my Lord." In her mind she recited a hundred times the holy name of her Lord. With her hands clasped, she stood in an attitude of prayer and paid her whole-hearted *Pranamas* to Krishna. "Oh my God, oh my Krishna, save my honour. Do not put me to disgrace, a devoted servant of thine."

Taking the vessel full of holes in her hands, she prayed again, "Save me, oh my kind Lord, if I am put to disgrace none will put a trust in your Holy Name, for I have depended on you with the whole might of my soul.

"The scandal is rife in the air, they call me the wicked one. I do not know if I am good or bad. To thee have I dedicated my whole soul. I do not know any other religion, I do not know any other duty. The world has no other attraction for me than that it gives me an opportunity to worship thy holy feet.

"I am put in the greatest of perils, but through your kindness, I hope to cross the bridge of hair and to carry the vessel full of water, inspite of its hundred holes, for what is impossible becomes possible through your kindness.

"I knew your kindness to me once, when, placed in danger, I had prayed to you with all my soul. You then assumed the form of Kali and protected me. This time also, danger will be no danger to me through your kindness, Lord of the Universe thou art, yet how strange that I have become an object of scandal, loving thee.

"Wherever I go my enemies pursue me. I cover my face with a veil to hide myself from infamy which shadows me everywhere in this city. But oh my God, my Krishna, hear of my resolve. If I fail to carry this vessel with water, I will drown myself in the Jumna. Though dying, I will have no peace in my mind, for they will cry shame upon me and abuse thy Holy Name saying—"Look at that bad woman who loved Krishna." You are the best judge in the universe and know the metal I am made of. I do not know what I am. Loving you with all my soul, I have earned the name of a bad woman. They brand me as one in love with Krishna.

"But this scandal and all this abuse I take as my ornaments. I pride in them, I take delight in them, since I have earned them by loving one who is the highest, the best and the greatest in the universe. Public scandal and shame weigh nothing with me, for I have dedicated my life and soul unto thy feet.

"The bridge of hair,—how slender is it? How will it stand my weight? But mayest thou protect me at this hour of great trial?"

Praying to Krishna in this way and bowing down to her elders, she started. Jasoda and other venerable ladies of the house blessed her.

Sula the poetess, sings, "Take care, oh Radha. Do not forget Him for a moment and proceed in a spirit of humility. Fill the pitcher and show the strength of one who is really pure. Let your enemies be ashamed of themselves."

(Ll. 1-30.)

Radha crosses the Bridge and Brings Water.

Chorus.—See how the much-abused Radha fills the pitcher with water.

When she stepped into that bridge of hair, she trembled for a moment. Just then the image of Krishna became vivid before her mind.

With her whole soul resting in faith in Krishna did she proceed in that bridgeway. People cried victory to her. The whole air resounded with the great uproar caused by their joy. They clapped to cheer her up and the Queen Jasoda rejoiced above all. She walked quite at ease and came to the other bank. But some of the spectators said, "Let her cross the bridge again : our belief will be confirmed."

Physician.

"Why once, do cross the bridge seven times to give them satisfaction."

At these words Radha crossed the bridge seven times. After this she filled the pitcher with water. Not a drop leaked and the women in the Vrinda groves were struck with wonder.

With the physician and Radha, Jasoda returned home and the fame spread in the country that there was no woman so chaste in the whole city as Radha.

Those who dedicate their souls to Krishna—what can the scandal-mongers and detractors do them by trying to expose them to shame? Krishna Himself protects those who put their trust in Him.

Sula the poetess sings, "One who hears this tale of 'The removal of scandal' will find himself safe against the tongue of scandal and at the end find rest in His holy feet." (Ll. 1-18.)

KRISHNA REVIVES.

Chorus.—Arise, oh son of Nanda.

Then did the physician sprinkle a few drops of water over the body of Krishna, uttering some mystic words. Krishna opened his eyes, to the great joy of the queen who thought as if she was restored to life. King Nanda caressed him and said, "Arise, my Krishna, arise from bed." Krishna now sat up perfectly restored to health.

There was a general rejoicing in which all partook, except Jatila and Kutila.

When Krishna was all right again, the physician said, "Oh, queen, you have got your Krishna back. I must have due reward for my pains. Kindly give me what you consider to be fit and allow me to depart."

Jasoda.

"Whatever you will demand, I will give you. Just name what you wish."

Physician.

"I do not care for riches. At the time of my bidding you farewell, I have one boon to seek from you.

"Treat me as your own Krishna with affection and I pray to God that in all my future births I may get a mother like you. May you suckle me when a child and may you bind my hands with rope when I do anything wrong! Treat me in the same way as you would treat Krishna. The desire of my heart is that I may always live in the company of milkwomen of these sacred groves."

The physician bowed before the queen and strangely disappeared.

Now with clasped hands, Sula, the poetess prays, that as minstrel she should receive the present of a pitcher for singing this song of "The Removal of Scandal."

(Ll. 1-32.)

PRAYERS FOR THE HOST.

"My last prayer is,—'May my host who has called us to his house be blessed with wealth and children! May fortune constantly shower her favours on him, and may all his dangers be over by the blessings of Shiva and Durga! May wealth accumulate in this house and may Lakshmi and Narayan be always worshipped here with steady devotion! May the cows give profuse milk and the evening lamps burn steadily in this house for ever. At the last hour of his life, may his soul find a place in Heaven and may all the Gods shower their blessings on him! May Narsing protect him from the influence of Jakshas, ghosts and goblins, and may he be free from fears of serpents and tigers.' "

Sula says, "Let all sing praises of Krishna. Here ends my Gopini Kirttan." (Ll. 1-16.)

LAMENT OF THE DAUGHTER OF SHAH SHUJA

PREFACE TO THE LAMENT OF THE DAUGHTER OF SHAH SHUJA

Though there are slight discrepancies in the accounts given by different historians in the details of the episode relating to the tragic end of Shuja, brother of Aurangjeb, yet apparently there is a striking agreement between these descriptions as regards the more important incidents of that tragedy. There is no doubt about the fact that Shuja fled to Arakan after his defeat in his war with Aurangjeb, and that he was thrown into the Bay of Bengal with some members of his family, by the King of Arakan—Sudharma, who had at the outset received him kindly. All historians and ballad-makers are agreed upon this point. Bernier says that after his defeat Shuja fled to Arakan through the Bay of Bengal, on board a ship belonging to the Portuguese. Mr. Stewart contradicts this statement on the authority of some Mahomedan writers and says that Shuja went to Arakan not by sea but by land *via* Chittagong,—through the north-eastern hills of that district. He and his people rode on elephants and reached the capital of the Arakan King who had already sent a representative to give him a cordial welcome. It is an undoubted fact that Shah Shuja carried with him a vast treasure. This is hinted to by the accounts of Mahomedan historians as well as the ballad itself. The Mahomedan historians, whose version was adopted by Mr. Stewart, relate the incidents of this journey *via* Chittagong. They say that it was a season of high Monsoon, and though Shuja had tried his best to find a ship which would carry him to Mecca, no sea-going vessel, nor even a sloop, dared cross the high seas in that season. So the prince was later on obliged to give up his project of visiting Mecca. He went up to the river 'Naf' which is the western-most boundary of the kingdom of Arakan Raja. The Rajmala, which is an authentic State-account of Tipperah relates the episode of an interview between Shuja and Govinda Manikya, the ex-king of that country. This does not agree in its details with the accounts of some of the Mahomedan historians, following which Mr. Lewin, one of the Deputy Commissioners of the Chittagong Hill-tracts, identified the place of the alleged interview. The Rajmala gives a different account. It states that the interview did not take place on the way in the hilly districts but in the court of the Arakan Raja itself. These are however very minor points of disagreement. From all these different sources of information we find the following fact very clearly put. Beating a retreat from the battlefield Shuja went to Arakan by land *via* Chittagong. He met there the ex-king of Tipperah, Raja Govinda Manikya. He was at first very warmly received by the Raja of Arakan. There however arose a quarrel later on between Shah Shuja and Raja Shudharma, leading to small warfares, and Shuja with his wife and some other members of his family latterly met a watery grave in the Bay. These are facts about which there can be no doubt. In a poem written by Alwal we find reference to this quarrel between prince Shuja and King Shudharama. The poet was implicated in the affair and imprisoned by the Burmese king on the evidence given by a man named Mirja. I give below an extract from Rajmala containing references to Govinda Manikya's interview with Shuja.

"Govinda Manikya came to Arakan (being driven by his step brother prince Chhatra Manikya who had usurped his throne) and Shuja also paid a visit to that country losing his kingdom which was seized by Aurangjeb. Govinda Manikya was seated on a throne in the Arakan Raj Court, when Shuja appeard there. The Raja instantly rose from his throne and offerred his seat to Shuja. The Maharaja of Arakan saw this and privately asked Govinda Manikya as to why he gave the throne to a prince who was a *Mlechchhya*. Prince Govinda Manikya said, 'Hear me, O great king. This prince Shuja is a famous man. He has under him many a prince of the status of myself and your worthy self. Many prince would not dare sit near a minister of this great Badsah.'

The king of Tipperah sat on another throne and when the court dispersed, Govinda Manikya and Shuja went together. They talked with eaeh other on the way and Shuja said ' You have given me a high status in the court of the Arakan Raja but you know my present condition, what can I give you as a reward ?'—saying this he took away his valuable Nimcha which was dangling on his breast and offered it to the Raja with his best compliments. Besides this he gave the Raja a very precious diamond-ring.

Shuja married a daughter of Raja Shudharma. Just at this moment Shuja became seized with a wicked motive. He secretly intrigued to kill the king of Arakan and with this object in view he collected forty picked wrestlers. He made them wear the costumes of ladies and seated two of them in each of the palanquins, counting a score in all, and these were covered on all sides. Each palanquin was carried by eight strong men. The report went out that the princess of Arakan was going to pay a visit to her father's palace. They crossed six gates without any hindrance, but when they reached the seventh, the chief guard stepped forward and asked why should so many palanquins enter the inner apartments. The palanquins were stopped accordingly, and the king's guards made a search, whereupon the wrestlers were all detected and a fight ensued in which all of them were killed. Prince Shuja privately left Arakan, creating by these acts an enmity with Raja Shudharma which resulted in the cruel massacre of Prince Shuja and his family.

A short time after the King of Arakan asked Govinda Manikya to return to Tipperah. He made him a gift of picturesque thrones made of eight metals for the gods he worshipped, besides a large pitcher containing valuable articles of Burmese workmanship. From Arakan Raja Govinda Manikya came to Chittagong where he got the report of Chattra Manikya's death. He returned to Udaipur, the capital of Tipperah, and ascended the throne once more without any hitch.

The diamond-ring which Prince Govinda Manikya had got from Shuja, he sold, and with the money he erected a Masjid which was named after the donor and is still called Shuja Masjid. Govinda Manikya founded a village close to the Masjid and he named it Shuja-Ganja or the market belonging to Shuja."

Out of the income from Shuja-Ganja the Masjid is being still maintained. In Chittagong there is also a Masjid called Shuja Masjid and there is a ward in the town called Shuja-kat-gaḍ. In the face of so many evidences commemorating his visit there, no one can doubt that the prince had lived in the town for sometime. We are not therefore inclined to credit the account of Bernier on this point.

There were however many reports afloat in the air regarding the procedures of Shuja after his defeat. Coloured versions of these reached the ears of Aurangjeb who for a long time was not quite at ease regarding the possibility of his elder brother returning to Delhi with a force. The rumour ran that Shuja had gone to Constantinople and collected a large army there. Another rumour went to the effect that he had already come to Persia and was intent on leading an expedition against Aurangjeb. There was a persistent report that the king of Pegu and Siam had given him two big ships bearing red insignia and he was coming with his army on board these ships *via* Port Surat. These rumours were all unfounded but they were sufficient for Aurangjeb to pass many a sleepless night.

Bernier refers to the battle which Shuja fought with the Arakan king, and Stewart also confirms the statement. The latter says that after his defeat Shuja was made a captive by the Burmese king and thrown into the Bay of Bengal with his family. This account agrees with that given in the ballad. Raja Shudharma in the Burmese language is called 'Sanda-su-dhamma'. In the works by Daulat Kazi, the author of Lor Chandrani, and of Syed Alwal references are to be found about this Raja Shudharma. The following extract from Saiphul Mulluk gives a short account of Raja Shudharma and also of a foreigner whom we unmistakingly take for Shah Shuja.

"In this world the city of Arakan is peerless and its great prince Shudharma is favoured by Fortune........ On the report that a foreigner was coming, the Raja was right glad and gave him a warm reception."

About this foreigner the following further details are given :—"His country lay in the west extending to the Indian ocean to the South and the Himalayas to the North. He was a hero of heroes and there was no one like him in the world."

Many ballads were composed about the princess Paribanu 'Begum' of Shah Shuja of which we find mention in the 'Rajmala' by late Mr. Kailash Chandra Sinha. I believe that if a thorough search is made in these backwoods of Bengal these ballads may be still recovered. The short one that we publish here relates to the love of the Burmese king for a daughter of Shah Shuja. Though the Mogul prince had married a daughter of Shudharma, it was held a great indignity on the part of Shuja to receive a proposal of marriage of his daughter from the Arakan King.

According to time-honoured custom the kings and princes could marry any woman even of a low birth, but a daughter could by no means be given to a person of lower status. Hence the proposal of Shudharma was received with great indignation by Shah Shuja, who had not felt any scruple in marrying Shudharma's daughter, and the dispute possibly arose from this incident.

The short ballad contains humorous references to the peculiar customs of the Burmese people. The food 'Nappi' has been always an object of ridicule by the people living in adjacent districts of Bengal. We have given a foot-note explaining what the ingredients of this favoured food of the Burmese consist of. The ballad has deep-seated pathos underlying it inspite of the occasional humour which enlivens it. It is a pity that our historians do not care to collect information from the popular sources. Their chief materials are derived from historical treatises of the Mahomedans which are naturally scanty and prejudiced. Though these treatises give an idea of the political atmosphere of the country generally speaking, they are silent about the history of the people. There is no doubt that the ballad-literature of our country is occasionally tinged with marks of ignorance and superstition of the unlettered peasants but often do we find a truthful narration of facts unbiased by political or communal motives and as true materials of history. They are therefore, invaluable. Though the ballad is very short it is important because of the fact that it throws side-light on a chapter of Mogul history which has been hitherto obscure on many points. If the whole body of ballads concerning the unhappy prince Shuja be collected, it will indeed be a valuable find.

Babu Asutosh Chaudhury sent me this ballad from Chaudhurypara Lane, Tamakumundi, Chittagong on the 12th of August, 1927. He collected it from various sources. First of all, he got a few scraps from a gypsy singer. In last March he collected the major portion of it from a blind singer named Makbul, an inhabitant of the village Char-chaktai in Chittagong. A whimsical singer named Belait Ali, who occasionally visits a mosque in the town of Chittagong, helped Ashu Babu with a few lines, but though it is known that he has got the ballad by heart yet he would not sing it, if it does not please him to do so. Last of all a 'manjhi' of a certain boat (Sarenga) which passed by a canal close to Station Satkania, sang it in the deep hours of night, and Ashu Babu completed the ballad of which he had already collected scraps from this song.

DINESH CHANDRA SEN.

Lament of the Daughter of Shah Shuja

Chorus.—

(1)

Oh! how ill-fated am I!

Oh! my parents! How could you take these foreigners into confidence treating them as your kinsmen and become guests at their place?

Captive am I at the hands of the Burmese.

Oh! God, numberless are the woes to which I am doomed by Thee.

I lost my mother, I lost my sister, and oh! my father! I have lost thee too.

The Burmese king now by a trick has robbed me from your custody.

(2)

Oh! how ill-fated am I!

At an evil hour didst thou come, oh! father, to this land of the Burmese!

Thy prestige, thy high status thou didst lose all, and at last thy life!

Whom didst thou dread in your own land and flee here with all your jewels and stones?

Where are your jewellery and diamonds gone now? Alas! in whose custody are they?

(3)

Oh! how ill-fated am I!

We wandered from place to place.

Who was that wicked friend, oh! father, who counselled thee to come at last to this cursed land—to Arakan.

My mother, my sister were drowned in the Bay, oh! how cruel!—

Thyself sharing the same fate!

(4)

Oh! how ill-fated am I!

Suffering from unbearable pangs my heart does not yet burst.

My heart burns as does the charcoal on an earthen pot.

I prevented you, father, over again, from sending me to Burmese king's palace as a guest. The result of your not listening to my advice is that I am like one buried alive here.

(5)

Oh! how ill-fated am I!

I feel no pang of hunger or thirst and cry day and night.

I abhor to touch the meals which the Burmese king takes.

There is one female cook in the whole palace and all the members dine the meals cooked by her.

Cups full of '*nappi*' are presented. How can I swallow these abominable things!

(6)

Oh! how ill-fated am I!

Night and day my tears do not dry and my pillows are wet with them.

The Burmese king has given me a black '*khami*' to wear.

Ten Burmese women sit by me and show me how to wear on my ears the golden '*nadham*.'

(7)

Oh! how ill-fated am I!

I was a flower of heaven but I have lost my high place at the hands of the Burmese king.

There in the grave under the high seas my parents lie in eternal rest.

In this land of the 'Harmads' and the Burmese, who is there, alas! to enquire about me?

Note.—' Nappi ' is prepared by rotten fish. The Burmese fishers after having caught a large number of fishes from the Bay by their nets, take away the big ones and leave the smaller ones to rot on the shore. These are lobsters, crabs, 'chenua' 'Kukur-jihwā' (the dog's tongue), 'hatyia' and 'fyshya'. When after eight or ten days these small fishes become thoroughly rotten, two Burmese with two wooden clubs begin to beat the heap from which a foul odour issues in all directions. They thus turn it into a soft clay-like thing, all the different fishes being mixed up together. Then balls are prepared out of it, which the Burmese consider to be a delicious ingredient to be taken with all kinds of their curry. Usually 'nappi' is sold for eight annas a seer but sometimes the price rises up to ten and even to twelve annas. The Chittagong hill-tribes, the Jumias, and Chakmas also take 'nappi' as a favourite food.

THE LAY OF THE TWELVE SHRINES

PREFACE TO THE LAY OF THE TWELVE SHRINES

The *Baratirtha* or the twelve shrines, as the Sutanari tank in the jungles of Madhupur is called, is associated with an old legend which the rustic bard, whose name is not known, describes in this ballad. I do not attach any historical importance to it. It is based on the popular belief that the tank was excavated by one Raja Bhagadatta and that waters from twelve shrines situated in different parts of India were brought and poured into this tank to sanctify it in popular estimation. Bhagadatta had a brother named Ramchandra whose piety and goodness were ill rewarded by some calumniating ryots, and the legend narrates that the curse of Ramchandra fell upon the people of his country which was depopulated later on and became a deserted tract. Up to this, there may be some grain of truth in the ballad. The rest is a product of popular fancy.

The District Gazetteer of Mymensing gives the following reference about the Madhupur Jungles and the legendary king Bhagadatta.

"The Madhupur jungle is a large tract of hard red soil, stretching from Dacca down to Jamalpur. It forms one of the natural divisions of the District of Mymensing.

According to Dr. Tayler, these jungles along with Tangyail once belonged to Kamrup (Pragjyotishpur in the phraseology of the Mahabharata) of which Mymensing was originally a part.

The earliest information about these kingdoms comes from accounts of Tibetan and Chinese travellers in the sixth and seventh centuries. In their day, Mymensing was more Buddhist than Hindu. The old ruins chiefly tanks in the Madhupur jungles are possibly of the eighth century and are associated with the name of Bhagadatta who has sometimes been confused with the famous Kamrupa King of that name. Kamrupa was in its prime in about 803 A.D."

Pargana Joanshai referred to in the ballad was founded by a Mahomedan convert from the Kastail Dutt family, who took the name of Manowoor Khan popularly called Manohar Khan. Other accounts say that he was a descendant of Fateh Khan who got the possession of this Mahal at the death of Isha Khan. Nur Hyder Chaudhury might have got re-settlement of the Pargana as a descendant of Fateh Khan in 1787. The descendants of these Dewans are no longer in possession of their lands. The Gazetteer makes a confusion of names. Manohar Khan was a descendant of Isha Khan, as we have seen from the ballads of these two Dewans of Jangalbari. Isha Khan was no doubt the son of a Hindu convert but this family had nothing to do with the Kastail Dutts alluded to in the ballad. We have already had occasion to refer to the warfare conducted by Isha Khan under the flag of the Tipperah Raj against Fateh Khan, King of Sylhet. The details of this warfare are described in the Rajmala of Tipperah (p. 156). Nur Hyder Chawdhury might have been a scion of the family of Fateh Khan who was probably connected with Sher Shah.

The ballad does not refer to any tradition identifying Bhagadatta with the famous hero of the Mahabharata as the Gazetteer has said. The popular notion suggests what is really the case—*viz.*, that this Bhagadatta is altogether a different personage, having a brother named Ramchandra.

The ballad is composed in animated verses containing couplets which are sung in chorus.

The language, though crude, is poetical and the author has condensed much matter within the narrow compass of this short ballad. He occasionally flings an arrow of satire at some of the customs of the Hindus, but there is no venom in it. He has evidently found a cause for lampoon in the prevailing custom of the Hindus to drink filthy water of the shrines, considering it to be an act of religious merit. The ballad-maker says that the earthly reward derived from this act of virtue is very often an attack of cholera. He also passes a remark with sneer on the practice of a large number of Hindu women assembling in the shrines on festive occasions, giving opportunities to Goondas to carry away the young and the beautiful ones from amongst them. Every unprejudiced mind must subscribe to the viewpoint taken by the Moslem poet. I have admired this piece of rural poetry for its brevity, straightforwardness and outspoken humour. At the same time, he bestows due eulogium on the Hindu princes and does not show any canker owing to communal prejudice.

The ballad was collected by late Babu Beharilal Roy and it is mentioned in the concluding part of the ballad that Saju Baity, a rhapsodist, added some refrains to the song for making it effective when sung.

DINESH CHANDRA SEN.

The Lay of the Twelve Shrines

Pargana Nachhirabaz is verily the back-wood of Bengal. There in the old fort of Joanshai the fair of twelve shrines has sat—*hey ! hey ! hey !*

It was during the period of dark moon in April. The rays of the sun were so strong that they seemed to burst one's head. At such a time I spread an umbrella over my head and went to see this fair of twelve shrines—*hey ! hey ! hey !*

The place was surrounded on all sides by tall Saal and Gajari trees. And in the midst of them lay a pond sanctified by the waters of the twelve shrines—*hey ! hey ! hey !*

Here the Hindus bathe in this pond and think that they have ensured their path to heaven thereby. It is the filthy water which they drink in pious faith, and cholera in its epidemic character breaks out as the result—*hey ! hey ! hey !*

In the neighbourhood there is no other pond nor any river. They search for water, but failing in their quest their very breath seems to be stopped in thirst—*hey ! hey ! hey !*

The Vaishnava women and others of that sex bathe in that pond. There is no want of bad men to seduce them. So not unoften they lose their caste, falling into the trap of the wicked and the vicious—*hey ! hey ! hey !*

Now, my audience, I am going to tell you the history of the origin of this shrine. I shall relate it to you as I heard it from my elders—*hey ! hey ! hey !*

Near the pond one comes across bricks and other relics of some old building and behind the mound containing these, there lies the big tank now blocked by weeds, called the *Sutanari Dighi* and close by there are two smaller tanks

Chhota Kodalia and *Bara Kodalia,* which also have almost been silted up—*hey ! hey ! hey !*

The mango groves and jacktrees still indicate the spot where once there was a spacious garden—*hey ! hey ! hey !*

One occasionally finds here charcoals and burnt wood attesting to the fact that there was once a settlement of blacksmiths in the place. It still bears the name of the *Kamarer Bagh* or the ward of blacksmiths—*hey ! hey ! hey !*

Here also lies the trace of a *daha* or a depression once filled with water. It is called Durga Daha or the place of the immersion of the goddess Durga—*hey ! hey ! hey !*

The shrine was established by a king named Raja Bhagadatta. He had a younger brother Ramchandra whose mind was pure as crystal—*hey ! hey ! hey !*

Raja Bhagadatta was happy with his people and Ramchandra preserved the peace of the Raj armed with weapons, his body protected by a steel armour—*hey ! hey ! hey !*

Their old mother was so infirm that she could scarcely walk. She once requested her son the Raja to do something by which her place in heaven might be ensured and her sins pardoned—*hey ! hey ! hey !*

The Raja clasped his hands as a mark of respect and said, "You are to me a goddess in the earth. What can I do to make your sins pardoned by the gods? Pray, tell me only once the means of your atonement. I shall instantly carry out your order"—*hey ! hey ! hey !*

The mother said, "Hear me, my son. I want to make a gift of gold to Brahmins and perform the Pindi ceremony sitting by the side of the twelve shrines"—*hey ! hey ! hey !*

At this word of his mother the Raja wonderingly said, "I am sorry to hear your words, oh mother! Your health is shattered. Pale is your face without any sign of blood. Your head trembles as you speak, and the legs totter as you walk. Your eyes are dim and ears are nearly deaf. How can I take you to the twelve shrines in this condition" —*hey! hey! hey!*

"I clasp your feet, oh mother! and wish you to comply with what I am going to say. I will myseif go to the twelve shrines and from each of them bring mud and water. Here shall I get a tank dug for you and in it shall I put the sacred mud and water of the twelve shrines. There you will bathe every day and thereby your path to Heaven will be ensured ; the water of the pond will have a cooling effect on your body and bring peace to your mind. The people of this city of mine will bathe in this holy pond and they also will be saved from sin. You will acquire virtue by this act and the people for generations to come will remain thankful to you"—*hey! hey! hey!*

The dowager queen said at this, "Well, my son, I accept your suggestion. Let your words be fulfilled. It will remove all cause of my pain"—*hey! hey! hey!*

In his private chamber, did the Raja call his brother Ramchandra. He held him by the hand and said, "I have consulted the almanac. I find that next Wednesday is a very auspicious day. I will leave my city in order to visit the twelve shrines and it is my resolve that I will have a pond dug here, wherein the water of the twelve shrines will be sprinkled, and there will my mother bathe every day and have her wishes fulfilled. It will take me a long time to wander abroad and during this time, you must sit on my throne and rule the kingdom in such a manner as the tradition and the fame of our administration may be preserved"—*hey! hey! hey!*

The younger brother Ramchandra sorrowfully said, "What you will command I will do. What I am thinking of is as to how shall I be able to live parted from you for such a long time. You will suffer the hardships of this long journey and I will enjoy the pleasures of life sitting on the throne. This is the one cause of my sorrow"—*hey! hey! hey!*

Bhagadatta said, "Don't sorrow, my brother. This body of mine has come out of my beloved mother's. She is to be adored by me. If I cannot gratify her wishes, my wealth, my power, my palace I will consider as of no value. I tell you, my dear brother, Ramchandra, give me leave with sweet words and without sorrow. Rule the kingdom justly and take the charge of our dear old mother"—*hey! hey! hey!*

"I have got one thing more to say.. You are to excavate a tank before I come back, so that on my return I may find it ready"—*hey! hey! hey!*

Raja Bhagadatta now bade farewell to his brother and started for the twelve shrines, and Ramchandra employed men for excavating the tank—*hey! hey! hey!*

The new Raja pardoned confirmed criminals and released them from jails, treating all with compassion. He tried by all means to keep his people in peace and happiness as his elder brother had advised—*hey! hey! hey!*

The ryots were permitted to pay him tribute by rice-dusts in the place of rice. When it was required to bring the ryots to his court for some reason or other, the order on the court-peons was that they should be brought on the back of elephants. "Do not cause them pain by obliging them to walk" was the order. So the peons took elephants to the huts of the peasants along with the warrants—*hey! hey! hey!*

Even those who were inveterate ruffians were treated tenderly, and the King would not use any rough word to them. Thus did the young brother follow the advice of his elder brother even to a fault—*hey! hey! hey!*

After a long time did Raja Bhagadatta return home. He told his mother the tale of his long wanderings and poured the water of twelve shrines into the pond. The mother was right glad to bathe in the pond, and seated on the landing ghat did she gladly make gifts of gold, silver and cows to the Brahmins. The Brahmins were sumptuously fed in the palace. They were given new cloths to put on besides sums of money much beyond their expectations. The Raja again sat on his throne and began to rule his kingdom justly—*hey! hey! hey!*

One day the king called his subjects and asked them, "How did my country fare during the time my brother ruled?—Were you not happy?—*hey! hey! hey!*

The subjects clasped their hands and said, "How can we venture to tell you all that we suffered? The memory of those days still pinches us like sharp thorns. Ramchandra, your brother, ruled the kingdom like one void of all sympathy. He took away all our rice, not leaving even the rice-dust for our share; our women in abject poverty had to gather fuels from woods and sell them for a bare sustenance. He used to send constables with warrants to the houses of the poor people and bring them dragged by rope to his palace. Their very bones were shattered by the blows the constables gave them at every step—*hey! hey! hey!*

Alone when the Raja was seated in his room, the younger brother gently came and spoke thus to the elder, "I have remitted the dues of the ryots and given them the paddy justly due to the State in order to make them happy. I showed them all consideration and brought them, when there was a need for them, seated on the back of elephants"—*hey! hey! hey!*

Then did the younger Raja curse the subjects in this way,—being hurt by the act of the ryots, "Your luck is burnt and henceforward you will perceive the effect of my words. You will die for want of food and seeking rice you will wander forth in the forest infested with wild beasts and the thorns will pierce your feet"—*hey! hey! hey!*

From thence the curse of the prince has followed the ungrateful ryots. They were reduced to extreme poverty and all their happiness disappeared—*hey ! hey ! hey !*

Then followed events which will no doubt interest you, my audience. I am going to tell you more about the tank Sutanara—*hey ! hey ! hey !*

The queen mother called his sons to her and said, "Before I die, my sons, I have a desire to be fulfilled by your help. If you care for money, I should not like to disclose it, but if you care for virtue alone, I shall be glad to tell you what my wishes are—*hey ! heg ! hey !*

The Raja said, "Do not worry yourself about the question of money. For your sake, good mother, I can spend the riches of my whole treasury"—*hey ! hey! hey !*

The mother said again, "Think well within your mind before you make a promise. If after giving me words you fail to carry them out, you will go to hell. So think thrice before you make a promise"—*hey ! hey ! hey !*

Bhagadatta said, "Here do I solemnly promise that whatever you will say I will do. Your order will be obeyed at any cost"—*hey ! hey ! hey !*

The mother then said, "I have spun one full *Nata* of thread. I have just taken it out from the spinning-wheel and have twisted it round a spindle. Measure it at its full length and dig a tank in my name which would be covered by the length of the thread. If you can do it, I will say that not only are you a prince but that you have the heart of a prince also"—*hey ! hey! hey !*

Then did the Raja take the spindle in his hand and ordered his Munshis to follow him. He fixed a spot where the tank was to be dug and at one end of it he planted a pole. He took one end of the thread and tied it to that pole. Then slowly did he advance with the thread in his hand and it took him four dandas (about an hour and a half) to go the full length of the thread—*hey ! hey ! hey !*

The ministers said, "We are afraid to council Your Majesty, but we cannot help doing so. If a *dighi* is to be dug of the size covered by this thread, the resources of our royal treasury will fail"—*hey ! hey ! hey !*

The Raja said, "I have promised to my mother and there is no help now. Even if my life goes out, not to speak of my kingdom, I must carry out my promise"—*hey ! hey ! hey !*

Then flocked three thousands of coolies, who carried each a basket full of earth. The strong amongst them with large spades in their hands began to cut blocks of earth and the comparatively weak men with small spades made up their shortcomings by shouting as loudly as they could—*hey ! hey ! hey !*

Near that new *dighi* there was a small pond with a little water. There the day-labourers washed their spades after their day's work—*hey ! hey ! hey !*

Each one of the coolies took a spadeful of earth from this little pond and threw it off. So the small pond grew in size and there was this sign left of their washing the spades. In this way two more tanks were dug without any cost and they were called *Bara Kodalia* and *Chota Kodalia* (the tank dug by the large spades and the tank dug by the smaller spades)—*hey ! hey ! hey !*

When the tank Sutanari was fully excavated, one standing at one of its ends could not command the view of the other. It was a wonderful reservoir of water of which the like was not seen in the locality. Its crystal water looked blue and transparent and in the midst of the tank was built a rest-house with a tower called *Gambhira*. Men and beasts and birds with coloured wings flocked there night and day for drinking water—*hey ! hey ! hey !*

This was the glorious memorial of the virtuous queen, and after her death a thick jungle grew round the tank, which was not cared for till the passage of air was shut on all sides by the jungle, and the liquid treasure of the *dighi* lost its pure quality—*hey! hey! hey!*

The king died; the ryots who loved him are no more. The splendour of his court and its pomp are now reduced to a dream. On the spot where once stood the palatial buildings foxes have made their parlour. In that spot if one would care to explore it, one might yet find unnumbered wealth and goods of the ancient palace. Many people did explore it and get treasures where others in similar attempts failed and cursed their lot—*hey! hey! hey!*

This Lay of the Twelve Shrines is finished here. It was composed in the year 1873 (1280 B.S.). Fazu Baiti, the Gayen (minstrel) of the village Basuria, has added some refrains to it for facility of singing. May God's name be blessed and may He help us!

THE FIGHT AT MANIPUR

PREFACE TO THE BALLAD OF MANIPUR FIGHT.

The beautiful valley of Manipur has on its north the hills inhabited by the Nagas, on the south the mountain-recesses where the Kukis, the Lushai and the Sutis have lived a primitive life from a pre-historic period. On the east of Manipur is Burma and on the west lies the country called Cachhar. The border-line of Manipur on the east demarcates it from Burma, and disputes often arose in the past as to the extent of this boundary-line, leading to warfares and political troubles which eventually brought on the interference of the English—a subject which is dwelt on at some length in this ballad. The State of Manipur contains fifteen lacs of bighas (about 5,00000 acres), of which only ten lacs have been brought under cultivation.

Beautiful is this valley of Manipur, surrounded by hills and lakes, the crystal waters of which shine forth, reflecting the romantic and picturesque scenery of landscape on all sides. The lake Logatak and the Ilai have on their south grassy meadows full of *Kash* and *Kush* reeds which delight the eye with their green verdure, undisturbed by trees or jungles. There are small rivulets and streams, the Ziri, the Mukru, the Borak, the Irang, the Lengba and the Lemitaka, which rush on with tremendous force during the rains but in the dry season become shallow and can even be crossed on foot. Near the hills known as the Lematol, lies the city of Imphal which is better known as Manipur—the capital of the Rajas of that country. At the foot of Imphal, flows the river Manipur in her rapid course, to meet the famous Irawady of Burma.

The beautiful valley of Manipur presents in its charming jungles the tall *Nageswar,*[1] *Parul,*[2] *Banshibat,*[3] *Arjun,*[4] *Indrajaba,*[5] *Tamal*[6] and oak trees with their luxuriantly

[1] Mesua ferrea. [2] Nonia Saveoleus. [3] The holy fig tree under which Krishna used to play his flute. [4] Pentaptera Arjuna. [5] The China rose. [6] Xanthocymus pictorius.

rich leafy branches, which afford shelter to the beautiful birds *Bhimraj*, *Shyama* and *Maina*. These birds which sell at high prices in the Tiretta Bazar of Calcutta are available at Manipur for little or no price. The whole country thus seems to be a nest of singing birds. In the Census Report of 1901, we find six thousand men, out of a population of 2,21,000, whose avocation is music. Besides these, every house of Manipur claims one or two amongst its members, as amateur musicians. In Calcutta where we had a population of about 9 lacs at the time, there were only seven thousand men who followed music as profession. It is no wonder that a country so rich in its natural beauty as Manipur supplies a perennial inspiration of the Muse amongst her people. Manipur-forests abound with cobras, elephants and royal tigers. White elephants are also to be now and then seen in the jungles. People of Manipur consist of the Manipuri Hindus who belong mostly to the *Kshattriya* race. There are also Nagas and other hill-tribes who have adopted Hindu practices and live on lines of amity with their neighbours—the Hindu Aryans. The Hindu women are famous for their beauty and skill in artistic work on silk. Inspite of their tender looks, they are hardy ; the dance of Manipuri women is a sight worth seeing by all visitors to Manipur. As the Hindus are Vaisnavas, their women have, in response to the call of their tender emotional religion, acquired an æsthetic culture which add to their various natural attractions. Sexual morality is on the whole above blame. In case of a breach of morals, it is the men who are subjected to punishment, the women escape with impunity. The Kukis, the Nagas, the Kochas as also the Aryan population have simple habits, brave hearts and sturdy patriotism. Says Mr. Mukundalal Choudhury, author of the history of Manipur, "The Manipur Hindus have polite manners. They are courteous but not flatterers like the Bengalees. The courage of the up-country Hindu, the gracious manners of the Bengalee and the simplicity of the Assamese have combined to form some of the characteristics of Manipur people." (p. 19. 2nd Ed.)

The income of the State is between twenty five and thirty lacs a year.

After giving this introductory note on Manipur, I shall dwell at some length on the ballad published in this volume.

We read in the *Srimat Bhagavata* (19th Skanda, 22nd Canto) and in the *Adi* and *Aswamedh Parvas* of the Mahabharat how Arjun, the third of the Pandava-brothers, went to Manipur during his exile and married a daughter of the King Chitrabahan named Chitrangada,—a subject which has formed the theme of one of the poems of Rabindra Nath Tagore. Chitrangada's son Babrubahan ascended the throne of Manipur, as Chitrabahan had died without any male issue. The Rajas of Manipur trace their origin from Babrubahan. It is a tale of the pre-historic period, and legends and myths have no doubt mixed together in the account given in the Epic and the Bhagavata. Some of our modern scholars have disputed the claims of this Manipur, to their alleged connection with the Mahabharat legend, and have tried to identify the Manipur of the Pandavas with a country of the same name situated in another part of India. But we need not enter into this vexed question, more or less of an antiquarian interest, as the subject-matter of this ballad belongs to a very recent political event.

The ballad is clear enough in all its details. But the elaborate history of Manipur by Mukundalal Choudhury, on which it is partly based, deals with the story from a somewhat different view-point. On reading the ballad one would suppose that Tikendrajit was probably more to be blamed than the British Government which sat in judgment over him and sentenced him to death. The ballad seems to attempt at a partial justification of the British authorities, whereas the history of Manipur finds fault with the Government officials for passing the cruel sentence. The reader will certainly find in the ballad the spirit of one who believes in British justice. The author writes with all sympathy about the unfortunate hero of the ballad Tikendrajit. But he places the facts in such a way that if he was, indeed, wrong in his view, it should not be attributed to any motive. His motive is simple enough and undoubtedly shows that he wrote from conviction. He gave the popular version of the tale as believed by his conntrymen, at least the Mohammedans, whereas the historian of Manipur cleverly handles all the political materials to which he had access and tries to show the inner workings of administration, which were certainly beyond the range of popular knowledge. There can be no doubt that Tikendrajit was an outstanding and remarkable personality. He was a hero of a hundred fights and everywhere he was triumphant, sometimes against innumerable odds. His courage, statesmanly manœuvres and integrity were praised not only by his countrymen but also by his numerous European friends. When he was a mere lad of eighteen, he killed lions and royal tigers in single-handed fights. It is said that he had killed innumerable bears, lions, wild buffaloes and more than two thousand tigers during his life. "The ways of our hero Tikendrajit while hunting were wonderful and strange"—says the historian of Manipur. "He would give no credit to those hunters who killed a tiger by gun-shots and arrows. When a tiger would come in sight, he would at once jump down from his horse and valiantly approach the animal face to face. If the tiger would not still be induced to come, he would pelt stones at it with a view to excite its anger. When the tiger so excited would jump down upon him, he would cut it into two by a stroke of his sharp sword. Many a time he encountered great dangers during such adventures." (p. 210). When he was only twenty one years old, he defeated the Nagas with extraordinary courage and skill, befriending the English, which won for him universal admiration, and as a reward for this daring act of bravery leading to British success, the Government gave his father Maharaj Chandrakirtti the title of K.C.S.I., together with a present of 2,000 guns, a medal and rupees ten to each soldier who had fought in that memorable battle, and a very valuable gold medal decorated with stones to Tikendrajit. He also helped the English in their fight with the Burmese King, and the British authorities were bound by ties of gratitude to this valiant general for his manifold activities on their behalf.

A man of intrepid charactar, Tikendrajit adhered to his principles above all things. He was a voracious eater of meat in his younger days, but when during his initiation into the Vaisnava faith, he was ordered by his father Chandra Kirtti not to touch any meat in his life, he obeyed that order to the last day of his life. His annual income was more than Rs. 60,000 a year but his charity was so great that he became involved in heavy debts by giving away more than what he had with an open-handed liberality, which made him so dear and beloved in his country.

If one will read the documents annexed to the History of Manipur, one will have grave doubts as to whether Tikendrajit was guilty of the murder of the Commissioner Mr. Quinton and his comrades. Before this tragedy had taken place, the Government was secretly considering if they would send Tikendrajit to exile.

Why the British Government became hostile to one who was their great benefactor and friend will be evident from the speech of Sir John Gorst, Under-Secretary of State for India, made in the Parliament.* "Just

* Hansard's Indian debates, Session (1890-91) pp. 329-32.

let the House consider who the Senapati was. He was a man of the greatest ability and the greatest force of character among the ruling family of Manipur. He was a man who was extremely popular among the people, who had the reputation of having impoverished himself by generosity, which is one of the greatest virtues to which an Oriental can aspire···Government have always hated and discouraged independent and original talent and promoted docile and unpretending mediocrity. This is not a new policy. It is as old as Tarquinious Superbus, and although in these modern times we do not lop or cut off the heads of the tall poppies, we take other and more merciful means of reducing any person of dangerous pre-eminence to a harmless condition. Why, in my own life I have known numbers of cases of this kind. I remember 30 years ago how the British Government spent their blood and treasure in the Colony of New Zealand for the purpose of destroying the power of the Maori King instead of governing the natives of New Zealand through his instrumentality. I remember how a few years later a British Government destroyed the power of the Betewayo in South Africa as soon as he ceased to be necessary as a counterpoise to Transvaal. But I can give you examples of the same policy more recent. Why did you expel Arabi from Egypt ? Because he was thought to be practically dangerous to the peace of the country. I can give you even a closer parallel taken from that Government of which the Right Honourable gentleman (Lord Lansdowne) was so distinguished a member. Why did you arrest Zebher and intern him in Gibraltar ? There was a man of great ability in a country over which you had no power, but acting from a political necessity you would not permit him to exercise his influence in the Soudon, although General Gordon your agent in the Soudon asked to have him there....It is a mortifying thing to confess but I think Governments are very likely to be right in following the tradition. It is perhaps better that great ability and independence should be a disqualification for State service. It is perhaps better for the peace and safety of the world that you should depend on mediocrities.''

However inconsistent and incompatible such views might be from the point of view of higher ethics, this has been the course adopted not only by paramount Powers but by petty chiefs and even Patriarchs in old family-life, all the world over. Even a Zemindar does not brook the ryot who exposes the manœuvres of administration and organises his neighbours to revolt, however righteous his cause may be. The Dutt of Bali in Bengal who declared that he had merely escorted the five Brahmins from Kanauj and had never been their slave, was branded as a low-caste Kayastha and he sank down to the level of a Non-Kulin. The scion of the Gupta family among the Vaidyas who did not alight from his horse to show King Lakshman Sen an abject and servile humility was deprived of his Kulinism and was sneeringly called Asva Gupta ('Horse Gupta,') a name of infamy still borne by his descendants. Dandapani, one of the Kulin Vaidyas, lost his high status, as he married a girl after his choice without consulting his father. Independence and honesty of purpose have often been condemned and discouraged by men in power not only in politics but also in society in every part of the world. The Government wanted to banish Tikendrajit. In the opinion of Sir John Gorsts this was a right view of matters. In the news-papers a report was published that Lord Landsdowne had expressed himself to the following effect: "The British Government is the supreme power in this country. I am the representative of Her Majesty and though we are here, Tikendrajit completly ignored us and without taking any permission from us, removed a Maharaja from his throne and installed another on the *Gadi*. This act can never be forgiven. He must be removed from Manipur."

The Government in thier attempt to banish the lion from his den met with a stern rebuff and the unfortunate assassination of the British officials was the result. Yet it is true that it was the old Thangal general who believing in an old prophecy gave orders for killing the five European officials. And as ill-luck would have it, Tikendrajit who had been deliberately and earnestly trying his level best to avert the tragedy could not obstruct the course of fate "which sent the five Europeans to their place of Eternal Rest, extinguished the lamp of the royal house of Kulachandra from the Manipur palace, blew out the life of the old Thangal general already in its last flicker, and last though not the least, destroyed the life of the greatest man of Manipur who had at the time barely reached the age of thirty two."

The poet inspite of his evident loyalty to the British Government expresses a doubt about what the issue of the fight would have been, had the Raja of Manipur accepted the help of the hill-tribes, which they had freely offered, and resolved to declare war against the Paramount Power (Canto 14, ll. 30-32). Here our poet shows his village-wisdom and a sense of proportion which is on a par with that of the bard of the Mainamaty songs who vaunted that the whole territory of the Emperor of Bengal was so large that it would require one 22 *dandas* to travel it on foot!

This ballad of the fight at Manipur was written by Munshi Mohammad Asraf Hossain about the time of the occurrence of the event, and I include it in this volume of Eastern Bengal Ballads with the permission of the author.

DINESH CHANDRA SEN.

The Fight at Manipur

Hear, my friends, the history of Manipur, a country which had ever preserved its freedom. In the east of India stands Manipur and to its south lies Burma. Now let me describe to you how the kingdom went under the domination of the English, and how Churachand became its king. Of old, there was a king in this land named Chitrabahan, who had a daughter named Chitrangada. The five Pandavas were in exile, and Arjun, in the course of his wanderings, came to Manipur. He was received with a hearty welcome at the royal court. He married the princess Chitrangada and a son was born to them named Babrubahan. As the king Chitrabahan had no male issue, the kingdom passed on to the grandson after his death. Five thousand years had elapsed since then; and during these long centuries, the kingdom had passed through many hands. Then it came under the sway of a race called the Nagas, whose leader Pamheva conquered the land by force of arms. He reigned under tho name of Garib Newaj and fought many a battle against the Burmese. He died after a long reign, and the kingdom passed on to a Raja named Jay Singha.

At this time, the king of Burma attacked Manipur and Jay Singha became frightened at his prowess. But the Burmese were at enmity with the English, and Jay Singha therefore sought the help of the latter. From Chittagong came six bands of sepoys and it was thus that the English first came in touch with the people of Manipur.

(Ll. 1-28.)

(2)

It was sixty years after this that Gambhir Singha became the king of Manipur. He was on the most friendly terms with the English who had about this time fallen out with the Ruler of Burma. It was the year 1824. The Burmese king attacked Cachhar and did not spare Manipur. But with the help of the English, the King became victorious. The war was brought to an end by the treaty of Yandavor ; and then a son was born to the King Gambhir Singha named Chandrakirtti. Chandrakirtti was only a year old, when the king Gambhir Singha died. The widow and the son of the deceased king were committed to the care of Narasingha, a general of the departed king. Narasingha became the regent and conducted the affairs of State with great ability and foresight. Devendra Singha, a brother of Narasingha, however, turned a foe to the latter and he was assisted in his evil designs by one Nabin Singha. They put their wits together and persuaded the Queen that Narasingha aimed at the life of her son; for, by killing him, he would be able to usurp the throne. The Queen foolishly believed in the words of the miscreants. The credulous woman could not see through the designs of Devendra who wanted to take the life of Chandrakirtti, after first getting rid of Narasingha. She readily lent her support to the plan of putting the general to death. Gradually Narasingha came to know of everything and the Queen with her son, thirteen years old, was now in great danger. The mother and the son fled off to Cachhar, and at this time Narasingha ascended the throne. He was a pious man and used to visit alone the temples of the gods without any attendant or bodyguard. He was one day offering prayers to the gods when the rogue Nabin raised his sword at him, but thanks to his good luck, he could foresee the design and caught the sword with his right hand. The mortal wound, however, brought on a disease to which he ultimately succumbed and then the kingdom went to the rogue Devendra. Chandrakirtti had by this time attained the age of nineteen and he made bold to go to his own country of Manipur. His subjects came in large numbers and rendered him every assistance. With their help he fought his way back to the throne. In the course of his reign, he entered into friendly treaties with the English. During the period of Gambhir Singha's reign, the English kept an Agent at Manipur; and from that time onward the Residency has been maintained all along. (Ll. 1-48.)

(3)

War with the Nagas, the Burmese and Barachawba.

In 1879, a war raged between the English and the Nagas. The Nagas displayed remarkable courage and the English General sought the help of Manipur. At the Durbar, Chandrakirtti asked of all his men as to who could go to assist the English. Prince Tikendrajit responded, saying, "If Your Majesty pleases, I can." The king then gladly sent him out with two thousand men; and after a month and a half of fighting the Nagas were defeated and they henceforth owed allegiance to the English. Thanks to the valour of Tikendrajit, the prestige of the English was maintained, and as a mark of recognition, the king was decorated with a K.C.S.I., and was further rewarded with two thousand guns. Tikendrajit was given a gold medal, and the shepoys too got a medal each, with other rewards, for the English, as you are all aware, know how to appreciate merit.

In 1885, another war broke out between the English and the Burmese, and the Maharaja sent out many soldiers under one 'Mr. John.' After a reign lasting for thirty-five years, King Chandrakirtti left the mortal world, leaving behind him eight queens and ten sons to mourn his loss. The names of these sons were Surachandra, Kesarjit, Bhairabjit, Padmalochan, Kulachandra, Gandhar Singha, Tikendrajit, Bhuban Singha, Jhalakirtti, Jilla Gamva. Maharaja Chandrakirtti had installed Kulachandra on his *Gadi* during the latter part of his life, and Jhalakirtti was appointed the general of the army. Arrangements were set on foot for the coronation of the Maharaja when the sound of war-drum was heard from a distance, which was a challenge from the sons of Narasingha. The king's death was followed by this disaster and the princes were all puzzled, but Tikendrajit mustered an army and prepared himself for fighting the enmy, while the other brothers all went to attend the funeral of the father. Barachawba and Mekjin were the names of Narasingha's sons, who had resolved to regain their father's throne. The two armies fought a hard fight for four days and then Barachawba retreated with his brother. After some time, Jhalakirtti died and Tikendrajit was appointed Commander-in-chief in his place. The fittest man was now at the head of the army and four months passed off happily. Barachawba invaded the land again and Tikendrajit went to encounter him for the second time. It was a terrible fight and Tikendrajit began gradually to lose heart. Surachandra now sought the assistance of the English who sent a hundred men. Reinforced by these men Tikendrajit rushed to meet his foes with great vigour, and suddenly the latter began to retire. The two brothers were then taken captives by Tikendrajit, but fresh trouble was now ahead. The third brother of King Surachandra was Bhairabjit who did not look upon the honours conferred on the General and the Crown Prince with good grace,—for both of them were his step-brothers. His thoughts night and day were fixed on devising means to harm his half-brothers. His evil counsels won over many of the courtiers, and a party was formed against the General and the Crown Prince. The king himself was a very simple man and he could not see through the designs of Bhairab. A year passed on in this way and then an event happened of great political significance to which I beg to invite your attention now. (Ll. 1-74.)

(4)

War with the Son of Ayalkarai, the Kukis, and Jogendra Singha.

King Chandrakirtti had a minister of the name of Bhuban Singha, whose son was Ayalkarai. Ayalkarai now found that an opportunity had come to him and he led an expedition against Manipur. The inhabitants of the place were sorely agitated over this attack and a great battle ensued, ranging through the whole country. The sound of guns and cannon dinned in the ear and many people left the land in panic. Ayalkarai was a very strong man himself and the king was seized with fear. Tikendrajit and Padmalochan were the two prominent figures in the field and the fight went on day and night without cessation. Many soldiers on the Maharaja's side lost their lives,—and Tikendrajit and Padmalochan were dismayed. Then the two brothers conferred together and divided the army into two battalions. With one Padmalochan left the field, and with the other Tikendrajit began gradually to retire and by this clever move he could now enter into the fortress. Ayalkarai found no trace of his enemy and followed Tikendrajit into the fort. Here too there was no sign of the existence of his foe. He now fondly believed that Tikendrajit had retired in despair, and he was confident of gaining the throne. All on a sudden the roar of guns was heard, as Tikendrajit had again combined with Padmalochan and attacked him from both sides.

Ayalkarai lost all his men and had to bid adieu to his hopes of gaining the crown. Indeed, he himself fell in the battle with four of his sons.

The whole country rang with shouts of ovation in honour of the General whose achievement also received the commendation of the Agent. The envious Bhairabjit was highly mortified at this fame of his enemy. He was a well-read scholar and always kept close to the king and helped him in the discharge of State-duties, for which he had become his father's favourite. The king fondly believed Bhairab to be an honest man. Too much of show often proves the lack of substance but in the present case the vagaries of Bhairab passed off undetected. Many a day went on in this way till there arose dissensions between a certain official of the State and the Kukis. Tamahu was the name of their chief. He came to the royal house and demanded justice for the Kukis. The king's decision was unfavourable to them, and for this they stopped paying rent and other dues. Finding that trouble was ahead, the king tried to bring them round by importunate persuasions, but mild words did not prevail on Tamahu who at last said that his men would submit only if the king dismissed the official with whom they had a friction. On investigation it was found that the official in question was free from all blame and hence nothing could be done against him. So the Kukis rose in rebellion. Soldiers were sent out to quell them, but in the first battle the royal army was defeated. The losses were heavy, for many were slain and countless taken captives. Then went forth Tikendrajit and a terrible battle ensued in which Tamahu was defeated. He was captured and brought to the royal court but did not yield even at this crisis. He was sent to prison. After four months, he was found remorseful and humiliated, and then was let off.

In 1888 appeared another enemy in Jogendra Singha in Cachhar. He went out to attack Manipur and with him were five hundred men. On his way he had a skirmish with the English in which he lost his life, and thus Manipur escaped a danger from outside. This act, on the part of the English, was of course, quite befitting a friendly power, and the Maharaja paid them his respectful thanks.

(Ll. 1-72.)

(5)

Troubles begin.

The king, won over by the dodges of Bhairab, began to trust him more than others. Prince Kulachandra was in charge of the judiciary and Bhairab found out many faults in his work. The king, listening to the evil counsel of Bhairab appointed him in the place of Kulachandra. It was a great insult to the latter and Tikendrajit was mortified at this act. Two ryots had once insulted the General for which he had punished them. This was just the loophole for Bhairab. He exaggerated the matter before his father, making, so to speak, a mountain of a mole-hill. Things came to such a pass at the instigation of Bhairab, that the king became rather displeased with Tikendra. But the supporters of this warrior-prince every day grew in number and at this Bhairab burned with malice all the more. Here in Bhairab's mind was kindled a fire which was destined to burn the whole of Manipur. The king now was guided by the counsel of this wicked prince and this resulted in the humiliation of many respectable people. On a day in 1890, King Surachandra was fast asleep when Jitta Singha and Prince Bhuban came out with many people. They climbed the walls of the palace with the help of ladders and reached the royal harem. There was the firing of bullets on all sides which awakened the Maharaja. He understood the situation and was seized with fear, for he was never known for any special aptitude for war. His body-guards too were not of any use. He was putting on a turban when a bullet struck it. The bullet pierced the turban and burst out, a few paces off from him. Stricken with panic the king made good his escape through a window along with four of his attendants. Jitta Singha joined Tikendra and other brothers of the king and also the retainers who had been driven out. They all flocked together and the whole palace rang with the hub-bub. Bhairab joined the king along with eighty men, and reflecting that it would not be safe to return to the palace, they ran off to the Residency. Meanwhile Tikendra had made himself master of the fort, the store of ammunition and the treasury. Cries of "Cheers for the General" shook the sky, and the men assembled under him remained ready to meet any attack that might be made. Seeing all these, Kulachandra ran away along with a number of soldiers. This was apparently a harmless step, but the object of Kulachandra was achieved by a clever dodge. The Residency was very close to the royal palace and the firing of guns could easily be heard from there. Mr. Grimwood woke up from sleep, but could form no idea about what the noise was due to. He made the soldiers of his personal staff put on their accoutrements and guard the house. At half past two in the morning the king reached the Residency along with his retainers. To the queries of the Agent he could give no answer and all of them spent the night in the Durbar Hall. On the morrow all the loyal soldiers and subjects flocked beside the Residency. The Agent helped the Maharaja with some soldiers and asked him to go out to take possession of the royal palace, but none was ready for the venture. Finding that things were in such a pass, the Agent scolded the men severely. The crest-fallen officials now went to the king and began to give him advice. There were many men, and many were the counsels given by them. At last spoke the old Prime Minister Thangal General. "If you care for your prestige, my prince, just take up your sword. I am the oldest of your ministers, and your predecessors did all abide by my counsel, and may I not expect you to do the same?"

But none else counselled war and the king too declined taking up arms. Then after two days he wrote to Tikendrajit a letter which ran thus—"I have a great wish to go to the holy city of Brindaban on pilgrimage. I have no mind to take up the reins of the State again. Let Kulachandra be installed on the throne and make arrangements for my starting for Brindaban. Bhairabjit has indeed served you ill. Remember your father and do forgive him for the sake of your father's memory."

Tikendrajit wrote in reply, "My respectful salutations to your Royal Highness. I do reverently bear on my head the command of my royal brother, and shall be glad to make arrangements for your trip to Brindaban. I hope, your Royal Highness will graciously pardon all the faults of this humble subject."

Now happened a strange event, but all was due to the will of the Almighty and who can stay His decrees? Mr. Grimwood went to the royal palace and had Prince Kulachandra called to him. On receipt of the message, Kulachandra hastened there and proclaimed himself king. Brothers, relatives and friends,- all acknowledged their allegiance and the General Tikendrajit was proclaimed Crown Prince. Having returned from there, Mr. Grimwood began to make arrangements for the journey of the ex-king to Brindaban. It was the eighth day in the month of Aswin (September) in the Bengali year 1928. King Surachandra had abdicated and was starting on pilgrimage to Brindaban.

(Ll. 1-104.)

(6)

Three brothers accompanied him with sixty retainers. There were also thirty-five Goorkha soldiers. On the eve of his departure, the whole of Manipur was one vast scene of grief. The people heard of the king's abdication. Tears gushed down their eyes and their hearts burned in sorrow. They came in groups, all in tears, and honoured him with presents. The king raised his hand and poured forth his blessings. He embraced Tikendrajit and gave him the keys of the doors of the royal palace. To Kulachandra he presented the royal sword and then he doffed his royal garments. At this the people recalled the old story of the Ramayan and said that it was as if Ram was giving his kingdom to Bharat. The old king left Manipur for good and all acknowledged allegiance to the new ruler. From here the ex-king went to Calcutta, and Government police became his escort. Now let us see what he did here. He made a petition to the English Government, asking their help for regaining his lost throne. He, further, said that he had no intention of finally leaving his kingdom. He only wanted to pay a visit to Brindaban. Mr. Quinton was then the Chief Commissioner. With six hundred men he went to Manipur and wrote to Surachandra from there. He then finally installed Kulachandra as king and said that those who had been his enemies would now receive condign punishment. Surachandra was not competent to quell his enemies and that was why Kulachandra was de king in his place. Having come to know all these, the Government of India sent instructions to the Chief Commissioner to arrest Tikendrajit by some clever trick not involving war and then to send him into exile on the pretext of some alleged offence. Mr. Grimwood informed the Commissioner that Tikendrajit was not the man to let himself be easily arrested. Then it was decided in council that Tikendrajit was to be called to the Durbar and there put under arrest. It was the desire of the Government not to shed blood, but to punish the miscreant after capturing him by means of a clever dodge. They came to this decision at a conference held at Sangamai, in which seventeen Englishmen were present. Maharaja Kulachandra was in great suspense, for, the order confirming his installation had not yet arrived. The Crown Prince Tikendrajit got information that the Chief Commissioner was going to Manipur to capture a tiger there, Kulachandra had also come to know about the petition of Surachandra for re-installation on the throne. Rumour was afloat in Manipur to the effect that the Chief Commissioner was coming along with Surachandra and a retinue of eighteen hundred sepoys, and that Surachandra would again be on his throne. This matter was discussed in the royal court too and these reports were known to all. The Chief Commissioner would soon be coming and it was supposed that Surachandra too was in his company. This report was a cause of great alarm to Kulachandra. He accordingly got ready to resist the coming of the ex-Maharaja.

(Ll. 1-66.)

(7)

As soon as the Commissioner arrived at Kohima, news reached Kulachandra ; and having got ready a force of thousand soldiers, he wanted to send it on to stop the further progress of the Commissioner's party. Mr. Grimwood came to know of this dangerous resolve and tried to dissuade Kulachandra from the wrong course. The Maharaja afterwards informed the Agent that it was not his intention to fight the English. What he wanted was to prevent Surachandra from entering the kingdom, and that was the sole reason for the advance of the sepoys. "That the British will not join any party," said the Maharaja, "we can well realise. It is an internecine strife, and so far as we know, the English Government will not interfere." Then he wrote a letter to the Commissioner enquiring if Surachandra was with him. "Why is it," he further asked, "that you have such a large army with you? What brings you to my country?"

"Surachandra is not with me," answered the Commissioner. "Indeed I have an army of body-guards, but these I have kept with me in obedience to the orders of the Viceroy." It was in the month of Chaitra (March) in the year 1297 B.S., that the Commissioner wrote this letter from Sangomai. He further wrote in the letter—"I shall arrive at Manipur at ten in the morning to-morrow, and there will be a Durbar at the Residency the day after. You will kindly attend there along with your ministers and your brothers." The Crown Prince Tikendrajit was ill and also fasting on account of *ekadasi*. Still he went forward with his armies with a view to receive the Commissioner and pay him respects. They met on the banks of the Kairang and the Prince paid his respects in a fitting manner. The Commissioner went to Manipur along with the Prince and reached the Residency on the 9th day of Chaitra. There was usual firing of guns in honour of his arrival, and Maharaja Kulachandra was himself present to welcome him. It was decided that the Durbar would be held in the afternoon. The official proclamation was written in English and the King and the Crown Prince were in the royal palace, and the work of translating it into Bengali was given to Babu Rasiklal Roy. Necessary arrangements were made for the arrest and body-guards were stationed in proper places. In the afternoon, the Maharaja, the Crown Prince, and ministers were all present at the Residency. There was yet some time for the proclamation to be translated into Bengali and for this they had to wait outside in the sun. The Crown Prince had been ailing already and the heat of the sun increased his illness. He returned home, saying that it was not possible for him to keep standing any longer, and the Commander-in-chief followed him. Then the Maharaja went up the steps of the Residency along with Prince Jilla Singha and the Prime Minister, and here they met Mr. Grimwood, who asked of them information about the Crown Prince. The Maharaja told him everything in detail and sent a man home to call the Prince back. On his pointing out that it was beneath their dignity to keep standing outside, they were all allowed to stay in a room inside the house. News arrived from the royal palace that Tikendrajit's illness was getting more and more serious, but Mr. Grimwood said to the Maharaja that unless the Crown Prince came, the Commissioner would not grant them interview, nor let them know the orders of the Government. He said that there would be another Durbar on the next morning at eight and they must all be present there. Said the Maharaja—"I will of course turn up, but I can give no assurance as regards the Crown Prince, for I am told that his ailments are getting more and more serious. I will however try my best to bring him."

Then the Maharaja went back to his palace, and Mr. Grimwood started on his way to call on the Prince. When Mr. Grimwood reached his palace, the Prince did not come out. The Agent asked him to do so, for he wanted to see how ill the Prince was, so that he might explain matters to the Chief Commissioner. Still the Prince declined coming out, and Mr. Grimwood was sorely mortified. He repeated the visit on the next morning and sent word that he wanted to see the Crown Prince. Even now Tikendrajit expressed his inability to come out. The Agent suggested that the prince might come borne in a palanquin, but the latter did not consent. Highly aggrieved, the Agent went back to the Residency. At eight there was a Durbar which no one from the royal house attended. Kulachandra wrote a letter to the Agent saying that the Crown Prince was ill, and "no useful purpose," continued the Maharaja, "would be served by my going,—for, if I am alone, I am sure not to be granted an interview by the Commissioner "

At noon the Maharaja despatched another letter asking information about the orders of the Government. The Commissioner sent Babu Rasiklal to watch the condition of the Crown Prince. Then he wrote a letter in answer to that of the Maharaja and sent it through Mr. Grimwood and Mr. Simson. The contents of this letter were—" From to-day, Kulachandra is confirmed as the Maharaja but as Tikendrajit's conduct with the ex-king Surachandra was refractory, he is to be banished, and Kulachandra must assist in getting him captured and sent to exile." Grimwood wanted a warrant for the arrest of Tikendra and the Maharaja was in a fix. He said to the Agent that he could do nothing without consulting his ministers. Mr. Grimwood asked him to finish the conference in half an hour Then the Maharaja began his Durbar and the Head Clerk of the royal palace explained the substance of the letter. Maharaja then asked of the Crown Prince his opinion on the matter. " If you think it proper," replied he, "do send me away." The ministers counselled otherwise. They asked the Maharaja to send a petition to the Chief Commissioner. This he did and in the letter thanked the British Government for acknowledging him as king and informed that the Crown Prince was then ill, and that he would be sent away as soon as he came round. The petition was handed over to the Agent who however wanted to have the Prince arrested at once. Then all of them implored Mr. Grimwood to use his influence with the Commissioner so that he might spare Tikendrajit and capture him when he was all right again. The Crown Prince now wanted to see the Agent himself, and was carried to him in a litter. Mr. Grimwood was now convinced about the genuine character of his illness. He then spoke about the Prince being sent on exile, adding that he would get an allowance wherever he stayed and would be allowed to return if he behaved well. The Crown Prince said, "Whatever be the decision of the royal court I will bow to it. But may I know from you why the Commissioner wants to exile me?" "It is," answered the Agent, "due to your misbehaviour with Surachandra that you will be banished from your land." Then he added another request for going to the Residency. "I cannot," said the Prince, "go now. I shall be there as soon as I am all right." Rasik Babu who had been to the Prince's place saw that people were removing various articles from there and he saw also an array of soldiers. All this he reported to the Agent, who, it is said, got information also from the Head Clerk of the royal palace. Afterwards the Head Clerk fled away and so did the subjects living in the vicinity of the royal palace. There was a general rumour abroad that the Residency would be attacked.

(8)

The First War with the English and their Defeat.

This night, the English were all very anxious and then they sat at a conference. The orders of the Government could never be set at naught and it was decided to arrest Tikendrajit in the early hours of the morning. Five hundred English soldiers prepared for battle and this the Prince knew from his spies. At daybreak, the English army was divided into three regiments. To the north went Mr. Brackenbury and to the west Captain Bucher with whom went Mr. Lowguard as lieutenant. The north gate was being guarded by the sepoys of Manipur, and they imploringly submitted to Mr. Brackenbury that if his men behaved ill with them, they would be bound to resist. Mr. Brackenbury said that he had some important matter to talk over with the Prince which the sepoys did not believe. They went inside the fort and from there fired at the English who were repulsed to the bank of the river. They too now lay down on the ground and began to fire from behind the *bandh*. As regards Captain Bucher, he set a ladder at the walls of the Prince's house and having surmounted them entered his room. Here too Manipuri soldiers were quite ready and the two parties began to fight. Quarrels thus set in at those places, and the men of Manipur began to fire at the Residency. Mr. Chatterton went to quell these people. Let us now follow the movements of Captain Bucher. Having taken possession of the Prince's palace, he proceeded to arrest him. But on entering the room where the Prince was supposed to be, he found to his surprise that the Prince was not really there. To the west of the royal palace Mr. Chatterton captured seventeen Manipuri soldiers. Many shots were fired at the royal temple and a part of it was destroyed. The cloth of the sacred image of Brindabanchandra, the tutelary god of the royal family, was spoilt, and this sacrilegious act was resented by all the inhabitants who became mad with indignation. There was a great commotion at the royal palace and suddenly there broke a shrill cry from there. Then bands began to play and the hearts of all the people began to dance to its tune. Guns and cannon were fired all at the same time and a terrible fight set in. A shot struck Mr. Brackenbury which laid him low. Mr. Chatterton was terribly attacked and the men of Captain Bucher were in a frenzy. Then information was sent to the Residency to the effect that unless Mr. Chatterton and Captain Bucher were given reinforcement, they would have to surrender at once. Mr. Skiney went with sepoys to their assistance, and people at the Residency were greatly frightened.

There was a terrible battle in which the casualties were heavy on both sides. The sepoys of the English were ultimately defeated and took shelter in the Residency. The soldiers of Manipur now invaded the stronghold of the English, firing at it from three sides. They cut off the telegraphic lines and at four o'clock the English were in a sore plight. Their sepoys climbed the walls and began to fire in self-defence. But even this could not damp the spirit of the men of Manipur. Terrific was their onslought and the stable was burnt down by cannon-balls. A part of the Residency too was destroyed and as the day drew towards its end, it appeared that the English were in danger of being captured by the people of Manipur. There was now talk of peace, and the Chief Commissioner was seriously puzzled over it. Suddenly he blew a horn signifying cessation of hostilities. Tikendrajit who was calm and sedate even in trouble, could hear the sound and he sent messengers all round. Suddenly the hostilities came to a close. The people of Manipur were sorely indignant at this abrupt cessation of battle and in their deep chagrin they began to bite their lips. When they now saw their own kith and kin amongst the slain, their hearts blazed up with the thought of revenge. Some thought, "Why is Manipur in such a plight to-day? Why have the English brought such woes on her? And why have hostilities been stopped when the enemy was in their last gasp?" The suspicions of these people were now on the Prince himself. Some said that the best way would be to avenge these wrongs by killing Tikendrajit and there were men who went mad over these thoughts. Having heard all these the State Officials began gently to explain the facts of the case to the people who were soon calmed. Then the Commissioner wrote a letter which ran, "On what terms are you willing to suspend warfare and allow me a respite to consult the views of the Viceroy? I will have, of course, to repair the telegraphic lines. Please let us have an answer as early as possible." Five Englishmen went near the godown with a view to getting the reply to the letter. Here they began to confer with one another. One advised flight, while another pointed that the Nagas and the Kukis would fall upon them and destroy them outright. One of them feared that the fire of the cannon would kill them too, while another held that cannon-balls would not reach so high. A third gentleman said that they would easily be able to fire the cannon. "When we find them removing the cannon, we shall snatch these from them from our position on the hills"—was the next suggestion. Another proposal was that they ought to make peace, to which an objection was raised that it would be compromising their prestige. The consultation was thus going on when a man of Manipur came there with a letter which he delivered to the Commissioner. The letter was in Bengali and its contents may be outlined thus,—"Unfortunately there is no one in the palace now who is competent to write in English. All that we can gather from your letter written in English is that you want to make peace. I am prepared to cease hostilities, if your soldiers lay down arms." Having listened to the contents of the letter, Mr. Quinton asked them as to what the Maharaja meant by "laying down" (literally "abandoning") arms. Mr. Cousins interpreted it to mean handing over arms to the men of Manipur. Mr. Grimwood demurred to this interpretation, and his view was that it meant simply cessation of hostilities. The Chief Commissioner decided to refer the matter to the Crown Prince. (Ll. 1-126.)

(9)

Englishmen killed.

Mr. Grimwood asked the bearer of the letter if they could call on the Crown Prince. "Why, certainly you can," answered the bearer. "Do swear to me and say if there is any possibility of danger there"—repeated Mr. Grimwood. "Well," said the bearer, "you are as good as gods to us, what chance is there of your being treated ill?"

"This bearer," said Mr. Grimwood to his fellow countrymen, "is known to me. I believe him to be a trusted servant in the royal house." Then relying on their words, the five men, Messrs. Quinton, Skiney, Grimwood, Simson, and Cousins, went out at eight o'clock in the evening along with a Gurkha soldier. When they reached the royal palace, the Crown Prince was asleep in the storehouse. Having received information he came down and held a conference with the Europeans. When this meeting was in progress, the subjects and the soldiers were looking on. They whispered amongst themselves, some blaming Tikendrajit, though none dared speak his disapproval out. They were all eager to know the result of the Durbar. Said the prince—"Have an end of this matter at once. Let your sepoys all lay down their arms. Your movements have filled us with apprehension and that is why we make such a request." The English thought these proposals insulting and the Chief Commissioner did not agree. He said that the Durbar would be renewed on the morning of the next day and they now separated. As soon as the Prince was out of sight, the people began to make clamour. Mr. Grimwood asked the minister to escort them till they were outside the house. The minister asked the permission of the Prince who said, "Go you must. Do accompany them till they are at a safe distance from here." The Englishmen came near the door to go outside when the men of Manipur shut it. Some hurt them with the butt-end of a gun, some threw brickbats, while others hurled slabs of stones. "Out with them—kill them"—was the cry and some one struck Mr. Simson whose life was saved only because of a Jamadar named Jatra Singha who took out his own turban and bound up the wounds. The Englishmen came down, and like mad men the people of Manipur pursued them. One of them struck Mr. Grimwood with his lance and the wound proved fatal. The Jamadar, the minister, and a few officials tried their best to save the Englishmen from being harmed. Jatra Singha pushed the door open and the noise of the great hubbub reached the ears of the Prince who came back and the Manipuris fled pellmell. He talked to the Chief Commissioner and kept the junior minister in charge of the Englishmen. This minister appointed ten guards to look after the men under his care. The senior minister Thangal had been holding a conference, and after the breaking of the meeting gone back to the fort. When report of these events reached his ears he was sorely puzzled. At this time there was a knock at his door and somebody came in after taking due permission. It was an old man, who said that the writing of the sacred scriptures could never prove false. The prime minister asked him to explain in detail what he meant. Said the old man, " Why, you can consult the holy books yourself. It is written that there will be grim warfare in the land of Manipur and that the gods will be appeased with the blood of five enemies. If the five enemies be now buried together, it will be all for our good." The prime minister replied that he had indeed heard such a folktale but it was not written in any book. "I beg to recall that prophecy to you now," answered the old man, " this is the battle predicted and these are the five enemies. One of them has already been sacrificed and but for the intercession of the Crown Prince, the remaining four would have shared the same fate by this time. Now is the time for immolating human beings, but the Crown Prince is both a fool and a knave." So saying, the old man began to tremble in the excess of his emotion. The prime minister asked him to be calm. " Even to-day have I lost two of my sons"—the old man moaned out and began to beat his bosom with both hands. The minister replied, "That the English have done wrong cannot he gainsaid. But they now seek our shelter and there can be no killing a suppliant. It cannot be helped of course; many people come to seek protection when in misery and difficulty. They have provoked hostilities with us and having no other alternative, have climbed down now. For achieving their own ends nothing is too bad, too low for them. Had they got the Crown Prince in their clutches, they would have sentenced him to transportation, or even taken his life."

Another man argued thus, "Listen to me, great minister. The Crown Prince has done the duty of a Kshattriya by stopping warfare." The minister retorted—"Talk you of duty in connection with them? Had the Prince been defeated, would they have come to any terms?" Then the old man who had first come in appealed to the minister, —"Do slay the English and vindicate the honour of Manipur." Then premier Thangal pondered over the matter for some time and after this called out to Jamadar Usarva—"Hand these men over to the executioner and let their mouths be stopped for good." The naughty old man was highly elated at this and went to call a headsman, but alas! what a heinous act the prime minister was going to do? It is written in the sacred scriptures of the Hindus that a guest must be welcomed and treated with hospitality even though he might be a deadly enemy. And what a sin this great sinner Thangal committed and he yet professed Hinduism! He would indeed eat the hard fruits of his sin. The pity of it was that a large number of innocent people had to share the punishment with him. Be that as it may, it must be noted that this impious Thangal left an indelible blot on the fair name of Hindu. And it rends my heart to narrate the event that followed,—the six unfortunate men lost their lives for nothing. Jamadar Usarba thought within himself, "Hundreds of men have been beheaded by the orders of this minister, but horrible indeed is his command of to-day." He, therefore, went with Jatra Singha into the house of the Crown Prince and let him know of the matter. The Prince was startled at the intelligence. Said he, "It will be all over with us, I am afraid. Let us hurry off to him."

The Prince came to Thangal and enquired, "Do tell us if you have given the order for killing the Englishmen." On the minister's answering in the affirmative, the Prince remarked, "Alas, alas, why did you pass this terrific order ? It is a grievous sin to kill one who is under protection. And to-morrow there shall certainly be peace." Thangal retorted saying, "You are an urchin and what do you understand of these things ? If it is within one's reach, what harm is there in killing an enemy ? I have been a minister for three generations having served with your grandfather Gambhir Singha and also with your father and I can claim to have some experience of State affairs." "But don't you know," answered the Prince, "what harm the slaughter of the English will do to you ? And over and above this, being a Hindu, will you go against the tenets of your religion ? It is I who have given protection to the Englishmen. I have had to resist a hundred attempts at their lives—then don't you know that these English are of mighty strength ?" "Why," persisted the minister, "we can well drive them beyond Cachhar. It is because of you that all these troubles have occurred, and strange it is that you, of all men, should side with the English ! It is, on account of the attempt at your arrest, that so many men have lost their lives and the country is in such peril. What hopes can you entertain of peace ?" The Prince replied, "We shall all be ruined. Do listen to my advice when there is yet time." The Prince fell into sleep before he had finished and the minister called a bearer Youngkarba and asked him to deliver the Englishmen to the executioner. He said that such were the orders of the Crown Prince, and finding the Prince asleep there the bearer believed in the minister's words. He thought that the Prince had fallen asleep after delivering the capital sentence. He now entered the Durbar room and communicated the orders to Jatra and Usarba who were in charge of the Englishmen. Then came an iron-smith who made them wear shackles and a watchman took them out of the room. Then the royal headsman Dhana Singha by name cut off their heads with a weapon called *tadantang*. The heads of the five men were collected together and buried. The one Gurkha who had come with the English also lost his life in the same way, and the barbarians of Manipur began to dance gleefully. They fancied that their heinous acts had the sanction of the holy scriptures, and being very much elated, the wild men began to indulge in orgies of merriment. The presiding goddess of luck in the house of Ghambhir Singha was shocked and she left her old place in horror. (Ll. 1-174.)

(10)

Let us now see what happened at the Residency after the five men had started for the royal palace. Those who were in sound body took their meals, and some of them fell asleep. Of the wounded, Brackenbury and some Gurkhas succumbed to their injuries at ten o'clock at night. When it was found that the five men had not returned even at two in the morning, Captain Bailo became very anxious and woke Mr. Chatterton up. They fixed their gaze towards the royal palace. The Durbar house was only about a hundred yards off from the Residency, and it being but a day previous to the full moon, everything looked beautiful in the light. They began to ponder over the cause of the delay. It was four hours that they had gone there and what could they have to do so long in that den of the devil? But it did not strike anyone that they ought to go forward and see what was happening. Alas, if they had only done their part of their duty, the five men might not have lost their lives. Had the men at the Residency been on their guard, could Thangal have been so daring? The noise would have awakened Tikendra and he would certainly have stopped the slaughter. But alas, what was fated came about. And suddenly cannon were fixed at the Residency itself. Hundreds of guns were shot and four cannon roared. The walls of the Residency were razed to the ground and the inmates were all at their wit's end. They thought that the five men had been imprisoned, and there being no one left competent to guard the Residency, the Manipuris met with no resistance.

They advanced and surrounded the place from all sides. The doors of the store-room broke down and they rushed upon the wall which fell down with a mighty crash. The English were in great panic and went out through the windows to save their lives. They rushed along the way to Cachhar, Mrs. Grimwood showing the way. She had many a time passed along that route and was, therefore, well-acquainted with the roads. Two hundred Gurkhas accompanied them, but innumerable articles and guns were left behind. The dead did not receive the last funeral rites, and the wounded lay uncared for. The Manipuris did not attempt to check their flight. Their interest was only to seize the store-room. The Residency was the home of their enemies; they burnt it down and then went back in gleeful spirits. The English left the place at two o'clock, and met with no impediments in the course of their flights. The day after, they were soon pinched with hunger and thirst and were in a sore plight. They were now very much unnerved and restless. Each went wherever he liked and many a person lost their lives for want of food and water, and others were killed by the wild tribes such as the Nagas, the Kukis, or by wild animals like the tiger. Mrs. Grimwood was dressed as a Gurkha and began to walk with a turban on. On the way some subjects of Manipur fell upon them and Captain Bucher killed five of the stragglers with the help of a gun. They all plodded their way on and after some time fell in with a number of sepoys. The sight of these struck terror in their hearts, but it was none other than Captain Cowley who, according to previous instructions, was on his way to Manipur with two hundred sepoys. They now all joined together into a party and walked on to Cachhar safely. Of those who in their extreme terror and nervousness had left the ranks and strayed away, many fell into the hands of Manipuris and were put under arrest. Among those men, who found their way back to Manipur, were Messrs. William, Melville and Brien. (Ll. 1-78.)

(11)

From Cachhar, Tamu and other places, the English got information of the tragic occurrence at Manipur. The Viceroy Lord Landsdowne was highly shocked by the fell news which had been sent to him by wire. It was believed that the five men were still in custody, and hence attempts were at first made for their release. Mr. Grant received orders at Tamu to proceed to Manipur with eighty men. It was arranged to despatch soldiers on all sides and gradually news was orally circulated from mouth to mouth. Everything was now known to all. Rasik Babu wired to the Viceroy saying that Mr. Quinton along with five others had had their heads chopped off. The Viceroy was awfully bewildered by this news and sepoys were despatched from all sides. Mr. Grant had, however, already started from Tamu, and nobody asked him to hold back. The Viceroy issued a proclamation saying that the Manipuris had been guilty of heinous offences, that the crimes would all be duly avenged and that no efforts would be spared to make good the loss they had inflicted. Arrangements were set on foot on a huge scale. Soldiers were sent from the Punjab and so also from Assam, and English soldiers rushed towards Manipur along the routes from Assam and Burma, ravaging the places that fell on their way.

(Ll. 1-34.)

(12)

Let us now return to the Prince who had fallen asleep after forbidding Thangal to take the lives of the Englishmen. His rest was disturbed by the noise and by the roar of cannon and he quickly rose up. He shouted aloud a command to give up arms at once, and then came to know of the massacre of the English and also of the burning of the Residency. The Prince was at his wit's end at this information; his countenance was covered with gloom and his head bent down in shame. When Maharaja Kulachandra came to know of all this, he too was confounded. The Crown Prince and he began both to lament together, for they well realised that the country had been plunged into deep misery. Thangal was, however, undaunted and advised the Maharaja to tell lies. He made the latter send information to the Viceroy, telling him that the men had all fallen in battle. And he, further suggested that they should prepare for war. But none heeded his advice. The Crown Prince asked the Head Clerk of the royal household as to what ought to be done, —for things had indeed reached a crisis. Baman Babu,—the Head Clerk—said that they had now to depend only on the Almighty, as their situation had become too critical for human control. The Prince wanted to write out a letter to the Viceroy explaining everything. He then called in Janaki Babu and Rasik Babu and showed them everything around the house. He also pointed out to them the places where temples had been destroyed. Next he set the British prisoners free, who numbered two hundred men. He provided them with food, clothes and escorts to lead them out of the country. Janaki Babu, Rasik Babu and Baman Babu—these three stayed behind at the request of the Prince who with their help wrote out a letter to the Viceroy and had it sent through messengers.

(Ll. 1-72.)

(13)

Arrival of the Lieutenant-Governor Grant, and the March of the English.

Mr. Grant reached Manipur with his eighty men. Nobody thought that the English would come so soon, nor did any one exactly remember now the precise cause of their quarrel. He fell upon the subjects that he came across on his way to Manipur. None could resist the onslought of Mr. Grant, and then a group of people having cut down trees blocked his way with these trees. But this was of no avail against Mr. Grant. The Manipuris were struck with panic and gave way. A party of hundred men next attacked Mr. Grant but he drove them three miles off The news of the massacre of the captive Englishmen reached his ears but he could not believe in it. For had these men been really killed, then the Government would certainly have called him back. He reflected thus and continued in his march. It was he that vindicated the prestige of the English. He had to surmount many obstacles on the way before he was able to reduce the royal fort of Thobal. This fort was fourteen miles from the capital and lay on the way to Tamu. The Crown Prince sent Mr. William, one of the captives, with an escort of body guards to Thobal. Mr. Grant introduced himself as Howlett, and William advised him to retire along with his men. The redoubtable general now began to work his way, fighting the Manipuris and performing impossible feats. At Palel the Manipuris sustained a defeat, of which, however, neither the Maharaja nor the Crown Prince knew anything. They did not contemplate the prospect of war and did not send any troops anywhere. It is at such a critical time that ministers give each a separate opinion. None listens to others and each blames the rest, thus forming a veritable babel. The plight of Manipur was now known to all, and the Manipuris residing in other countries blazed in resentment at this. There were no less than thirty-five thousand Manipuris resident in Cachhar alone and they now rushed to their native country in groups. Those who were in Sylhet, Silchar, Shillong and Dacca, were also filled with indignation at this terrible situation of their motherland. The English Government were clever enough to explain the real situation to them and they were calmed. There were many hill-tribes residing around Manipur and these too, finding the opportunity, began to cause trouble. The British Government had got information of all these and were engaged in making preparations on a grand scale. They wanted to attack Manipur from three sides, that is, from Cachhar, Kohima and Tamu, and in all these places huge arrangements were set on foot. From Bengal soldiers were sent out on ships and they reached Kohima along the Brahmaputra. Eight thousand soldiers and ten cannon, sixteen thousand soldiers and two doctors were sent to the war along these three routes. A terrific intelligence now reached Manipur. It was given out that thirty thousand soldiers were coming there, and General Thangal repeatedly urged the Maharaja to make preparations for war. Many leaders of hill-tribes offered their assistance. The subjects too made their request to the Crown Prince, but he heeded none. Thangal asked permission at the royal court to mobilise a large army. He said that since the hill-tribes promised help, he could, if he were allowed, get together a lac of men for the purpose But the permission was not given and the tribal leaders all said that the Maharaja and the Crown Prince were both out of their wits. They made preparations, each as he liked, but no good came of it for want of a commander-in-chief. (Ll. 1-72.)

(14)

The English enter Manipur and the Maharaja flies away.

General Colet was the leader of the forces sent out to Manipur. On the 20th April, he left Kohima with all his men. Before he had reached Manipur he sent a messenger to the Maharaja saying, "Should you look to your own good, do not make any attempt to fight with us. If you surrender and seek our protection, you will be well treated. But if you want to make war, know this that death awaits you."

No one showed any enmity to Colet, but his ranks were thinned by fever and cholera. When he was close to the capital, he received an answer to his letter. Wrote the Maharaja, "I had never had any mind to make war on you. It is due to the caprices of destiny that such a disaster has happened. Even now I don't want to fight. I was all along on friendly terms with you, and it is unfortunate that those cordial relations with the English should have been broken. I am just leaving the capital and shall return when there is any prospect of peace." The army from Cachhar and Silchar arrived and they had severe skirmishes with the men of Manipur. When the army from Tamu reached Palel, they had a severe encounter with the inhabitants. These people were without guns and cannon and still they fought in a manner which amazed the English. This day many Manipuris were sent to their graves and henceforth none else offered any resistance to the English. It was on the 13th of Baishakh (April) in the year 1298 B.S., that the Maharaja fled away from his capital. The Crown Prince, the generals and the high officials all left the country. Even the subjects went away with their valuable properties. The English took possession of Manipur without a struggle. Had the Maharaja and the Crown Prince offered more fight, who knows what would have been the fate of the country ?

From three sides the English soldiers reached the vicinity of the capital, all at a time. There were no men for five or six miles and the soldiers fired their guns in the direction of the capital in a warlike fashion. The liberty of Manipur was now a thing of the past! The English went at first to the Residency where there were some graves of Englishmen. They found to their indignation that these graves had been demolished. After a good deal of search all around, the soldiers managed cleverly to bring away a few inhabitants who acknowledged allegiance to the English and sought out a few human heads. These, of course, belonged to the unfortunate five and the conquerors duly buried them. They were aflame with anger and grief, and General Colet now issued a Proclamation saying that the reign of Kulachandra was now over, that the English were henceforth rulers of Manipur and that those who proved recalcitrant would get proper punishment. He issued another Proclamation offering a reward of rupees five thousand each for the arrest of the Maharaja and the Crown Prince ; two thousand for Thangal, a thousand for each of the generals and the *subedars*. People went out in quest of these men and a strenuous search was made extending to the lands of the Magas, to China and Siam. Colet issued a third Proclamation, this time inviting the subjects to their respective homes. He announced that the guilty would be duly punished and that no one in the land would be allowed to keep arms. People were asked to hand over their guns to the English within a week. If any one were found to possess any gun after that period, he would be hanged or transported. (Ll. 1-78.)

(15)

Arrest, Trial, Punishment and the New Regime.

After this the minister Thangal was trapped by a device and brought captive to the English court. The Maharaja was hiding himself in the land of the Kukis and he was caught after a few days by some Manipuris. Arrangements for his trial were set on foot, but there was no trace of the Crown Prince. Balaram Singha was a Hekim (a medical practitioner) at Manipur, and in his house the Crown Prince lay hidden. He one day asked Balaram to inform the authorities about his stay in the latter's place. Balaram advised concealment, on which the Prince said—"Arrested I must be some day or other. Why, let somebody else get five thousand rupees on my account!"

Unwillingly did Balaram lodge information about the Prince, and *subedar* Kalendra Singha at once came up. "Spare me to-day," said the Prince, "for, it is my birthday. I will go to-morrow." Yet, for the sake of money Kalendra took him away on that very day. In the prison, they all lay as captives, and preparations for their trial were in progress. They were tried by a special tribunal, and all the accused were sentenced to death. An appeal was preferred to the Viceroy who commuted the sentence on Kulachandra to exile. The death-sentences on Tikendrajit and on Thangal and his accomplices in the murder were upheld. Those who had taken up arms against the Queen

Empress were sentenced to transportation for life. These orders were given out on Thursday, the 29th of Sravan (July), and then, a scaffold being made ready, the accused were all hanged. Thousands of people came to witness the scene and there were even Naga and Kuki women amongst them, so universal indeed were the feelings roused on this occasion. They came to have a last sight of their own Crown Prince, and tears gushed down their breasts at the piteous sight! Thangal was raised forcibly to the scaffold but the Prince seemed to offer his neck with great readiness. When the hanging was done, all the people of the land were in deep mourning. The other convicts were bound and sent up to the Andaman Islands. (Ll. 1-50.)

(16)

Let us now see what new arrangements were made. There was a man in Manipur named Chowbie Jain, and he had a son called Churachand. They were the descendants of Narasingha, and this Churachand was installed on the throne by the English. He was made to ascend the throne in 1907 when he was only five years old. He is still alive, holding the rank of a Raja. He was bound to the English by a treaty comprising various conditions. If the Raja of Manipur happens to visit British India, eleven guns will be fired in his honour. Only the king's eldest son will henceforth be entitled to the throne. A brother could succeed, if only the king died childless. But everyone shall have to get his title approved of by the British Government. A revenue of fifty thousand rupees shall have to be paid annually to the British Raj. The reigning prince must always give his consent to the acts of the British Government who, in their turn, would consider the State as a Protected one. (Ll. 1-10.)

INDEX

N

O

P

APPENDIX

OPINIONS ON

DR. D. C. SEN'S EASTERN BENGAL BALLADS.

Times Literary Supplement (London).

His (Dr. Sen's) journeyings should become a legend, and the Bengali imagination, centuries hence, should see one figure eternally traversing the Gangetic plain, now beaten upon by the fierce sun, as he makes his way across the red, deeply fissured fields of Vishnupur, now floating on the rain-swept rivers of East Bengal. He has coaxed a cautious peasantry into opening their store of traditions.

....

And Dr. Sen throughout his long and successful career as discoverer, has never done his country greater service than by saving these stories that would have so soon faded out from the world.

he Oriental List (London).

Great as Dr. Sen's other services to the cause of Bengali Literature have been, it is doubtful whether any of his previous work is a more valuable contribution to our knowledge of Bengali life and thought than this collection of ballads, which but for his enterprise and the praiseworthy efforts of his collaborator, would, in all probability in the course of the next few years, have been lost beyond recovery.

Dr. Sylvain Lévi.

What shall I say of Dineschandra Sen's Eastern Bengali Ballads. I must confess that I have a peculiar fondness for the man and for all his publications. He carries all his work, however technical it may be, in such a rapt of enthusiasms; he has such a love for whatever is Bengali, and his mystical love is not afraid of the most minute technicalities. No living man has probably contributed more to make Bengal understood, realised, felt, enjoyed by the Western mind.

Sir George 'Grierson.

I may say that they have been long waited for and that they entirely fulfil the expectations aroused by the publication of the first volume. They throw important light on the history of Bengali Language and Literature, and contain much charming poetry that revives memories of my own happy days spent in India. Mr. Dineshchandra Sen's enthusiasm and scholarly treatment compel me to offer to him and to the Calcutta University my congratulations on the successful production of this valuable work.

William Rothenstein.

I plunged at once into your book and finished it only too quickly. It is of the greatest possible interest and full of beauty and of drama. Through every ballad moves that marvellous being exalted, grave, shy and passionate, reserved and bold—and how nobly beautiful—the Indian woman. She has remained unchanged through all the phases of Indian culture, religious and social. Her lovers carved her in stone and marble at Barhut, Sanchi and Amaravati, painted her, sinuous, radiant and bejewelled at Ajanta and Bagh and delighted to honour her in thousands of humble studios in Jammu, Jaipur, Delhi and Agra, Muslim as well as Hindu, well into the 19th Century. I am interested to find some among your Bengali Ballads date from the middle of last century. Indian Art is unique in having preserved a robust primitive spirit throughout what in Europe were late and sophisticated periods; I notice the same quality in the late literary examples you give. No revival seems able to preserve the strength and directness of the true Indian tradition which is still alive in your latest ballads.

Francis H. Skrine.

The Professor has rendered eminent service to his country in rescuing the charming ballads of Eastern Bengal from oblivion. His labours, indeed, may well be compared with those of Sir Walter Scott and Joseph Ritson, who did the same for the melodious songs of the Scottish Border.

E. F. Oaten.

To the western critic, stumbling by good fortune upon Dr. Sen's Book, these ballads, straight from the unsophisticated people's heart, come fresh and stimulant as the breeze that revives the jaded traveller from Calcutta, as he sits in steamer and ploughs across the monsoon gusts of Eastern Bengal.

Lord Ronaldshay in his introduction emphasises their importance as the seed from which Modern Bengali has sprung. They will also prove valuable as a source of historical information. But one cannot but dwell here on their intrinsic value as literature since it is to be hoped that Bengal will eventually value them most as such.

Jules Bloch.

My opinion of the work may be guessed beforehand from the eagerness with which I have for long followed Rai D. C. Sen's admirable labours, happily supported by the help of the Calcutta University. He has revealed a great part of Bengal to itself and to the world.

Extracts from a letter addressed by H. E. Lord Lytton, Governor of Bengal, to Maharaja Sir Prodyot Kumar Tagore.

Government House, Calcutta, 25th June, 1924.

"It is clear from these publications (Eastern Bengal Ballads) that the line of research now being pursued by Dr. Sen is of great interest and importance. If, as Dr. Sen states, these poems range in date from the 16th to the 19th century, they must obviously possess great literary and historical significance. A glance at the poems so far published shows that they throw much light on the social history of that part of Bengal, where they took their rise. Their importance as additional material for the history of the rise and development of modern Bengali needs no emphasis.

Dr. Sen asserts that he has evidence that a considerable volume of ballad-poetry still remains to be collected from the singers, and other sources, not only in Mymensingh but also in other districts of Bengal. The financial difficulties of the University, however, make it impossible for Dr Sen to arrange for a systematic search for these ballads on a reasonable scale. It is obvious that, with one solitary worker in the field collecting the ballads, progress must be slow. Dr. Sen has, therefore, appealed to me for financial assistance to enable him to prosecute these researches with additional agents and on a systematic plan. For this purpose a sum of Rs. 5,000 is required immediately, while a larger amount still will be required to meet the cost of printing the ballads subsequently. A total sum of Rs. 15,000 would place the work on a sound footing for some time, enabling Dr. Sen to carry out systematic researches on a wider scale, and subsequently to edit and publish the poems in a worthy manner.

After a life-time of devotion to his mother tongue Dr. Sen assures us that nothing but the limited financial resources available to him prevents him from enriching the Bengali language by a large volume of hitherto unknown poems of a remarkable and important character. I am sure that the wealth and culture of Bengal will regard it as a pious and patriotic duty to assist Dr. Sen to complete what may prove to be the most remarkable of his many services to his mother tongue, and they will regard it as a point of honour that the proposed extension of his work would be financed not from official sources, but from the private generosity of those whose literature his researches are enriching. As the sum is a comparativety small one, I do not think that a general appeal to the public is necessary or desirable. If the facts are brought to the notice of a limitted number of gentlemen interested in the language, literature and history of Bengal, I am sure they will readily provide the amount that is necessary for the prosecution of Dr Sen's researches. I know that an interest in literature and the arts is traditional in your family, and that you personally appreciate the value and importance of Dr. Sen's work. I, therefore, feel that I can confidently appeal to you to undertake the duty of collecting the Rs. 15,000 required."

Some publications of the Calcutta University on Language & Literature.

1. **The Origin and Development of the Bengali Language**, by Dr. Sunitikumar Chatterji, M.A. (Cal.), D.Lit. (London) with a Foreward by Sir George Grierson, K.C.I.E., I.C.S. (Retd.). In two Vols. F cap pp. 1179. Rs. 20.

Is the ... sematic and detailed history of a Modern Indo-... ...itten by an Indian. A work " worth to be na... ...e of Beames and Bloch."

2. ... **Literature in the Nineteenth Century**, by Dr. S. K. ..., M.A ... Demy 8vo., pp. 530. Price Rs. 8-6.

... historic ... ew of the course of Bengali Literature from its ... ence after Bharatchandra's death to its rejuvenation under the ... influence.

... y commended by J. D. Anderson, Sylvain Levi, F. E. ... Jules Bloch and others.

... **Selections from Avesta and Old Persian**. First series, ... I.J.S. Taraporewala, B.A., Ph.D. Demy 8vo., Rs. 5.

... character with translation juxtaposed. No ... this work on Avestan. Distin-... Hillebrandt, Jolly, Keith, Jacobi ... spoken ... of its usefulness to ... nts of

...

B. ... Mazumder, Rs. 7.

Co... chapters on the ethnology and geogra... and variation of vernaculars in India due to ... Non-Aryan ... "A fine study of accent in Sanskrit and Bengali and of the ... metrical system is of special value as the author has own distinction as a poet in his native language.